The Life and Death
of
"SUSPECT"

PREVAILING TOWARDS
REDEMPTION

A TESTIMONY BY:

Gabriel I. Hinojosa

ACKNOWLEDGMENTS

First and foremost, I want to thank God, my Lord and Savior Jesus Christ, for saving my life and giving me purpose when I had none. Without His grace, this story wouldn't exist.

I want to give honor to Amazing Church Colorado, our covering and protection, and to Pastor Brandon Brown and Pastor Tiffany Brown for speaking spirit and truth into me when I was still unsure about my journey with Jesus and activating my spirit.

To my family who never gave up on me, even when I gave up on myself, your love carried me when I couldn't stand. Especially my sister Bernadette Lara and my mom Elizabeth Hinojosa. You mean the world to me. My brother Chris, I can't express how much I appreciate you from the bottom of my heart for taking my kids in and raising them when I couldn't.

Thank you to my mentor and brother, Kevin, for pushing me to stay accountable, for showing me what real leadership looks like, and for always being a solid presence.

To my friends and peers in recovery, your stories inspire me every day to keep fighting for others.

To the entire Prevailing Towards Redemption team, you are the hands and feet of this mission. Thank you for walking beside me to help those suffering from addiction and homelessness find their way back to God.

Thank you to my beautiful wife, Melissa, for all the love, support, and help in making my dream become a reality.

This book is dedicated to everyone who is still lost in the storm. There is hope. There is redemption. If He could do it for me, He can do it for you too.

All glory to God.

Author's note

Reader Discretion Advised

This book is a deeply personal account of my life. Within these pages, I share genuine experiences, some of which are raw, painful, and explicit in nature. These moments are not written for shock value, but to reflect the truth of what I have lived through and, by the grace of GOD, overcome.

I believe in the power of honesty and testimony. My hope is that my story will bring healing, understanding, and inspiration to others who may be walking through their own struggles, and that they may see what Jesus Christ, our Lord and Savior, can do in their lives as He has done in mine.

Please proceed with care and compassion, knowing that what you are about to read is not fiction, but my reality, my life. All glory to GOD.

With love, courage, and wisdom,

Sincerely,

Gabriel I. Hinojosa

Heavenly Father,

I come before you with an open heart, seeking your mercy, your grace, and your redemption. Wash me clean of all that is not of you, my sins, my doubts, my fears and make me whole again in your love. Thank you for never turning away from me, even when I've strayed and was completely and utterly lost. Redeem my past Lord God and use it for your glory.

I ask for your strength today God. You've placed a calling on my life to write this book not for my fame, but for your name. I cannot do it alone. Fill me with divine inspiration. Give me clarity of thought, discipline in the process, and courage to tell the truth. Let every word I write be guided by Your Spirit and speak life and provide living water to those who read it.

And most of all, Lord, I surrender all that I am. I give you my plans, my voice, my future, my everything. Take control of my life. Use me as a vessel (Isaiah 42:6) empty me of self so that you may fill me with purpose. Lead me where you want me to go and speak through me, act through me and let everything I do reflect your love, power and greatness father.

I am yours and yours alone God - mold me, guide me and use me.

In Jesus' mighty name I pray,

Amen.

INTRODUCTION

Now, where do I begin... Well, here goes nothing.

My name is Gabriel Ismael Hinojosa, though in the streets I was known by my nickname, "SUSPECT." I'm currently living in Colorado Springs, Colorado, and I began writing this while in custody at the El Paso County Jail, better known as CJC, the Criminal Justice Center. I'm 38 years old as I write these words.

I am Hispanic, and for as long as I can remember, I wanted to be a gangster. That desire shaped my life into one of crimes carved from the streets and soaked in adrenaline, where every heartbeat raced to the rhythm of gunshots and sirens. Fueled by drugs that blurred the line between euphoria and madness, I watched mountains of dirty money pile up as fast as loyalty crumbled. Women drifted in and out like smoke, seductive, fleeting, drawn to the danger, the shine, the lust, the power, yet never staying long enough to see the wreckage underneath, the wreckage I tried to sweep under the rug and forget.

Behind every car and gold chain in this so-called "game" was a soul unraveling, caught in a vicious loop of deals gone wrong, enemies made overnight, and nights that ended in blood or betrayal. It was a kingdom built on sand, thrilling, intoxicating, and destined to fall. To be honest, I don't know how I managed to survive. I should be dead on multiple occasions. But the story I'm about to tell you is true. While some names and places have been changed, the accuracy of the timelines and events remains as I recall them.

Please keep in mind: there will be graphic and unsettling details. This was my life, the life I lived and the life I created. I ask you to approach these words with an open heart and a curious mind. This is more than a story; it is a path I walked, one I had to endure, through pain, loss, and agony. Yet within those moments of truth came growth, and - ultimately, transformation.

As you journey through these pages with me, may you find pieces that speak to your soul, echoes that stir your spirit, and glimpses of light that remind you that we are all, in our own way, becoming who we are destined to be.

Welcome to my journey. I am honored to share it with you. This is my spiritual path, laid bare in its rawest form. May it meet you wherever you are on yours. The truth is hard to accept, but in the end, it will set you free.

"Let the redeemed of the Lord tell their story,
those He redeemed from the hand of the foe."
—Psalm 107:2 (NIV)

CHAPTER 1: PERCEPTION

As the smoke clears, reality sets in. I find myself at the intersection of Palmer Park and Powers, stuck at the light, anxiety gnawing at me. My heart is racing as I sit alone in a truck with a 16-foot trailer and yes, it's stolen.

Nightfall creeps in, and it's about that time to "go to work." Not work in the normal sense, but the kind of work that means making money by any means necessary. I'm sitting at the light on Palmer Park, headed east, but my body is screaming for rest. I can't even remember the last time I actually slept.

Still, I need energy for what's coming. My eyes locked on the gas station across the street, just past the lights. That's my next stop.

I'm sure I can park for a few minutes, get high, hit a few rails, and chase a few 30s oxys to push me where I need to be, to get my adrenaline pumping.

At this point in my life, my days blurred into nights under the weight of two poisons: meth and oxy 30s. Meth lit my brain like wildfire, rushing, urgent, a synthetic euphoria that pulled me into a relentless, jittering high. I'd chase hours of energy that stretched into days without sleep, convinced I was alive, when in truth I was breaking down in ways I couldn't even see.

Then came the oxy. The little blue pills whispered peace. They promised a calm, soft landing after the storm. But that peace was a lie, just another chain, another trap, another way to keep me bound.

They softened the harsh edges of meth's chaos, numbing the comedown and wrapping my body in a false sense of calm. Together, they became a twisted dance, one to lift me up, the other to slow the fall. But in truth, I was sinking deeper each time, trading pieces of myself for fleeting relief.

Behind every high was only a hollow man. Behind every moment of escape, a widening distance from my soul. I thought I was in control. I thought I could manage it. But addiction is a liar, it whispers comfort while quietly stealing everything sacred.

If only I had known, then what I know now.

Back to the story—

I'm sitting at 7-Eleven, tucked away where nobody can see me getting my fix. Hidden from plain sight, loyal to the foil. Let's just say I reached my goal, and now I'm officially lit.

With a deep inhale, then the slow exhale, I reach for my smokes, Marlboro Reds, to be exact. I pull one out and raise it to my lips, the paper dry and familiar between my fingers. The ritual is second nature, a small comfort in the middle of the chaos.

With a flick of the lighter, a tiny flame danced to life, casting a brief orange glow on my face. I touched it to the tip and heard the soft crackle as the tobacco caught fire and drew in slowly. The smoke curled into my lungs, warm and bitter, then slid back out in a lazy exhale, swirling into the air like a ghost with nowhere to go. For a moment, everything was still, just the burn, the breath, and the weight of silence pressing around me.

I closed my eyes for a moment, shutting out the noise, the static, the weight of everything pressing in. My thoughts were scattered like broken glass, but I began picking up the sharpest pieces one by one, forcing them into something that resembled a plan. Focus, I told myself. Breathe. Lock in.

My heartbeat thudded like a drum in my ears. I could feel the tension in my jaw, the twitch in my fingers. Focus. Gotta focus. No room for doubt. No time to spiral. Just me, the moment, and whatever came next.

I straightened my spine, narrowed my eyes, my mind a battlefield, and dragged myself back to the front line, where it was me, myself, and I.

There are a thousand ways this night could play out.

First option—cruise through a few neighborhoods, real slow. Eyes peeled. Look for dropped packages on porches; you might catch one just delivered, still warm in the box. Hit a few mailboxes too, see if there's anything worth flipping, like checks or cards, whatever. But nah... too risky tonight. Cops have been out heavy lately.

Option two—garage hopping. It's messy, but it's worked before. Some folks leave 'em wide open, like they're inviting trouble. Tools, bikes, sometimes even full-on generators just sitting there in the shadows, waiting. I've scored big that way in the past... but something about tonight feels off. Gut says no.

Option three—then there's the trailer I'm in. Stolen, yeah, but clean for now, and nobody knows it's stolen yet—or at least I don't think so. But it still has tags on it; it looks legit if you don't stare too long. Who would even know? Who would look twice? I could hit a construction site, maybe grab some 4x4s, generators, hell, even a dirt bike or a couple of crotch rockets if the stars align. Something big, something that pays. That trailer is not just dead weight; it's potential and lucrative. I just need to move smart, fast, and keep my head clear.

I see someone coming out of the store, and I clock her the second she steps out, her heels clicking sharply against the pavement, her hips swaying like she owns the night.

She's got that look, you know, high-end everything. Designer purse hanging loose on her arm, the kind that costs more than some folks' rent. Nails done, hair did, and that smug little air of someone who's never had to worry about a damn thing. Then I saw it. There it is: the BMW. Brand new, deep black, sitting on chrome rims like it's floating. She presses the fob, and the lights flash once, clean and quick, like money talking directly to me, honestly. She's not alone, though. Here comes her man. He's tall, flashy with his jewelry and all, but soft.

I can see it in the way he walks. Pretty-boy swagger is what they call it, but no weight behind him at all. I size him up quickly. If it came down to it? Yeah, I could take him. No doubt. One clean hit and he's down. But at this spot, at the gas station, cameras are on every corner. Too much risk. Too many eyes. Still, I feel that itch crawling up my spine. That go feeling.

"Screw it!" I say to myself. Go hard or go home, right? What's there to lose now? I've already been sitting here too long, engine idling low, paranoia kicking in. Then she slides into the driver's seat, heels first, purse still swinging. He takes shotgun, laughing like life's a joke only rich people get. I wait for a bit, then drop this truck into gear. No more thinking. Just motion. Just instinct. I'm gonna follow. See where they go. See what the night wants to give me.

They roll out eastbound on Palmer Park Boulevard, smooth and steady, headed toward Marksheffel. I follow behind them, but not too closely, not too far away, just another vehicle in the stream of nighttime traffic. But I'm no ordinary driver, and this isn't an ordinary truck. As I mentioned earlier, let me paint you a picture real quick...

White work truck, trailer hitched and rattled quietly behind me like it belongs there. I look at the part to the letter: high-visual yellow vest catching the glow of every streetlight, dirt-smudged work pants, steel-toe boots planted firm. Gloves and a clipboard on the dash. Hard hat on the seat. The tools were scattered just messy enough to sell the story. If you looked at me through a window or passing mirror, you'd swear I was just another city employee grinding the late shift.

Out here, it's not just about hiding in plain sight; it's about becoming plain sight. I don't dress like a thug or a gangbanger. That's a rookie move. I don't wear a mask; I wear a uniform. I become the role. Whatever you think I am, that's exactly what I want you to believe. I control the lens.

It's psychological warfare, and every detail matters. My posture. My stride. The way I turn the wheel or even hold a cigarette—two fingers, slow drag, just enough ash before the flick. If even one thing is off, one thread out of place, one wrong gesture raises a flag. And flags get noticed. Noticed gets watched. Watched gets questioned. And questions? Well, that's when we all know it falls apart. Period.

You gotta walk the talk. And not just say it, embrace it. Your clothes. Your voice. Your ride. Your scent. Your shadow. The way your boots hit the pavement. The way your eyes move when someone looks too long. Everything is a tool, or a form of leverage. The average person sees a worker headed to a job. I know better, because I built this mask. And I built it airtight.

The growl of the truck's engine purred low under my hands as I tailed the sleek, black BMW ahead of me. It shimmered under the early evening moonlight, sitting on polished rims that caught the light like blades. bass from its sound system pulsed through the air, rattling its own frame like it had a heartbeat of its own, loud, arrogant, alive. I watched it glide through the neighborhood like it owned the pavement. Two people inside, laughing. Carefree. Money. I figured that's the only reason people act that way. Maybe it's more than just money. It made my fingers twitch with just the thought of it.

The idea slithered up the back of my neck, cold and sudden. I could cut them off. Ditch this truck I'm driving and jack the Beemer. Make them get out with their phones, wallets, everything. Even the clothes off their backs if I wanted. Leave them humiliated, helpless on the side of the road. I'd be gone before they even remembered how to breathe, let alone call for help.

I took the last drag of my cigarette and flicked the butt out the window, watching it spin in the wind. That's when I saw them, just out of the corner of my eye.

Boxes.

Dozens of them. Sitting pretty on porch after porch after porch, untouched and unclaimed in the soft glow of suburbia. Cardboard treasure chests, waiting for me. Silent. Forgotten. My eyes lingered on a few big boxes that stood out from the rest, taped up like they held secrets.

My mind shifted.

A side mission?

Cars like that BMW... they're everywhere. But those packages... they were mysteries. Could be junk. Could be gold. Could be something worth more than anything in that car.

I turned the wheel slowly and began to turn around without causing any kind of dismay. I let the BMW keep cruising. We will meet again, I'm sure of it.

I had a new plan now. And it started with a quiet street, a bundle of boxes galore, and no one was watching or even thinking about what was going to happen until it happened.

I'm grabbing these packages. No fear. No hesitation. That's the rule. The only rule that matters. Hesitate, and you're caught. Second-guess yourself, and you're done. Game over. The world doesn't pause for indecision, and neither do I.

Fear? Please. Fears for people who still have something to lose.

Me? I was bred for this. Built like steel and sharpened by the grind. Cold mornings. Hot tempers. Hard lessons. This life doesn't hand out participation trophies. You either take what's yours or get eaten alive.

I never had silver spoons or safety nets. Just grit and guts. And a gut feeling that always points me toward the prize.

I make the turn, tires humming low across the pavement as I slide into the mouth of the cul-de-sac like a predator entering a den. The street curls in on itself like a closed fist, tight, quiet, and private. A perfect little suburban loop lined with freshly cut lawns, trimmed hedges, and porch lights still glowing amber in the dusky half-light. Dinner's probably on inside these houses. TVs are murmuring. Parents coaxing kids off tablets. No one's looking out. No one ever looks until it's too late.

My eyes scan fast. Target-rich environment. Five, six, no... eight houses, each with at least one box sitting like bait at the front door. Company logos, bright white shipping labels, sealed clean with tape. Could be anything. Electronics. Designer clothes. Jewelry. Tools. Meds. All unguarded. All for the taking.

The truck coasts to a stop at the far end of the circle, engine idling low like a beast on a leash. I kill the headlights and motor simultaneously and sit, waiting for movement and ready to move. Always ready to move.

Heart's thudding now, but it's not fear. It's power. Pure adrenaline, jet fuel in the veins. I reach into the back, grab the duffel bag. Empty for now, but not for long. I can't forget my clipboard. This ain't just theft. This is art. Timing. Movement. Silence. I'm a shadow with a heartbeat. A ghost in a hoodie. One step out onto the pavement, and the night swallows me whole.

Game on.

I got out of the truck, calm and collected, the duffel bag slung low over one shoulder like it's just another day on the job. In my other hand is the clipboard, prepared to make it look like I'm writing something down, just in case I encounter someone. Clean. Official-looking. Blank paper tucked beneath a clear sleeve; a pen clipped on tight. It's not for writing. It's for show. My mask is my uniform, because people trust the familiar, and nothing says "authorized" like a clipboard and a confident stride.

The air is thick with the end of summer and the beginning of fall, the wind blowing cool through the trees. The scent of cut grass and backyard barbecue lingers—All-American, all asleep.

I approach the first house like I belong there. No rush. No shifty eyes. Just another delivery driver finishes his route. I glance left, then right. No curtains twitching. No dogs barking. The porch light above casts a soft, golden circle over the welcome mat.

The box is medium-sized, brown with black barcodes, and that little smirk of a smile from Amazon is printed across the front. I crouch smoothly, not a thief, just a worker. I scoop it up one-handed, thumb the clipboard like I'm checking it off, and move on. No hesitation.

I hit the second house just as clean. This time, two boxes. One heavier item, such as books or canned goods. I grunt under the weight just for show and walk these back to the truck. Clipboard tucked under my arm now, pen between my teeth. I'm painting a picture. If anyone's watching, they're seeing what they expect to see: a tired courier getting the job done.

Third house. Fourth. Rhythm locked in. We are going for gold here, guys.

Grab. Check. Move.

The fifth house breaks the pattern.

It's darker; the porch lights are off. A narrow walkway with cracked steps and overgrown bushes brushes my arms as I pass. There's a ring camera on the doorframe, red light blinking. I don't flinch. I tilt the clipboard just enough to block my face and keep moving. I lift the package with my back turned, the duffel open, and make a smooth drop.

By the time I hit house number six, I'm in the zone. The wind at my back, duffel halfway full, clipboard still riding shotgun. My footsteps are silent against the concrete. No barking dogs. No shouting neighbors. It's almost too easy.

I round the last bend of the cul-de-sac, breathing steady, pulse still hammering with that sweet edge of danger. Not fear, just clarity. Every sense is on high alert. I'm not just watching the street. I am the street. I'm watching for movement in the windows, extra lights flicking on inside the houses.

From the porch of house seven, I lift a thin, flat package. Maybe a laptop. Maybe a gaming console. Jackpot. I can feel it. I scanned the windows again. Nothing. Clipboard taps with a pen. Turn.

I'm almost back to the truck when I hear it...

—a faint creak.

Somewhere behind me, a door opens. Dogs start barking.

I don't stop walking.

Clipboard tucked tight under my arm, I cross the lawn with the practiced ease of someone who's done this before. No rush. No panic. Just fluid motion, like I'm still on schedule, still part of the system. I reached the truck without a hitch. The duffel swings off my shoulder and lands heavily on the passenger seat as I open the door, a muffled thud as the weight of stolen goods settles like bricks.

I slide into the driver's side slowly, with the tired appearance of a man finishing a shift. The door opens just enough. I hold the inside handle as I pull it shut—soft and silent. No slam. Just a clean click that disappears into the dark. No reason to make noise now. No reason to draw eyes.

My fingers find the ignition. Key in, twist, the engine rolls to life with a low, familiar rumble, like a growl under my feet. I rolled the window down halfway. The night air slips in, warm and sharp with the smell of cut grass, faint barbecue smoke just as before.

I don't peel out.

I ease off the curb like I'm just another working stiff finishing a long shift, clipboard still balanced on my knee, the glow of the dashboard painting my arms in cold blue light.

But then I see it.

Click.

A porch light flares to life.

In the rearview mirror, the soft gold halo cuts through the dark like a spotlight on the house I'd just passed. My eyes snap to it like magnets. It's the same place. The one with the overgrown walkway and the same angry dog I heard barking. Maybe someone looked out. Maybe they heard the barking. Maybe they saw me.

For a second, I try to stay chill. Play it cool. Keep driving smoothly and slowly. I can feel my pulse picking up again, heavy in my neck. Something about that light, how sudden it was, how it stayed on. It's not a motion sensor. It was flipped on. Someone's coming outside now.

My gut tightens. A cold ripple climbs my spine.

Screw it. I'm overthinking it. I gotta get gone.

I punch the gas, not flooring it, but just enough to feel the truck lunge forward, the engine growling low like it knows we need to move. The tires grip hard against the pavement as we peel out of the cul-de-sac's tight loop and roll back into the open.

In the rearview mirror, something shifts.

A shape. In the doorway.

At first, it's just a silhouette—tall, motionless, backlit by the sudden blaze of the porch light. But it's not just anyone. There's weight to it. Posture. Like someone trying to decide whether to shout or step forward. The kind of person already on edge, already reaching for a phone.

I don't want to look.

But I must look.

My eyes flick back to the mirror, just for a second, locking on that cracked door, half open now. No sign of the dog. Maybe it's inside. Maybe not. It doesn't matter. I'm already gone. But the image sticks, burned into the back of my mind like a scar.

As I hit the main street, the glow of suburban calm fades behind me, replaced by the hum of traffic and amber streetlights. I try to slip into the flow, casual, invisible. Nothing to see here. Just another tired delivery guy with a clipboard and a schedule.

But I'm off rhythm now.

My mind's chewing on that porch. That light. That door. That look. The way the dog barked and then stopped, as if it were listening for something more.

Too late.

The truck veers slightly as I try to merge. Not wildly, but enough. A sedan's in my blind spot. My eyes snap to the mirror just in time to see the high beams of the car behind me swell into view—too close, too fast.

"Come on…" I mutter under my breath, jaw tightening.

My right-hand jerks off the wheel, snatching the clipboard and slamming it hard against the dash. It slides once, then skids crooked and comes to a stop against the windshield like it's ashamed of itself. My left hand clenches the wheel harder, knuckles pale in the streetlight's flicker.

Deep breath. In. Out.

Mission complete.

Or so I think.

Until I glance back up at the mirror and see it.

The car I cut off.

Boxy shape. Unmarked. Steady. No horn now. No aggression.

No. No, no, no.

Is that a cop?

I cut off a cop?

My heart stutters. Not full panic yet, just enough to turn the air sharp and dry in my throat all at once. I stared too long in the mirror, watching the grill of the vehicle hold steady in my lane. It doesn't speed up. Doesn't fall back. It just sits there, like it's reading me. Like it knows.

Calm down and breathe.

Breathe.

I ease off the gas.

One eye on the speedometer, the other in the rear.

I bring it down exactly to the limit.

Not over.

Not under.

Right on the money.

Hands at ten and two. Shoulders relaxed, or pretending to be, or as relaxed as I could be with the extent of drugs I'm on. Face calm, or at least blank. That much I know for sure.

The clipboard sits silent on the dash, nothing on it but a crumpled page and smudged fingerprints. I don't dare touch it now. That could become evidence.

The city lights stretch out ahead like a river of possibility. One after the other. After the other. After the other.

Behind me, the cruiser keeps following.

No sirens. No lights.

Just presence.

And the game, well, ladies and gentlemen, the game has just begun.

CHAPTER 2: FLIGHT OR FIGHT

EPSO's better known as the El Paso County Sheriff's Office. Their cruiser is clear as day in the rearview, headlights locked onto me like a predator that hasn't decided when to pounce. I can't believe I'm in this dumb situation again.

I can feel the weight of its presence pressing in, cold, silent, and way too close for comfort. The pulse of my heartbeat in my ears is louder than the low hum of my engine.

What do I do? What the hell do I do now?

Okay, okay. Think. Think stupid. You got this. Think like someone with nothing to hide, like someone who's not two heartbeats away from flooring the gas pedal and pushing it to the limit.

Up ahead, the traffic light hangs like a judge's gavel, ticking down to red. If I time it just right, I can hit the gas and slip through the yellow before it flips. I'll know for sure then. If he blows through the red just to keep on my tail... then we've got an issue. Then I'll know this isn't paranoia. This isn't just another bored deputy on a slow patrol.

Nope. He's as ready as I am.

The light shifts amber, bleeding into red like a wound spreading, and I press on the gas. Not enough to draw attention, just enough to slide through.

And then I check the mirror, where my eyes have been glued all along.

The cruiser doesn't hesitate. No blinkers. No siren. He blows through the red light like traffic laws don't apply to him and turns with me. Still behind me. Still watching. He's probably running the tags.

I'm screwed. I'm screwed, that's all there is to it.

No way around it. No talking smoothly. No ducking corners. I'm in deep, and not the kind of deep you dig out of.

Stolen trailer. Stolen truck. Stolen packages stacked like felonies, one on top of another. Drugs in my pocket somewhere. Gun next to me, loaded and ready to ruin what little I had left going for me. Which was basically just my freedom. And from this view, I don't want to get locked up. Who knows how dirty this gun is?

Every second I keep breathing is just the clock winding down.

And those EPSO cruisers are still there. Still glued to me like a curse.

Okay. Think. THINK, idiot.

Left on Piros. It's coming up fast. Side street, low lights, barely any traffic at this hour. Could be cover. Could slip away somehow. But how?

I hit the signal for the turn like a good citizen and ease into it.

Breathe, dummy. Just breathe. Pretend like my heart isn't trying to hammer its way through my ribs.

I glance in the mirror, and sure as hell, the minute I'm sure of it...

BAM.

The sky behind me explodes in the famous red and blue. The cherries. That unmistakable glow of everything coming down. Reflected off the side mirrors. Bouncing across the windshield. Coloring the inside of the truck.

This is it.

No more pretending. No more maybe-this, maybe-that.

Time to decide. Run or surrender. The weight of everything I've done is sitting in the passenger seat, looking at me like it already knows the ending.

I grip the wheel tighter. Breathe once.

Just once.

And then...

I ease the truck to the right side of the street. Slow. Smooth. Like I've accepted it. Like I've made peace.

But I haven't.

I stopped. Full and complete. The engine is still humming like a heartbeat that won't quit. I don't kill it. I'm not ready for this to be over. Not yet.

Outside, the red and blue lights dance off the houses, spinning reflections in glass windows and car doors, like the whole neighborhood's holding its breath.

Then—SLAM.

A door swung shut behind me with that sharp, unmistakable crack of authority. That was him. The cop. His boots hit the pavement, footsteps growing louder, more measured. Confident. Like he's done this a thousand times before.

Like he thinks it's just another bust. Just another thug with no options left.

Eh—that's probably right.

The window's already down because I never planned on talking. Just pretending. And here he comes, creeping into my view, flashlight in one hand, the other hovering close to his hip.

"License and registration."

His voice is calm. Too calm. He thinks this is going by the book.

I don't look at him. I keep my eyes forward. My hand moves slowly, faking the reach, fumbling toward the glovebox like I'm digging for papers.

But in my head? A different voice cuts through everything.

GO.

Just one word. Louder. Raw. Pure evil.

GO! WHAT ARE YOU WAITING FOR?

Screw it. I'm not going out like this. Not tonight. Not cuffed in the back of a cruiser while they catalog every felony stacked like a laundry list of chores. Not while I've still got a foot on the pedal and steel beneath me.

Boom.

The shifter slams into DRIVE.

Pedal to the floor.

The truck roars like a beast unchained, a diesel growl tearing through the silence of suburbia. Tires screech, trailer follows, and I'm gone.

"BYE, FELICIA!"

Rear tires chirp, biting pavement as I rocket forward. Side mirrors rattle. My chest is a jackhammer. Eyes glued to the rearview. The cop's silhouette is shrinking fast, caught mid-sprint, still yards from his car. He's reaching for the door, scrambling to catch up. But I'm already three blocks deep before he's even got the engine started.

I'm ghost.

Streetlights whip past in blurs. Trash bins tumbled as I cut a corner too sharply. The trailer sways, wheels shrieking under the load, but I don't ease off. Not for a second. Not until I see destruction or hell. Let him come. Let the sirens scream. They'll have to catch me first. And tonight? They're gonna earn it.

AHA!

I grin through gritted teeth, sweat slick on my brow, knuckles white on the wheel.

Got 'em.

At the very least, I've bought myself a head start, a couple of seconds of freedom bought with pure madness. Pedal pinned, engine howling, this beast under me screams louder than the sirens behind.

I'm all in now. No hesitation. No half-measures. Just diesel-fueled desperation and a stolen life trying to outrun fate.

Around the bend, VROOOOM, tires squeal, trailer groans. The hitch wobbles but holds. I power up the hill, fast as she'll take me. The cab shakes, the frame rattles, the rearview bouncing so hard I can barely see the lights chasing me.

But I know they're there.

"Here he comes…"

I glance back. The cruiser's eating pavement. EPSO's finest isn't backing off, and his engine is a pit bull's snarl behind me, getting louder, closer, meaner.

Then—

"CRAP!!"

Up ahead is an intersection.

Piros and Constitution. And the damn light is red.

Still red. No sign of turning. No time soon.

"Please… PLEASE…" I mutter, like the traffic signs are listening. "Don't let anyone cross. Don't let me hurt someone. Please don't let anyone be in the way of this. Not like this."

But I'm not stopping.

Neither is the cop.

This isn't a brake-and-bargain situation. This is all or nothing. I punch the gas even harder, the hill peaking under me. Trailer still dragging behind like a cinder block tied to a rocket.

And then—

AIRBORNE.

The truck and trailer leap off the crest like a wild animal. For one breathless, weightless second, I'm flying. Tires off the ground. Time slows. The lights, the noise, it all fades.

I shut my eyes. Then crack one open.

"Look, dammit! LOOK!"

I scan left. Scan right. Empty.

WHEW.

No cars. No kids. No one. I blast through the intersection, tires slapping pavement again with a sickening, bone-rattling thud. The front-end slams down hard, and the rear? It isn't so graceful. The trailer hits like a hammer, jumps the hitch, throws the truck into a wild fishtail. The whole frame groans under the force. Tires screech. Sparks fly from the undercarriage steel.

I yank the wheel, overcorrect, damn near jackknife the whole thing. I fight to keep the nose straight, arms wrestling the wheel like it's trying to buck me out of the windshield. The trailer's dragging me now. It's just dead weight, not any potential or lucrative like I was thinking earlier. Sloppy. Unstable.

"This trailer's gonna kill me before the cops do..."

I grit my teeth and my eyes dart for options. I need to ditch it. Cut it loose. I need to lose weight if I want to survive this. Because this isn't just a chase anymore.

This is survival.

Of course, this cop isn't slowing down. Still on me like a heat-seeking missile. Full throttle. No hesitation. Sirens wail like death screams behind me.

I glance back. Cruiser headlights locked in, bouncing with every bump, climbing the same dips, sliding through the same turns. He's not even trying to back off.

"Isn't there a law or something where they can't pursue high-speed chases in residential areas? What happened to public safety?!"

But maybe he just doesn't give a damn.

We're tearing down Piros, a quiet street that has become a battleground. Bikes scatter. A few adults dive behind cars, waving arms, yelling, cursing.

Lawn chairs flip over. Dogs bolt into yards. Pure chaos in every direction.

And then—**BANG! BANG! BANG**!

Gunshots.

"OH, HELL NO—HE'S SHOOTING!"

Glass explodes beside me. The driver-side mirror shatters in a burst of sparkling dust. Something rips through the truck wall, then silence...

"He's actually trying to kill me!"

Heart hammering. Mouth dry. Eyes wild. I duck instinctively, one hand still on the wheel. The other—

"Where's my piece?! WHERE?!"

I start reaching, scrambling under the seat, checking everywhere, trying to feel for it. Everything got jumbled when I launched this beast off the hill. The gun vanished into the black hole of panic and bad timing.

I can't believe this right now. I can't...

"UGH!"

Still can't find it. Every second spent searching is another chance for a bullet to find my skull. Gotta move. Gotta think.

"Okay... okay..."

If I can't shoot back, I can at least fight dirty. I look around both sides of the street, lined with parked cars. Sedans. Pickups. A trash truck. Even a classic Impala sitting low on busted tires. Tightly packed. No breathing room.

An idea sparks like fire to gasoline.

"Wanna play hardball, huh? Let's play ping-pong."

I yank the wheel left, just enough to clip a silver compact.

CRUNCH!

Metal scrapes and sparks fly. The impact jolts through my bones. I swerve again.

BAM! into a parked van. The trailer swings wide, slamming into trash bins, fence posts, and mailboxes, sending up splinters and garbage like shrapnel.

I'm bouncing side to side now, pinging off this car, pong off that one, using the whole street like a demolition alley. Every impact throws sparks and noise back at the cruiser behind me. Glass explodes. Mirrors snap. Alarms blare.

The cop's got no clean path now, just wreckage and chaos in his lane. I glance in the mirror, and he's swerving, trying to dodge it all, but he's losing ground. I see the hesitation.

"That's right... BACK UP!"

Another shot.

BANG!

This one punches into the tailgate. The trailer jerks. I nearly lost it. I yank the wheel again, tires screaming.

"You wanna kill me?! YOU BETTER BE READY TO DIE WITH ME!"

I'm not driving anymore. Honestly, I'm wielding this truck like a weapon. Like a thousand-pound middle finger to the law, the world, and the grave that's been chasing me since day one.

CHAPTER 3: IN THE BAG

Well. This should make him back up a bit.

Alright… here goes nothing.

The red four-door Camry appeared out of the dark, parked crooked on the shoulder like the owner got out in a hurry. No time to think. The trailer behind me, already fishtailing, swung wide and slammed into it. Metal on metal. A crunch that screamed through the air like a gunshot. Glass exploded across the road. The impact jerked the wheel in my hands; I lost control for a half-second, tires shrieking against the pavement, but I kept pushing it. No choice. Not anymore.

Two black Honda Accords up ahead. Parked tight, one on each side of the street like twins. I gritted my teeth and didn't even blink.

SMASHED.

The trailer crashed through them like a rampaging rhino, debris showering the air, sparks lighting up beneath me like fireworks. The truck shuddered, fighting back under the strain, but I was able to hold it together, white-knuckled and fueled by sheer adrenaline.

In the mirror, the cop was still there. Unbelievable. This guy was going for bust of the year, but you had to give it to him; he had dedication. Lights flashing, sirens screaming loud like a banshee in my ears. He wasn't giving up. Not an inch.

Faster.

Faster.

I was flying now. Barreling down Piros Street like a bullet from a gun, the houses blurring past, fences bending in the wind of my passing.

And then I looked up. And my stomach dropped.

You'll never guess.

This street ends. No outlet.

OMG. No way. It's a cul-de-sac.

The road curled inward like a dead-end grin, trees looming, driveways yawning, and no way out. No way to brake in time. Not at this speed. Not with that cop right behind me and a trailer running like an angry bull at full speed with one mission… kill and destroy.

But maybe.

Just maybe.

Between the two houses up ahead. A narrow sliver. Barely a car-width. A cracked sidewalk. A backyard on the other side, maybe open ground.

"FLOOR IT, DAWG!"

The voice came from somewhere deep inside me, primal and raw. And I listened.

My foot slammed the pedal to the floor. The engine roared. I lined it up by instinct alone, ignoring the sparks, the grinding howl of tires that had nothing left to give.

BOOM.

My world exploded.

I lost consciousness for a moment. Just a second. It had to be just the impact. A short flicker in my mind, like someone yanked the plug and shoved it back in.

Smoke.

Thick, grey, and bitter, smoke poured from the hood in a twisting column, smothering the windshield. The engine wasn't roaring anymore. No more speed. No more chase. Just the angry hiss of something broken and bleeding oil onto someone's living room floor.

Wait.

Living room?

I blinked, disoriented, head swimming, heart pounding. I look right.

And there he is.

The cop, running full tilt past the passenger side, one hand already going for his radio, the other reaching for his sidearm. His eyes locked on mine like a heat-seeking missile, not knowing I'm still conscious.

My eyes go huge, like half dollars.

I drove through the house.

No. Not around it. Through it. I must have jumped the curb, lost control mid-air, and bulldozed straight into the living room. Wood, drywall, picture frames, and couch cushions are around me in a cyclone of debris.

My stomach dropped. The world slows to a molasses crawl.

Seconds. Mere seconds. That's all I have.

I shove the truck door open and stumble out. My pistol follows, hits the concrete floor with a loud metallic clack, and I grab it without even thinking.

One decision. One instinct.

Get out and get out now.

I don't look back. I squeeze between the truck and the house, and I'm in the front yard. I decided to go through the side gate into the neighbor's backyard. Fresh-cut grass. Wooden fence. Kids' toys littered across the lawn. My boots smash against the damp dirt, lungs burning, my brain running on fumes.

K-9.

The thought punches me in the chest.

What if they bring dogs?

I sprint to the furthest corner of the yard, practically dive into it, and rip off my hoodie. I hurl it over the fence into the next property. One shoe comes off, and I chuck it to the left, deep into the shadows, far away. The other I hurled to the right, toward the opposite direction. Decoys. Scent trails. I don't know if it will work, but I must try. Right?

And then I see it.

The porch.

Stacked along the railing, like some kind of twisted gift from fate: black trash bags. Big ones. Ten, maybe twelve. Heavy-duty. Yard work leftovers, stuffed with leaves, clippings, whatever. They are piled in a loose pyramid, almost chest high.

Heart hammering. Blood roaring.

Think, stupid. Think.

I sprint over, now dressed head to toe in black, but it was my first layer, just in case. You never know when you need to disappear in the dark. I throw myself into the center of these bags. The bags rustle and collapse around me with a low crunch. I drag them close, one, two, three, bury myself beneath them, feel the plastic hug my body like a second skin.

I must freeze. I must be still. I must control my breathing.

Dark. Pitch black. I close my eyes and rely solely on my hearing.

BREATHE.

In your nose. Out of your mouth. Deeper and slower. Do not panic.

I can hear the sirens getting closer now. More of them. Tons of them. Echoing off every house on the block. Voices too, some yelling, "Where did he go? He must have gone this way," and arguing amongst themselves. The static of their radios, conversations with dispatch. A woman screaming somewhere. Children are crying in the distance.

And that's it.

My world goes black again, not just the outside world, but inside of me too. My body shuts down under the weight of adrenaline and panic and, of course, the drugs. I slip away into the dark, my breath slowed, heart pounding so hard, hard like a beating drum.

I blackout.

I come to in a haze, head throbbing, throat dry, heart pounding like it wants to crawl out of my chest. Dazed. Confused.

Where the hell am I even at? Black plastic bags crumble beneath me as I shift. Trash, sharp-smelling and wet in spots, surrounds me like a nest. A metallic taste coats my tongue. Blood, maybe smoke, sweat—I don't know. My clothes are damp and filthy. I blink hard, I force myself upright, groaning, as I shift the bags off me, like shedding skin. My hand flies to my pocket. No phone. I pat my pants. Nothing.

"Gush," I groan aloud.

All I have is this gun.

Heavy. Cold. Comforting in the worst way.

I glanced at my watch. 2:37 a.m. I've been out for hours. I try to stand, but the world tilts and crashes again, and my leg buckles. A flash of pain shoots up from my knee. I fall hard back onto the ground, broken plastic crunching beneath me, falling face-first with my hands trying to catch myself.

The dogs go wild. Sharp, angry barks explode from the other side of the fence. My breath comes fast. Shallow.

I clench my teeth, push myself up onto one good leg, dragging like dead weight.

I gotta move. I gotta get the hell out of here.

I limp toward the side gate, half-hanging on one hinge, bent like it's been kicked too many times. My body, beat up, feels heavier than it should. I weathered the storm, but just barely, a small miracle in a storm of bad luck.

My phone… it must have bounced somewhere in the crash. Maybe in the truck. Maybe in the house. Maybe in the street.

Maybe in someone's hands right now. Hopefully, the cops don't have it.

Great. Dumbest move of my life. Legs busted. No phone. The whole damn city probably knows how to look for me.

It's cold enough that my fingers are going numb, and my brain's moving slower with every step. I feel like I'm slipping—mentally, physically, maybe permanently. I don't even know where I am anymore.

My only choice now? Keep moving. Limp faster. Don't look back.

CHAPTER 4: PARANOIA

No coat. No shoes. Dogs are barking somewhere behind me, loudly, like they smell the guilt on my skin. My leg's jacked up from the crash. I don't know how bad it is, but it's bad. The kind of pain that doesn't stab, it burns. It feels like someone took a bat to my knee and then lit the bone on fire. I'm limping hard, dragging one leg behind me like a corpse I haven't buried yet. I've been hiding, curled up behind a trash bin in someone's yard for God knows how long. Drifted in and out of sleep. My body gave up on me a few hours ago. Muscles frozen stiff, fingers numb, jaw locked from the cold. The only thing still moving is the pounding in my skull. I need to get high and take this pain away. That's all I could think of.

I can't believe I'm not in cuffs yet. Or a body bag. I push myself up off the ground, eyes darting, lungs rattling. No time to go back for the hoodie or the busted shoes I kicked off after the chase. No time for anything. Constitution Avenue is just across the way. If I make it there, I can get to Alison's. My room. One of five scattered safe spots I use like drop-off points around town.

I hobble to the gate. My handshakes as I push it open, the cold biting down to the bone. The front yard is still too quiet. I pause and listen. Somewhere, maybe a block away, a siren wails in the distance. The cops are still out there. Not just searching, they're hunting.

I move like smoke. Slow. Thin. Vanishing between shadows. Every step is war. My limp is loud, clumsy, a spotlight in a sleeping neighborhood. Someone must have seen the chase earlier. Probably filmed it. Cops will be pulling Ring camera footage for next week. I keep my head down, trying to move like I belong, like I'm just another lost soul wandering this godforsaken part of town.

But let's be real for a second. A guy barefoot, limping, out at this hour? I might as well be wearing a neon sign that says, 'ARREST ME.'

I reach the edge of the park and freeze when I see the headlights. Instinct kicks in, and I dive headfirst into the bushes. Thorns rip into my arms, tear across my cheek. My heart is hammering like a riot in my chest. I peek through the branches. Just a regular car. A civilian.

Still, I can't carry this gun anymore. I must lose it. I claw at the dirt like a madman, nails breaking, fingers cramping, until I've got a hole deep enough. The gun, with its cold steel still smelling like regret, goes into the earth, and I pack the dirt back with shaking hands. No ceremony. Just bury it and forget. Too familiar.

Paranoia slithers up my spine. Every sound is a cop. Every car is unmarked. These bushes stretch along the wall for a few blocks. If I stay low, crawl like a cat, I might make it to the other side without being seen.

So, I started moving. No cover but the shrubs and the dark. The wall beside me scrapes against my coatless arms, and branches whip at my face. I feel the sting of scratches stacking up like IOUs. I'm bleeding more. Cars pass. One, two, three. Too many for this hour. I duck, heart skipping. My breath is ragged, steam ghosting from my mouth in short bursts. I feel like prey.

I keep crawling. Every inch is war. My body's screaming at me to stop. To lie down and disappear into the cold. But that's not how this ends.

I get close to Allison's. Closer than I've been to safety all night. I know the way back. Her place is around the corner; the porch light is always off. I've got a room there, one of my ghost nests. A spot I pay for with favors and drugs.

But first, I have to cross Constitution. A main road. Wide open. Bright streetlights and the occasional gas station crawler. If I cross clean, I'm good. If not...

Then I saw them.

Three cop cruisers. Parked right at the Maverik gas station. Lights off, engines running. Like sharks beneath the surface. Just waiting.

I stopped. Frozen. My whole life, every decision I ever made that led me to this exact moment, punches me in the chest.

You're stupid. When will you learn?

Then I ran.

Limping. Sprinting. Practically I threw myself across the road like a wounded animal. My foot hits the pavement wrong, and pain flashes like lightning. I keep going. Across the lanes. Into a yard. Through the bushes. I threw myself into the shadows and curled up, trying to vanish into the dirt.

I wait.

Time slows. Minutes feel like hours. I watch. Listen. Sirens in the distance, but nothing close. No doors open. No footsteps. No shouting.

Maybe they didn't see me.

I can't breathe. My chest is full of razors. I get to my knees, legs trembling. One more corner. Just one more corner and I'm there. I stagger forward, dragging my busted leg behind me, leaning against the fence posts and walls as I go. Blood drips down my shin.

I don't even care anymore.

I reached Allison's door.

KNOCK. KNOCK. KNOCK.

I pound on it like it owes me money. My lungs are shredded. I'm shaking, barely upright.

"OPEN UP!"

I slam my fist into the door again. Harder. Louder. Each second feels like a year.

I put my head down and fell to my knees, starting to feel defeated as I collapsed forward, forehead pressed to the door, breath steaming against the wood. I feel everything catch up at once: pain, panic, exhaustion, guilt. The weight of the night crushes me.

I whisper, barely, "Please…"

Then, finally, through the haze of defeat and cold and blood and desperation, I hear it.

Click.

The lock?

Then the door cracks open, just an inch.

And from the dark, a confused voice I didn't know I needed to hear cuts through it like a razor edge.

CHAPTER 5: ALLISON'S HOUSE

The door creaks open slowly, like it is afraid of what's on the other side. I look up. It is not Allison. Not even close. Just some stranger, face tight with confusion, eyes scanning me like I might be dangerous or dying. Hell, maybe I am both. Judging by her appearance, she has no idea who I am, and I don't know her either, but given my current state, I can't blame her.

"Allison. Where's Allison?" My voice is hoarse, dried out, barely pushing past the blood in my throat.

"She's... in the room," the woman replies, hesitant, almost guilty, like she is holding onto a secret. Or maybe it is just fear.

I step forward, or more like stumbling, through the open door. I don't have the strength or time to explain myself. I am too exhausted to hold my ground, too busted up to pretend I am okay. The door-keeper lady hesitates, blocking my way like she has some kind of authority. I glared at her, blood crusted on my temple, half-limping with one dead leg.

"Move," I mutter. She blinks, stunned. I don't have the patience. "Just move, lady."

She steps aside.

I take two more steps, and everything shuts down. My knees give out, and I collapse, body hitting the floor like dropped meat. Cold hardwood against my back. A blur of motion around me, and someone lifts me up just enough to lean against the wall. Another set of hands appears with a cold Pepsi can, hissing open, and a cigarette. They place it between my lips and light it.

I take a drag like it is the first breath I have had in weeks. Their fingers are rough but careful. A flick of the lighter, a flare of flame, then the tip catches, hissing softly like it knows what I have been through. I drew in deep, the smoke biting my throat, burning its way down into my lungs like a rush of fire and fog. It doesn't heal anything, but it slows the chaos. My pulse steadies. My head clears, just a little. Like I have been drowning for hours and finally surfaced for air, bitter, filthy air, but it is mine.

The release of smoke from my lungs, and everything slows.

Man, I think, this is what I needed. Just a smoke.

Then Allison.

She bursts into the room like a bullet through glass.

"Suspect?! What happened??"

I am silent. Blank. Numb. I take another drag. Sip of soda. Trying to piece my thoughts into something that makes sense.

"SUSPECT," she says again, this time louder, more frantic. "What happened to you? Where's the truck? How did you get here?"

I cough out the words: "Crawled here, basically."

And then it all spills. The whole nightmare, the packages, the chase, the sirens, the crash, that damn truck splitting the front of a house like rotten wood. The panic. Running. Every second feels like a warzone.

I was playing GTA in real life. No save points. No try again. No second lives. No spawning.

Real life.

"I don't even know if anyone was hurt," I say quietly, looking down at my hands. "The house. The cars... Oh, man..."

Shame creeps in like a fever.

How many lives did I just jeopardize?

I started to shake. It is not cold. It is the weight of it. I feel the sting in my eyes, a tear slipping free, and I wipe it away fast, blaming it on the pain in my leg.

Can't cry. Not here. Not in front of these strangers. Not even in front of Allison.

Man up.

Suck it up, buttercup.

The words echo in my skull, my father's voice, hard and sharp like gravel under boots. You made your bed. Now lie in it. He would yell at me every time I made a mistake. His idea of love was discipline. Pain was just "weakness leaving the body." I used to hate him for that. Still do, sometimes. But damn, I miss him.

Another engine rumbles outside. Someone else is pulling up.

I push myself up, every muscle screaming in protest. One step. Then another. I limp toward the room. Don't look back. Don't break.

Inside, I wash the blood and dirt from my face, swap out the filthy clothes. I catch my reflection in the mirror, eyes hollow, soul bruised.

I made it here. But at what cost? The next day hits too fast, like a slap across the face before you are even fully awake. My body feels like it has been through a meat grinder, every joint aching, every muscle screaming. But the real pain comes from yelling.

"SUSPECT!"

A sharp and familiar voice cuts through the fog in my skull. I peel my eyes open just enough to see Becca's silhouette standing over me, her energy loud and chaotic like she has been up for hours stewing on this.

"Wake the hell up!"

She is already in full-blown meltdown mode. I can smell the stale perfume and cigarettes off her hoodie before I can even focus on her face. Her hair is tied up in a messy bun. Eyes bloodshot. She looks as though she hasn't slept for days. She is pacing now, hands flying as she talks to me. "Where. Is. The. Trailer?!"

I sit up, head pounding like a war drum. My ribs protest every movement. "Becca… chill. I told you last night. I had to use it, and I took it. I told you I was gonna…"

"You're a LIAR!" she snaps, cutting me off.

Now she is in my face, voice rising with each syllable. I see the storm behind her eyes, not just anger, but panic, fear, and guilt. Maybe because it is her grandpa's trailer. Not just some random piece of junk. This was a big ask, a stupid risk at that, and I took it.

"You sold it, didn't you?! Don't lie to me. SUSPECT. You're always full of it! You sold it for whatever dumb move you're into now, didn't you?! Where is it?!"

"I didn't sell it, Becca."

"You sold it. Where is it?" Her voice breaks slightly. "My grandpa is on my neck about it. You don't understand, he's threatening to call the cops…"

"I didn't freaking sell it, alright?!" I snapped back, louder than I meant to. My throat aches from the force of it, but I am too far gone to care. "I crashed it. You think I wanted to? Everything hit the fan. You think I'm proud of what happened?! Just call the cops, say it got stolen… You don't have to say my name, but they have it!!"

She stares at me for a bit, breathing heavy, lip curled like she is ready to spit venom. Her face is twisted up in that way where it is hard to tell if she is about to scream again or cry. Becca stands over me, five-foot-five of chaos in a crop top and attitude. Blonde hair frames her face in a messy knot that somehow still manages to look good in the morning light. She has that kind of body that men lose focus on a slender waist, long legs, and those 38Cs she loved to flaunt when she wanted something. Bought and paid for, bold and unmissable. She knew what she had, and she knew how to use it.

But beauty only goes so far when it is soaked in bitterness and the next level of drug habit.

Her skin used to be smoother, used to glow when she smiled for real, before the weight of late nights, cold mornings, and whatever she was putting up her nose started showing in her face. We have messed around before. Had those nights. Laughed, smoked, even talked about maybe being something more. But it never got serious. And deep down, I think we both knew why. I am not that guy. I am not for her. I am not for anyone. I am chaos. And she keeps trying to fix chaos as if it were just a puzzle missing a few pieces.

But right now, none of that matters. All she sees is the trailer gone. And all I see is a friend who trusted me, and I burned her for it.

"I'm sorry," I say quietly, trying to pull something honest from the wreckage inside me. "It got bad out there. I didn't have a choice."

"You always have a choice," she says, and her voice is colder now. Flat. Hollow. "You just never choose me."

That one lands harder than I expected.

She turns and walks out, slamming the door behind her. The echo of it feels final, as if something has just come to an end. Maybe it did.

I lay back down, staring at the ceiling, smoke from last night still clinging to my lungs. The room is quiet again, but my head is not. It is full of engines, sirens, broken promises, and burned bridges.

And now I have one more person pissed at me.

One more trail of damage I probably will not clean up.

Welp, another bites the dust. Females, especially the ones I attract. I cannot win for losing.

I start to get myself up and get ready for the day. Shave my head. Get clean. I cannot step out looking anything less than a million bucks.

Now, it is about 5:30 or 6:00 p.m. With everything that happened, I am just about ready for the night to fall and carry me away with it into whatever comes next. There is a weight in the air, thick and familiar, like the calm before something stupid. Or necessary. Or both.

The streetlights were already flickering to life outside my window, casting long orange shadows across the floorboards of my room. I sat there for a moment, hunched at the edge of the bed, one shoe halfway on, staring at nothing. It was about time to go to work again, whatever "work" meant tonight.

Then came the knock. Three taps and a pause, the kind you recognize without needing to look. My boy Craig, or that is what we will call him, leaned against the doorframe when I opened it. Hoodie half-zipped, breath smelling faintly of Black & Milds and bad decisions. His grin? Wolfish.

"Yo," he said. "Come with me. Let's see what's up with these females. And get this money. I need to grab a printer and blank checks. You riding?"

It sounds ridiculous to you, but the way he said it, it felt like just another night.

I blinked once. Nodded. "Aight, I'm in."

We left my room, and the hallway swallowed us, dim and pulsing with bass from some upstairs speaker. As I stepped out, dragging my leg behind me, still messed up from the night before, I shouted over my shoulder, "HEY! I'll be back!"

Allison appeared in the doorway, framed by peeling paint and the soft yellow glow of the hallway light behind her. Five foot six, maybe an inch taller when she was barefoot and defiant like this. Her long, brunette hair was a little tangled, the kind of mess that came from hours of pacing or lying in bed, staring at the ceiling and thinking too much.

Skinny, almost fragile looking, but not in a way that made you worry. More like someone who had not had a full meal or a full night's sleep in days, because she was always halfway in her head, halfway watching me, and halfway unable to get out of the house. The drugs did not help either.

She wore one of my old T-shirts, oversized and worn thin at the collar, its sleeves hanging off her narrow shoulders as if they didn't belong to her. And she had this look, half mad, half scared, all heart. As if she wanted to stop me but knew she couldn't. Like she was hoping that maybe, just maybe, if I kept coming back, someday I would come back for her.

She never said it out loud. Never had. But it was there. In the way her eyes lingered when I laughed.

The way she said my name made it sound like it had weight to it. In the way she stood there now, biting her lip like she was holding back all the things she wished I would notice without her saying a word. Allison wanted us to be something. Something real. And maybe in another life, maybe even in this one, if I did not keep walking out that door. But really, that is not me. Not now.

But the night was already pulling me in.

"SUSPECT, behave please," she called after me, using the nickname everyone used to call me by. "Come back, please," she added, quieter this time and barely above the creak of the door hinge. But Craig was already halfway down the stairs, and the night was calling. I did not turn around.

I just kept walking.

The door slammed behind me, the sound echoing down the street like a warning I did not bother to hear. Craig and I moved fast but casually, that careful balance you learn in certain neighborhoods. Look too nervous, and you get noticed. Look too bold, same outcome. We slid down the cracked sidewalk toward his car, eyes moving, heads on swivels. I scanned left, then right. Just shadows, streetlights, the buzz of a flickering sign in the distance. No undercover agents were in sight, but that did not mean they were not there. The air smelled like hot pavement, spilled oil, and the last breath of summer.

We climbed into the ride, some old Impala with the suspension of a boat and the soul of a graveyard, and Craig cranked the system.

Bass hit like a heartbeat too loud in your ears. No talking. Just smoke from cheap cigarettes curling up into the roof and the hum of tires eating the road. The city passed us by under a canvas of stars, uncaring and cold. We rolled down Powers Boulevard, creeping up on Barnes. I caught a flicker of motion in the side mirror. Instinct. I glanced again.

What do I see?

Of course. A cop.

"Yo," I said, calm but already tasting metal in my mouth as I turned the music down. "Ay, brotha... don't freak out, but there's a cop behind us. Keep cool, my boy."

Craig looked.

And what does this idiot do? I will tell you what this idiot did.

Before I could say another word, he threw the car in park at the light and jumped out of the driver's side like it was a damn movie. Just bolts. Sprinting like a madman down Powers southbound, arms and legs everywhere, hoodie flying up in the wind.

I sat there frozen, hands still in my lap, mouth wide open, and stuck there in disbelief.

What the...

Then the cherries lit up. Red and blue bounced off every surface, painting the inside of the car like a crime scene. Another cruiser came in hard from the back of the other patrol, squealing tires, blocking us in with surgical precision.

I couldn't jump out if I wanted to. I was caged in.

The radio squawked. A flashlight beam hit the back window. I could feel a second heartbeat in my throat now. Fast. Panicked. The taste of everything is going sideways.

And here I was in the passenger seat, leg still jacked up, and I just knew Craig had just picked me up. That's all it was. Now he was gone, just left me with a car, a cop, and a thousand questions I didn't have answers for.

So yeah.

That's my story.

Period.

The red and blue lights carved through the darkness like sirens from hell, painting the cracked windshield with lit panic. Tires crunched gravel. Doors slammed. Boots shuffled, and I could hear them getting closer.

And then I heard it.

Knock. Knock. Knock.

A hard rap on the passenger window snapped me out of my freeze. My hands were slick with sweat, chest tight, vision tunneling. I turned slowly, like maybe if I didn't make eye contact, they would forget I was here.

The cop stood just outside the glass, one hand on his belt, the other tapping the butt of his flashlight against the door. Calm. Way too calm.

"Sir, roll your window down," he said through the glass. His voice was firm, rehearsed.

I hesitated, then fumbled with the handle and got the window halfway down. Cold night air rushed in just enough to take my breath away.

"Let me see some ID," he said, leaning in just enough for me to catch the caffeine on his breath and the tension in his jaw. Then he glanced toward the driver's side, the door wide open, the seat empty where the driver once sat. The one who bolted.

He drew a long breath. That tired, cop breath, like he had seen this story too many times.

"So, why'd the other guy get out and start running?"

I swallowed. Hard. My tongue felt dry, like it had been sandpapered raw. "I-I don't know," I stammered. "You'll have to ask him."

The cop's eyes narrowed, reading me. Measuring.

"Whose car is this?"

I shrugged, heartbeat hammering loudly in my ears. DOOM. DOOM. DOOM. "Don't know. His, I assume." I tried hard to keep my composure.

"What's his name?"

I blinked. "I don't know, man, honestly. He was just giving me a ride, and we were talking, and then he left. This all happened so fast, I don't know anything about anything."

The cop watched me a second longer than I felt safe. Then he nodded his head slowly up and down, like he had decided something. Maybe he thought I was just scared. Maybe he thought I was lying through my teeth.

"Alright," he said, voice low. "So, what's your name, son? Let me see some identification."

I reached for my back pocket, but my hands didn't seem to work right. Wallet. Where the hell was my wallet? My fingers were trembling, fumbling over lint and loose change, struggling to even hold on to it.

Then the reel started playing in my head.

Robberies.

Kick doors.

Setting up drug dealers.

The carjackings all over town.

That night with Dre in the alley.

It all surged like a flood, smashing against the inside of my skull. Every wrong turn, every moment I should have walked away, every bad choice wrapped in adrenaline and easy money.

I'm cooked. I'm hit. I'm done.

"SIR, your name and identification?" the cop barked, sharp now, sensing the static in my silence.

I forced myself to breathe. In through the nose. Out through the mouth. Keep cool. Keep it together.

They don't know anything... yet anyway. Probably. Maybe. I don't know.

But one look at me, sweaty, jumpy, lips dry, and I was pretty sure he knew something. And that was enough.

My fingers finally hooked the edge of my wallet, slick with sweat. It slipped once before I gripped it tight, breathing deeply through my nose and out my mouth, like they tell you to do in rehab, juvie, or yoga. Not that any of that ever worked.

I pulled my ID out with shaky hands and passed it to the officer.

He took it without a word, eyes flicking over the plastic like he already knew what he was going to find. As he turned back toward his cruiser, I caught a glimpse of the other cop, the quiet one, slowly circling the car. His flashlight beam cut through the windows like a searchlight, looking for anything incriminating. He struck the glass, peering in, searching for God knows what.

Weapons.

Drugs.

Blood.

Whatever gets you cuffed first, am I right?

The first officer muttered, "Be right back," and walked off.

I sat there, frozen. Watching him in the mirror. Watching him slide into the squad car, the door slamming like a cold cell door. He was only in there for a minute, maybe less. Long enough to kill the last bit of hope in my gut.

When he stepped back out, I saw it in the way he moved. Purposeful. All business. His stride was heavy. Slow. Final with every step. He was already pulling his cuffs from his belt. I watched him in the side mirror, coming straight for me like a fiend I owed something to.

"Sir, can you step out of the vehicle?"

My spine went stiff. "For what?"

"Step out and put your hands behind your back."

"No, seriously, for what?" I replied.

He did not answer. Just turned me, firm but not rough, like he had done this a hundred times. I felt the cold steel clamp around one wrist, then the other.

He spoke without looking me in the eye.

"We have a warrant for your arrest."

My throat tightened. "For what?" I asked again, louder now, panic creeping into my voice like a rising flood.

"We'll talk more back at the station," he said, like a robot. Already moving through the motions.

The words barely registered as he began reading me my rights, his voice flat and scripted. Something about remaining silent. Something about lawyers. The rest blurred.

My heart was pounding so loud it drowned out everything else.

My brain lit up with what-ifs like flashbangs:

What if they've already hit the house?

What if they got Dre, too?

What if the fools from the carjacking ID'd me?

What if they found the burner in the glovebox?

What if they know everything?

Too many maybes. Not enough time.

He guided me toward the back of the cruiser, hand on my shoulder. Not gentle, not angry. Just doing his job, as if I were already a number. When he opened the door and pushed me in, the stale air inside hit me like a wall. I started sweating, couldn't shake the fear of not knowing.

The door slammed behind me. No handle. No escape. Just me in the back seat, wrists cuffed, heart thundering like a war drum, staring out the window as each streetlight passed by.

Ugh. I was just free. Why did I even leave with this fool?

CHAPTER 6: CRIMINAL JUSTICE

The cruiser rolled into the back lot of Sand Creek Police Department like a hearse pulling up to the morgue. A row of concrete walls, steel doors, and buzzing floodlights greeted me like the gates of hell. We stopped. The engine cut. No one said a word.

The back door opened, and I was yanked out into the night air, cold and metallic, tasting like rain and regret. My knees buckled slightly when my feet hit the pavement. My leg was still messed up, but I kept moving. What choice did I have?

He didn't take me through the front. I was sure this was a side door. It opened with its security clearance, and just like that, the holding cell was right there.

The inside was worse. Fluorescent lights buzzed overhead, flickering like broken promises. The whole place reeks of bleach, mildew, and old sweat, the kind of smell that sticks to your skin long after you are gone. Scuffed tile floors. The feeling of other people's bad choices echoes off the walls.

The steel door creaked open like the beginning of a nightmare. Inside, a box made of concrete, steel, and hopelessness.

No windows. No clock.

Just time and silence.

The walls were stained with age and sweat, a sickly off-white paint that made everything feel sick. One long metal bench, bolted to the wall. A stainless-steel toilet sat in the corner, no privacy, no seat, just humiliation and me. The floor was cold and damp under my shoes, like it had just been mopped but never dried.

They uncuffed me, searched for me, took my shoes and socks, handed me sandals, and shoved the door shut as I walked in.

CLANG.

The sound was final and loud. It felt like game over. Like being sealed into a tomb. The buzz of the electric lock was the only goodbye I got.

I sat on the bench, my elbows on my knees, my head hanging. My skin itched from the drugs sweating out of me. My jaw was clenched so tight my teeth hurt. Every nerve in my body was screaming, twitching, tensing, trying to jump out of my skin.

My heart would not slow down. I could feel my own pulse in my ears, in my throat, in my fingertips. All of it spiraled in my head, faster, sharper, louder. No peace. No silence. No escape.

The bench was cold beneath me, and the temperature inside the cell was even colder, but my skin burned as if I were on fire from the inside out. I felt like puking. Like screaming. Like sleeping for a year. But I just sat there. Staring at the floor. Waiting for someone to come. With every voice I heard, I thought they were coming around the corner. Nothing. No one came.

They left me there. Left to sit and think and realize what was happening. I don't know.

And my mind...

My mind was a broken projector spinning out clips I didn't ask to see of all the crimes I had committed in the last few months.

I lay down on the bench and let it all set in. I must have been sitting in that cell for hours. Or maybe it was minutes. Time has a funny way of slipping through your fingers when you are stuck in a box, just your thoughts echoing off concrete walls.

At some point, I fell asleep. Or blacked out. Maybe both.

Next thing I knew, I heard the click of keys. The groan of the lock sliding back. Then I heard it.

"Mr. Hinojosa," the officer said, swinging the heavy door open. His voice wasn't angry. Just tired. Routine. As if he had done this too many times and already knew how the story would end.

"Come with me."

Ugh... here we go.

I stood up slowly, everything stiff. Bones aching, muscles sore, head pounding like I had swallowed a war drum. My mouth was dry, my stomach sour. The crash from the high had settled in full now, and all that false confidence, all that numbness, was gone.

And with it came the storm.

I'm an idiot.

I'm so stupid.

Why can't I ever just be… normal?

Why can't I walk a straight line like everybody else? Get a job. Be a dad. Pay bills. Just exist without blowing everything up.

I followed the cop down the hall, his footsteps calm, mine dragging. The floor was sticky from a dirty mop. Fluorescent lights hummed overhead, making my skin look gray and hollow in the reflections.

My mind was louder than anything around me.

Why do I keep doing the same things over and over again?

Every time someone reaches out, I push them away. Every time life hands me a second chance, I throw it off a cliff, light a cigarette, and watch it burn.

WHY.

My chest got tight. My throat was clenched. I blinked hard.

Why do I keep using?

Why do I keep getting high and feeding this demon inside me, this thing that gnaws at everything good in my life? The dope doesn't make it better. It doesn't fix anything. It just makes it worse.

And now the crash is here. And I've got nothing to break the fall.

Nevaeh Alisianna.

Her name hit me like a freight train.

My daughter.

Her little face, her hair, her laugh, the way she looks at me like I'm a superhero, like I can do no wrong. And here I am. Again. Locked up. Again.

She needs me. And I'm not there. I'm not there enough. I know I tried to be, but I was always too busy running the streets.

And my mom…

She stayed when no one else did. She cried when I disappeared for days. She held me through the pain, bailed me out, and prayed when everyone else gave up.

And what do I do?

I leave her phone calls unanswered. I lie. I vanish. I get high. And I smile in her face like I'm fine, like I'm clean, like I'll do better, like I'm still her son.

But I'm not. Not really. Not anymore.

Tears wanted to come, but I swallowed them. Locked them behind the same door I locked everything else. But they were there, or at least I thought they were there. I'm so dead inside, I probably couldn't squeeze a tear out if I wanted to.

The hallway stretched ahead, long and endless. Every step was heavier than the last. Not because of the cuffs. Not because of the cop. But because of everything I had built and broken and taken advantage of.

My life didn't fall apart just tonight, just right now.

I tore it apart over time.

Piece by piece.

And now I was walking straight into the wreckage, and whatever was waiting for me behind the next door.

No excuses left. No high to blame.

Just me and the truth I had been running from since I could remember.

I followed the detective down a dim hallway, the kind where the fluorescent lights flicker like they're trying to stay alive. Cold concrete underfoot. The smell of stale coffee and sweat in the air. He opened a heavy metal door and gestured with two fingers.

"Have a seat."

I slid into the steel chair, back straight, palms flat on the table. Heart thudding in my chest, but I wore the face of someone who had done this before.

"Here we go," I thought to myself.

The detective sat across from me. Worn leather jacket. Coffee-stained folder in one hand. A stare in his eyes that could peel paint off the walls.

"I'm the lead detective working your case," he said, slow and deliberate. "Let's start with something simple. Where were you last night?"

I blinked once. "Where was I?"

I let the question hang in the air like a cloud of smoke. Then leaned back, casual.

"I was at home."

He narrowed his eyes.

"Okay. Sir, I'm going to be as forward as I can. Last night, there was a high-speed chase. Long story short, the vehicle in question drove straight through someone's house. The suspect fled on foot and got away."

He locked his eyes on me. "Do you know anything about this?"

I knew it. I just knew it.

I let out a low chuckle, shaking my head slowly. "What? Nah, bruh. I don't know what you're talking about."

"So, you're saying this wasn't you?" he asked.

I smirked, cool and easy. "That's exactly what I'm saying... SIR."

He laughs with me, but it is not a friendly laugh. It is that kind of laugh that says he has cards in his hand that I have not seen yet.

I start to second-guess myself. Maybe I played it too hard.

"Well, SIR," he says, laying it on thick, "funny thing about that..."

He flips open the folder.

"We found prints."

Another laugh. This one is sharper, like a knife pressed to skin.

"And a phone."

He leans in.

"Your fingerprints are on it. We were able to link the phone to you and your Facebook account. Your messages. And your last known location." His smile sharpens. "We have a pretty good idea it was you, Mr. Hinojosa."

I breathe deep, lungs heavy. I am hit. Hit like good weed on a bad day. I feel it. They know too much.

I think fast.

"That is really weird," I say, voice calm. "Because my phone was stolen days ago.

So, unfortunately, SIR, you have got the wrong guy."

Inside, I am grinning like I just played the ace of spades. Outside, poker face locked tight.

But he does not flinch.

He laughs again, louder now. "Alright," he says, "you might be right. Thing is, I figured you would say that."

He slides a photo across the table, slowly, like he is flipping over a royal flush ace high.

The image hits me like a sucker punch to the gut.

It is me.

Or someone that looks exactly like me, behind the wheel of a busted-up truck, caught mid-frame by a street camera blowing through a red light with a trailer dragged behind it.

"This," the detective says, tapping the photo, "is from the beginning of the pursuit."

I freeze. I do not blink. But the chill crawls up my spine like a spider.

Still, I do not crack.

"That is a good one, sir," I say, words clipped and firm. "But to be honest with you, I was home.

That guy might look like me, sure, but I am completely outraged by these accusations."

I lean forward now, steady.

"And in all reality, SIR, I was not there. Not involved. In this so-called incident. In any way, shape, or form."

Silence stretches.

"So... I am going to have to ask for a lawyer."

He stares at me for a long moment, face gone dark, cold, and blank.

Then he stood up. "Okay. That's how you want to play, huh?"

He opened the door behind him.

"Stand up. Let's go."

No more smiles. No more jokes. Just the sound of my cuffs clicking behind my back as he marched me to the holding cell, the cold steel door slamming shut like the end of a bad dream.

Hours dragged by. The walls in this cold cell felt like they were closing in, breathing against my neck. I paced back and forth, counting cracks in the concrete like they held some secret

I was missing. Time slowed. Thoughts didn't.

What the hell just happened?

Eventually, exhaustion took over. I lay down on the slab of steel they called a bed, no mattress, just a mat thinner than my patience. My mind kept racing and spinning, twitching, clawing for an escape. But I was too tired. Too sober. All I could think about was getting high, zoning out, and floating far from this nightmare.

Sleep hit like a fist.

I don't even know how long I was out before I heard the sound.

CLANK.

The cell door slid open with that rusty, metallic scream that makes your spine twitch.

"Let's go, Mr. Hinojosa," the cop said. Voice like gravel. No sympathy.

I sat up slowly, rubbing my face. It took me a second to get my brain working again. "Where are we going?"

Like I didn't already know.

"You're going for a ride," he said and slapped the cuffs on me without another word. That cold metal around my wrists, a feeling I knew all too well. It felt like home in the worst way.

He walked me through the maze of the facility. Past holding cells. Past junkies rocking in corners. Past the worst version of myself, reflected in every dirty window we passed.

The air outside hit me like a slap. Bright sun. Was it morning? Loud traffic. Freedom, just out of reach.

They put me in the back of the patrol car. Doors slammed. The engine rumbled. And we were off.

Destination?

CJC.

The Criminal Justice Center.

I slumped in the seat, stared out the window, and my heart sank into the pit of my stomach.

I was back.

Back at the place where hope goes to die. Booking. Intake. Fingerprints. Mugshot. Same damn routine. I felt like I was stuck in a loop I couldn't escape. Like I was born to fail.

God, I'm the dumbest idiot alive. Seriously.

Charges?

Stacked a mile long. Bond? Sky-high. The sheriffs didn't look at you like humans anymore. Just another screw-up. Another number on the list. At least most of them did.

Funny thing is, I know a good handful of them, and we've got rapport with each other. This is where they call me a "frequent flyer."

Eventually, they tossed me a jumpsuit.

County orange.

Like some sick joke, it was the same size and fit I had last time. Too big in the shoulders, too tight in the neck. It felt like a noose, disguised as clothing.

More waiting. Hours blurred together. Time didn't move in here; it stagnated. Like the air.

Finally, they assigned me a bed. I walked the long, echoing hallway to my cell. Every step felt like I was walking deeper into a grave, blanket and sheets in my arms. No pillow. Don't want you to get too comfortable now.

I got in, dropped my bag on the bunk, and sat.

Then I just sat.

And I felt it start to crush me. All of it. The silence. The smell. The weight of knowing I did this again.

I made my bed, but I didn't lie down.

I just stared out the window, four by twelve inches.

And the questions started to pour in like rain through a busted roof.

How?

How did I get here?

How did my life come to this again?

Why can't I learn from anything?

Every time I swear, I'll change. Every time I say I'm done. And then I fall back into the same pit with the same demons whispering in my ear.

Why am I like this?

What the hell happened to me?

When did I stop caring?

And that's when it hit me hard, the part that really hurt.

It wasn't the charges. It wasn't the cell. It wasn't even the time I might have.

It was the mirror.

Because the man I saw now, I didn't recognize him anymore.

He was angry. He was lost. He was dead. Just a soft shell of a man. Hollow.

There's a demon in me. A darkness I can't seem to kill. It feeds off pain. Off rage. Off guilt. Revenge and joy in others' pain. Every time I try to shake it, it drags me back in.

The demon inside me isn't some horned beast with red eyes and a pitchfork.

Nah.

It's colder than that. Smarter. Meaner.

It's a whisper in my own voice, telling me to do the wrong thing and making it sound like survival. It wears my face when I look in the mirror, only twisted, smirking like it knows something I don't. As if it's already seen the ending and is laughing at the idea that I could ever change.

It isn't loud.

It waits.

Lurking in the quiet moments. In boredom. In the anger. In the long nights when sleep doesn't come and the cravings scratch behind my eyes. That's when it wakes up. Crawls out from wherever I buried it last time and stretches like it's been resting all day.

It feeds off my pain. Off every L I ever took. Every time I was told I wasn't enough. Every fake friend. Every broken promise. Every time I told myself I'd do better and didn't.

It reminds me.

It catalogs every mistake and plays them back like a highlight reel.

And when it speaks, it doesn't yell. It doesn't threaten.

It seduces.

"Just one more hit, you'll feel better."

"Just one more hustle, and you're straight."

"Just one more lie, and you'll get out of this."

And I believe it. That's the worst part.

I believe it. Because it's dressed up in logic. In fake comfort. In promises, it never keeps.

That demon isn't a monster in the dark. It's the part of me I thought I needed to survive. The fighter. The hustler. The one that never shows weakness.

But it's a liar. A parasite wearing armor made from every time I got hurt and didn't know how to deal with it.

It's not in me.

It is me.

And sometimes, I wonder if I was born with it, or if the world gave it to me piece by piece.

However, it is strong either way. Stronger than my will most days. Stronger than my guilt.

And it is patient. It will let me clean up, get right, and smile in the mirror again, just to pull me back down when I least expect it.

And when I am lying there, broken, ashamed, alone, it does not comfort me.

It laughs. Because the demon does not want me dead. Nah. That is too easy.

It wants me to be trapped.

Alive, but lost.

A ghost of the man I could have been.

Evil thoughts.

Bad choices. One after another.

And now I am here again, behind cold steel, drowning in questions I do not have answers for.

Why? Why? WHY?

That is the one that echoes loudest.

WHY?

CHAPTER 7: FAMILY MATTERED

I was born on Sunday, June 19, 1983, in Colorado Springs, Colorado, under the shadow of the Rocky Mountains, at Fort Carson Army Hospital. That Sunday happened to be Father's Day. Fitting, perhaps, for a child arriving in a life already shaped by the rhythms and sacrifices of military service.

My mother, Elizabeth M. Hinojosa, a Colorado Springs native, was barely more than a girl herself. A beautiful young woman, hopeful and strong in the way women often are when they carry a child. My father, David R. Hinojosa, born in Detroit, Michigan, was stationed far away in Panama when I decided it was time to enter the world. But duty did not stop him. He flew back just in time, his uniform still creased with the weight of his post, to be there when I took my first breath.

I was his Father's Day gift, the kind you cannot wrap or measure in boxes, the kind that makes a man feel something deep and trembling inside. My father saw me before I even saw him. When he held me, the room seemed to pause, as though new life alone could still the world. My mother, exhausted but radiant, looked on with quiet awe. In that moment, there were no bases, no deployments, no borders. Just the three of us. A unit. A beginning.

They say the room was filled with light when I cried. Not the sterile glow of hospital lamps, but a tender light, as if joy itself had come to peek in. My mother's arms wrapped around me as though I had always belonged there. My father, who had spent his life learning how to march, salute, and sacrifice, stood still for the first time in a long while. Not for duty, but for love.

We did not stay in Colorado for long. That is the way of military life: always moving, always packing pieces of your life into boxes stamped with base names and zip codes. Shortly after I was born, we left for Panama. My first passport would bear a stamp not of memory, but of promise, the promise of a journey just beginning.

The first few years of my life were spent in Panama, a humid and vibrant land where the air was thick with the scent of earth and salt, and the sounds of life rose in wild, rhythmic layers. I was barely a toddler, unaware of borders or languages, yet the world around me felt alive in a way that imprinted itself deep in my bones.

Our house sat in a quiet stretch of military housing. Modest by today's standards, but comfortable, even spacious for a young family in the 1980s. From the outside, it looked ordinary, beige, practical, and uniform. But behind the house, the magic began.

Our backyard was not just a yard. It was a jungle.

Not a patch of overgrown trees, but a dense, tangled rainforest teeming with life. Birds with painted feathers screamed from the canopy. Monkeys swung through the trees at dusk, and lizards the size of a child's arm darted across mossy rocks. At night, insects and unseen creatures created a symphony, as if nature itself hummed a lullaby just for me.

My father, ever the adventurer, could not resist. Armed with a machete and a rope tied to a thick tree trunk, he would vanish into the green abyss behind our house, the rope his only guide back. To him, it was an adventure. To me, he was a hero, a man slicing through vines and mystery like something out of a storybook.

While he explored, my mother brought life to the kitchen. Fresh seafood from the Panama Canal became our meals. Ingredients so fresh they still smelled of the sea.

I remember eating ceviche bright with lime, sharp with peppers, alive with fish that had only hours before been swimming. Our meals were not just food. They were tradition, culture, and love, served on hand-painted plates.

Some afternoons, my mother would take me to the local casinos. Not like Vegas, quieter, subdued, but still full of flashing lights and the hum of hope. I would tug on her hand, wide-eyed, and say, "Money pull!" pretending to gamble like the adults, mimicking the slot machine lever with tiny fingers. The lights, the sounds, all part of a colorful mosaic of early memories.

Life in Panama was wild and structured. A boy could play beneath palm trees while tanks rolled by on the road. Soldiers saluted as monkeys chattered in the trees. Discipline and unpredictability danced together, and I grew up in the space between.

But permanence, like the jungle itself, was an illusion. Eventually, it was time to pack up again. The jungle behind our house, the laughter in the kitchen, and the casino lights all became distant memories. We moved to Watertown, New York.

It was colder there. Quieter. The wildness I had known was replaced by snow, straight streets, and structured days. In Panama, the air smelled of rain and was clean. Watertown smelled of frost and chimney smoke. Even as a child, I could feel the shift, not just in the weather, but in life itself.

And there, my parents would welcome a new life into the world. My sister, Bernadette, was born May 27, 1987, premature yet perfect, a tiny miracle wrapped in hospital blankets. My mother had complications, and Bernadette was so small she had to wear doll clothes. Two years later, on August 8, 1989, my brother Christopher arrived. I became the eldest, the one who had known the jungle before the snow. Our family of three had become five.

New York was not home, not really. But for a time, we were together—a young family navigating the shifting tides of military life, from Panama's wild beauty to the quiet streets of upstate New York, holding onto each other as the world changed around us.

Every so often, my grandmother, Grandma Jessie, would visit. She was my father's mother, a strong, no-nonsense woman from Detroit, Michigan, where my dad had grown up. Her voice carried the grit of the city, but her presence brought a sense of comfort. Strict, yes, but the kind of strict that only comes from blood and history.

When she visited, our world seemed to slow down. From my point of view, we gathered around the table, laughed at old stories, and ate until we could not move. Yes, there were arguments amongst them, but it did not concern me. There were no uniforms or schedules, no looming relocations. Just warmth, noise, food, and love, the quiet kind that filled the spaces between words.

Life felt easier then. Simpler. No bills, no responsibilities, no weight on my shoulders, no chaos. I was just a kid, free to play, to watch cartoons on quiet mornings, to chase shadows in the snow. The grown-ups handled the world, and I lived like a child. A normal, carefree child.

We moved to Berlin, Germany, during a time when the world seemed to be holding its breath. The Cold War's grip was loosening, and the Berlin Wall, a scar of concrete and barbed wire that had sliced the city in two decades, was finally beginning to crumble.

I still remember walking the streets in those early days of my life, guided only by the sound of hammers and cheers, as people from both sides chipped away at a wall that had once felt permanent. It was a sight to see.

My family now lives in Germany, where we are stationed as part of my father's military service. There was raw, electric energy in the air, a mixture of hope, fear, and the dizzying sense that history was shifting beneath our feet.

My father was a drill instructor in the United States Army, tough as iron and sharp as they come. But even steel bends.

During basic training exercises, something went wrong. A split-second misstep, maybe. The kind of injury that not only ends a drill but also rewrites your body. They had to take a tendon from his leg and graft it into his shoulder.

I remember the surgery. They put him in a full cast from his torso up to his shoulder and down his arm, keeping his arm fully extended for months. I remember the way he gritted his teeth through the pain, refusing to let it slow him down.

He never talked much about it, just a stiff nod when someone asked. But I could see it, the way his walk changed, the way he rotated his arm with caution, like it was borrowed.

Still, to me, he was larger than life. A soldier not just in title, but in presence. Even though he was wounded, he stood taller and harder than anyone I knew.

CHAPTER 8: GROWING PAINS

I was eight years old in 1990, a wild ball of energy with scraped knees and a buzz cut, living in Berlin during a time when the world around me was rearranging itself. Vanilla Ice's "Ice Ice Baby" was blasting from boom boxes, and I thought it was the coolest sound ever made. I remember my friends and I would dance like maniacs to it, trying to moonwalk on the concrete and breakdance in our sneakers until we were dizzy and breathless with laughter. We did not know it then, but we were the soundtrack of a world changing around us.

Football, not just any football but American football, was everything to me, and my dad instilled that in me. I was small but fast and never seemed to run out of steam. My dad, a drill instructor in the U.S. Army, had already begun grooming me for the game at an early age. He saw something in me, some raw potential that needed to be shaped. Plus, I was his son, and he played football when he was young. He was hard as a nail, sharp in voice and sharper in expectations. There were no shortcuts and no excuses. If I dropped the ball, we ran drills until the sun went down. He was not just teaching me a sport; he was instilling discipline into my bones, one push-up at a time.

We lived on base in a block of apartment-style housing, uniform rows of concrete buildings with faded paint, tall and square. Behind our building stretched a wide-open playground that might as well have been my home. It had swings that squeaked, monkey bars with the paint worn off, and a giant ship-like playground. A giant field rolled out like a sea of grass. After school, I would live out there, running, tackling, and playing made-up games with kids from all over the United States. We did not need much. Just a football and daylight.

School was different. German. Foreign. Exciting. The language felt sharp and fast in my ears, like stepping into a puzzle where the pieces kept moving. I picked it up slowly, clumsily, but I wanted to belong. I wanted to understand the kids I saw on the other side of the fence, speaking something that felt like code. My world was English at home, but the streets and classrooms whispered in German, and I listened hard.

Sunday mornings were for Catholic school, where I would receive my Holy Communion, and church, where we would kneel in pews under stained-glass windows, the light streaming in like colored fog. My hands were clasped together, but my mind drifted to football plays and playground dares. I believed in God, yes, because that's what I was told. But did I know Him? I knew football, and I also believed in catching the perfect spiral pass.

Those years feel like a memory sealed in streetlights, amber in color, bright, loud, and slightly distorted.

A young boy, dancing to Vanilla Ice, dreaming in English, learning in German, and sprinting across a field that never seemed to end.

There was this old playground behind our apartment block on base, the kind of place that felt bigger than life when you were a kid. It had everything you could want: swing sets that could launch you into orbit, monkey bars that turned your hands to blisters, and a giant field where we played until the sky turned orange.

But the crown jewel of that playground, the thing that made it legendary, was this ship.

Not a real one, of course. It was a wooden structure, faded and weathered by years of sun and rain, built like a pirate ship, complete with portholes, a ship's wheel, and best of all, a crow's nest. For those who do not know, a crow's nest is the lookout post at the very top of a ship's mast, meant to give sailors a wide view of the ocean around them. Up there, you were the eyes of the entire crew. The one who spotted danger first. The one who found land.

On that day, I scrambled up the ship and into the crow's nest, pretending I was a fearless explorer with binoculars slung around my neck, scanning the high seas for enemy vessels. I was full of energy, imagination, and just enough recklessness to make life interesting.

Then I heard them.

Trouble.

Two girls I knew, slightly older, maybe nine or ten, were walking toward the playground. We lived in the same building. Our parents were friends. I knew their names, had seen them at backyard barbecues and base events. And to me, at that age, they were beautiful and pretty in the way that made your stomach flutter even though you did not know why.

They spotted me up there, perched high above the playground world, and they started shouting.

"JUMP, GABE! JUMP! Come on! Do it!"

Their voices were full of laughter and challenge, ringing out across the empty swings and silent field. Other kids playing around the park stopped in their tracks to see if I would actually do it.

I looked down. From where I stood in that wooden bucket, it felt like two stories up, maybe more. My heart thumped in my chest. My fingers clutched the edge of the crow's nest as I leaned out, testing the drop. For those who do not know, a crow's nest is the highest point above the rest of the playground ship, a small circular platform encircled by wooden slats, like a barrel bolted to the tallest mast. It was just big enough for a kid to crouch or stand inside, hands gripping the rim, eyes peeking over the edge. From down below, it looked like a birdhouse for humans, narrow, weather-worn, and slightly tilted from years of rain, snow, and rough play.

To me, though, it was more than just wood and nails. It was the highest point in the world. A place where you could look out and see everything: the swings, the sandbox, the whole neighborhood, even the edges of the base where the trees began. Up there, the air felt different. It felt thinner, freer. It was a throne for the king of the playground, a watchtower for spotting enemy ships, a launchpad for the bold.

Getting up there took guts. You had to climb a winding ladder or scale the ship's side like a pirate, hands slipping on worn beams, feet searching for the next grip. And once you were up, standing in that narrow space with the sky above and the world below, it felt like anything was possible.

The crow's nest was not just a part of the playground. It was a rite of passage. A place where dares were made, dreams were imagined, and sometimes, just sometimes, crazy leaps of faith were taken.

They kept going. "Come on, Gabriel! What are you waiting for? JUMP!"

I hesitated. For a second, my brain said no way. But then something shifted. Maybe it was pride. Maybe it was the need to impress them. Perhaps it was just being young, filled with blind courage and a child's logic.

So, I said to myself, why not?

This was my moment. My chance to be the cool guy. The brave one. The kind of kid who did things others would not.

I climbed out of the bucket, carefully placing one foot on the narrow wooden railing, the other dangling over open air. The wind tugged at my shirt. I closed my eyes.

And then I leapt.

For a second, it felt like flying. The kind of flying you only experience in dreams. Eyes shut, arms out, soaring through the air with a whoosh in my ears and nothing but sky beneath me. Time stretched, like the world was holding its breath.

Then BOOM.

I hit the ground hard, legs bent, arms flailing to catch my balance. My sneakers dug into the dirt, and I stumbled but didn't fall.

I landed it.

I freaking landed it.

My eyes flew open, and I stood there, breathless, half-shocked, half-thrilled, just pure amazement. The girls were screaming, laughing, and cheering. Even I could not believe it. My knees were shaking, but I did it.

For that one moment, I felt invincible. Like a superhero. Like the legend of the playground.

That first jump opened something inside me, like a window I did not know existed. Not just between me and the two girls, but between me and everyone who saw it. Children from all corners of the playground came running, their sneakers pounding the ground, their faces lit with disbelief and awe. For a few seconds, I was a legend.

They surrounded me, wide-eyed and buzzing, like I had pulled off a magic trick. The girls were there too, laughing, clapping, their eyes bright. I stood in the middle of it all, soaking it in, breathing hard, chest puffed out.

Then I heard the first one's voice, then another.

"Do it again!"

And then the yelling began to rise, building in rhythm and volume like the drumbeat before a battle.

"AGAIN! AGAIN! AGAIN!"

I froze, caught between the pride swelling in my chest and the dull ache creeping up my right leg. It did not hurt badly, but something felt tight, a pain that had not been there before. Still, I brushed it off. I was the kid who flew out of the sky and landed it. I could not back down now. Not with half the playground watching.

So, I smiled, because what else could I do?

I dusted myself off, turned around, and headed back toward the ship. Each step toward the crow's nest made the crowd louder. Cheers. Shouts. Hands in the air like I was walking into a stadium. I limped slightly, trying to hide it. My leg was whispering warnings, but I was not listening. I had a show to give.

I climbed the ship again, hand over hand, heart pounding. The wood was warm from the sun, rough under my fingers. I made it back to the crow's nest, my little command post in the sky, and stood inside for a moment, breathing deep.

Below me now was a crowd. This was real. Kids of all ages, faces turned up, shouting like I was a hero in a movie.

"DO IT! DO IT! DO IT!"

I hesitated for just a second. My leg throbbed a little more now. I could feel it.

I already did it once. I can do it again. What is the worst thing that could happen?

I climbed onto the edge, the wooden rim cool beneath my sneakers. My arms stretched out like wings. I closed my eyes, sucked in one final breath, and let go of fear, of hesitation, of common sense.

And I jumped.

Through the air I went, flying again. But something was different. Off. The landing came faster than before. My body hit the ground, not with grace, but with weight. My legs folded awkwardly beneath me, and—

SNAP!

The sound was unmistakable.

Hot pain shot through my body like lightning. I screamed and crumpled to the dirt, grabbing my leg, eyes wide in shock. My breath caught in my throat as I looked down and saw it.

My leg twisted in a way no leg should twist. The world around me blurred. Kids gasped. Some screamed. The chant died instantly.

I broke my femur.

I could not move. Could not speak. The pain was so sharp it felt like the world itself had torn open beneath me.

And just like that, the legend of the flying boy came crashing down.

For a moment, everything went still.

No chanting. No clapping. No laughter.

Just me on the ground, screaming. That was it.

The pain was beyond anything I had ever known. It was not just pain. It was fire, white in my vision, radiating from my thigh like someone had driven a hot metal rod through my leg. My screams tore out of me uncontrollably, raw and full of panic, louder than I ever thought I could yell. My hands clawed at the dirt, trying to grab something, anything, to ground myself.

Around me, the kids scattered. The crowd that had cheered for me just seconds before now exploded like a shaken anthill. I saw them sprinting in every direction, faces pale, mouths open, screaming things I could not understand over the sound of my own voice. They moved fast, too fast, like roaches when the kitchen light flipped on. But a few stayed. The two girls were there, eyes wide, frozen in shock. One of them had her hands over her mouth. A couple of my football friends were there as well, their scraped knees hovering close, unsure of what to do.

Then I heard one of them yell.

"GO GET HIS DAD!"

Someone took off running. I lay there, gripping my leg, staring in disbelief at my thigh, which was already beginning to swell, the skin stretching tight like a balloon under the surface. It no longer even resembled my leg. Just this bent, unnatural thing attached to me.

I was sobbing now, voice hoarse, begging for it to stop, trying to wake myself from a nightmare that was not ending.

And then, through the tears and chaos, I saw him.

My dad.

Coming from the far end of the field, running, or at least trying to. He had just had surgery on his shoulder and was still wearing a cast, limping with every step from the tendon they had taken out of his leg. But he was coming, teeth clenched, eyes locked on me like a missile. And he was not alone. A few of his buddies, Army strong, all of them, were running behind him, faster and catching up to get to me.

He could not carry me himself. He could not even walk right. But he got to me, collapsed to his knees beside me, his breath ragged.

"Gabe! Gabe! Look at me, son. Look at me!"

I tried. My eyes met his, and I saw the terror there. Not fear of the blood or the break, but fear for me.

Two of his friends gently slipped their arms under me. Even that movement made me scream again.

"Easy, easy," one of them said. "We got you, kid. Hang in there."

They lifted me up like I was made of glass, careful to keep my leg as still as possible. The world tilted as they carried me across the field, through the playground, back toward the apartment building. I could hear my dad limping behind us, still trying to stay close.

Inside, everything was a blur. My mom was crying as soon as I got home. I was lying down carefully on the couch. The cushions were soft, but every breath still felt like someone was stabbing me. The room spun. The voices of adults overlapped, calm but edged with worry.

Then came the sound I will never forget, the wail of the ambulance siren in the distance, growing louder with each passing second.

The paramedics arrived quickly, efficiently, and moved like they had done this a thousand times. One of them pulled out a pair of trauma shears.

"Sorry, buddy," he said, voice steady. "We have to cut these off."

My jeans were gone, sliced clean down the middle. When the paramedic peeled them away, he winced.

"Femur's broken," he muttered to his partner. You could see it pushing against my skin. It was not punctured; it was just pressing underneath.

A needle went into my arm, something cold and heavy settling in my veins. My vision began to blur, the pain softening just slightly around the edges. The last thing I saw was my dad's face, pale and strained, standing behind the paramedics with one hand on his cast, the other clenched into a fist.

I woke to the sharp scent of antiseptic wash and the low hum of fluorescent lights. The ceiling was dull off-white, tiled in neat squares, and I stared at it for a long moment, confused about where I was, until the pain finally caught up with me. It was dull at first, then roaring, lightning that shot from my thigh to my chest. I tried to move, but my body would not listen. My leg felt limp. Heavy. Not just pain, something deeper. Broken.

Then I heard voices.

"Hey, hey... he's waking up," my mom said, her voice cracking, like she had been crying for hours. She was at my bedside in an instant, brushing the damp hair off my forehead. My dad stood behind her, mad and upset, his jaw clenched as if he were chewing gravel. And next to them was a man in a white coat, clipboard in hand. The doctor.

"Welcome back," he said calmly. "You gave everyone a scare."

I blinked at him, disoriented. "What... what happened?"

The doctor glanced at my parents, then pulled a chair up beside my bed.

"You were in an accident. A bad one," he said. "You snapped your femur clean in half mid-shaft. It took a considerable amount of time to realign the bone. We had to pull your leg and stabilize it temporarily, but you are going to need surgery. We will have to insert a rod, which we call an intramedullary pin, to keep everything in place."

The words hit like weights: snapped, surgery, pin. However, I could not get them to settle.

My dad leaned in. "Doctor, what does that mean for his future? For sports? Football?"

There was a pause. The kind that dangles in the air like a loaded gun.

The doctor set the clipboard down. "I will not sugarcoat it. The fracture is severe, one of the worst I have seen in someone your age. Even after we repair it, the bone's integrity will never be the same. A hit, especially the kind of impact you get on a football field, could shatter it again."

He turned to me, eyes serious, voice low. "Son, you do not play football with an injury like this. One wrong tackle, one helmet to the leg, and you are right back here... or worse."

I stared at him, numb. My mouth opened, but no words came out. Just a faint, dry whisper. "But I play football."

"Not anymore," he said, and it was not cruel. It was final. "Once the surgery is done, you will be in traction for at least six months. And even then, you will have to learn to walk again."

My stomach turned. The room tilted. A cold sweat broke out on my forehead.

Learn to walk again?

My dad's face dropped. He looked like someone had kicked him in the chest. My mom let out a soft sob and clutched my hand tighter.

I wanted to scream. To punch something. To run. But all I could do was lie there, broken, crushed beneath the weight of something far heavier than pain.

The doctor stood. "We are going to take good care of you. Surgery is first thing tomorrow. Rest. You will need your strength."

He left the room, and silence filled the space he had occupied.

Football. Gone. Just like that.

Everything I had worked for or even dreamed about, those Friday night lights, scholarship scouts, my name on the board, all gone in the snap of a bone.

I turned my head away from my parents, blinking hard to fight the tears stinging my eyes. My dad did not say anything and walked out.

This was not a nightmare. It was real. And it had only just begun. Staying in that German hospital felt like being trapped between two worlds: my old life dreaming of football and whatever was waiting for me next. Everything around me was familiar and foreign at the same time. The walls were sterile white, the lighting always humming above me, and the smell of antiseptic clung to everything. The nurses spoke in clipped, efficient German, and while I could follow some of it, talking about medications and pain thresholds in a second language was something else entirely.

Even in the haze of painkillers and recovery, school did not stop. Packets of homework were delivered to my bedside in manila envelopes, math problems, history readings, essays waiting to be written. At first, I hated it. But eventually, it gave me structure, a reason to push through the monotony. Something that made me feel like I was still me, not just a broken body.

My parents were my lifeline. They visited daily, always bringing food, but not just food, real food. My mom would unwrap warm bread rolls and fresh bratwurst, or the occasional PX cheeseburger, laying them out like a makeshift picnic on the tray beside me. My dad did not say much, but his presence was stern and steady. He was not a man to mess with. He would sit quietly, sometimes just watching me. I think he felt helpless, disappointed, and perhaps even more, but he never said so aloud.

Then, one day, the girls I had tried so hard to impress back at school showed up. They stood awkwardly at first, shifting from foot to foot, arms full of flowers. I couldn't help but laugh when I saw it; I really laughed, for the first time in weeks.

"We did not know if we should come," one of them said shyly. "But we felt bad."

I shook my head, managing a grin. "I am alright. It was fun though, flying in the air like that."

We laughed together, genuinely and quietly, like something normal had crept back into the room. For a moment, the cast, the wires, the IV lines, none of it mattered.

Eventually, I was discharged from the hospital. They wheeled me out in a full body cast that covered half my torso, one entire leg, and most of the other, all held in place with a stabilizing bar. It felt like I was wearing a cement shell. The doctors recommended strict bed rest.

But I was not built for lying still.

Within days, I was figuring out how to slide myself out of bed, land on the floor with a soft thud, and drag my body room to room like some stubborn army crawler. My mom flipped out the first time she found me halfway to the kitchen, arms shaking, grinning like an idiot.

"I am not staying in that bed," I told her.

Six months in traction and casts felt like a prison sentence, but when they finally cut me free, the hard part started. Walking again was its own battle. My muscles were weak, like rubber bands left in the sun too long. I initially used parallel bars, then a walker. Every step was awkward, every joint stiff, my legs relearning movements they had once done without thinking. The pain was constant. Some days, it felt like my bones were grinding against each other. Other days, it was the ache of frustration, knowing I would never move the same way again.

The field. The roar of the crowd. My dream of playing football. Gone.

Football was not just a sport; it was a passion for me. It was the future I had envisioned through my dad. And now, it was gone. Dead. Like a door that had slammed shut, locked from the other side, and the key thrown away.

Around that time, my dad received his own news. After years of service, surgeries, and silent suffering, the Army handed him a medical discharge. It was the end of his military career. Just like my football dreams, his chapter had closed too.

So, we packed up what was left of our life in Germany and headed back to the States.

We went to Colorado Springs, Colorado, where all my mom's family lived. The air hit differently there, crisp and dry, thin enough to burn your lungs if you breathed too quickly. It was something you had to get used to. The mountains towered in the distance, vast and unmoving, watching silently from afar.

We settled into a modest house on a busy street. It was not fancy, but it was ours. I started at a new school. No one knew me as "the football kid" anymore, or "the guy who almost lost his leg." I was just the new kid. It was a different kind of freedom. Painful, yes, but clean. A blank page.

The leg healed, though it hurt sometimes, and it stayed with me as a quiet reminder of everything I had fought through. Some days it was worse than others. And when the weather turned cold or the pressure changed, my leg would throb deep in the bone, like it remembered and would not let me forget.

But I was walking. I was living.

And I was far from finished.

CHAPTER 9: TROUBLE BEGINS

By the time I was in the fourth grade, nine or maybe ten years old, I was no longer the same kid I used to be. I had grown sharper, quieter. The innocence most kids carried like a backpack was long gone, discarded and lost somewhere between the hospital bed and the rice grains that dug into my knees due to my father's discipline.

I was in Ms. Elaine's class that year. She smelled like mothballs and talked with her hands, always snapping her fingers when she wanted silence.

But no amount of finger-snapping could shut up Fabian. He was the class clown, the fast-talking, track-running, always-smirking type. African American kid with skinny legs, slick words, and the kind of cocky charm that made teachers chuckle and girl's whisper. He sat right behind me, always behind me. And every day, he'd poke me. The tip of his pencil would jab into my back, the soft spot just beneath my shoulder blade, like a bird pecking nonstop in pure madness. Tap. Tap. Tap.

"Stop," I'd hiss, barely turning my head.

But he didn't. He just grinned, wide and white, feeding off my anger like it was fuel. The more I tried to ignore him, the harder he leaned in, laughing, whispering something to the others. And they laughed too. Always laughing.

I snapped once, turned around in a red haze, and yelled, "Cut it out!"

Ms. Elane didn't see his pencil. She only saw me.

I bit my tongue and sat back down. My fists clenched so tight my knuckles cracked. The classroom lights buzzed overhead like flies.

That was the day something inside me shifted.

When I got home, the house was quiet, cold. My father wasn't back yet. Maybe still at work. Maybe waiting for one of us to screw up so he could remind us of what discipline was. He didn't hit with love. He hit with precision. Like punishment was a ritual, something sacred embedded inside him. Belts. Wall sits. Kneeling on raw rice until your legs went numb and your mind left your body.

I walked past the kitchen and into the hallway. That's when I saw it.

His knife.

It sat on the hallway bookshelf, half-sheathed in cracked leather. Not big but not small either, small enough to hide. I had seen it before, once, when he cleaned it carefully, methodically, like it was a living thing.

And at that moment, staring at it, a switch flipped. A thought, like smoke, slithered into my mind.

"He won't laugh at me anymore. Not after this."

I didn't know what I was going to do, not really. But I knew the feeling. The heat behind my eyes. The roaring in my ears. I wasn't scared. I was focused. Like the world had finally made sense.

That evening, when the house settled into its usual rhythm, there was distant television chatter of the news, the clatter of dishes from the kitchen, and the hum of a ceiling fan overhead. I slipped the knife from the hallway dresser and took it downstairs to my room. It felt heavier than I expected. Solid. Cold. Real. Not like a toy or a threat. Like a promise. I tucked it under a loose board beneath my bed, wrapped in an old T-shirt. My heart hammered in my chest the whole time, like it was trying to warn me. I didn't listen. I didn't do anything else that would make it obvious. I just... existed. Helped set the table. Sat quietly through dinner, chewing slowly and nodding when spoken to. I kept glancing at my father while he sat in the living room drinking his beer, waiting and almost hoping that he'd notice. That he'd march to the hallway and scream for us all to line up, screaming, "Who took it?" so I could gauge my options, plan my next move.

But he didn't.

He didn't even pay attention to what we were doing unless we made noise or played around at the dinner table. Later, I told them both goodnight with the usual rehearsed smile and walked calmly to my room. Downstairs, the air felt heavier, like the walls themselves were in on it. I shut the door softly behind me, then sat on the edge of my bed, staring at the floor. I could feel the knife under there. It was like it had a presence now, breathing with me, pulsing in sync with my own thoughts.

I lay back and stared at the ceiling, wide-eyed in the dark.

The idea kept playing over and over in my mind. This ends tomorrow. He won't laugh again. He won't even look at me. Not after this. He wouldn't see it coming. That smug face, that cocky walk, the way his pencil stabbed at me like he owned me, it'd all be gone in an instant. Just like that. One move. One moment. And I'd make sure the whole class saw. That they all knew exactly what pushed me there.

That I wasn't weak. That I wasn't someone to laugh at anymore. That night, sleep didn't come easy. My body felt electric—nervous, twitchy. My thoughts raced like I was running a marathon in my skull. But underneath all of it, something colder began to bloom.

I was anxious, yeah but ready. Too ready.

By the time my alarm buzzed the next morning, I was already awake. I moved slowly, carefully, and controlled. No rushing. I didn't want to look suspicious. I slipped on my clothes, layer by layer, then went to the mirror and stared into my own eyes as I looked for approval. For a long second, I didn't recognize myself. My face looked older somehow. Harder.

"This is it," I whispered to the reflection. "Game time."

I reached under the bed, pulled the knife from its hiding place, and slid it into my front pocket carefully. My hands trembled, but my jaw was locked tight. This was more than revenge. This was freedom. Freedom from Fabian. From the laughter. From being the kid who just takes it and goes home bruised, inside and out.

Today, I would speak in a language everyone understood.

And no one would ever forget.

"Let's go," I muttered under my breath, yanking the front door shut behind me. The morning air slapped my face, and it was sharp, cold, thick. My backpack hung heavy on my shoulders, not from the weight inside but from the dread. Same walk. Same steps. Same street. Different day.

But the story didn't change.

Every morning, I played it out in my head, how he'd start, how I'd try not to react, how I'd pretend I was above it. But pretending was just another word for swallowing broken glass and smiling. By the time I got to school, the building loomed like a cage, not a sanctuary. The hall smelled like overcooked cafeteria food and wet sneakers. The buzzing of students blurred into a dull, constant hum. I moved through it like a ghost. I reached the classroom, pulled off my coat with slow, deliberate movements, hung it neatly beside my backpack. My hands were already trembling, just slightly. Not from cold.

Please, not today, I thought. Just give me one quiet day.

I sat down. Trying to blend in.

The teacher droned on. Chalk squeaked. Pages turned. But all of it was background noise.

Thirty minutes of clockwork, and there it is, it began.

The sharp click of his pen behind me. The quiet laugh. The whispered joke, too soft for the teacher to hear but loud enough to drive a spike into my spine.

I clenched my jaw. My pencil tip snapped against the paper.

"You good?" the kid beside me whispered.

I didn't answer. Just nodded once and stared ahead.

I could feel his breath now, close. His words, soaked in venom and boredom, slithered over my shoulder.

"You always flinch like that? You scared, or just stupid?"

I gritted my teeth. Don't turn around. Don't feed it.

But I could feel the heat building. A slow burn behind my ribs.

"Dude, stop," I muttered, half-turning.

He laughed. Loud. On purpose. Some of the class turned to look.

He wants a show.

And I was done playing the quiet one.

One more hour until recess. Sixty minutes. I could do this. I did it. But something about today felt different. Like someone had been sawing at the last thread of my patience all week, and now they were down to the final strand.

The bell rang.

The sound cracked through the air like a gunshot.

I stood fast. Shoved my chair back with the sounds of screeching. I started toward the door with my head held high, my feet moving quickly.

And just as I reached the exit outside and

BAM.

He slammed into my back, shoving me hard.

"Move it, loser," he told me.

I staggered forward, my shoe slipping on the tile. I caught myself with a hand on the doorframe. My breath hitched. My heart spiked. And something deep in my chest, something I didn't recognize, snapped.

I straightened slowly. Every muscle in my body is buzzing. I wasn't thinking anymore—I was feeling. Years of humiliation, shame, fury, and silence condensed into one moment. One action. One decision.

I reached into my pocket.

Fingers closed around cold steel.

The knife. Just a little thing. Just in case. I never thought I'd use it.

But now it was in my hand.

The outside blurred. My pulse pounded in my ears like war drums.

He turned to look at me.

And our eyes locked.

He saw it.

The blade.

His face changed in an instant from smug amusement to raw, white panic. His mouth fell open, and his eyes stretched wide like he was seeing me for the first time.

He ran.

But I was already moving.

Knife in hand, arm swinging, footsteps slamming the ground.

"GET BACK HERE!" I yelled louder than I knew I could shout.

Gasps filled the playground. Screams followed. I wasn't chasing him anymore; I was chasing everything. The laughter. The silence of teachers. The "boys will be boys." I was chasing justice. Revenge. Rage. He leapt down the stairs two at a time, barreling through the playground. I followed, hot on his heels, the knife glinting in the daylight. Kids scattered, some screaming, some frozen in place, too shocked to move.

I reached the jungle gym just as he tried to climb, his foot slipping, his hands scrambling for a grip.

I raised the knife.

Swung.

And then

My arm stopped.

Not by choice.

It was gripped tightly by a hand. A strong one.

I turned my head.

The assistant principal.

Her face was contorted with fury and horror. Her voice was screaming something, but I couldn't hear it, as if my ears were filled with static. The only thing I could feel was her iron grip on my wrist and the trembling in my legs.

The blade still shook in my hand. Inches from his back.

She yanked me backward.

I kicked. Screamed. I don't even know what I said. Maybe I wasn't even speaking English anymore. Maybe it was just noise.

But the moment was broken.

She dragged me away. My shoes scrape against the blacktop. My knuckles were white around the handle of the knife until finally, it was ripped from my hand.

And I stood there, breathless, empty, surrounded by silence and eyes.

Everyone had seen it.

Not just what I did.

But who I really was.

CHAPTER 10: THE ROCK

As I got hauled off to the principal's office, literally dragged away from the playground by the wrist, I could feel every pair of eyes burning into my back. My shoes scraped against the pavement, the loose gravel biting into my heels as I stumbled to keep up with the furious march of the adult yanking me along like a sack of bad decisions. No laughter just whispers. That awful hush that falls over a crowd when something juicy is going down. I did not dare look back.

The authority figure, the Assistant Principal, was fuming. Her voice cut through the air like a serrated blade, barking words I only half-heard through the ringing in my ears. Something about rules, consequences, and "completely unacceptable behavior." My cheeks burned hotter with every step, the shame knotting in my stomach like a fist.

By the time we reached the front office, my legs felt like jelly. She practically shoved the door open and pointed to a hard plastic chair beneath the fluorescent lights. I sank into it, numb, humiliated, my heart thudding against my ribs like it wanted to escape me entirely. She stood over me, arms crossed so tightly across her chest I thought she might snap in half. Her eyes narrowed behind her thick glasses.

"I'm calling your parents."

That line stopped everything.

Until then, I had been wrapped in my own whirlwind of anger, embarrassment, and confusion. But that pierced through it all. My chest tightened. My mouth went dry.

My parents.

My dad.

Oh God. I had not even thought about that. The man who could silence a room just by walking into it. The man whose fuse was short and whose temper was nothing less than a thunderstorm. He was not the "disappointed" type. He would be livid. Explosive. The kind of mad where words came sharp and loud, where the whole house felt like it had to hold its breath.

I could already see his face when my mom picked up the phone and told him. That slow inhale. The pause before the eruption.

I sank lower in the chair, my shoulders curling inward like I could somehow disappear into myself. Maybe if I stayed really still, I would turn invisible. Maybe this was all a mistake. Maybe—

She was already dialing. Each beep of the number pad echoed louder.

I wondered who answered.

And I sat there, the back of my throat tight, knowing I had messed up badly, and the worst part was just beginning.

My father did not believe in being soft or emotional. "Today is the first day of the rest of your life," he would say, loud and clear. He was a former Drill Sergeant in the U.S. Army. Combat boots are always lined up by the door like a warning. A man who barked orders instead of speaking. A man who believed fear was the closest thing a child should feel to love. Discipline in our house was not a punishment. It was a lifestyle. A religion. And he was the high priest.

We were not spanked. We were beaten. At least I was.

Belts were his favorite, followed by buckles, until they were deemed ineffective. Not the thin kind either, but thick leather, heavy with years. You would hear it before you felt it. The sharp crack as he snapped it once in the air, a warning shot. And then it came down, whip-like, across your legs, your back, your arms. He did not aim. He did not need to. Pain was the message. Accuracy was not required.

But that was just the warm-up.

Sometimes, he made us kneel, bare-kneed, on a bed of uncooked macaroni, rice, or beans in the corner of the living room. Hands on our heads. Eyes forward. You stayed there until your knees went numb. Until they split open. Until grains of rice pressed so deeply into your skin that you carried the indentations for days. My legs would burn, shake, and go ghost-white before the blood returned in slow pulses. But you did not cry. Crying made it worse. Crying made him even madder.

And then there were the wall sits. That was his version of mercy.

Back flat against the wall, legs bent at a perfect ninety degrees, like an invisible chair was beneath you. Sometimes for hours. He would place a stack of books in your outstretched arms, just to make it worse. Arms shaking, thighs on fire. If they dropped, even one, you started over. From the beginning. No exceptions.

He liked silence. Preferred it, actually. If you screamed, he would hit harder. If you pleaded, he would say, "This is life, son. Pain is only weakness leaving your body."F

He was always teaching. Just not the kind of lessons anyone should have to learn.

So, by the time I was nine, my body already knew pain. Intimately. My mind knew shame, the way some kids know lullabies. I walked through the world braced for the next blow, waiting for the next order, the next reason to be punished.

But after a while, I stopped flinching.

And something else began to grow in that space where fear used to live.

Anger.

Not the loud kind. Not the kind that throws things or yells in public. Mine was quiet. Controlled. Measured. It lived under the surface like a second heartbeat, ticking away, waiting. Watching.

Cruel and unusual punishment. That is what it was, flat out. Not in a courtroom sense, no judge, no jury, just the sentence handed down by this man. And this man was my father.

David R. Hinojosa.

They called him The Rock, and not because he was dependable. Not because he held the family together. Not to say he wasn't those things, but he got his nickname from the streets while growing up in Detroit as a kid. They called him The Rock because when he hit you, it was like a rock. A rock that hit you so hard your head would strike the ground before your body. He was cold. Hard. Unmoving. Immune to emotion. Immune to pain. And he expected the same from me.

That was what had been instilled in him, running in the streets with gangs at an early age. My father did not have a dad growing up. He had a mother, a grandmother, and two brothers, and he attended Catholic school. He ran away at eighteen to the Army to get away from Detroit, or he would have died in the streets. At least, that is what he told me.

To him, I was not his son. I was a recruit. A private in his personal war on weakness.

"Pain is just weakness leaving the body," he would growl as I struggled to breathe, chest heaving after he forced me through another set of pushups, sit-ups, and drills. Sometimes until I puked. Sometimes longer. "No pain, no gain."

And if I hesitated? If my knees buckled? If my voice cracked?

"Suck it up. Drive harder. Push through. Every day."

I remember his face when he said those things. Not angry. Not loud. Just stone cold. Like he believed it was love. Like breaking me was building me. He would look me in the eye, sweat pouring down my face, legs shaking, and say calmly, "Today is the first day of the rest of your life." As if that somehow made the punishment a gift.

But it was not discipline. It was not training. It was control. It was domination. I was not learning strength. I was learning fear.

There was no room for mistakes. No room for questions. No room for me.

He treated error like betrayal. Weaknesses like a disease. He measured manhood in scars and silence. If I cried, he would stare at me like I had just confirmed his worst fear: that I was soft. That I was failing him. And in his eyes, failure was the ultimate sin.

The truth? I did not grow stronger. I grew harder, and not in the way he wanted. I did not become disciplined. I became numb. Numb to his voice. Numb to his rules. Numb to his version of love. What he thought was forging a soldier was forging a rebel, and soon, everything he stood for would become everything I fought against.

But he could not see that. He could not see the hate quietly blooming in my chest like a bruise that never healed. The more he pushed, the more I pulled away. Until one day, I stopped listening entirely. And you will soon see as the story continues.

Yes, my father was The Rock, unbreakable and cold. But my mother was softer, though no less strong. She was the shelter, the only safe place I had growing up. Where he barked orders, she whispered comfort. Where he built walls, she opened doors. Her name was never shouted. It did not need to be. Her presence alone carried a quiet gravity that filled a room with warmth.

She had a voice like a lullaby, even when she was exhausted. And she was always exhausted. But she never let it show, not to me. Not when I needed her.

She was the type of woman who smelled like warm laundry fresh out of the dryer, whose hands were always busy folding clothes, cooking, wiping my face, and moving my hair from my eyes after one of Dad's so-called "training sessions." She would press a cold washcloth to my bruises without saying a word, but her eyes told the story. They burned with a fire that she kept hidden from him.

Her love was armor. Her touch, an infinite lifeline.

When my dad went into his military mode, barking, demanding, punishing, and yelling to grab him a beer because he did not want to get up from his throne, she was the one who stood between me and the storm. She did not raise her voice often, but when she did, it cut through his fury like a blade. I can still hear her sometimes:

"He's a boy, David! Not one of your soldiers. Leave him alone!"

And even when her words did not change his actions, they reminded me I was not crazy. I was not weak. I was not alone.

She had this look, this deep, maternal knowing in her eyes, like she understood things she would never say out loud. She knew how far he could go. She knew the lines he was always on the verge of crossing. And she did everything in her power to keep me on the safe side of them. She was my first protector. My first act of resistance was learning to love like she did, gently, fiercely, without needing to prove anything.

She made our house a contradiction. It was a war zone with a hidden sanctuary. She kept it together: the meals, the clothes, the smiles in front of friends and family, as if it were a duty. But I saw the cracks. I saw the way she paused when she thought no one was looking. The tired sighs. The eyes that stared just a little too long out the window.

Still, no matter how broken she might have felt inside, she never let me see her shatter.

To this day, when I think of strength, I do not think of fists or barked orders. I think of her. Of warm hands. Of whispered reassurances. Of love that stood its ground.

She had my back. Always. Especially when he did not. And that, I think, is the only reason I survived that house with my soul still intact.

So, hopefully it is her who shows up to get me. I sit in the cold, too-quiet office, the ticking of a cheap wall clock slicing through the silence like a dull knife. My backpack is slumped by my feet. I keep my eyes focused on the speckled tiles on the floor, tracing the cracks like they might spell out my future, though I already know it will not be anything good.

I cannot even begin to imagine what comes next. School is probably done with me, at least for a while. And my father? I do not even want to think about the explosion waiting at home from that man. Then I hear the familiar shuffle of footsteps in the hall, slow and loud as the steps get closer. The door opens with a soft creak.

It is her. My mother. Thank God.

She walks in, shaking her head, lips pressed in a tight line. Her face is carved in that all-too-familiar look of disappointment. No surprise. Not concerned. Just that quiet disapproval that stings sharper than yelling ever could. She does not look at me, just hands a clipboard back to the secretary, signs something with a flick of her wrist, and then finally lowers herself into the chair beside mine.

She does not say a word.

For a few seconds, it feels like the whole room holds its breath. I can hear her breathing deep, controlled. She keeps her eyes fixed ahead, her jaw clenched so tightly I can see the muscle twitch.

I want to say something, but I do not.

But what do you say when you are the disappointment in the room?

The woman at the front desk barely looks up from her monitor as we both sit there. Her tone is practiced, almost bored, like she has said the same thing a hundred times already today.

"One second, ma'am. I will go get the principal. She has been waiting for you."

My mom says, "Ok, thank you," just as she shifts her weight from one foot to the other. As she sits there, she looks more nervous than I feel. I can only imagine what she thought I did. She turns to me slowly, and her eyes, cold and sharp, land hard on mine.

"What did you do, boy?" she asks, low and clipped, before I can even open my mouth. Her voice cuts through the quiet like a blade. There is no room in it for excuses, explanations, or even truth.

I looked away, suddenly fascinated by the scuff marks on the tile.

Before I can say anything, the office door creaks open and in steps Principal Hernandez. His face is stern, unreadable, but his eyes flick to me and narrow just slightly. That is all I need to know. I am already guilty.

"Mrs. Hinojosa, follow me, please."

She walks with the same hard stride I have known since I was little, the kind that always meant someone was about to get it. I trail behind her like a lost puppy, my footsteps quieter than they have ever been.

We are led into a small room with stiff chairs and pale blue walls that pretend to be calming. Nothing about this room feels calm.

"Please, have a seat," the principal says, gesturing to the chairs across from his desk. My mother sits stiffly; hands folded in her lap like a statue carved out of concern and despair. I sink into the seat beside her, my fingers twisting the hem of my hoodie.

Principal Hernandez folds his hands on the desk and begins.

"Mrs. Hinojosa, today we had an incident involving your son, Gabriel." He pauses, like he is deciding how much weight to drop at once. "He attempted to stab another student. Fortunately, he was unsuccessful."

The silence that follows is deafening. My mom is not moving. She does not even blink.

"We will be suspending him from school, effective immediately," he continues. "We are also waiting to see whether the parents of the other student intend to press charges. That will determine how we proceed further. Hopefully, you and your husband can get this under control."

"Of course," my mother says finally, her voice flat and formal. "My husband will definitely speak with him once we get home."

My stomach sinks.

I know what that means.

Not a talk. Not a lecture. Something else entirely. Something that starts behind a closed door and ends in silence and bruised pride.

I stared down at the desk, trying to wipe it all away. But the truth hung in the room like thick smoke, choking whatever hope I had left.

The walk to the car felt like silence before a storm, thick, charged, and impossible to ignore. Each step echoed with the weight of what was coming. My mom didn't say a word, and I didn't dare try. What could I say that would make any of this better?

I already knew how this would end.

Once we got home, my dad would light me up. No questions. No explanations. No mercy. They did not call him The Rock for nothing. That was what everyone called him, not because he was strong, but because he was unmovable, unshakable, and when he came down on you, it hurt.

We reached the car. I climbed into the passenger seat, the door clicking shut with the finality of a prison cell. My mom started the engine but did not shift into drive right away. She just sat there for a moment, gripping the steering wheel like it was the only thing holding her together.

Then she spoke.

"What's wrong with you, boy?" she said, her voice trembling. "You know your dad's going to beat you, right?"

Her words hit harder than I expected, but her voice broke on the last word, and then the tears came.

"You just don't learn," she whispered, shaking her head, tears trailing down her cheeks like tiny rivers of disappointment. "You just… don't."

"But Mom—" I started, desperate for her to see me, to hear something, anything that might soften this moment.

"I don't care," she snapped back quickly, her voice sharp through the sobs. "I don't want to hear it."

And just like that, silence swallowed us whole.

The car began to move, but time stood still. Outside the window, the world passed by in a blur—trees, people, traffic—but none of it mattered. All I could hear was her crying. And all I could feel was the guilt clawing at my chest.

It still hurts, even now, just thinking about it. Thinking about all the hurt and pain I caused her.

She did not deserve any of this. She was the kind of woman who wanted nothing but the best for her son, who worked too many hours, smiled too little, and prayed too hard. And what did I give her? Shame. Fear. A reason to cry in silence while the world kept turning.

We pulled into the driveway just as the sun began to dip behind the trees, painting the sky in burnt orange and bruised purple. The car came to a stop, and for a moment, she did not move. Then she turned her face toward me, eyes red, mascara smudged, and said with no emotion left,

"Go to your room, boy. Stay there until your dad gets home."

I nodded, swallowed the lump in my throat, and opened the door. My legs felt weak, like they might give out before I reached the front door. But somehow, I managed to make it up the steps.

The house was quiet. Too quiet.

I walked down the stairs like it was death row, every step heavier and more serious. My hand shook as I opened my bedroom door. I stepped inside and closed it behind me. The click of the latch sounded like a countdown.

I sat on the edge of my bed, staring at the wall, my heart pounding so loud I could hear it in my ears.

The Rock was coming. And I was afraid.

Truly afraid.

So, I had to think.

Think, stupid. Think.

What can I do to stop this beating?

My eyes darted around the room like a trapped animal, searching for an escape that did not exist. I paced. My breath was shallow, chest tight, hands clammy. I could feel the panic building in my throat like a lump I could not swallow. My father's fury was inevitable, looming like a thunderstorm ready to break wide open.

Then an idea hit me.

Layers.

Layers might dull the sting. Layers might slow down the belt. Layers might save me.

It was dumb. It was desperate. But it was all I had.

I dove toward my dresser, yanking drawers open, tossing clothes across the room in a frenzy. Sweatpants over jeans. Basketball shorts underneath. Three pairs of underwear. Thick hoodie over a long sleeve, over a T-shirt. Another hoodie for good measure. I looked like a stuffed animal version of myself, but I did not care.

Genius, I thought. Always trying to stay one step ahead.

Each layer was a thin, pitiful shield against what was coming, but it made me feel like I had some control, even if it was a lie.

Then I heard it.

The low growl of my father's truck turning onto the street.

The sound made the air leave my lungs. I stopped cold.

Gravel crunched under his tires as he pulled into the driveway. My whole body went still. I crept to the window and peeled back the curtain with just a sliver. The truck door slammed with that all-too-familiar violence, sharp, final, angry. I watched as he stepped out, his silhouette cut dark against the fading sun. His shoulders were squared, steps heavy and deliberate.

I could already feel the tension rise in the house. Even the air seemed afraid.

He was home.

I heard the front door creak open, then shut. Muffled voices. My mom's tone was quiet, strained, like she was trying to hold the walls up with her words before they collapsed under his anger.

Then it came.

"BOY! GET OVER HERE, NOW!"

His voice ripped through the house like a shotgun blast.

My stomach drops. My knees are weak.

My mouth goes dry.

This is it.

No amount of layers can stop what's coming now. I can feel the belt already, phantom pain rushing in before I've even moved.

Still, I turn and shuffle toward the door like I'm walking the green mile. Every step feels heavier than the last, as if my clothes are soaked in fear and are dragging me down.

I open the door slowly, the hallway stretching long and dark in front of me before the stairs. His shadow moves behind the light at the end. Waiting.

Waiting for me.

And all I can do now... is walk into the storm.

I gathered every shred of courage my young self could find and stepped out of the basement. The narrow stairs groaned beneath me, each creak up each stair loud enough to betray my heartbeat. Here goes nothing.

At the top of the steps, he was waiting. My father stood in the kitchen like a thunder cloud ready to break.

"What's this your mother's been telling me?" What did you do at school, boy?"

His voice was low but vibrating loudly with rage.

I tried to answer, but then I saw it, the beer cold sweating in one hand, the belt coiled in the other, buckle hanging. The sour reek of alcohol filled his breath. He placed the beer on the kitchen table with deliberate care, as though the beer deserved more respect than I did. Before I could get a word out, his hand shot forward, iron-hard around my arm, and he yanked me off my feet. The belt cracked through the room, one strike after another after another. Leather snapped against my padded clothing with a sound that sounded empty.

I noticed, but did he?

The shock dulled the sting, but I knew the rules. I screamed anyway. I couldn't let him even think I layered up the noise from my mouth; it had to be accurate because silence only ever made it worse. I flung my free hand up with instinct, trying to shield myself. His eyes narrowed. He froze for a breath as he got tired, then dropped the belt to the floor with a heavy thud and threw me to the ground.

"What's all this?" he growled, noticing my layers voice dropping to a dangerous rumble.

"Think you can stop me, boy? "HUH? As he somewhat laughs.

The air around him seemed to tighten, heavy with beer fumes and anger as he ripped off all my clothing until I was naked. He gripped harder, punching me into the floor, dragging me upward until the room tilted. His open hand struck again and again—shoulder, ribs, back, each blow a punctuation mark in a sentence I couldn't escape. Each strike exploded against my skin, sharp as gunfire. Pain bloomed hot, but shock turned into pain. I screamed louder, and this time it was real, no acting.

I tried to shield myself from what I could, but it didn't work.

Time stretched into a blur of noise and heat over my entire body. My own cries echoed back at me like they belonged to someone else. Then, as suddenly as it began, it ended. He let me go. I dropped to the floor and stared at me as he hovered above.

"Get out of here," he said, already reaching for the beer and walking to his throne in the living room in front of his TV.

I lay there for a second, trying to catch my breath and wipe the tears and blood on my face.

"Move! Now BOY!" He yells!

My legs barely worked, but I forced them to obey. I stumbled back down the stairs, every step a retreat into darkness of what I called my room.

I heard her voice first, sharp and cracked with anger, trembling beneath the weight of something deeper. My mother. She was yelling again. Not at me this time, but at him.

"How could you do that to your own son?" she screamed, her voice rising and falling like waves crashing against stone. "You beat him like he was nothing!" Through the thin walls of our house, I could hear every word. Each one landed like a second beating this time inside my chest. I sat quietly in the corner of my room, shirtless, staring into the cracked mirror hanging crooked on the wall. The reflection was almost unrecognizable. My body looked like battlefield cuts, welts, and angry bruises painted across my skin like a map of every mistake I'd made. Dried blood clung stubbornly to my lip, and my ribs ached with every breath. My left eye had started to swell shut, an ugly purple halo growing darker by the hour.

I cried silently, so no one would hear. Not even me. The kind of crying that does not make a sound, just hot tears slipping down your face, soaking onto the floor as you lie there, too tired to wipe them away. My brother and sister had not said a word to me since it happened.

They barely looked in my direction. I could see it in their eyes—fear. Not of me, but of what might happen to them if they ended up like me. I had become a warning, a living lesson in what not to do.

That night, I did not even crawl into bed. I lay on the floor, my skin stinging against the cold concrete of the basement and stared at the ceiling until my body finally shut down and sleep took me like a thief.

The next morning, everything was gone.

No TV. No Nintendo. Just a note scrawled in my dad's handwriting:

"Chores. Full house. Yard too. Done by dinner. No excuses."

And so that is what I did. For days. While my classmates went to school and talked about lunchroom drama and after-school games, I scrubbed floors and raked leaves until my hands blistered and bled. Every creak of the front door made my heart race; a part of me hoped they would come home early, while the other part was terrified they would.

About two weeks before my suspension ended, he called me into the living room. His voice was calm.

"Take off your clothes," he said.

I froze. Confused. Ashamed.

He stood there, arms crossed, scanning me like I was some kind of project he was inspecting for damage. I stripped down to my underwear, humiliated, as he paced slowly around me. He paused at my back. I could feel his breath, low and steady.

"Oh man," he muttered. "Look at this." He reached out and traced a welt with his finger. I flinched. Not because it hurt, although it did, but because I hated him touching me like this, like I was some broken thing he was proud of.

Then he said the line that would haunt me long after the wounds healed.

"I love you, boy. Why do you make me do this to you?"

He did not wait for an answer. He just shook his head like he was the victim of all this.

"You will live," he said, almost carelessly, as if the words did not carry the weight of the pain he had caused. Then, without even looking at me, he turned his head, pulled a crumpled pack of cigarettes from the pocket of his flannel shirt, and tapped one out with the same casual rhythm he might use if nothing had just happened. He lit it with a flick of his old Zippo, the one with the eagle engraved on the side, and brought the cigarette to his lips with the kind of slow, practiced ease that only comes from years of repetition. The flame briefly lit his face, casting sharp shadows across his jaw before he snapped the lighter shut.

He exhaled a cloud of smoke that drifted lazily through the stale air, like it had all the time in the world. His eyes did not find me again. They were already locked on the flickering screen of the television. It was some old western rerun, like a lullaby for psychopaths or cowards, you choose. He sank into the worn leather of his recliner with a low grunt, one arm slung over the side like a king settling back into his throne. His other hand found the sweating can of Budweiser on the table next to him. It was his scepter, and he took a long, slow sip, never breaking his gaze from the screen.

And just like that, I was dismissed.

Discarded.

Forgotten.

What had just happened was a scene from a show he had already seen before and was not interested in watching again.

CHAPTER 11: MAN'S BEST FRIEND

When I went back to school, everything had changed. I could not quite explain it at first, but I felt it the moment I stepped out onto the schoolyard. The air felt calmer, as though the chaos I used to expect had packed up and left. No cruel whispers behind my back. No glares. Even the bully who once made it his mission to make me flinch barely looked in my direction. It was like I had turned invisible. But not in a bad way. It's more likely that people just didn't want to disturb me. I was a new version of myself, and somehow, they all sensed it.

With that quiet came space. Space to breathe. Space to grow.

That was when I found art.

I do not remember the first time I picked up a pencil and pen with intent, but I remember what it felt like. Like my insides finally had a language. I was not just making lines and shapes; I was pouring myself out onto canvases. My sketches turned into drawings, and my drawings turned into something more. One day, my art teacher asked me to keep one of my pieces. Two weeks later, I saw it framed, and they said it would be behind glass at the downtown art museum gallery.

I stood there, not really believing it was mine. People would walk by and stop. Some tilted their heads, squinting, analyzing the colors and shadows. Like I knew what I was doing. The teachers at school heard too. "You have real potential," they told me. I did not know exactly what that meant, but I held onto it like a secret treasure.

Fifth grade came quickly. So did music.

I picked up the cello first. I loved how it sounded low and warm, like a heartbeat in a quiet room. But it was heavy and carrying it home was a nightmare. I would shuffle down the street with the case banging against my legs, trying not to trip.

So, I switched.

The violin was too high and sharp, like a scream held too long. The viola, though, fit. Its tone sat right in the middle, like it knew how to listen. My instructor noticed how naturally my hands moved across the strings.

"You have a feel for this," he told me one day. "Stick with the viola."

So, I did.

But school, art, and music were not enough for my parents. They did not like me having too much free time. They said it gave me space to "drift." So, they enrolled me in the Shaolin Temple. A local martial arts school tucked away behind a strip mall, but inside, it was all polished wood, incense, and discipline.

I learned forms. I learned stillness. I learned how to push through pain without blinking. I rose through the ranks quickly, not because I was stronger or faster, but because I cared. I listened. I respected the art. And for the first time in my life, I felt like I belonged somewhere. The training made me feel light, like I could carry the weight of everything else, school and expectations, even silence and still walk with balance. It was peace in motion.

Then came the dog.

His name was Tippy. A small, scruffy Shih Tzu with big eyes and a tongue that always stuck out just a little. At first, I was not sure what to do with him. He was energetic, needy, and always getting underfoot. But over time, he started sleeping next to me. Sitting by the door when I got home. Waiting for me like no one else did.

Tippy became my shadow. My sidekick. My friend.

My parents kept me on a tight leash with rules, routines, and curfews that never changed. But Tippy did not care about any of that. He did not want anything from me except my presence. When I was painting, he curled up at my feet. When I was practicing music, he tilted his head and listened. And when I had rough days where the quiet at school felt too loud inside my head, Tippy was just there. He did not speak. He did not need to. Sometimes, love does not come in grand gestures. Sometimes it is in a soft tail wag. A nose pressed into your palm. A heartbeat beside you when the world feels like it is drifting away.

Tippy was that for me.

In a life full of expectations, disciplines, and performances, he was the one thing that let me be completely myself. And that was more than any trophy, painting, or praise could do. It was what I needed most.

We named him Tippy because of how he danced light as air, always on his hind legs, toes barely touching the floor like a dancer who had not yet come back to Earth, floating on a cloud. Every time he saw me, he rose up, pawing at the sky, tail wagging wildly like it had a mind of its own. It was his way of saying, "You are home," and no matter what kind of day I had, it never failed to make me smile.

He followed me everywhere. Literally. If I went to the kitchen, he was at my heels. When I went to the bathroom, he waited outside the door, tail gently thumping. He even curled up next to my viola case when I practiced. It was like he understood the sound meant something. He was more than a pet. He was the one soul in the world who never asked me to change or be more than I was. Tippy was freedom in a fur coat, and my shadow made of flesh.

But we lived on Circle and Fountain, a busy intersection pulsing with the rhythm of city life. Cars zoomed past our house as if they were late for something important, even when they weren't. Our driveway had a gate, but Tippy was clever and always found a way to get to me. I had learned to brace the gate with a piece of wood every time I left, a makeshift blockade to keep him safely inside when I ran errands. Candy runs to the gas station across the street, which was a regular thing, but I always double-checked the gate. Always. Even that day.

It was late afternoon, the sun dipping low behind the trees, houses, and light poles. I remember stepping out of the house with a couple of crumpled dollar bills in my pocket, already dreaming of some kind of candy and maybe a bag of hot fries. I shut the gate behind me, slid the wooden brace into place, and gave it a little nudge to make sure it was solid.

Or so I thought.

As I crossed the first half of the street, the sounds of the city surrounded me—the whirring engines, distant music from a passing car, someone yelling down the block. It was all normal. Just noise.

I proceeded to cross and reached the middle. Then came screeching tires.

A hard, sudden slam of brakes.

And then a loud yelp.

Not just any sound. A sound that sliced through the noise like a blade.

My heart stopped. I turned around.

There, in the middle of the street, not far from the yellow divider line, was a tiny form crumpled awkwardly on the asphalt. Brown and white fur. A crooked tail.

Tippy.

No.

I ran back, feet pounding, cars honking, someone yelling, but all I could see was his little body lying still. His chest rose in tiny, rapid spasms. His eyes were wide open.

The man who hit him got out of his car, concern written on his face, trying to say something. But it did not reach me. I could not process his words. The world slowed down, and I reached down to pick up my best friend from the road.

He had followed me.

He always followed me.

Somehow, some way, he had pushed through the brace, nosed open the gate, and chased me across the street. He must have been right behind me, unnoticed, silent in his determination to be where I was. His loyalty was his last act.

I looked up and saw my dad watching from the porch.

I did not feel my legs moving as I stepped out of traffic. I barely felt the weight of Tippy in my arms, though his small, warm body hung limp, cradled against my chest like a soaked towel. His soft fur was wet and sticky with blood, mostly around his mouth, where it leaked out slowly in horrifying drips. His eyes had lost that spark, the one that always lit up when he saw me.

Tippy.

And now here he was. Crushed. Broken. Yelping in short, choking bursts that sounded more like pain, trying to speak.

I stumbled across the street, heart pounding in my ears louder than the screeching brakes I still could not forget. I looked up, and there, standing just outside the porch, framed in the doorway, was my father.

He locked eyes with me.

And he knew.

I did not have to say a word. He could see it in my face, red, full of tears, frozen in panic. And he could see it in what I was carrying.

"Dad!" I screamed, my voice cracking as I crossed the curb.

He stepped forward like someone waking up from a dream. His hand went to his head.

"Oh my God, boy…" he muttered, shaking his head slowly. His voice was low, shaky. Not angry. Not loud. Just like he was processing what he was seeing.

I could not speak. I just kept crying. The kind of crying that feels like it starts in your stomach, where your whole body shakes, and you cannot breathe between the gasps.

"Come on," he said, his voice soft but steady now. "Bring him. Come on."

I followed him.

"Boy," he said softly, voice deep and steady, "listen to me."

I froze, clutching Tippy tighter, shaking my head as if I could undo the moment by refusing to hear it. My chest heaved, my throat raw from crying.

"Sometimes," my father continued, his eyes locked on mine, "there is nothing left to do but let go."

The words landed like stones. Heavy. Final.

"No!" I shouted, my voice cracking. "He's still breathing! We can save him. We have to try!"

My father's jaw tightened. He looked at Tippy, then back at me. His eyes glistened, though his face stayed hard. "Son, he's hurting. You see it. I see it. Keeping him like this… it's not saving him. It's only making him suffer."

I shook my head violently, tears blurring everything. The world tilted. My knees pressed into the grass, damp and cold, as I buried my face in Tippy's fur. His shallow breaths rattled against my chest, each one weaker than the last.

"I can't," I whispered. "I can't put him in that box."

My father stepped closer, the shovel still in his hand, dirt clinging to the blade. He crouched down, his shadow falling over me. For the first time in my life, I saw him not as The Rock, not as the unbreakable man who barked orders and demanded silence, but as something else. A man who knew loss. A man who had buried too much already.

"You don't have to," he said quietly. "I'll do it."

I looked up at him, my face streaked with tears, my arms still wrapped around the only creature who had ever loved me without condition. My father reached out, slow and deliberate, his rough hands trembling as he touched Tippy's side.

"Say goodbye, boy," he murmured.

The world seemed to stop. The birds, the cars, the wind—all of it faded until there was only me, my father, and the fragile heartbeat pressed against my chest.

My mouth hung open, but no sound came out.

He stepped closer, wiping his brow with the back of his hand, his eyes locked onto mine.

"Tippy's got a broken neck," he said, the words like stones hitting the ground. "He's in pain, boy. That yelping you hear, that's him crying for help. That's him suffering. It's time. Be a man."

I shook my head.

"No… no, Dad, he followed me. He's tough, he'll make it. He just needs a vet. He needs something."

"They can't help him, son," my dad interrupted gently. "He's too far gone, boy."

I opened my mouth again, but nothing came. My knees felt weak, my chest tight, like something inside me was caving in.

"He's not gonna get better," my dad said, slower now. "He's not gonna come back from this. We can't let him keep hurting like this."

My whole body shivered as I stood there, not from cold, but from the shock of reality landing like a punch I was not ready for.

"I…" I tried. "But he's still here. He's still breathing, Dad."

"Breathing isn't living," he said quietly.

Tippy was still yelping, but farther apart than before. Just tiny twitches. His breathing had become shallow, like the last flickers of a flame. My dad looked down at him for what seemed like an eternity. Then, without looking back at me, he said the words that crushed the last hope I was clinging to.

"Say your goodbyes, son."

That was it.

That was the moment I knew.

That was when it hit me. This was real. Tippy was not going to get better. We were not going to the vet. There would be no medicine, no bandages, no coming back.

This was the end.

The dam broke. I dropped to my knees beside the box, sobbing uncontrollably. I looked down and touched Tippy's soft fur, still warm, still familiar. I ran my fingers behind his ears like I always did, and for a brief moment, his eyes fluttered open just enough to find me.

He knew I was there.

"Now put your dog in the box and bury him. Finish up the job, boy."

My dad's voice cut through the silence like a blade, sharp, heavy, and unflinching.

He stood over me, hands rough and dirt-streaked, the shovel still clutched loosely in one hand. His face was hard to read, shadowed by the fading light and something deeper, something I did not understand yet. Maybe he was trying to stay strong. Maybe he was just trying to stay numb.

I looked up at him, my face wet with tears, lips trembling. My knees dug into the dirt next to the cardboard box where I placed Tippy while he was barely breathing.

"Dad… he's still alive," I sobbed. "Please… he's still—he's still breathing!"

I could not stop crying. The words came out twisted, strangled by the knot in my throat.

My dad exhaled sharply through his nose. His eyes flicked down to the box, then quickly went away.

"Boy," he said, louder now. "Just get it done. Now."

I froze.

"There's no other choice here. And don't come in until you're done."

And just like that, he turned his back on me.

He walked across the yard, each footstep crunching on gravel and grass. At the porch, he bent down, grabbed his half-finished beer, and without another word, stepped through the back door.

He shut it behind him. Not slammed. Just closed. Firm. Final.

I stared at the door like it might open again. Like he might come back and say he was sorry. That he had changed his mind. That we were going to take Tippy to the vet, no matter what it cost. That he could not let me do this alone.

But the door stayed shut.

The light through the kitchen window glowed warm, almost golden. Inside, I could hear the faint clink of a bottle on the table, the creak of a chair as he sat down.

Out here, it was cold, and nightfall was approaching.

The kind of cold that had nothing to do with the weather.

I turned back to Tippy.

His body was still curled the way I had laid him. His little tongue peeked out slightly between his teeth, dried blood staining the corners of his mouth.

He was still warm, crying, and looking at me.

I don't remember how the shovel got back into my hands.

This was not just death. This was wrong.

This was burying him alive.

And it broke me.

My fingers tightened around the wooden grip, splinters biting into my palms. I looked down into the grave and felt my knees wobble.

"I can't do this," I whispered. But no one was around to hear me. The back door was still closed. My father was not coming back.

He had said, "Don't come in until you're done."

That was the rule. That was the end of it.

And this, this right here, was the first time I realized that being a kid did not protect me from anything. Not grief. Not pain. Not responsibility. Not choices that should have belonged to someone older, stronger, anyone else but me.

But it was just me.

This box.

And Tippy.

I knelt beside him again, unable to hold back another flood of tears. His breathing was ragged, every exhale catching in his throat like it did not want to leave. His eyes, once so full of light and mischief, barely held anything now but a quiet flicker.

"I'm so sorry," I whispered, brushing my hand along his back.

He flinched.

My heart cracked into pieces I could never put back together.

"I love you," I choked. "You weren't supposed to follow me. You were supposed to be safe." I pressed my forehead to his and closed my eyes, breathing in the last of his scent—his fur, still warm, still familiar, even beneath the blood and dirt and fear.

Then I stood up.

"Hurry up, boy!" I heard from inside the house.

I lifted the first scoop of earth and hovered over the box. My hands were shaking so badly that I thought I might drop them, but I didn't.

I could not stall any longer.

Not because I was ready, but because I did not want to feel the wrath of The Rock. I would never be ready. But I had to end his pain. Right?

Even if it meant starting mine.

The dirt fell in a soft, cruel whisper.

He whimpered.

I cried louder, followed by screams.

It was a sound I did not know I had inside me, something different and desperate, like an animal. It tore from my lungs as I spilled screams into the sky, but it did not stop my hands from moving.

Another scoop.

Then another.

Each one felt like I was throwing away part of my soul. Burying more than just a dog. Burying a piece of myself. There is supposed to be a part in your life when you still believe life is fair. Parents always protect you. That love alone can keep something alive. But that is a lie.

By the time I dropped the final mound of soil and packed it down with the back of the shovel, the sun was gone.

So was Tippy.

And so went something else I would never get back. Something more than time. More than innocence.

I could not believe what I had just done. My hands were still shaking, dirt caked under my nails, the smell of raw earth filling my nose. I had just buried my dog alive.

Alive.

Not because I wanted to. God, no. I loved that dog. He trusted me. He looked up at me with those wide, confused eyes as I dragged him into the hole, his legs too weak to stand, but his tail still trying to wag. He did not know. He thought maybe we were playing. Maybe we were going somewhere. I do not know.

I still hear his whimper, soft, muffled under the shallow grave. Like a cry that does not die with the body.

What kind of person does that?

Or perhaps the better question is, what kind of person would make their own child do that?

Because it was not my choice. I had no choice. It was his. My father. Cold as the steel shovel I dropped at my feet again. "It's suffering," he had said. "It's time. Be a man." As if manhood meant playing executioner to your best friend.

I was eleven.

Eleven, with knees buckling in the dirt, tears streaking my face, and a heart torn in two. One half begged for mercy. The other locked itself away somewhere, gone, trying to survive the weight of his command.

That day, something broke in me. Something died. And that part of a human being I had held on to was buried too, in that shallow grave.

Sometimes I wonder if my dog was luckier being gone.

CHAPTER 12: BECOMING SUSPECT

Beige brick walls, cracked pavement, busted lockers that never quite latched right. But inside, it was chaos. Pure chaos. Kids are trying to act older than they are. Drinking and smoking were cool. Teachers seemed like they did not care, and fights—well, fights broke out like wildfires. Over a look, a word, or nothing at all.

That was when I met Issac.

He was in my grade, same age, but felt years older. Something about him carried this tough, unpredictable energy, like a lit match flickering close to gasoline. He had that "I don't care" attitude that made other kids want to be around him, and adults want to pretend he did not exist. He already had tattoos, real ones, not drawn on with pen ink. Said his cousin did them in a basement with a needle and a bottle of Indian ink. He showed them off like they were war medals.

Issac told me he was in a gang too. Not like the kids who said they were but weren't. He did not brag or throw it around carelessly. He just said it once, flat, like someone saying they had asthma or divorced parents. Normal to him. He was not trying to impress me. That was probably what pulled me in.

There was something about the way he moved through the world, like he already knew it was not going to give him anything, so he stopped asking. And he did not care who did not like him.

Especially not my dad.

Issac tried coming over to my place once. Just once. My dad opened the door, looked him up and down, and shut the door in his face without a word. I did not even find out until later. My dad never told me he came. That was how it always was. He made decisions for you, and you lived with them.

So, I stopped asking, and I would just go. I started walking to Issac's house before school and would hang out there after school. He lived a few blocks over, in a two-story house with a porch that sagged like it was giving up. His mom worked nights and was hardly ever there. No dad around, from what I could tell. Just a haze of cigarette and marijuana smoke, old rap CDs playing, and the occasional older cousins and their girlfriends passed out on the couch from the night before. His sister Janice was older too, but she was never home. She was always out and about.

But it felt real. Honest. No pretending. No one there told me to shut up, or sit straight, or hide how I felt. So, I would wake up early, sometimes before the sun, just to walk to his place, hang out, and catch the bus from his stop. We would eat dry cereal straight out of the box, kick empty beer cans down the stairs, and talk about music or other trivial things, like which teacher probably had a drinking problem.

It was stupid, but it was the closest thing I had to feeling seen.

Issac was not a good influence. I knew that. But he was there. He listened. He did not make me feel like I was too soft, or too quiet, or too broken. He made me feel like maybe all the messed-up things in my head were just part of the deal, like we were both born into lives already halfway on fire, just waiting for it to flourish and burn. When you are a kid in a house where nobody talks about feelings, where silence is your second language, someone like Issac feels like a lifeline. And I needed it. I wanted it. I yearned for it.

One day after school, I was at Issac's house like usual. We were sitting on the broken porch steps, passing a half-smashed Sprite bottle between us for some game we made up. That was when the screen door creaked open and his cousin stepped outside. He was older, probably eighteen or so, tatted up from neck to wrist, eyes heavy-lidded but sharp underneath. He had that way about him, like a wolf that did not need to growl to be dangerous. He looked at me, chin up, like he was sizing me up for something more than just conversation.

"What's up, Lil' homie," he said, voice smooth but firm, the kind that made you sit up a little straighter without realizing it. "Here's the deal."

I did not say anything. Just looked at him. He lit a joint, took a drag, and when he lit it, the tip flared a dull orange, then settled into a smoldering red glow, crackling faintly as the smoke curled upward in slow, lazy spirals. I recognized the smell. I had smelled it before, but I had never placed it. Then it hit me. This was what it smelled like late at night when my dad was the only one awake, or when his friends were around. It smelled like burnt leaves and gasoline, with a chemical undertone.

Then he passed it to me as if it were part of a ceremony. The smoke hit hard. Harsh and dry, like sandpaper dragged down my throat. I felt an instant wave of warmth behind my eyes, a numbness in my lips, and a sudden, woozy lightheadedness, as if I was no longer quite standing on the ground. My chest burned. My tongue went heavy. I exhaled, and I could not help myself. It hurt, and I coughed. Eyes dazed, he laughed.

"Good stuff, huh, homie?"

I tried to stand tall in front of him, especially when this felt like some kind of test. But his eyes did not leave mine.

"You wanna put it down for our barrio or what, ay?" he asked. Calm. Almost casual. But there was weight behind the words. "We've been watchin' you, being around and all, and you've been solid. You know you're really becoming part of the familia, right?"

As he passed the joint back to me, I took it, hesitated for half a second, then hit it. The smoke burned on the way in, rough and dry, but I did not cough. I held it down, nodded like I understood what he meant, even though part of me did not.

But another part of me?

It wanted to belong.

We talked. Or mostly, he talked. About loyalty. About being real. About not backing down when it counted. Issac chimed in now and then, but mostly he just nodded along, like all of us did, as if this was a sermon and we were at church. The joint kept coming back around. Eventually, there were beers, and then shots. Someone pulled out a bottle of something cheap and sharp that felt like it melted the back of my throat.

Later, there were more people. Older kids, a few girls, music loud enough to rattle the windows. Somebody lit a cigarette and passed it to me. Then another joint. I don't remember much of the middle part, just the scene—the smell of sweat, weed, and cheap cologne. I laughed a lot. I danced a little. I tried to act like I had done all this before.

But I hadn't.

It was the first night I did not go home.

No call. No check-in. No explanation. And no one came looking.

I woke up sometime around 6 a.m. in the basement, with the music still playing. I was crumpled on a couch that smelled like smoke and old pizza. My mouth tasted like ash, my head a dull drumbeat, pounding. There were people still passed out all around me—one guy on the floor, someone snoring in a chair. Issac was curled up in the corner, hoodie over his face, even though he had his own room.

I did not even brush my teeth. I woke up Issac and told him we had school, and he jumped up. We splashed water on our faces and slipped out the door. The morning air hit me like ice. I walked through the neighborhood like a ghost, clothes rumpled, eyes red, stomach turning. And then I went to school. Straight from the party. Straight into the first period. Like nothing had happened.

But something had happened.

The next morning after the party, while we were walking to school, I asked Issac what he thought about what his cousin had said. About me getting put on the neighborhood. He did not answer right away. Just kept walking, hoodie up, hands in his pockets, his breath little clouds in the cold morning air. Then finally, he said, "You know it's a big deal, right? Like… once you're in, you're in for life. Ain't no switching sides. Ain't no backing out. You ride or die, homie."

He said it was like a warning, but there was something else underneath. Respect maybe. Or pride. But definitely a warning. We didn't discuss it again that day. Just went to school like it was any other day. Walked into the first period stinking of smoke and old sweat, eyes low, heads down.

Later that day, after school, I went home.

The house was quiet.

No lights on. No note. No questions.

Nobody was there.

I dropped my bag on the floor and collapsed on my bed, shoes still on, my body sore and hungover. I must have passed out hard because when I opened my eyes again, it was dark outside, and I could smell dinner cooking in the kitchen. I shuffled to the table. Sat down.

Nobody said a word.

No one asked where I had been. No one said they were worried. No one even noticed that I had not come home the night before. I sat there, chewing on my mom's homemade meal, while the TV buzzed in the background and my parents pretended, I was still the quiet kid.

That night, lying in bed, I stared at the ceiling and made up my mind.

A few weeks would pass, and thoughts of joining this gang were the only thing I could think of.

I was going to do it.

I was going to join.

Not just because I wanted to be tough, or cool, or reckless, but because it felt like someone finally saw me. Like someone wanted me. Like I was about to belong somewhere, for real, for the first time in my life, I would be accepted.

The next day could not come fast enough.

I woke up early, heart racing like Christmas morning. The sky was still dark, the world was still quiet, and I felt wired, as if something big was about to shift. I threw on my clothes, grabbed my backpack, and bolted out the door before anyone in the house even rolled over in bed. The air was sharp and wet, and my breath came out in fast puffs as I walked toward Issac's place. My stomach twisted, nervous, excited, scared, but I told myself this was it. I made my choice. There was no turning back.

I got to his house and walked in without knocking. That was just how it was there. The front door never locked properly, and nobody cared who came in or out as long as you didn't steal anything or start trouble. If you did, you were dealt with. I went up the stairs, two at a time, and found Issac in his room. He was standing in front of a cracked mirror, ironing his Dickies on a wooden chair, a half-burnt joint hanging from his lips. His speakers were bumping rap music, the bass so deep it made the floorboards vibrate. Smoke circled around him with intention. He was shirtless, tattoos creeping up his chest and shoulders like vines, a look of total calm on his face.

He saw me in the mirror and raised his chin. "What's good, fool?"

I swallowed, took a breath, and said it.

"I'm in. I wanna do it. I'm ready."

He froze for a second, then turned around fully, eyes wide.

"For real?"

I nodded.

A slow grin spread across his face, and he dropped the iron, walked over, and pulled me into a hug. A rough, hard hug, the kind where he slapped my back twice like it was a rite of passage.

"That's what's up, carnal," he said, grinning. "We will talk to everyone later tonight."

In that moment, with the smoke, the music, and the weight of his arms around me, I felt something strange. Not fear. Not guilt. But relief. Like I had finally stepped out of the shadows. Like maybe this was the only kind of love I was ever going to get—the kind you earn with loyalty and respect. The kind that did not ask where you were last night, because they already knew.

"We'll talk to my cousins once we get to school," Issac said, pulling his hoodie tighter around his head as we climbed the steps onto the bus.

The ride was its usual blur—cracked vinyl seats, someone blasting music from a speaker in the back, the low hum of tired conversations and tired faces. I barely heard any of it. My mind was already ahead of me, skipping past first period, past lunch, to what came after. I felt like I was walking into something bigger than me. Something dangerous, yes, but real. Something solid I could finally grab onto.

The bus screeched to a stop in front of East Middle. Doors hissed open. We stepped off into chaos.

Kids were everywhere, spread out in packs and cliques across the front of the school. You could tell who they were just by the way they stood. Athletes in tight huddles. Girls with lip gloss, chola makeup, and feathered hair leaning against the wall. Nerds are already halfway through their textbooks. And then… the ones you knew not to look at too long.

Off to the right, under a stretch of busted chain-link fence, were Issac's cousins. You could not miss them. They did not blend in; they owned whatever space they stood in. Baggy pants, fresh fades, and bald heads, faces half-covered by bandanas or sunglasses, tattoos visible even in the early morning light. Around them, girls, laughter, smoke curling from half-lit cigarettes and joints. And other gang members were not talking; they were just posted up, scanning the crowd as if they were watching over something sacred.

We headed their way.

I felt my heart start to hammer in my chest, not out of fear exactly, but adrenaline. That cold fire that rises up your spine when you are about to do something that cannot be undone. As we got closer, Issac started throwing up gang signs, dapping people up, doing that slow, casual "what's up" dance that looked so effortless, like he had been born into this life. I did my best to keep up, mumbling greetings, nodding where it felt right. My palms were slick with sweat, tucked deep into my hoodie pocket.

Then Issac stepped to his cousin, the same one from the porch. His name, what they called him, was Kane. He leaned closely, whispered something in his ear.

Kane glanced over at me. His eyes landed hard and stayed there. No smile. No nod. Just measuring. Then he looked back at Issac, nodded once, and said,

"Orale." Low and solid, like a promise.

"Let me get with everyone," he added. "We'll set something up for when y'all get outta school. Koo?"

Just like that, they peeled off. All of them. The cousins, the girls, the older homies. They did not go to class. They did not need to. They did not even go to that school. They were just there because everyone was there. That was their domain, the concrete, the steps, the fences. School was just another stage for them.

They walked off slowly, deliberately, like kings heading back to the palace. I stood there, watching them go, my mind racing but strangely clear.

This is it, I thought.

Time to step into the spotlight. Whatever that meant.

No more shadows. No more being overlooked. No more sitting quietly at dinner while the world burned around me. I was about to be part of something, something bigger than me, something that had weight, history, and blood. I did not know exactly what was coming after school, but I knew it would be my initiation.

And I did not care.

Because for once, I felt like I was seen.

The day dragged like wet cement.

Every class felt pointless. The teachers' voices were just noise, floating above me like a radio on in the next room. My mind was not in the building. It was outside, with Issac's cousin Kane, with the crew, with whatever was waiting for me after the final bell. My leg bounced under every desk, heartbeat pacing like it was trying to outrun something. Lunch came and went, tasteless. I barely spoke.

Issac, though? He was lit all day.

He had that spark in his eye, the kind that said he had already been somewhere dark that morning, and he liked it. He leaned in during sixth period, when the substitute teacher was not looking, and started talking in a low voice, his tone carrying heat and adrenaline.

"Yo," he said, grinning like he was telling me about some wild dream. "I put a strap to some lame and a couple snow bunnies earlier. Made 'em eat the pavement at the gas station."

I turned slightly in my seat, trying not to react, but his voice had me locked in.

"No right way but this way," he said, shaking his head slowly, like he was proud. "You either in, or you in the way."

I watched his eyes. They were not bragging. Not like some kids do, puffed-up lies just to sound tough. His eyes were calm and cold, as if what he was saying was just another Tuesday. He leaned back, arms stretched out and kept going.

"Saw them walking by the 7-Eleven. Rich kids. Backpack lookin' fat. They had money, had money, but not untouchable." He laughed, no humor in it. "So, I walked up, pulled my piece, nothing fancy, and put it right in the dude's ribs. Told 'em to get down, face to the ground. The look on his face? Man..." He shook his head again, eyes glazing over a little like he was replaying it in his mind, savoring it. "Took his wallet, her purse, all that. Had 'em begging, bro. Cryin'. Crying, man. Snow bunnies always fold quickly."

He glanced at me, grinning. "You'll get your turn. Don't even trip."

My stomach flipped. Not from fear, exactly. It was something else. Something messier.

A mix of awe and doubt. Just like... really?

Because at that moment, Issac was everything I thought I wanted to be. Fearless. Respected. Feared. He walked through this world like it could not touch him. And here he was, looking at me like I was next in line to wear the crown. But somewhere deep in my gut, something was twisting. A quiet voice asked, 'Are you really ready for this?'

I ignored it.

I had to.

The moment the final bell rang, I was no longer a student. I was not just some quiet kid from a silent house with a broken past.

I was about to be something else.

And ready or not, the spotlight was coming.

It was not just the idea of joining the gang that had my heart racing. It was the identity. The name. Just the thought of being able to say, I'm a gangster, and have people believe it— that got me high before anything else ever could.

I no longer wanted to be invisible.

I wanted people to feel something when I walked by. I wanted heads to turn. I wanted whispers in the hallway, sideways glances, people stepping back not because they liked me, but because they feared what I might do. I wanted to be a force, the kind that brings havoc and grief behind it like a shadow. The kind you do not laugh at. The kind that makes people sleep with one eye open.

Yeah, I wanted that.

More than anything, I wanted to matter.

The bus let out that sharp hiss as it pulled to a stop. Doors clanked open, and we stepped off into the late afternoon sky. The sun was low, bleeding through the trees like it knew something bad was about to happen. The air smelled like heat off the asphalt and someone barbecuing cheap meat down the block. Issac walked next to me, quiet for once, hoodie halfway off his head. He had that look—focused, serious, like his brain was working ahead of us.

As we passed the old liquor store on the corner, he glanced over at me and said, "You know there's no quittin' once this life starts, right?"

His voice was not loud. He did not have to be.

"This ain't some club you check in and out of. Ain't no, Yo, I'm done now, thanks for the ride. Once you in... you in, bro. For life. Blood in, blood out."

His words hung in the air, heavier than uncertainty.

I swallowed, feeling the nerves twist in my gut, but I did not show it. I could not. I nodded, eyes fixed ahead, like I had already made peace with the devil.

"I hear you, bro," I said. My voice came out steadily. Cold. It felt like I had been waiting for this my whole life.

We turned the corner onto his street. The houses here all looked the same, tired, sagging under the weight of forgotten dreams. Lawns gone to patchy dirt, windows half-covered by sheets or old blinds. But it felt alive. Like something was happening here. Like this was the only place that had not lied to me.

As we got closer to Issac's house, I could already hear the bass thumping from inside, that low, heavy rhythm that made your ribs vibrate. Something was waiting for us behind that door.

Something final.

I did not flinch.

Because at that moment, I was not a scared kid.

I was the storm coming.

The door swung open, and the music hit me like a wall, bass so deep it rattled the windows, some West Coast beat thumping loud enough to shake your bones. The air inside was thick with the smell of weed smoke, cheap cologne, and something electric, a tension buzzing under everything, as if the whole house was holding its breath. Girls were already there, leaning on walls, sitting in laps, laughing too loudly, drinking straight from bottles, smoke curling from their lips. One of them handed me a beer without asking, smiling like she already knew who I was. Like my name had been whispered before I even walked through the door.

And all I could think was...

This is the life.

This was the world I wanted. Music, smoke, girls, respect. A room full of people who did not ask questions, did not judge, did not pretend. Nobody cared about school, curfews, or rules. They moved how they wanted, talked how they wanted, lived how they wanted—wild, loud, and unafraid.

And now I am part of it.

I was all in.

We settled in the living room, couch cushions sunken in for too many years, ashtrays overflowing, empty cans already piling up on the coffee table. A circle formed naturally. No one told anyone where to sit; it just happened. I dropped down on the edge of the couch, next to Issac, and cracked my second beer. It was warm, bitter, but I did not care. My hands shook just a little, but the buzz in my chest drowned it out.

People were dapping me up. Nodding. Smiling.

"Ey, this the one?"

"This Lil' homie right here?"

"Been hearing good things, fool. Solid."

I did not know half their names, but they all acted like they knew me. As if I were already one of them.

The night moved fast.

We smoked blunt after blunt, the smoke rolling thick across the ceiling like a storm cloud. Jokes flew, girls danced in the kitchen, someone started freestyling over the beat. I remember laughing so hard I could not breathe at one point. But under it all, there was still that pulse—that quiet current running beneath the fun.

Something was coming.

I could feel it.

By the time the sun had dipped, and the house was glowing with nothing but red and gold light from the hallway lamp and the TV screen, the energy shifted.

That was when Kane stepped forward.

He was standing by the kitchen doorway, arms crossed, a half-lit blunt tucked behind his ear, a thick gold chain catching the light. He did not smile. Did not blink. His presence quieted the room like someone hit pause on the night.

"This was all for you, Lil' homie," he said, his voice deep, steady, final. "You ready?"

The whole room turned towards me.

The laughter stopped.

The beat kept playing, but softer now, like it was holding its breath too.

I looked around at Issac, at the faces watching me, at the smoke and the girls and the bottles and the walls that suddenly felt like they were closing in with gravity.

My heart was pounding, but I did not hesitate.

I nodded once. Just once.

"Yeah," I said. "I'm ready."

Kane stared at me for a second longer, then nodded back.

"Then let's get it."

And just like that, the game changed.

Forever.

"Let's go outside," Kane said, his voice like an executioner.

Issac was already standing, eyes locked on me. Next to him were Slow Poke, Knuckles, and Vicious—all older, harder faces carved by the street life. They moved with that kind of stillness that meant danger. Nobody rushed. Nobody smiled.

I stood up, chin up and chest out, without a word.

This was it.

The air outside was colder than it had been all day. The sun had dipped, and the sky was bleeding out in streaks of dark orange and purple. Streetlights flickered to life down the block, casting long shadows across the cracked concrete and oil-stained driveways.

Everyone followed.

The music cut out the second the front door swung open, like even the beat knew it was not time for noise anymore. The laughter, the smoke, all of it faded. Girls came out too, leaning against the car hoods and fences, lighting cigarettes with curious eyes, like they had seen this before and already knew what was coming.

My heart was hammering.

I followed Kane down the driveway. His gold chain flashed under the streetlight as he motioned toward a circle already forming at the end, the same spot they fixed their cars, rolled dice, smoked, and now… broke boys into men.

"This your time, Lil' homie," Kane said, his voice low, almost respectful. "You wanna ride with us, this is how. You get jumped in."

He looked me dead in the eye with full seriousness.

"No backing out now."

I nodded. Swallowed hard. "Alright," I said. "That's what's up."

Someone in the crowd muttered, "Time to shine."

Another one called out, "Knuckle up!"

Then I heard a girl's voice, soft but clear: "Hope he don't fold."

I took a deep breath. I could take a beating. I knew I could. My dad had swung on me since I was old enough to talk back. I had been hit hard before. Bruises faded. Pain was just weakness leaving the body. Right?

But this?

This was different.

I stepped into the circle.

Knuckles cracked his neck. Vicious pulled off his shirt, tattoos crawling across his chest like war paint. Slow Poke smiled, not friendly, but excited. Issac just looked at me, his jaw tight. He was not going to save me. That was not how this worked.

"One minute," Kane said. "No tapping out. You make it through, you in."

I nodded again in agreement.

And then…

BOOM.

I did not even see the first hit coming.

 Blindsided.

A white flash of pain exploded across the side of my face as someone's fist cracked into my temple. My knees buckled. I staggered sideways and caught a boot to the ribs. Then a shoulder drove into my chest. I hit the pavement hard, gasping, already bleeding.

But I did not stay down.

Couldn't.

I scrambled up and threw a wild punch, caught someone—maybe it was Knuckles—in the chin, but then another hit came from behind and I tasted blood in my mouth. My vision blurred. The voices around me became one loud ringing, a mix of cheering, shouting, laughing, maybe even screaming. My head snapped back from another punch, this one straight to the nose. Blood poured down my lips. My eyes watered. Everything was spinning.

Still, I stayed on my feet.

Because this was not about winning.

It was about surviving.

Hands grabbed at my hoodie. Fists slammed into my stomach, my back, and the side of my head. I could not breathe. My body screamed. My brain was fog. But I kept swinging, kept moving. Every hit was a voice in my head—my dad's, my silence, every time I was ignored, forgotten, unseen.

BOOM. BOOM. BOOM.

The circle pulsed with violence.

And then, just as fast as it started, it stopped.

I dropped to one knee, spitting blood on the concrete, eyes swollen half shut, chest heaving. Someone grabbed my arm and yanked me up.

It was Kane. He stepped in and called the wolves off.

He looked me over, blood dripping from my nose, shirt torn, breath ragged, and then he gave a nod—a nod of acceptance. "You did that," he said. "You in. See, it wasn't that bad, huh? We got you now, my boy."

He said it as we started to walk back into the house. The crowd clapped, a few shouts went up, and someone popped a beer. Issac stepped forward, grabbed me in a tight hug, and slapped my back twice.

"Welcome to the family, fool."

The girls were watching.

The music kicked back in.

And even through the pain, even with the ringing in my ears and the fire in my ribs, I smiled. Because for the first time in my life, I felt like I belonged. Even if it meant bleeding for it.

We stumbled back inside, the night air still clinging to our skin, the echo of cheers and adrenaline still humming in my chest. My face was sore, swollen, and cut open in a couple of places. My knuckles hurt. I could barely breathe from the hits to my ribs, but none of that mattered.

I was in.

I was one of them.

Kane looked to the couch. "Sit down," he said, his voice steady and calm, like we were just about to talk business over beers. "Now that you in, you gotta rep the neighborhood."

He reached over to a beat-up shoebox on the coffee table and pulled out a makeshift tattoo kit: a needle, lighter, thread, ink, and a bottle of cheap rubbing alcohol that looked like it had been used a hundred times before. It was all new to me. No gloves, no stencil, just memory and muscle. The smell of alcohol and cigarette smoke wrapped around me as Issac wiped down my arm, then tied off a needle to a pen with tape. My heart was still racing—not from fear now, but from the rush, from being seen, from being real. Becoming a gangster.

"This is your set now," Kane said as the first poke hit my skin. "Ain't no erasing it."

The needle dug in slowly. Poke by poke. My arm flinched, but I did not make a sound. Just took it, eyes locked on the ceiling fan spinning fast above us but not balanced. We were still drinking, beers cracked open, a blunt in rotation. And that was when it happened.

POP! POP! POP!

The first shot was loud, but it did not register right away.

The second shot shattered the front window.

Glass exploded inward like a grenade, and the whole room dropped.

"Get down!" someone screamed.

The music kept playing. Beer cans spilled. A girl yelled and dove behind the couch. I hit the floor, cheek against the cold tile, heart pounding so hard it felt like it would punch through my chest. My ears were ringing, not from the shots, but from the silence that followed.

Issac jumped up, reckless, fast.

He ran straight to the door, pulled it open without thinking.

He did not even duck.

"White four-door Cadillac," he shouted, eyes wide, pointing down the street. "Took off down the street. The plates were paper, and music was blasting. It was them, bro. Them from earlier."

Knuckles was already by the window, brushing glass off his arms. His eyes were on fire. "That's those foos that just came to town selling all that weight," he growled. "They've been startin' it with us since they moved in. Walkin' around like they own this town."

He spat on the floor. "Time to ride."

Nobody hesitated.

Cans were kicked aside. The shoebox hit the floor. Girls moved out of the way without a word. They knew what this was. Kane did not say anything. Just turned and walked to the back room. The house was dead quiet except for the sound of the back door creaking open and slamming shut behind him. When he came back, he had it in his hand. A .38 snub nose, all chrome, short-barreled, dull around the handle like it had seen its share of nights like this one. He checked the cylinder. Fully loaded. No words. Just muscle memory.

Then he looked at me.

Held the heater out.

"Ready?"

My hand shook for a second as I reached out. The steel was cold, heavier than I thought. It no longer felt like a prop. It felt real. Like life or death. Like crossing a line that had no edges on the other side. I looked at Kane. Then Issac. Then the blood on my knuckles and the almost unfinished tattoo on my arm, still raw and bleeding. However, the other two tattoos were completed.

"Ready as I'll ever be," I said.

And I meant it.

Because there was no going back.

The street had called, and I answered.

Kane burst through the front door like a wild dog off the chain.

"Let's go. Now."

Outside, Janice was already in the driver's seat of the old Suzuki Sidekick, the paint faded, muffler loud, and the passenger door creaking when I pulled it open. Kane slid in behind me, knuckles already tightening his gloves, his jaw clenched like steel.

"Give him shotgun," Kane barked.

Without a word, I climbed into the front seat, legs still shaking from the shock, but hands steady. Issac, Knucks, and Kane all piled in behind me. The weight of the strap in my hoodie pocket felt like it was fused to my ribs with the pain in my side. The air inside the SUV was thick—sweat, gun oil, blood, fear, and rage. A cocktail only the streets could shake up.

Janice did not say a word. She just drove.

Fast.

Like she had done this before. Plenty of times.

We tore through neighborhoods lit by flickering streetlights, the Suzuki humming low and angry under us. Houses blurred past, people on porches faded into the background. Kane's eyes scanned every car we passed. Knuckles was dead silent, cracking his fingers. Issac had the window half down, elbow out, scanning for that white Cadillac.

Nervous as hell, yeah.

But not second-guessing.

Not now.

I had made my bed. Now I was lying in it with brass and fire.

"I think I know where they chill at," Issac said, his voice low, steady.

So, we did.

We hit three different spots, looped around alleys, cut across parking lots, and kept our headlights off at times, just creeping. But nothing. No Cadillac. No music. Just the silence of empty streets and the weight of unfinished business. We were almost ready to call it.

Turning back onto Circle Drive, driving slowly, hearts sunken just a little like we failed, and then we saw it.

Boom.

There it was.

White four-door Cadillac on rims.

Parked sideways on the curb with the doors open, music thumping, some drunk fools laughing too loudly. They were in a yard, red Solo cups in their hands, smoke in the air, girls on lawn chairs. Just wild and careless, like they had not just put bullets through someone's home. Like they had not just tried to kill us.

"They're partying?" Kane said, squinting. "These lames are partying?"

We slowed down, keeping our distance about a block back. Lights off.

They did not notice us. Why would they? They thought they got away with it. They were moving in and out of the house, someone grilling in the front, loudspeakers leaning up against the porch, a cooler tipped over in the grass. It was just another night for them. Another flex.

But to me?

It was war.

My mind started spiraling—every buried scream, every busted lip from my dad, every time I cried into a pillow so no one would hear. Every time I felt invisible. Worthless. This was no longer about gang retaliation. This was me standing at the edge of the world with a smoking pistol in my lap.

And I was not praying anymore.

I thought, don't pray for me. This ain't me anymore. Pray for the demon I've become.

He's the one without remorse.

He's the one pulling the trigger.

Janice's voice cut through the silence like a match to gasoline.

"NOW!"

She floored the gas.

The tires screamed, and gravel spat from under the wheels. My body snapped forward in the seat as we charged down the block, the house getting bigger and bigger in the windshield. The bass from their party was still thumping like nothing was wrong. I rose up in the seat, one knee on the cushion, my hoodie lifted, the pistol gripped tightly in both hands.

FOCUS. STUPID. FOCUS.

The gun felt alive in my palms.

My heart was beating so loudly I could not hear the music anymore, just the echo of every broken part of me screaming for release.

READY. AIM.

I raised the .38 through the open window.

Time slowed.

One guy looked up, a solo cup still in his hand, just as I locked onto the crowd.

POP! POP! POP! POP!

The hammer danced under my finger.

POP! POP!

Smoke curled up past my eyes. Girls screamed. A bottle shattered. Someone dropped in the yard, clutching their stomach. Another guy ducked behind the barbecue grill. The air was filled with screaming and the stench of fear. The pistol kicked harder than I expected. The last shot rang out like it had nowhere else to go but through me.

Click.

Click.

Empty.

I dropped back into the seat, chest heavy.

Janice swerved hard, tires screeching as she pulled a wide left and peeled off down the block, engine growling. Nobody said a word for the first few seconds. Just wind and silence—the kind that follows the devil when he leaves the room and leaves a stench. Honestly, they tried to take us out, so I thought it was a fair trade. People would soon learn what I said had substance.

The tires screeched one last time as Janice cut the wheel and slid the Suzuki Sidekick into a narrow alley behind a house I had never been to before. She hit the button and the garage door creaked open, slow but loud as hell to my ears, like it was announcing us to the whole city. My hands were still trembling, but I held the pistol tight, barrel hot, the smell of burned gunpowder still clinging to my sleeves. We pulled in, and the door dropped behind us, closing us off from the outside world with a dull thunk. Just like that, we vanished.

No sirens. No cops.

Just silence.

Inside, it was dim. A single lightbulb hung from a cracked wire, casting shadows over a rusty bike, stacks of dusty boxes, and a broken futon. Nobody said anything for a minute. Just breathing. Just the hum of the garage door motor cooling down. I sat in the front seat, staring straight ahead, heart punching at my ribs like it wanted out. I could not feel my fingers.

I couldn't feel my face. My mind was spiraling, fast, replaying the moment the first shot cracked, the look on that guy's face as he turned, the sound of glass and screaming and chaos.

It didn't feel real.

It felt like I had left my body somewhere back on Circle Drive. Kane finally broke the silence, voice low and calm, like we hadn't just opened fire on a front yard full of people. "We'll wait here. Lay low. Think things through."

Issac slapped my shoulder, grinning. "You did that, fool."

Knucks laughed, wiping sweat off his forehead. "Yo, that was wild. The way they ran. Like roaches when the lights come on."

I tried to laugh, but it caught in my throat.

Outside, the city continued to breathe as if nothing had happened. Inside, I was choking on what I had just become. I didn't know where we were. Some houses they used for nights like this stashed away in the middle of nowhere, low-key. Nobody turned the lights on inside. Janice cracked a window and lit a cigarette, the cherry glowing in the dark like a quiet red eye watching us.

Hours passed.

I stayed quiet. Watching. Listening.

Panicking on the inside, still cold and silent on the outside.

This was where I learned about the art of composure. Of holding your fear in your gut and locking it down behind your teeth. I kept still. Didn't fidget. Didn't breathe too loud. Just nodded when they praised me.

"Real one right here," Kane said, pointing at me. "Ain't even flinch."

"Man," Knucks said, grinning, "we might have made a monster tonight."

Then someone inside shouted.

"Yo! Hurry up come see this!"

We all rushed into the living room. The TV was on. News at Ten. Cheap background music, news ticker crawling across the screen.

"Breaking news out of the Southside of Colorado Springs. Police are searching for suspects involved in a drive-by shooting that occurred just hours ago off Circle Drive…"

The anchor's voice was smooth, detached, like they were reading the weather.

"…the shooting injured two individuals at a house party, both of whom are in critical condition. No fatalities have been reported yet. Police are urging anyone with information to come forward."

Then the shot cut to a grainy phone video with sirens blaring, yellow tape fluttering in the wind, and people crying in the background.

Kane pointed at the screen. "Welp," he said with a crooked grin.

"Ay, SUSPECT!" Knucks yelled, laughing hard. "YOU MADE THE NEWS, LOCO!"

Issac threw his arm around me. "Ayyyeee! That's you now, fool. That's you. SUSPECT. That's your name from now on."

The whole room cracked up.

I didn't.

Not because I was scared, but because something inside me had changed. I stared at the screen, at the wreckage we left behind, and I didn't flinch. Didn't blink. I was cold. Empty.

But it's not broken. No.

Just… transformed.

The kid who used to get beaten and punished? Clocked out.

That kid who used to cry in his room? Gone.

That kid who used to ask God why he felt nothing inside? Buried alive.

Suspect.

It didn't feel like a nickname.

It felt like a birth certificate signed in fire.

A contract written in every beating I took, every time I tasted blood and didn't cry, every second I sat alone in that cold basement while someone I loved locked themselves in the bathroom to escape their own life.

Suspect.

They think monsters are born in blood and rage.

Nah.

Monsters are built in silence.

In the pauses between screams.

In the loneliness, no one checks on.

In the questions no one answers.

"Why doesn't he cry anymore?"

"Why is he always watching?"

"Why doesn't he look scared?"

Because fear is a luxury.

And I spent mine already.

I don't dream anymore.

Not of better days. Not of escape.

I dream of control. Of never flinching again.

Standing in the wreckage and knowing I put it there, not by accident, but by choice. Yeah, that was me,

I AM SUSPECT.

CHAPTER 13: WRATH OF THE ROCK

Frantic did not even begin to scratch the surface. My heart was sprinting before my feet hit the sidewalk, before the sirens ever faded into the night behind me. I kept my head down the whole way home, hoodie up, jaw clenched, breath like broken glass in my throat. Every car that passed felt like it was slowing down. Every porch light that flickered made me flinch. My legs did not stop moving, but inside I was unraveling, stitch by stitch.

I did not go through the front door.

Couldn't.

My dad was sleeping right there in his throne as soon as you walked in, and I did not want to wake the giant. So, I crept around the back, stepping over busted fence posts and empty cans, past the old grill nobody had used in forever. The grass back there was half dirt, half neglect, full of cigarette butts and secrets that never got cleaned up. I pushed the basement door open slowly. No creak. I had oiled the hinges last summer, just in case I ever needed to disappear without anyone knowing I came back, and any sound would wake him. Inside was dark, but not the kind of dark that scares you. It was the kind that hides you.

That welcomes you.

Like it knew what I had done.

I closed the door behind me, locked it, and slid the bolt into place.

I stood there for a minute, forehead against the cold metal, breathing like I had just run from God. My hand was still shaking. Not from fear exactly, but from adrenaline that had not figured out where to go yet.

Then I went down the steps.

Slow.

One by one.

Each creak underfoot reminds me that this was still real. That I was still alive. That night had not been a nightmare. It would take adjusting to, but it was just my life now.

A month or so passed.

No news.

No whispers.

No knocks at the door.

No flashing lights.

It was as if the drive-by had never happened. It's as if the city just swallowed it whole and moved on. Another headline that never made it. Another bullet that did not belong to anyone. But I knew better. Still, I had to live. Had to act like things were normal. And normal for me was getting ready for school like I was about to walk a runway or should I say a hallway full of fake smiles and real enemies.

That morning, I moved like I had learned how.

Speaker thumping loud, something with bass heavy enough to rattle the windows. The kind of music that made you feel bulletproof even when your insides were unraveling. I had a blunt half-burnt in the ashtray, still smoldering, sending smoke trails into the ceiling. Took a pull every now and then, not just to get high, but to slow my heartbeat. Weed did not make me escape. It made me float just enough to keep the weight from crushing me.

With iron in one hand and a towel in the other. Pressing heat into a pair of black jeans, I kept them crisp like funeral clothes. They could probably stand by themselves.

Every line is perfect. Every wrinkle smoothed out like I was erasing the chaos of my life, one sleeve at a time.

I cleaned my shoes next.

Nike Cortez. Classic.

They had to be spotless. I took a toothbrush to the sole, dipped it in baking soda and water, and scrubbed it as if I were cleaning a weapon. Because in a way, I was. Where I am from, how you look is your first line of defense. You cannot show weakness. Not even a scuff mark.

Now, I dress to impress. Not because I was vain. To me, looking right meant feeling in control. And control was something I did not have much of these days. A wristwatch that no longer ticked but still caught the light just right. I checked myself in the mirror, straight posture, eyes low, expression blank. Clean. Controlled. Cold.

That was the image. Even if it was under the surface, my nerves were static. Even if every siren in the distance made my throat tighten. Even if I caught myself staring too long in the mirror, wondering if I still looked like a kid or something else now.

Something darker.

Something permanent.

Next thing I knew, my door opened with a no-knock warrant, no warning. It was not just opened, it was pushed open, hard enough to make the hinges rattle. And standing there, filling the doorway like a shadow out of my nightmares, was THE ROCK.

Not the smiling Hollywood version.

Not the one with jokes and eyebrows raised from wrestling.

This was The Rock of my life. A heavy, stone-faced killer, looking like a storm about to break loose.

Of course, he looked pissed.

His shoulders were squared so wide they blocked out the little strip of basement light. His eyes were hard, cutting straight through the smoke hanging in the room. His jaw was clenched tight enough to crack teeth. Maybe I woke him up with my music.

"BOY, WHAT THE HELL ARE YOU DOING DOWN HERE?"

His voice was thundering in a low-ceilinged room. It shook the whole basement.

"SMOKING WEED, HUH?"

If looks could kill, I would be dead already.

He had that look, not just anger, but disappointment mixed with it. The kind of look that makes you feel smaller than you already do, even when you are trying to stand tall. I stood there frozen, blunt still smoldering in the ashtray, the music still thumping low in the background like a heartbeat I could not slow down. My hands went to my knees, not because I was scared, but because I did not know where else to put them.

Hear me out real quick before I continue.

And here is the part that always burned me up inside.

He smoked weed, too.

Even grew it in the garden.

Big, green, proud plants hidden behind tomato cages like they were just another crop.

However, he never discussed it with me.

Never let me know anything. Never sat me down and said, "Here's what it is, here's what it does, here's why I do it, or here's why not to do it."

Nothing. It did not exist.

Just rules.

Just yelling.

Just anger.

Yeah, I understood he wanted the best for me.

Wanted me to succeed. Wanted better from me. I get that, I do. But the way he would come at me? Completely uncalled for. One hundred percent.

Ok, back to regular broadcasting.

His words hit like a belt buckle. His tone hit like someone slamming a door closed. As for me, standing there in the basement, smoke still coming from my lips, I felt like a stranger in my own life. Part of me wanted to yell back. Part of me wanted to explain. Part of me wanted to tell him I was already drowning, and his voice was just pushing me under faster. Instead, I stayed quiet. Let the bass from the speaker fill the silence. Let the smell of weed hang in the air between us like a confession. Even though we were both guilty of the same thing, somehow, I was always the one on trial with no deliberation.

He stared at me for a long moment, eyes dragging up and down my bare torso. No shirt, just skin and ink. The smell of weed still hung in the room, heavy and sweet, mixing with the iron tang of the old basement pipes. The bass from my speaker thumped low, like a slow heartbeat I could not steady.

Then his eyes locked on my tattoos.

That was it.

That was the moment he lost it completely.

"WHAT'S THIS ALL OVER YOUR BODY?" he roared, voice echoing off the cracked concrete walls. "OH, YOU'RE BAD NOW, HUH? I'LL SHOW YOU WHO'S BAD, BOY!"

His words hit first, sharp and heavy, anger flying from his lips. His whole body swelled with rage, shoulders squared, fists clenching and unclenching like he was already throwing the punches in his head. The air in the basement thickened, hot and still, like the seconds before a storm breaks.

At that moment, I knew it was game over.

No time to think.

No time to breathe.

No way out of this.

BAM.

A fist slammed into my face, full weight, full force, a shockwave cracking through my skull. My vision burst into white stars. My knees buckled. The room tilted, the bass from the speaker turning into a low hum as my body reacted to the blow. I hit the floor hard, the back of my head bouncing off cold concrete. The breath flew out of my lungs in a single sharp grunt. My ears filled with a high ringing, and for a second the whole room turned white, like I had fallen into a flash of lightning.

Before I could even move, his fists were already on me again. They followed me down, no hesitation, no warning just slamming into my face and chest with steady, merciless rhythm. Left, right, right, left. Face, body, face, body.

Each hit was a hammer.

My skull rattled. My ribs ached. My lips split open, and I could taste blood, warm and metallic, running into the back of my throat.

The music from the speaker had become a muffled heartbeat somewhere far away, swallowed up by the sound of knuckles on skin. I was dazed, confused, barely even there. Just a body on the floor in nothing but basketball shorts, skin slick with sweat, offering no defense. No shirt to grab. No armor to take the edge off.

He was a grown man.

My father.

And he was hitting me with full force.

Each blow came down with all the weight of him, all the muscle, all the anger, and all the disappointment. His fists cracked against my face, then my chest, then back again, a rhythm drilled into me like a drumbeat. I tried to lift my arms, but they felt like concrete. Dead weight. My hands hung limp at my sides. My body would not respond; my brain was too slow to tell it what to do.

Left. Right. Face. Body. Face. Body.

I could not block. I could not stop him. All I could do was absorb the pain, the noise, the smell of sweat and rage. All I could do was absorb the pain, the noise, the smell of sweat and weed and rage. My vision blurred at the edges of the room, tunneling until there was nothing left but the flash of his fists.

I was not fighting back at all.

I couldn't.

I was just a boy being hit full force by the man who raised him, my body going under him, my spirit slipping somewhere else, somewhere quieter, leaving only dead weight behind.

He grabbed me by the arm, not gently, not like a father should, but like he was yanking a body off the street. His fingers dug into my bicep, iron-tight, nails biting into skin. I was barely conscious, eyes flickering, mouth leaking blood. My cheek was already swollen, my ribs screaming every time I took a breath.

Then he dragged me out of the room.

My skin scraped the basement floor, concrete grinding against my back and spine, and I could not stop it. I could not move. It was like my whole body had short-circuited, every muscle gone, leaving only the weight of shock and pain. He was pulling me toward the hallway, toward the narrow staircase that led upstairs, the house above, the world that did not know what was happening beneath it.

That was when something inside me kicked back to life.

I came to—not fully, not clearly—but enough to fight, to scream, to kick with whatever strength I had left.

"LET ME GO!"

My voice cracked like a dying animal. "GET OFF ME!"

My foot connected with a wall, then the floor, but it did nothing. I twisted in his grip, flopped like a fish pulled from water, heart pounding so loud it echoed in my ears.

It did not matter.

He kept dragging me like I weighed nothing, like I was not his blood, like I was not even human. My heels banged against the wooden steps as we hit the stairs.

THUD. THUD. THUD.

Each impact sent a jolt up my spine. Pain flared through my chest, my face, my arms. I could not even imagine what he was going to do to me.

Or what was going through his head. All I could feel was raw terror, the kind that makes your throat tighten and your vision blur.

There was nothing left to reason with. Nothing to calm him down.

He was not there anymore.

This was not discipline.

This was not a lesson.

This was rage. Pure. Full of hatred.

"STOP FIGHTING ME, BOY!" he roared, spit flying from his mouth as he struck me again, a backhand across the face that snapped my head sideways mid-scream. My lip split wide open. Blood smeared across the hallway wall. My body went limp again.

He kept dragging me.

Up the stairs.

Into the unknown.

And all I could do was pray, not to be saved, but to survive.

"YOU'RE TUFF, HUH?!" he bellowed, voice vibrating through the house like a war drum.

"YOU'RE BAD, RIGHT?!"

His fist swung again, catching me in the jaw as he dragged me through the kitchen, one arm still hooked under mine like I was a disobedient dog, not his son. The tile scraped beneath my heels, my body limp, my vision blurred, blood trailing behind us like breadcrumbs. I saw flashes of the kitchen table. The sink. A pot left on the stove. The hum of the refrigerator mixed with the rasp in my throat as I tried to cry out. My voice was gone. Everything felt distant.

The kitchen lights were too bright. The air too still.

It all felt wrong.

He did not stop.

Did not slow down.

Did not speak except to grunt through his teeth like he was possessed. His grip tightened around my arm, bruising deep, now purple and red already blooming beneath the skin.

By the time we reached the top, I could barely keep my head up.

Then I saw it. The bathroom door. Wide open. Waiting.

Like a mouth about to swallow me whole.

No.

I kicked weakly. Dug in my heels.

And when we reached the doorway, I threw my hands up and latched onto the frame with everything I had. My fingers curled into the wood like claws. My whole body strained backward, desperate.

"I'm not going in!" I managed to scream. "I'M NOT—"

BOOM.

Another blow.

His fist crashed into my face, right eye, sharp and brutal. My head snapped back.

Dazed again.

My grip slipped.

The strength drained out of my fingers like water down the drain. My body folded. He yanked me fully into the bathroom, and this time I did not resist at all. I couldn't. He pulled me over the threshold and slammed the door shut behind us with a deafening BANG that echoed through the hallway like the end of something holy.

The lock clicked.

The silence after that?

It was worse than the beating.

This ill-minded maniac manifested completely with only my invitation granted to his torture chamber.

The bathroom was a trap so I could not run. Full tile and steam. The hiss of the faucet filled the room like a snake's warning. Hot water rushed into the porcelain sink, steam curling up around us, fogging the cracked mirror above. His fingers clamped around my wrist, hard enough to leave bruises. With his other hand, he reached into the cabinet and pulled out a razor knife. The handle was worn, the blade still folded in. A single flick of his thumb and—click—the steel slid free, gleaming under the flickering lightbulb.

He did not look at me. Not yet. He reached for the bottle of rubbing alcohol sitting on the counter and ripped the cap off. The sharp chemical scent hit my nose like a punch. Then he tipped it, pouring it over me, over my chest, my hands, all the places where the ink crawled across my skin. It splashed cold, burned hot, stung where the skin was raw.

I gasped, jerking back, but his grip did not move.

His jaw clenched.

His eyes were fire.

"I'M NOT GOING TO LET YOU MESS YOUR LIFE UP, BOY!" he thundered, voice cracking in the tiny room. The words rattled in my ears, heavier than fists.

The blade hissed under the hot water, steam rising off it like a ritual sacrifice. The bathroom had turned into a furnace of steam and tile. The faucet hissed like a snake coming alive, filling the air with scalding mist. The cracked mirror cut my reflection into pieces—his mouth stretched open, eyes wide and wet, skin slick with sweat and alcohol. His hand crushed my wrist like a vice, pinning me against the sink. In his other hand, the razor glinted as he ran it under the hot water, steam curling off the blade until it looked like it was breathing.

The smell of rubbing alcohol was everywhere, sharp and chemical, burning my nose and throat. It ran down my chest and arms in cold rivers, soaking every place the ink lived under my skin, stinging like a thousand pinpricks before the blade even touched me. I tried to jerk away, but his grip only bit deeper into the meat of my arm.

"YOU'RE NOT GOING TO BE ME!" he roared, voice booming against the tiles. His eyes were fever-bright, his jaw set, spit flying from his lips as the blade hovered in his fist.

Then all his focus came upon me, my skin.

Not a quick cut. No. He was dragging, searing that blade across my skin, like he was trying to peel my mistakes off me. The pain was instant, electric, burning all the way into my teeth. My back arched. My throat opened. A scream ripped out of me raw and jagged, bouncing off the walls until it did not sound human anymore.

"SHUT UP, BOY!" he bellowed, and his open palm cracked across my face, snapping my head sideways. My screams broke into sobs. Blood and spit spattered the tile. My eyes did not want to look, but the blade kept moving, hot metal, steam, and alcohol mixing with sweat, his breath heavy in my face as he held me down. I tried to kick, to claw at his arm, to push him back, but my limbs were water, just useless. My fists slid off his chest. My voice cracked into a cry I had never heard before. Nothing slowed him down. Another cut came, and another scream followed.

The smell of hot metal and chemicals burned my head until there was no air left. My heart thundered against my ribs. My vision narrowed to a pinhole. The edges of my vision darkened. My fingers slipped off the counter. My knees buckled. My head fell back.

I lost.

And then the bathroom, the blade, his voice, all of it turned into a faraway hum, like I was sliding under deep dark water.

I lost consciousness.

Now, I do not know what love is. And I am not talking in the way they write it in songs or whisper it in movies with perfect endings, but in the way a parent loves their child and wants to protect them from the world, to show them unconditional love and support them and build them up, not tear them down.

I also know what love ain't.

It ain't this.

It ain't waking up every morning with a knot in your chest, already bracing for his mood, his silence, or his storm. It ain't walking on eggshells in your own home to use the bathroom, holding your tongue just to keep peace, swallowing pieces of yourself day after day until there is nothing left but the echo of who you used to be.

Love ain't being invisible. It ain't someone looking right through you like you are just another piece of furniture, like something that is there but not really seen.

He does not even know me. Not the real me. Doesn't ask questions. Doesn't want to know.

He thinks he has me figured out, like I am a list of his chores, like I am just here to fit his life, to clean around the sharp edges of his mood while he drinks.

We talk, sure about chores and bills, and how I need a job. But not about dreams. Not about life. Not about how your day was. Not about fear. Not about the future. Not about the things that make us human.

He looks at me like I am supposed to be grateful he did not beat me. Like being tolerated is the same as being loved.

I feel it in my bones, that ache, that hollowness. The kind you cannot explain, even when you are sitting right beside the person who is supposed to hold your heart.

And maybe I do not know what love is. Maybe I have never had the real thing in front of me.

But I know this: love ain't forgetting who you are just to keep someone else comfortable.

I reach for the counter and feel the porcelain under my fingertips, cold, solid. My bloody fingerprints leave marks like a crime scene. The smell of blood is strong. The world tilts. I fell back to the floor.

I do not know if I am alive or only remembering being alive. I do not know if I am still on the floor or if the floor is inside me.

I wake up a little more and realize I am still here. I am still on the bathroom floor. I do not know if it has been hours or minutes, but I see my dad is gone, and I am in the bathroom on the floor in a pool of my own blood, trying to take in what just happened, staring at the ceiling, just lying there and crying with what tears I had left.

CHAPTER 14: EXIT WOUNDS

The bathroom looked like the aftermath of a crime. Blood smeared the sink in streaks, like someone had dragged a paintbrush across porcelain. Tiny droplets peppered the mirror. My hands were trembling as I clung to the counter, knuckles white, ribs screaming every time I drew a breath.

I forced myself to look up.

The stranger staring back at me had my face, but not my eyes. One pupil swallowed by a bruise, lip cracked and bleeding, hair clinging to damp skin. I did not even look human, just some animal that had crawled through a storm. I twisted the faucet and water rushed out in its familiar hiss. It was cold enough to make my teeth ache, but I splashed it over my face anyway, again and again, until the water running down the drain turned pink, then clear. Each splash sent a dull shock through my body, but it also made me feel more awake, more real.

I gripped the sides of the sink until my arms steadied. For a heartbeat, I stared at my reflection, waiting for some flicker of strength to show up. Nothing. Just me. Broken. My dad had just carved me like a pumpkin. I broke even more.

The floor seemed to tilt under me as I pushed off the counter and limped toward the door. My bare feet stuck to the tile where the blood had dried. Down the hallway, the house felt quiet, the kind of quiet that made your ears ring.

In my room, the air smelled like smoke and old laundry. My backpack lay in a heap beside the bed. I dropped to my knees, fighting dizziness, and started shoving things inside. Clothes. Cash from under the mattress. The photo of Isaac and me at the lake was taken some time ago. My hands were clumsy, fumbling, but I did not care how it looked. I just needed out.

I glanced at the clock on my dresser. If I left now, I could reach Isaac's before he left for school. If I moved fast, I might even catch him still at home. The house was still dead silent. My dad's truck was gone. He had either gone to work or was out somewhere, but it didn't matter. Best not to test my luck and be here when he returns.

I swung the backpack onto my shoulders. The weight dragged on my aching muscles. My breath came in shallow gasps as I crept down the hall to the back door. The brass knob was cold under my palm.

Slowly, I turned it. The hinges gave a small groan, but nothing else stirred. Outside, the yard was washed in early morning sunlight, the grass dulls and lifeless under a sky bruised gray. The fences seemed higher than they had ever been. I slipped through the back door, shutting it softly behind me. The air outside smelled of rain and metal.

I crossed the yard, heart hammering, and planted my hands on the rough wood of the fence. The edges dug into my palms as I hauled myself up, ribs flaring with pain. One leg over. Then the other.

I dropped onto the other side. Given what I had just endured, my knees bent to take the fall, and I was surprised I did not collapse.

I yanked my hoodie over my head.

Then I ran, as fast as I could, the fabric of my clothes snagging on branches and bushes. My ribs burned with every breath, but I kept moving, shoulders hunched against the cold. The sky was waking up, getting brighter by the second, and I knew the bus would be leaving soon.

I did not stop. I did not look back.

When I finally got to Isaac's house, I barely knocked before the door swung open. He was there, his eyes wide for half a second, then they hardened. He saw the bruises, the dried blood, the way I was standing like my bones were made of glass.

Behind him, the room came alive. They were all there. Kane. Diego. Lis. Even Ramon, leaning in the corner like he already knew what had happened. The air tightened, like it had just inhaled.

I stepped in without a word.

No one asked me to explain. I did not have to. It was all over my face. My busted lip. My black eye. The way I kept my left arm pressed tight to my ribs.

Isaac's mom appeared from the back, wiping her hands on a dish towel. She took one look and did not flinch, just nodded toward the bathroom.

"Come on, mijo," she said softly. "Let me clean you up."

She moved like someone who had done this before. Her hands were quick, practiced. Warm water. Antiseptic. Gauze and tape. She did not ask questions. She did not need to. I sat on the edge of the tub, flinching every time she dabbed a cut. I bit the inside of my cheek to stay quiet.

When she was done, she cupped my chin and looked me dead in the eyes. "You're safe now."

But I was not sure I believed that.

When I stepped back into the living room, the temperature had dropped ten degrees. The guys were quiet. Too quiet. Like wolves just before they bite.

Kane was pacing, arms crossed, jaw clenched so tight it looked like it might shatter. He glanced up at me, then down at the floor, then back again.

"Ay," he said, voice low and thick. "Tell me what happened."

So, I did. Everything.

"My boy... You want us to go get him?"

No hesitation. No questions. Just loyalty.

He stepped closer. His eyes burned with fire and rage. "We're down to put in work, carnal. We ready. Just say go."

The room shifted. All of them are watching me now. Not asking, just waiting. I looked around, and it was like staring into a pack of rabid wolves. Every one of them is ready to move, to fight, to burn something down if I gave the word. Their bodies are tense. Their eyes locked on mine.

My heart pounded in my ears. Not from fear, but from something darker.

Part of me wanted to say yes. Part of me wanted to see him crawl. Seeing him hurt the way I did.

But another part—the one that was still bleeding, still scared, still human—was not so sure. I swallowed hard. My throat burned. Nobody said a word. They just waited.

And I realized... this moment right here? This was where everything changed.

"Na, bro," I said, shaking my head slowly. "Let him be."

Kane looked at me hard. That kind of stare that drills into you, like he was trying to see if I meant it or if I just did not have it in me.

"You sure?" he asked, voice steady but tight.

I did not answer with words. Just gave him a nod.

That was enough.

He sighed through his nose, rolled his shoulders like a fighter pulling back from the edge. "Alright. But if you change your mind, you let me or anyone here know. We'll be there. All of us. We got you, carnal."

Another nod. Quieter this time.

He clapped my shoulder once with a tight squeeze, hard but with meaning, and that was the end of it.

I knew what they could do to him. What I wanted to. What he deserved. He had left me broken, bleeding on a bathroom floor like I was nothing. Part of me wanted to return that same pain, to watch him crumble the way I did. To make him feel what I felt.

I didn't.

Not because he did not deserve it, but because he was my father, and I did not want to carry that weight. His blood on my hands would stain more than skin. It would live in my chest; echo every time I looked in the mirror.

He would reap what he sowed, and it would not be from me or anyone I knew. I refused to become anything like my father.

We did not step foot near school that day. Did not even pretend. Instead, we stayed at Isaac's house, pretending like last night had not happened. Smoke curled through the air like it had a purpose. Music played low from the old house speaker, old songs, just Isaac and me, chilling, hanging out. We passed the blunt around like communion. Everything slowed down. The house felt safe. Warm. Like it was holding us in, just for a little while.

Later, we hit the park. Streetlights buzzing overhead, concrete still warm from the day's sun. We did not talk much. Just wandered. A few jokes here and there. Laughter was around, but I was trying hard to maintain and forget.

But it was enough.

For a while.

Night came.

The party started. Not a big one, just our circle, some girls we knew, a speaker in the corner, drinks in red cups, smoke in the air. Laughter bounced off the walls. Girls danced in the middle of the living room, moving to the bass like the beat owed them something.

I leaned against the wall, hoodie still on, watching it all through my swollen red eyes. Not really in it, but not out of it either.

It felt good. Felt like maybe, just maybe, I could breathe again.

Then we heard it.

Yelling.

Not inside. Outside.

Sharp. Slurred.

Everyone went quiet, like someone hit pause on the whole night.

I turned toward the window.

And there he was.

My dad.

Stumbling in the street like a curse let loose. Loud. Ugly. I was pretty sure he was drinking too. His shirt was stained, half-buttoned. His belt was hanging loose, as if he had forgotten how to fasten it.

"WHERE'S MY SON?" he roared. "WHERE ARE YOU HIDING HIM, HUH? COME OUT, BOY!"

My stomach twisted. That voice hit something deep.

Inside, nobody moved at first.

Then Kane stood. Slow. Controlled.

He walked toward the door. Not rushing. Just calm. Dangerous.

"Don't," I said, barely loud enough to hear.

Isaac stepped in his way anyway. "Let him handle it."

Kane's eyes never left the door. His fists clenched and unclenched like they had their own heartbeats.

Out the window, my dad was kicking over the trash cans, still shouting. His voice cracked, ugly and bitter. Neighbors' lights flicked on across the street.

He was unraveling in real time.

And all I could do was watch.

"GET OUTTA HERE, OLD MAN, BEFORE YOU GET HURT. YOU WANT SOMEONE TO PUT HANDS ON? HERE I AM," Kane said, loud and proud.

The words hit me like a fist. Then the metallic click of the gun as Kane cocked it swallowed me whole. That sound, locked and loaded, pulling free from his waistband, was not a trick or a bluff. It was a punctuation mark, dark and final, and I could not stand to watch it land.

I got up without thinking. My legs felt like somebody else's, clumsy and fast. I did not look back as I slipped into Isaac's room and closed the door soft enough to muffle the chaos. I lay down on the mattress, hoodie over my face, the bandage at my cheek catching the fabric. The house sounded huge and hollow. All I heard was muffled shouts, the scrape of shoes, then the dull thud of someone leaving.

Through the thin wall I heard them argue, voices blurred into a radio I could not tune. Then my father's slurred venom faded, footsteps stumbling away into the night. The front door slammed like a final verdict. I could feel the vibration against my ribs long after the sound died.

They came to the room right after, rushing in, loud at the doorway. "You okay?" "He left." "We handled it." I did not move. I did not want to hear it. I did not want to retell the scene I had already lived a hundred times in my head. I kept my eyes closed and let the smoke from earlier stick to the back of my throat.

My mind was not with them. It was on my mom. What she must have been feeling right then, all the years compacted into a single unbearable hour. The image hit me like a cold winter storm. I visualized her alone, listening to my father stagger through the house, the same man who had left me on the bathroom floor for dead. I imagined the weight she carried, the small private storms she swallowed every day so the rest of us could pretend to be normal. The thought made something in me go very quiet.

Lying there, I thought about the hands I never wanted to be. I thought about the kids I did not know, my brother or sister's faces. I had only seen them in family photos, lives raised separate from mine. The life I had chosen, the things I had been made to endure, had pushed me away from them. That feeling tasted like regret and iron. They had seen me and the way I was treated and wanted no part of that life.

If I could replay this life over, maybe I would play my cards differently. Maybe I would not have jumped off that playground and shattered my leg. Maybe my dad would not have stopped loving me. Maybe I would not have tried to kill the bully who was picking on me. Maybe I would not have jumped into a gang.

But here I was, counting breaths in the dark, feeling the bandage press against my jaw, and knowing the difference between hurting someone and letting the hurt define me.

CHAPTER 15: CHILD'S PLAY

The next few years were not just wild. They rewrote me.

Middle of sixth grade, I got kicked out for fighting in the bathroom. Not some petty shove match. No, this was blood on tile, fists to bone. I remember my knuckles more than the kid's face. Not proud of it. Just real. The school said I was a threat. Dangerous. They were not wrong.

No one in Colorado Springs would take me after that. My parents panicked. Their "last resort" became a private Christian school tucked at the edge of town, behind a church that smelled like dust and judgment. Uniforms. Morning prayer. Silent lunches. I was a wolf in sheep's clothing. I only stayed until the end of that year. They thought it worked. Thought the sermons and chapel would wash me clean. But I did not let it.

Next, the summer hit, and I hit back harder. The anger did not leave. It grew teeth. By seventh grade, I was worse. Meaner. Drinking. Smoking. Doing whatever it took to stay numb. School became a battlefield again. It did not matter where the place was. One fight, one hallway brawl, one more kid on the ground, and I was out. Again. Another year wasted.

Back to the Christian school. This time, I knew I was not alone in my damage. The place was filled with other kids like me, cracked open by life and stitched back together with anger and probation reports. It was smaller there. Quieter. But not safer. Just concentrated chaos in a white-walled prison. Most of us were bad kids with trauma and some kind of issue. We could not get it right. Some would, though. I cannot lie; there was a handful of kids who strived to walk the righteous path.

But me? I could not shake the street. Could not shake the hunger. I was not pretending anymore. I was the life I came from. My parents tried to fix it. Took my clothes. Took my shoes. Would not buy me anything. Grounded me. Yelled. Cried. But it did not matter. I made my own money and got my own stuff. Plus, the things I liked did not come home with me. They stayed at Isaac's house. And when enough was enough, I would just run. Out the window. Through backyards. Disappear for days like smoke in a breeze. Sleeping on friends' couches, abandoned houses, wherever felt better than home.

I became a reported runaway. Police would bring me back like some stray dog. Knock on the door, hand on my shoulder, my mom crying behind them. I would sit on the couch, silent, stone-faced, and emotionless.

But I did not care. I did not care. Every punishment felt weightless. Every consequence, numb.

I was untouchable. Not in the way that meant power. In the way that meant I was already gone.

I was getting older. Not grown, not yet, but old enough to start feeling the shift. Girls were now entering the picture. More than just hallway glances or dumb jokes between boys. Real conversations. Real attention. Things that used to feel far away started to circle closer.

I was different. Wired differently.

I was not used to being wanted. I was used to being used. Treated like something broken. Passed over, pushed aside, put back on the shelf like damaged goods waiting to be resold. That kind of history does not just fade. It settles in your bones. It changes how you look at everything.

Still, I wore the mask.

I kept a good poker face. Nothing bothered me. Or at least, that was what I let them see. That was the rule. Never let it show. Never let anyone see where it hurts. I could be bleeding inside and still smirk like I did not feel a thing. I was good at that. Too good.

I was still running with Isaac. Same crew, same streets. The days all blended together, one after another, like smoke. Same conversations. Same risks. Same empty laughs.

Then she came around.

It started small.

Lyla had a way of existing like the world bent slightly around her. She was not loud, never the one who pulled attention, but somehow you noticed her anyway, like a song you didn't know you loved until the hook hit.

She was petite, barely five feet tall, with a slim waist and delicate frame, but she moved as if she didn't care who was watching. There was quiet confidence in her walk, as if she knew something you did not and did not need to explain. Her skin had the soft, bronze glow of late summer, and her features were sharp yet subtle, with high cheekbones, full lips, and almond-shaped eyes that always seemed to be holding something back. Secrets, maybe. Or sadness. Or both. Her hair was long, thick, and brown, almost black when it caught the light. She wore it down most of the time.

Her voice was soft, but it had weight. Every word felt intentional. And when she laughed, it came out low and a little crooked. Not cute. Not fake. But real. Like she had been through some things and still found a way to let joy slip through the cracks.

Lyla had a presence. The kind that didn't chase the room but owned it quietly.

After school, I asked Lyla if she wanted to come to a party with us. I did not know why I expected her to say no; maybe because I still couldn't wrap my head around the fact that a girl like her even noticed a guy like me. But she did not say no. She smiled. A soft, almost shy kind of smile. Then she said, "Yeah… sure." Just like that.

That one word "sure" played on loop in my head all the way home.

Later that night, I did what I always did when I needed out. Waited for the silence. Waited for the weight of the house to settle. My room was dark, the hallway darker. I slipped out through the back like a ghost. Hoodie up. Heart pounding but quiet.

We did not have cell phones back then. Just memory and hope. Once we said we would meet at the old park, with its rusted slide and busted swings, we were there, on the dot.

To my surprise, she was there, waiting for me. Sitting on top of the monkey bars like she had climbed up just to be closer to the stars. Her silhouette glowed under the yellow wash of a streetlight. Hair down. Knees pulled up. She looked like she belonged to the night. When I walked up, she dropped down with a little hop, smiled again, and said nothing.

We did not rush anything. We just talked. Walked slowly around the edges of the playground. She kicked gravel with her shoes, and I kept my hands in my hoodie pocket, trying not to seem nervous. But I was. God, I was.

And then, without warning, she kissed me.

It was soft. Almost unsure. But it landed like thunder in my chest. After that, we did not need to talk. We just walked hand in hand toward Isaac's. My fingers wrapped around hers like they had been waiting to. Her touch was light but steady. As if she were choosing me on purpose.

When we arrived at the house, the party was already in full swing. Music loud. Lights low. The smell of weed and cheap liquor was already thick in the air. People were everywhere, laughing, dancing, spilling out onto the porch. I introduced her around, and she handled it better than I thought she would. She was not loud or trying to impress anyone. She just smiled that same smile and stayed close to me.

The drinks started flowing, and everything got warmer.

She leaned in at one point, close enough that I felt her breath on my skin and started kissing my neck. Slow and steady, like it was not her first time doing it, but maybe her first time doing it because she actually wanted to. Everything inside me lit up. I looked at Isaac across the room, gave him a nod. He raised his eyebrows, caught on immediately.

"Already, my boy," he grinned. "Get it in."

I reached for Lyla's hand. She took it without a word.

We walked up the stairs together. One slow step at a time. The sound of the party faded behind us, replaced by something heavier. A silence that felt full of things we were not saying.

We stepped into Isaac's room. The door clicked shut behind us. Lyla sat on the edge of the bed, legs crossed, hands in her lap. Her hair framed her face in soft waves. Her eyes met mine, and there was something in them—not fear, no hesitation, just realness.

I sat down next to her.

"You're beautiful," I said quietly.

She smiled. Then leaned in to kiss me again.

But this time she paused. Pulled back just an inch.

"Look," she said, her voice barely above a whisper. "I've never done this before… I'm nervous."

My heart slowed a little.

"It's okay," I said. "We don't have to do anything. Only if you want to."

She looked down at her hands, then back at me.

"I do. I really do. But… can we just take it slow?"

"Yeah," I said. "Of course."

Then she kissed me again. This time with less fear. With more of herself in it. I kissed her back.

I pulled off my shirt. My hands did not shake, but my thoughts did. She laid down next to me, tucked into the space under my arm like she had been there before.

And just like that, everything slowed.

The room no longer felt like a party. It did not even feel like Isaac's room. It was just us. Just warmth. Just her breathing soft into my chest, and me trying to breathe.

Then… she fell asleep.

Peacefully. Completely.

Like she trusted me enough to let go.

I stared at the ceiling for a while. Then at her.

I kissed her forehead, pulled the blanket over her shoulders, and laid back.

I laid there with her head on my arm, the room quiet except for the sound of our breathing. Her body was soft and still, wrapped in sleep, and for once, nothing hurt. I kissed her forehead gently, like sealing a memory, and pulled the blanket up over her shoulders.

I did not even mean to fall asleep, but next thing I knew…

Birds.

That early morning chirping through the open window, sun breaking through the blinds in soft gold streaks across the floor. I blinked, disoriented, and then I felt her stir beside me.

She sat up fast. Looked around. Then she freaked.

"Oh my God," she gasped, clutching her head. "What time is it? Oh my God, my parents are gonna kill me." Her voice was shaky, eyes wide with panic.

I sat up, rubbed my eyes, and swung my legs off the bed. Walked over to the door, opened it slowly.

The hallway was wrecked.

I checked the clock. 5:45 a.m.

The house looked like a bomb had gone off. People passed out in every direction, on couches, under tables, slumped against walls. Red cups, empty bottles, ashtrays full, someone's shoe in the kitchen sink.

It was a battlefield.

I turned back to Lyla. She was standing now, arms wrapped around herself, eyes darting like she was trying to make sense of what planet she had woken up on.

I reached out and took her hand.

"Come on," I said.

We stepped through the chaos quietly, carefully dodging bodies, stepping over legs, moving past collapsed memories.

Outside, the world was wet.

The pavement shimmered like it had rained just before sunrise, and the air was cold, not freezing, but sharp enough to bite. Without saying anything, I pulled off my hoodie and slipped it over her shoulders.

She looked up at me.

"I really enjoyed last night," she said, her voice quieter now, gentler. "Thank you… and thank you for being a gentleman, and just not…"

I stopped her, brushing her hand.

"It's okay," I said. "You don't have to thank me."

We walked in silence the rest of the way, just the sound of our footsteps and the occasional car in the distance. The streets were still half-asleep, wrapped in fog and morning light.

When we got as close as we could to her house, she hesitated, her hands reaching to return the hoodie.

"I should give this back," she said.

I shook my head.

"Nah," I told her. "Keep it. Looks better on you anyway."

She smiled. That same soft, simple smile from the playground. Then she turned and walked away.

And I just stood there watching her go, that hoodie hanging off her frame, hair catching the wind, her shadow getting smaller with every step.

Man.

I stuffed my hands in my pockets and turned around, making my way back to Isaac's.

It was cold.

But I did not mind.

Life had been a mess up to this point, loud, violent, lonely, but last night was something different. Something real.

And I could not help but wonder what was waiting around the next corner.

Because whatever it was, I was starting to feel ready.

CHAPTER 16: DISAPPEARING ACT

Ninth grade rolled in like a storm cloud, heavy and unpredictable. I was still doing my thing, still moving quietly, and selling drugs had started. Quick handshakes between classes. Teachers did not see it. Security was not sharp enough. I kept it low with my eyes forward, voice low, always three steps ahead. The game was good to me at this early age. It started out by stealing product from my dad when he passed out. I did not take all of it, but I took enough.

Lyla? She was starting to feel like a liability. We were still "together," whatever that meant in high school. She wrote my name in her notebooks, wore my hoodie even when it was hot, kissed me by the vending machines when no one was watching. But things had started shifting. It was not love anymore. It was surveillance. If a girl laughed too loudly near me, Lyla saw it. If someone handed me a note, her eyes followed it like a hawk. It was not about what I was doing. It was about what she thought I might do.

Arguments started stacking like library books. Whispered fights in the back of class. Heated words by the water fountain. Glares across the cafeteria table. She would ask questions with no right answer, like,

"Why was she talking to you?"

And if I said, "It's not like that," she would roll her eyes, arms crossed, lips tight like a locked safe. She wanted full control, and I was already juggling too much.

Then came that day in the hallway. I remember the sound of it more than anything. The third period had just let out. The hallway was loud, with shoes squeaking, lockers banging, voices echoing off the walls, and dice rolling on the floor. Lyla came cutting through the crowd like a blade. I barely had time to react before she was in front of me, eyes blazing, hands clenched.

"You think I'm stupid?" she snapped as I stood there. "You think I don't see how they all look at you?"

People turned to watch. I did not answer. Not here. Not in front of everybody. My silence made it worse.

"Oh, now you ain't got nothing to say?"

She reached into her bag, and before I could move—

BOOM.

Her book slammed into my chest. Hard. Hardcover. Geometry. All of it. It knocked the air out of me and hit the floor with a loud sound that echoed off the lockers. Everyone froze. No one said a word. It was just me, her, and the sound of my patience dying.

That was it.

She did not know me as well as she thought she did. Thought I would argue. Thought I would chase her down the hallway and apologize, tell her she was right even when she was not. She did not understand. My cut-off game was tough even at that age. That was the moment I felt the switch flip inside me. Like a circuit breaker snapping in the dark. I would just leave her with the ghost of me. Once I was done, I was done. No letters. No explanations. No scene. Just gone.

The next day, I walked past her like she was a ghost. Sat on the other side of the cafeteria. Changed my route between classes. Ignored her notes. Ignored her friends. I erased her name from my world like chalk off a blackboard. Let her argue with my silence. Let her throw words into the wind. I was done.

Let her feel the absence. She would be looking for me in the echoes now, talking to ghosts. Let her talk to the shadow I left behind.

She had thrown a book for the last time, and that was it. Silence.

And silence does not apologize.

That next morning, two days after I ghosted Lyla, I did not go to school. I got on the bus like I was supposed to, hoodie up, backpack on, head low, but I never stepped foot inside that building. Instead, I crossed the street and walked straight into Manny's world.

Manny lived in a two-story, four-bedroom house with peeling paint and cigarette butts in the flowerpots. His place was right across from the school, but it felt like another universe. His mom was white, and his dad was black, so he was of mixed heritage. He was a little older than me, seventeen going on thirty. Manny had the entire downstairs to himself. Already dropped out, already living like rules did not exist. No alarms. No lectures. No grades. Just smoke in the air and liquor on the table before noon.

His mom was part of the chaos. She would sit on the sagging, cracked leather living room couch in her robe, chain-smoking Newports, sometimes lighting the next one before the first was out. Her eyes were tired but wild, like she had seen too much and did not care anymore. She drank with us. Smoked with us. Laughed when we acted stupid. The rules that other parents had. She never followed them. She did not even pretend to, with her ashtray balanced on her knee. Sometimes she passed you a drink. Sometimes she passed out before dinner in the same spot.

That first day, I was supposed to be in my first-period class. Instead, I was on the couch with a blunt in one hand and a red Solo cup in the other. Music blasted from dusty speakers, old-school rap, distorted from too much bass. The house smelled like weed, fried food, and old couch cushions. You walked in and got hit with everything at once. No warning. No filter. Like the walls themselves had been partying for years.

I told myself it was just for the day. Just to get my mind right.

Then it turned into the next day.

And the next.

Before I knew it, school was a memory. Very distant. Unimportant. Like a show, I stopped watching mid-season. For six months straight, it was the same routine. I would ride the bus to school, cut across the lot, and walk into Manny's house like it was mine. I would crash there all day, get faded, eat junk food, play video games, and watch people come and go like we were running a trap house that just happened to have a spot on the couch just for me.

Manny's girlfriend, Naomi, practically lived there. Always in leggings and someone else's hoodie, chewing gum like it owed her money. She was always there, long braids, too much lip gloss, and a don't-mess-with-me attitude. The kind of attitude that made guys nervous and girls hate her. She spoke as if she had matured since she was thirteen. She laughed loudly, argued louder. Always had something smart to say. She did not smile unless she was drunk. And even then, it looked like a threat.

Because there was a secret. She also knew I was distracted by the way she looked at me, and I was.

By Priscilla.

Manny's sister.

But what nobody knew, not Manny, not Naomi, not even their mom, was that I was talking to Priscilla on the low.

Priscilla was different. She was not like the rest of them. Quiet, eyes always watching, always thinking. She would come in from work or wherever she had been, say barely two words, and disappear into her room. When the rest of the house was loud and wild, she would sit in the kitchen with a book or stand on the back steps with her headphones in. But she always noticed me. Ask me how I was, what I was thinking about. And when I finally started answering, really answering, it was like the world outside Manny's walls did not exist.

Sometimes, early in the morning, before the rest of the house woke up, we would talk. Real talk. Deep talk. About life, about escape, about how everything felt stuck and broken.

And sometimes, we would do more than talk.

We kept it secret. Not because we were ashamed, but because that house fed on drama. I do not know if it was guilt or a sense of survival, but we did not tell a soul. Manny would have lost it. Naomi would have had something slick to say. I honestly do not know how we managed to keep the party going like that every single day. No real money, no plans, just smoke, drink, and music. The house ran like a well-oiled machine, with different people coming in and out, but the vibe remained the same. A fog of numbed-out energy, like we were all running from something but forgot what it was. Always something to drink. Always somebody showing up with something to kill the time, kill the pain, kill whatever little part of us was still trying to fight reality.

The world outside kept spinning. School did not matter anymore. Time did not either.

It was six months of fading out slowly, surely, until I was not even sure who I was trying to be anymore.

And honestly?

I did not care.

Not then.

Now, Priscilla.

Priscilla did not belong in that house. Everything about her felt like it was from somewhere else, like she had been dropped into Manny's world by mistake and just never found the way out, even though they were family. She moved through the smoke and noise like it could not touch her, like she was made of something cleaner, something softer, something untouched.

She was mixed, half Black, half white, and she wore it on her skin like caramel poured smooth over bone. Not too light, not too dark, just golden in a way that caught the light differently, especially when she stepped into the sun through those dusty windows. Her complexion had that natural glow, the kind you don't often see, the kind that doesn't need makeup to make an impression.

Her hair was long, jet black, and bone straight. Not the kind of straight that comes from a flat iron or salon, but like it was just born that way. I used to catch myself watching her when she tied it up in a loose bun, little whispers falling around her ears, framing her face like she knew exactly what she was doing without even trying.

Her eyes were green. Real green. Not hazel, not brownish-something, not contacts. Green like wet moss after a rainstorm. They did not sparkle; they cut. Calm and slow-moving, but sharp, like she could see the part of you tried to hide from everybody else. I used to look away when she stared too long, not out of fear, but because she made me feel like I was being read, like I was some open page she was flipping through with those eyes.

She was not as thick as Naomi or as flashy as her friends. She was slim, quietly curved, with long legs and soft hips. The kind of body that did not scream for attention but never had to. She wore simple clothes, fitted tees, sweats, old hoodies. Nothing tight. Nothing loud. But the way she walked? Controlled. Like she was aware of every step, every move. Like the floor itself was lucky to feel her weight.

There were moments when she would look at me across the room and just see me. Not the smoke. Not the hoodie. Not the fake toughness I wore like armor. Just me. A kid skipping school, high before noon, fading deeper into the streets every day. That kind of look?

Like I was wasting time.

It was dangerous.

It made me feel like I could still be something more.

I kept going to Manny's every day like it was clockwork. By that point, it was home, or at least, it was the only place that did not ask questions. I would get off the bus, walk past the school as if it didn't exist. School was on one side. I was always on the other side. Slipping into Manny's front door before the first bell even rang. Light up before breakfast. Pour something strong before noon. Laugh at nothing.

Wait for Priscilla.

She did not always respond immediately. Sometimes she worked. Sometimes she was just in her room. But I would wait. I did not say it out loud, but that was the reason I kept coming back. The noise, the smoke, the chaos, that was just background.

Priscilla was the main event.

And then the rumor started. Somebody from school, probably one of the kids who came over just to smoke real quick between classes, said something. Said they saw me and Priscilla talking closely. Said we looked like something more than friends.

The thing about rumors? They do not need proof. Just oxygen.

And by the time it reached Lyla, it had already become wildfire.

She lost her mind over it. I started asking around at school like a detective with no badge. Running her mouth in the girls' bathroom. Pressing people who barely knew me like they had answers. But the thing was, I had vanished. And in a world without cell phones, without Instagram stories or Snap Maps or Find My Friends, if someone did not want to be found? They weren't.

I had become a ghost. The only thing Lyla had left was my absence, and it was eating her alive.

One afternoon, I was sitting on the ripped couch in Manny's living room, flicking ash into a half-full soda can, when Priscilla came out of the back room. She moved like she always did, slow, calm, like the world did not faze her. She wore an oversized hoodie and leggings, her hair tied up in a loose knot, her green eyes sharper than usual. She sat on the arm of the couch, close. Not saying anything at first. Just watching me. Then she asked, flatly, like she already knew the answer but wanted to hear it from my mouth.

"Who's Lyla?"

I paused. Not because I was scared, but because I hadn't said her name in so long, it no longer felt real.

"Old situation," I said finally. "Girl I was with before. We haven't talked in months."

Priscilla nodded slowly. Her expression did not change.

"She keeps running her mouth at school," she said, voice low. "Talking like she knows something. If she doesn't stop…"

She leaned in, eyes locked on mine.

"…I'll make her stop. Personally."

She did not blink. Did not smile. She just said it as if it were a promise she planned to keep. I exhaled smoke through my nose and stared at the ceiling, as if it might offer some kind of advice.

"I don't even know why she's in her feelings," I said.

We had not spoken since that day in the hallway. Since she threw that book at me. I left her with the ghost of me, and now she was mad that she could not find the body. Please.

Priscilla tilted her head slightly, studying me like she was piecing together a puzzle.

"Then it's her own fault," she said.

Can't hold onto a ghost. Especially one that does not want to be touched.

We sat in silence for a minute, the sound of bass thumping faintly from Manny's room down the hall, smoke hanging in the air like fog. Out front, I heard some of the school kids laughing as they lit up on the porch. The smell of weed drifted into the kitchen. Somebody knocked over a chair and cursed loudly. It did not matter. None of them mattered.

This secret was no longer so secret.

Me. Her name, Lyla, was sitting between us like a spark.

I started to realize something dangerous.

Priscilla was not just someone I was talking to. She was someone who had grown feelings for me.

One day, when we were all laid out, baked, and half asleep in the haze, the living room at Manny's was dim. The only light came from the flickering TV screen, which played the same burnt-out music videos on a loop. Ashtrays full. Smoke hung thick like fog; nobody bothered to clear it. Naomi was curled up sideways on the couch, flipping through her CD wallet. Manny was lying across the floor, arm stretched toward the blunt in the ashtray, too lazy to move. One of Naomi's friends was painting her nails, legs crossed on the floor, gum popping between her teeth like a ticking clock. I was sitting in the recliner. Quiet. Faded. Thinking about nothing and everything at once.

Then the front door flew open as if somebody had kicked it in.

BAM.

The entire room jolted like we had just been yanked out of a dream. The door swung so hard it slammed against the wall, and before we could even sit up straight, Priscilla came flying down the stairs, hoodie half-on, sneakers still tied tight, her breath ragged in her throat like she had just run ten blocks with her lungs on fire.

She was rushing.

Not walking, not storming, but rushing through the room like she had been possessed by something wild and fast and loud. Hair loose, cheeks burning, eyes lit up like she had just stepped out of a war and liked the way it felt.

"Yo! What the hell!?" Manny started to say, half-sitting up.

But she did not stop.

She jumped right over Naomi's legs, over Manny's feet, over a half-full ashtray on the floor, and landed right next to me. She had never done that before. Priscilla was not the touchy type. She never sat too close, never showed her cards.

But this time?

She grabbed my face, still catching her breath, chest needing air, and kissed me like the world had just ended and she had to leave proof that she was here.

Hard. Hot. Fast.

The whole room froze. Even the smoke paused mid-air.

My body stiffened for half a second, then relaxed into it. Her hands were shaking, her lips trembling like she was still full of motion. I was dazed and stunned. Then she pulled back panting, smiling, hair sticking to her forehead, and said it like she had just scored the winning shot in the last second of a championship game.

"Okay?! Okay? Listen, guys, she got beaten up! Whooped!"

The silence was shattered.

Naomi sat straight up. "Who?"

"Lyla," Priscilla said, like the name was nothing. Like she was talking about the weather.

Manny's jaw dropped. "Nah. Nah. What happened?!"

"She got what she was lookin' for," Priscilla said, eyes wild with adrenaline, voice sharp and fast like she had not taken a breath in five minutes. "I walked into that school, right? Yeah, the one I don't even go to. Walked in like I ran the place. I started asking where she was. A few girls pointed me down the hall near the bathroom, and I heard someone say it was third period." She mimed the moment with her hands, all quick jabs and animated motions.

"She looked at me like I was crazy. I tried to say something. I didn't even wait for her to finish. I grabbed her, slammed her against the lockers, and laid her out. No back and forth. No back up. Just me and her."

Her smile twisted. Pride sat on her face like war paint.

"Left her on the floor and ran all the way home."

She was out of breath again, finally letting herself sit still. Her body was still buzzing, her knees bouncing, heart thumping through her hoodie. Then she looked around, all cool again, like the chaos had not just happened twenty minutes ago.

"...So... do y'all think I'm gonna get in trouble?"

The room stared.

Manny just blinked, eyes wide. "Uh. Yeah."

Naomi's mouth was open, halfway between shock and respect. "Girl, you really did that?"

Priscilla laughed, leaned back against my shoulder like this was just another Tuesday. "She asked for it. Y'all heard what she was on. Talkin' slick, actin' like I was scared. I couldn't let that slide. Right?"

I looked at her as if her hair fell over her eyes, knuckles red like maybe they had caught skin, and I did not say anything at first. Because at that moment, she was not just the quiet girl from the back room anymore. There was something about that moment; she was something else now. She felt something and fell in love with it.

Priscilla, busting in, out of breath, blood still hot from the fight, shifted the ground beneath me. She kissed me like she owned it. Sat beside me like she belonged there. Not just some girl I was waiting for, but something more dangerous. Surer of herself. More real.

And the crazy part?

That made me like her even more.

I do not know what it was. Maybe it was the contrast. The way she always carried herself was so quiet, so chill, like she barely needed to speak to control a room. But now, here she was, fired up like a lit fuse, hands shaking from the rush, heart pounding out of her hoodie. Still had that same steady look in her eyes, just with a new kind of sharp behind it. She was not screaming. It was not loud. But you could feel the weight of what she did, like a secret carved into stone. She took care of business and came straight home, proud of it.

As I sat there, listening to her voice tell the story to the room, all animated now, her knees bouncing, her eyes dancing with wild energy, I realized something that hit a little deeper.

This was not new to me.

All the females I had been with? Fighters.

Every single one of them.

Girls who had hands before they had feelings. Girls who would not cry in front of you but would not hesitate to swing on someone twice their size for looking at them wrong. The type who kept blades in their purses and trauma in their back pockets. Beautiful, but dangerous. Sweet only when they felt safe, which was not often.

Even now, as I tell you this story and think back on the many chapters, I've lived through with girls like that, I realize it was not a coincidence. It was like I was drawn to that kind of energy. Like some part of me needed it. Maybe it was survival. Maybe it was just what made sense in the world I was raised in.

But the truth is, I did not want soft love. No picture-perfect romance. I wanted intensity. Loyalty with fangs. Affection that came with a warning label.

Always.

Girls who not only understood the chaos. They came from it. They knew how to move in it. They knew how to protect themselves, and if you were lucky, you saw it and understood.

Maybe that is why I was sitting there, half in love with Priscilla at that moment. Not just because she was pretty, and believe me, she was, but because she was real. She did not ask permission. She did not explain herself. She found the girl running her mouth, put her on the floor, and came straight to me like, Now what?

It was something primal.

She was not just another girl I was messing with. She was a chapter of my life about to be written in all caps. Loud. Raw. Unforgettable.

And I think I knew, even then, that stories with girls like Priscilla do not end softly.

They do not fade out.

They burn.

Chapter 17: FORCED RELOCATION

Every morning looked the same. Cold breath fogging the window, worn hoodie pulled low, and the school bus squealing to a stop like it had any business picking me up. I would still feel at home, as if I belonged. Still nod to the same bus driver who had stopped asking questions months ago. Routine was a disguise, and one I wore like armor. Every morning, I rode that same yellow coffin, but I never walked through the front doors of Wasson High. Not once in six months. I would step off the bus, cut through the parking lot, cross the street without looking back, straight into Manny's basement like it was second nature. That house had become my school, my refuge, my escape. And no one said a word about it.

Until they did.

It was after school. Late afternoon. The sun had dropped just enough to paint the walls gold, and I was still buzzed from the blunt Manny rolled up. I came in through the back door, hoodie heavy with smoke, and tossed my backpack, empty as ever, onto the kitchen chair.

My mom was standing there, in front of the sink. Stiff. Still. In her hand was an envelope, the kind with the school district's logo in the top left corner like a red flag. She did not look at me when she spoke. Just read it out loud like she could not believe the words on the page were real.

"This letter is to inform you that your student has been dropped from enrollment at Wasson High School, effective immediately. Your child must reapply through the district office to resume schooling."

Silence.

She looked up at me, finally. Her face was tight, jaw locked, eyes full of something between anger and heartbreak. Her voice came out low and sharp.

"Boy... your daddy is about to be home. Go to your room and wait."

I did not flinch. I did not even blink.

I had heard that line before. Too many times to count.

I knew the pattern, the storm that came with the sound of his keys in the door, the shouting, the pacing, the sermons I was supposed to absorb like commandments with gifted lashings. But something in me had changed. I was no longer that scared little kid. I was not waiting around for a man who only came home to correct what he did not care to understand. So instead of heading to my room, I just stood there.

In my head, I was already gone.

He was not home yet. That was his mistake.

I had a window, a small one, and if I timed it right, he would come storming in only to find air where I used to be.

He is not here now, I thought, and he is not going to catch me either. And when he tries, it will be too late.

I turned without a word, calm like the calm before a fire. I walked to my room, not to wait like she said, but to grab the bag I had been quietly building for weeks. Nothing heavy. Just the essentials. A change of clothes. A little money I stashed from Manny's weed runs. A toothbrush. The hoodie Priscilla had fallen asleep at once still smelled like cheap shampoo and cinnamon gum.

I paused at the door and looked around. Posters peeling. Everything was covered in dust. Schoolbooks I had not cracked open since spring. It no longer felt like my room. It felt like a museum of a version of me that no longer existed.

I heard her pacing from downstairs. Mumbling to herself. Crying maybe. But I did not go check.

I pulled the zipper slowly and tightly. Slid the duffel over my shoulder. Walked to the window and cracked it open just enough to feel the evening air brush against my face. The sky was pink and burning at the edges, like it knew what I was about to do. I looked at the door, at the hallway, at the stairs that creaked on the third step down.

"I'm not staying," I whispered to myself.

Because if I stayed, I would get swallowed. By yelling. By guilt. By promises I did not believe in. I would be grounded, beaten, and still forgotten. I would end up right back on that same bus, pretending like I belonged somewhere I had already been erased from.

And I could not do that again.

I was not scared. Not this time.

I climbed out the window slowly, feet hitting the dirt like a decision. The street was loud. The air tasted like fall, sharp and full of smoke. I heard a car turn the corner two blocks down, engine rumbling low. Could have been him. Probably was.

It did not matter.

I was already gone.

Down the side of the house. Through the alley. Over the fence behind old Mrs. Q's yard. Past the mailboxes. Past the world that forgot how to see me. I did not look back.

Because some moments are not about regret. They are about survival.

I was not running away.

I was finally running toward something.

Night was falling fast, like someone had thrown a switch on the sky. The shadows stretched longer than usual, and the air turned colder with every block I passed. I was on my way to Manny's house. They lived all the way across town, deep in the part where the streetlights flickered and the sidewalks cracked like old skin. It was a long walk, always was, but I was finally close. Just a few more houses. I am close now. Real close.

Then I saw them.

Cop cars.

Flashing lights painted the neighborhood in pulsing reds and blues, spinning across the front of Manny's house like some twisted warning sign. My stomach dropped. I froze halfway down the street and ducked back, slipping around the corner of a sagging fence, crouching low behind a trash bin that reeked of something long dead. I did not get any closer. Not right away. I just watched. Waited. Tried to breathe. From where I sat, I had just enough of a view. Enough to see what I needed to see. I wondered why the cops were there. Who they came for. What went down?

Then I saw it.

Priscilla. In cuffs.

Two officers held her tight, one gripping her arm like she was some kind of monster, the other scanning the house like it might explode next. They walked her out, slow and controlled, like a threat. She did not struggle. Did not cry. Her face was hard, unreadable, but her eyes gave it all away. That blank stare, like she had already left her body. Like something in her had died days ago, and her walking was just muscle memory. I knew her well enough to see the storm behind her eyes.

The second they shoved her into the back of the cruiser; my chest went tight.

It was the fight at the school.

I knew it without question.

I did not know it then, but I would never see her again. We were all products of the same place, children of the corn, born in the shadows of dead businesses and abandoned churches. Broken homes. Rusted swing sets. Lost causes. We did not come from love. We came from survival. Every single one of us carried something dark inside. Honestly, we all had demons inside us, and she let them out that day. They won. They destroyed Lyla and left her for dead in the hallway. Priscilla just stopped hiding hers, the way most of us did.

Man, if I only knew then what I know now.

That day at school, she let her demons off the leash, and they found Lyla. Tore into her like wolves. By the time everyone came running, it was too late. Lyla was laid out in the hallway, crumpled, beaten, broken. Blood smeared across the linoleum like some kind of sick art project.

That image, described to me and filled in by my imagination, was burned into my skull. Word got out fast. Her parents pressed charges. They got the surveillance footage from the school. Black and white. Grainy. But it's clear enough. Clear enough to see the truth. Especially when the camera caught Priscilla walking into the school and then across the street to a certain house. The rage in her. The fists. The way Lyla never even got a chance. And it was all caught on camera.

Priscilla was gone. I never knew where or what happened to her. I would not see Lyla ever again, either. Why would I want to? Buried under trauma, fear, maybe vengeance. I would not want to see myself either.

But something died in all of us that day.

We were not just kids anymore. Childhood had slipped through our fingers long before we even knew we were holding it. We were fractured things, almost like cracked glass held together by silence and survival, walking through the world like we had not already been cut to pieces. This town did not raise us. It starved us. Fed us violence and called it discipline. Buried tenderness beneath concrete and told us to man up, shut up, grow up. So, we did. We became what we were made to be. Monsters when we had to be. Survivors, when we had no choice. Ghosts long before we were dead. Some of us forgot how to feel. Others remembered too much, and it burned them alive.

I stayed there, crouched in the dark as the cruiser pulled away, the red and blue lights fading into the night. I did not move. Could not.

Because deep down, I knew the truth.

None of us ever really stood a chance.

Truth is, none of us was innocent.

We were born from chaos, shaped by it, fed by it, raised in its fire. It was not just around us. It was in us, stitched into our blood like a curse passed down through broken homes and unspoken trauma. Chaos does not choose sides. It does not punish the guilty or spare the innocent. It just devours you slowly, silently, and relentlessly. We were never outside its reach. We were its children, its fuel, and eventually, its meal. I had to head to Isaac's now, and that was another whole journey, back toward my side of town. SMH. Just thinking about it made my shoulders sink. It was going to take a few hours, easy, especially on foot. Streets are long out here, stretched from one side to the other like they were designed to wear you down.

Still, I did not hesitate.

I turned and started walking.

I was not going home. Not tonight. The Rock was there.

I did not want to hear him or get beaten. Plus, I did not want to hear the silence in those walls or feel that kind of stillness that makes your skin itch. Home has not felt like anything lately. Just four walls full of broken dreams and echoes of what used to be, or what was supposed to be. The air was always heavy, stale with old arguments and silence that meant more than words ever could. My dad was still there, mostly in the form of empty bottles, drifting from his throne like smoke. He used to be something, or even someone, to me. Now he was just a shadow with a short fuse.

Walking through that front door felt like stepping into a war zone that had already lost its reason for fighting. Nothing fit right anymore. Not the furniture. Not the conversations. Not me. There was always that awkward tension in the air, like everyone was pretending things were not broken. As if we didn't all see the bruises on skin, on hearts, on trust. I had run away more times than I could count, sometimes just down the block, sometimes further. But no matter how far I got, I always found a way, somehow.

So no, I did not want to go home.

Not to that house.

Not to that history.

Not to that version of me that still lived in those rooms, afraid to breathe too loud.

I would rather walk across the whole city than sit through another night pretending everything was fine.

So, I kept moving. Through cracked sidewalks and busted streetlamps, past rusted mailboxes and houses that looked asleep or abandoned. Every block felt heavier than the last, but I did not stop. Would not. I needed somewhere else to be. Somewhere real, even if it was just Isaac's beat-up porch and the sound of music leaking from his busted screen door. Even if it was only them. They were family.

Anywhere but home.

Anywhere but inside my own head.

I finally made it to Isaac's. The streets were quiet now. Too quiet. The only light was the flicker of a busted porch bulb hanging on by a thread at Isaac's. The house looked dead. No music. No voices. No signs of life.

They were all asleep.

Figures.

But out in the driveway, I spotted my boy, Restless, slumping in the front seat of his beat-up Monte Carlo. Engine off. Seat leaned all the way back. Passed out cold. His hoodie was pulled over his face, windows fogged up from his breathing, and the air smelled like old fast food and stale smoke.

I walked up and knocked hard on the window.

Bang. Bang. Bang.

He flinched, groaned, then peeled the hoodie off his face with a grunt, blinking like he had just woken up and did not recognize where he was. He looked around, confused. Then he saw me, and he smirked.

"Get in," he muttered, voice thick with sleep.

I nodded, walked around to the passenger side, and climbed in. The door creaked loudly, like everything else in this town. As soon as I shut it, Restless fished around in his hoodie pocket, slow and lazy, like the weight of sleep had not fully left him. Then he pulled it out. A thick, hand-rolled joint, slightly bent at the tip, like it had already lived through a few rides in his pocket. He held it up in the dim light spilling from the porch bulb, inspecting it like the light itself was a tool.

"Been saving this," he muttered, half to himself.

He struck a lighter. Flick, flick. The flame danced, catching the tip on the first try. The paper curled, the end flared orange, and he rotated it between his fingers, slow and practiced, letting the cherry burn evenly. The scent hit almost immediately, earthy, sharp, and thick with that sticky edge that could be tasted in the air. He took a long, steady pull. The ember flared again, casting a warm red glow across his face for a second as we sat in the dark. His eyes closed as he held the smoke in, shoulders sinking like he had just slipped underwater. Then he exhaled slowly, a cloud spilling from his nose and lips, curling like mist against the window.

He passed it to me without saying a word.

I took it, still catching the warmth from his fingers. Brought it to my lips, the lit end pulsing bright in the shadows. The first inhale hit hard, burning just enough to remind me I was still breathing. I held it in, lungs tight, eyes locked on the cracked windshield where the night outside looked like it was leaning in, watching.

Then I exhaled.

The smoke slid out slowly, curling from my mouth like it had a mind of its own. It moved lazily, as if it didn't want to leave, twisting and unfurling in the stale air of the car. It coiled upward, brushing the roof liner in thin ribbons, soft, almost delicate, like something alive. It caught the faint orange glow of the joint's ember, flickering like spirit trails in the dark. For a moment, it just hung there between us, suspended in silence, like time had paused to watch too.

Then it faded, like everything else around here does.

Outside, the night stayed still. The world did not care. But in that car, in that quiet moment, with the joint passing between us, for a moment we existed.

That was more comfort than anything waiting for me at home.

"What you doin' out here this late?" he mumbled, voice raspy, sleep still stuck in his throat.

"Can't go home right now," I said. No explanation. I did not need to give one. He got it.

"You tryin' to make some money or what?"

I did not even hesitate. "Well, yeah," I said, boldly. I leaned in, eyes steady. "Why, what's up? What's the plan?"

"In the morning, once the sun's up," he said, voice low, "I'm hittin' a lick. Nothing crazy. If you're with it, you'll get paid. Easy."

Sounds legit, I thought, trying not to overthink it. I needed the money. That was enough.

"What all I gotta do, bro?"

He took the joint back, puffed on it, and exhaled slowly. "Around eight, maybe nine. We slide by the mall, handle our business, and dip. I'll fill you in on the rest when we roll out. Koo?"

"Koo," I nodded. "I'm with it," I said it loud, like I meant it. Like, I was not scared. As if I wasn't still a kid pretending to be something harder than I was.

We sat there, passing the joint back and forth, the Monte Carlo filling up with smoke and silence. That peaceful kind. The kind that only shows up when no one is asking questions. The night got quiet. We both ended up slouching in our seats until we knocked out.

BANG. BANG. BANG.

"WAKE UP! Wake-e Wake-e!"

Kane's voice smacked through the fog of sleep, followed by wild laughter and loud pounding on the hood. I blinked awake, eyes burning. Restless groaned next to me, hoodie back over his face. I rubbed the sleep out of my eyes just as Isaac walked up behind Kane, laughing too.

"Y'all look like two dead dudes in there."

I opened the door, stepped out into the morning air. It was colder than I expected. I stretched, bones popping, head still fuzzy from the night before.

"Let's go inside, talk about the plan for today," Isaac said, already walking toward the porch.

As we all headed in, I paused in my steps.

"Hold up. I forgot my bag. Lemme grab it real quick," I said, turning back toward the car as everyone else went inside.

I walked back outside to the car. I opened the passenger door and reached for my bag, and that was when I saw one of them. Standing there.

I had not even noticed him at first. The driver looked bored, like he knew exactly how this was going to go.

He flicked on his red and blue lights. The light hit me in the face like a slap.

Now the doors opened and slammed.

As the other got out of the car, one of them started to talk.

"Hey, son," he said, calm but sharp. "What's your name?"

This real?

My throat went dry. Mind racing. Chest tight.

"Gabriel, sir," I said.

"Gabriel, what, son?" the other asked, stepping closer. His hand rested near his belt, fingers tapping.

I hesitated. Thought about running. Thought hard.

But it was already too late.

"Hinojosa," I said. "Can I help you guys?"

The first cop nodded like he was checking a box in his head, like I had answered the question correctly.

"Alright, Mr. Hinojosa," he said. "Please turn around."

What?

"For what?" I snapped, heat rising in my face. "I didn't do anything."

"Calm down," he said, already grabbing my wrist. "You've been reported as a runaway."

And just like that, click. Cold metal kissed my wrists, and he put them on tight, one after the other.

"You serious right now?" I said through clenched teeth, trying not to snap.

He did not answer. Just led me to the back of the patrol car like I was sleepwalking, like I did not even matter.

The door opened. I was pushed in.

Slam.

That sound echoed inside my skull.

I sat there, cuffed, breathing hard, watching him walk up the path to Isaac's house. He knocked twice. Isaac's mom opened the door; her face scrunched with confusion. He started talking. I saw her glance past him, straight at the cruiser.

At me.

That was when I realized I was hit.

This was not just a warning or a scare.

My parents had reported me.

This was real. This was the system sinking its teeth in.

I was not just running anymore.

I could not. I was caught.

CHAPTER 18: A NEW DAWN

I did not even know where we were going. No one told me a thing. I just sat in the back of the cop car, staring out the window, the early morning sun creeping over the tops of buildings as we drove. It was not until we pulled into the parking lot that I saw the sign:

Spring Creek Youth Detention Center.

My stomach dropped.

The car stopped. My door clicked open from the outside, and the cop motioned for me to get out. I did. No cuffs. Just silence. He walked me inside as if I were some packages being dropped off. Cold tile floors, the smell of industrial cleaner, and this humming silence that buzzed in my ears louder than anything.

They handed me over to the staff as if I were not even there. Just said,

"We need to hold him. Can't get a hold of the parents."

No charges. No explanations. Just that.

I did not say a word. I could not. My mind was already spinning.

I'm in trouble.

Dad is gonna lose it.

They escorted me to a holding cell with a steel toilet in the corner, no bed, cold bench. They took my shoes, socks, and belt. The door clanked shut behind me like a punch to the chest. Time crawled. I just sat there. Thinking. Staring. Waiting. Watching the light in the hallway change as the sun passed overhead.

I was picked up around 7:30 a.m. My parents did not arrive until 6:30 or 7:00 p.m. I know what that means now. My mom waited until Dad got off work. They talked. They planned. Took their sweet time to figure out what they were going to do with me. They weren't rushing to come get me. They were scheming.

When they finally walked in, the air shifted. I could feel the storm before they said a word. Their faces were tight, eyes sharp, voices low but full of rage. They signed some papers, and I was released.

We arrived at the car, and that's when it started.

"WHY HAVEN'T YOU BEEN GOING TO SCHOOL?"

"WHERE THE HELL HAVE YOU BEEN GOING THIS ENTIRE TIME?!"

I had nothing. Not a word. Just a flat,

"I don't know."

Over and over.

"I don't know."

Because what else was there to say?

The ride home was dead quiet. The kind of silence that roars. Dad gripped the wheel like he wanted to snap it in half. Mom stared out the window, her jaw clenched so tight I thought she might grind her teeth down to dust.

We pulled into the driveway. Everything looked normal. The porch light buzzed. The house stood there like it always had, except now something was off, though I did not know exactly what. I was pretty sure I should be getting dragged into the house and beaten, but I wasn't.

We walked in, and Dad did not even look at me.

"Go to your room," he said.

"Go to your room until we can figure out what to do with you."

That line hit harder than anything. Figure out what to do with you. Like I was some broken tool they were not sure was worth fixing.

The moment I got to my room, my first thought hit me hard.

Run.

I did not know where or how, but I had to get out. My heart was already pounding like it was trying to break free before I did.

I turned and bolted down the stairs, heading for the basement windows, the ones that looked out into the window wells. I had snuck out through those before. They were my escape routes.

But this time…

They were not just locked.

They were screwed shut.

Big, rusted wood screws drilled right through the frames, deep into the sills. And outside the windows? The wells were filled with rocks and boulders. Not anything small either. These were big, heavy ones stacked all the way up to the glass. There was no getting through them.

I just stood there, staring.

They were serious.

That was what took them so long. While I was rotting in that cold holding cell all day, they were not sitting around. They were turning my house into a prison.

And now, I was not just grounded.

I was trapped.

I lay down on my bed, staring up at the cracked ceiling, feeling the weight of everything pressing down. My room was no longer a room. It was a box. A cell. Four walls, a bed, a pillow, a pile of clothes in the corner, nothing else. No TV. No games. No house phone. Nothing to distract me from my thoughts. Just me and the silence. Let me tell you that silence was heavy.

Days passed like that, with me locked in my room, them moving quietly through the house. The air was thick and awkward. We were not speaking. We were not even looking at each other. I kept to myself, slipping upstairs to eat when I was hungry, when I had to, but mostly staying hidden away.

In my head, questions spiraled.

What are they planning?

What is coming next?

I felt like an animal waiting in a cage, the door shut, the owners deciding what to do with me.

Then it happened.

Late one afternoon, a sound erupted from the ceiling above me.

BOOM. BOOM. BOOM.

Heavy stomps. My dad. I froze. My blood ran cold. I knew what that meant. That was not just noise. That was my summons.

I got up slowly, hands shaking a little, and walked up the stairs like I was walking into a courtroom. They were both waiting in the living room. My dad's face was carved from stone. My mom would not meet my eyes.

"Get some clothes ready," my dad said flatly.

"We have an appointment in the morning at a new school."

A new school?

My mind stopped, confused, and my heart skipped a beat. That was not what I was expecting at all. Not juvie. Not boot camp. Not another lecture. A school? It did not feel like an opportunity. It felt like another punishment. Another cage with a different label.

I muttered something under my breath, but no one heard. They just stood there like prison guards reading out a transfer order.

I went back to my room and sat on the bed, staring at my pile of clothes, trying to make sense of it. The morning came faster than I wanted it to. It was still dark when my alarm went off, but I had not really slept anyway. Anyone who has ever been a kid knows that starting a new school is not exciting; it is devastating. It is like walking into a new arena where you are the only one without armor.

I got dressed in silence, pulling on the clothes I had picked out. My stomach was tight, twisting, my throat dry. Outside my window, the rocks and boulders still sat in the wells, the screws still drilled into the frames. My parents were up, moving around the kitchen, but everything felt distant, muted, as if I were underwater.

By the time we were ready to leave, the sky had just started to turn gray. The car waited in the driveway. And me?

I felt like I was being marched off to my next sentence, like this was intake at some juvenile facility, not enrollment at a school.

We pulled up to the building. It said, Community Prep. Basically, it was a private school for troubled kids. But do not let the name fool you. Community Prep sounds harmless, like a place with garden beds and group therapy circles. Somewhere you can learn how to make smoothies and manage your emotions.

But this place? It was not that.

The outside looked polished, with brick walls, clean windows, and a flag flapping in the breeze, as if this was just another respectable institution. But under that shine, you could feel the weight. This was where the system dropped kids off who did not make the cut anywhere else. The throwaways. The ones who already had their names typed in bold on school reports, police records, and permanent files.

They gave us a tour. I trailed behind like I did not even exist. My footsteps echoed too loudly in the hallway. I wasn't saying much, just scanning, absorbing, and bracing for whatever was coming. Already out of place.

The halls were quiet. Not the kind of quiet you get in a library or a church. This was a different breed. It was a managed quiet. Manufactured. It was as if someone had reached over and twisted the volume knob of the whole building down to low. Every sound I made, my shoes on the tile, the soft creak of a door closing behind us, landed heavy, like it was echoing through a courtroom.

Every door we passed, I could feel eyes drilling into me. Teachers peeked out from their classrooms, doing that quick double-take like their brains were trying to match my face with a warning they had read in an email. Then they looked away, fast, like they were not staring at all.

Students leaned against the lockers, arms folded, watching. Not friendly curiosity. This was sizing up. They were not wondering my name. They were trying to figure out my story. What did he do? Why is he here? Is he trouble or prey? Their eyes flicked over me the way you check a dog you do not know, cautious, ready for it to bite.

Even the janitor, walking around and cleaning, the old man with the stained work shirt, pushing a mop that squeaked against the linoleum, paused mid-stroke and squinted. His expression said it all. He had seen my type before. Kids dropped in like ticking time bombs, just waiting for the right moment to blow. He studied me for an extra beat before shaking his head and going back to work, slow and deliberate.

And I get it.

I do not blame them.

I am walking through their world like a storm cloud that drifted off course. My steps do not match the rhythm of this place. My face does not wear the blank, polite mask they are used to. I have different energy and a different weight. You cannot fake that. And they can feel it, every single one of them. I move like someone who's been dropped in from another planet. A different walk. Different energy. No disguise. Nothing polished. I do not carry a backpack full of honors, credits, or varsity dreams. I carry silence, suspicion, and history. And they can feel it. This is not just another new kid walking through the doors. I am the question they do not yet have an answer to.

The principal shakes my hand as if to show me he is not scared. Too bad for him, his eyes give him away. We meet the teachers, and they are smiling a little too hard, voices a little too soft. Like they think if they say the right words in the right tone, I might magically care about Algebra or American Lit. Then they handed me my schedule. Just like that. I am officially in tenth grade.

How? Honestly, I do not know. I have not really done schoolwork since sixth. Not real work, anyway. I would show up when I felt like it, maybe scribble something down, and somehow the credits kept coming. They passed me along like a hot potato, no one wanting to hold onto it for too long. Shoved me down the line to become somebody else's problem. And now, I guess, I am Community Prep's problem.

It is wild when you think about it. All this effort to pretend the system works. But I know better. I have lived in the cracks.

So here I am. Tenth grade. New school. Clean slate, supposedly. But let's be real. The slate is never clean when you already have a file in the office. I shake my head in disbelief, eyes still on the wrinkled piece of paper they just handed me.

"You are going to catch the bus to school," my dad says, like he is announcing something normal.

I look up, confused. "The bus?"

"Yes. The city bus."

Wow. That one hit differently. Not the yellow school bus with noisy kids and crusty vinyl seats. No, they meant the bus, the one that smells like urine and bad decisions. The one full of people going to jobs they hate, court dates, and halfway houses. That bus. I say nothing.

Just nod once, slowly, like that might help me process it. But really, I am thinking, this is a complete mess. They are just dropping me into it like it's nothing. Like, I am not already one wrong move away from falling off the map completely.

We got home, and they handed me a full-size city bus schedule. Folded up all neat like that makes it better. The kind of thing you see tourists holding downtown when they are lost. I stare at the little colored lines and numbers. None of it makes any sense. Just one more thing I have to figure out alone.

This is really happening.

My parents go quiet after that. Not cold. Just verbally distant, as if they had used up all their parenting energy on the bus conversation. The house is silent except for the occasional hum of the fridge or the clinking of silverware. We eat dinner like strangers sitting at the same table by accident. No eye contact. No "how was your day?" Just chewing and swallowing and scraping plates. I finish fast and head to my room. Close the door, press my back to it, and just sit there for a second, staring at the floor.

The next morning, I woke up before the sun. No alarm needed. My eyes just open like something in me already knows this day is not going to give me a second chance. I iron my clothes. Black pants, gray shirt, hoodie laid out just right. Gotta look clean. G'd up from my feet up, fresh to the death, like a million bucks. I was a gangster, nothing more, nothing less.

I am kind of a big deal, and my clothes and my first impression are a must. No matter where I am headed, I cannot show up looking like I have already lost. That is rule number one. Always look like you care about yourself, even when you don't. In the mirror, I check myself. Not for style. This is not about drip. It is about armor. Presentation. Control. If I cannot control anything else, I can control how I walk out that front door.

And with that, I am ready.

Gotta hurry. Cannot miss this bus.

I jog up to the stop, heart thumping, city bus schedule clutched tight like it is a passport to survival. Right on time. Miracle. I checked the pamphlet again, which was now creased and soft from being folded and unfolded too many times, and double-checked the route. Do not need any surprises today. The bus grinds to a stop, doors hissing open like a warning. I step on, drop the fare in the slot, and take a seat near the back. Headphones in. Hood up. Eyes on the window. The city rolls by in a blur. Liquor stores. Corner boys. Chain-link fences. All the familiar ghosts.

I get there early.

A low brick building with kids hanging around out front, clustered up in groups, hoods up, cigarettes lit, and talking. Some lean against the walls, while others sit on the curb, as if they have been there forever. I pause across the street for a second and take it all in.

This is Community Prep in the wild. No brochures. No smiling staff. Just raw, unfiltered energy.

I cross over and walk up slowly. A couple of people saw me. We make eye contact, nods exchanged, all quick and neutral. I introduce myself to a few people, keeping it light and not saying much. Names I probably will not remember, at least not yet. Everyone is smoking Marlboros, Newports, and some rollies. Smoke just hanging in the air like fog. It is early, but nobody looks tired. Just wired differently.

I cannot help but notice there are some pretty girls here, too. Not the kind that smiles at you in the hallway for no reason. No, these girls have sharp eyes, quick laughs, chipped nails, and real stories. One catches me looking and half-smirks before turning away. I look back, but yeah, I noticed.

Then the bell rings. Sharp. Sudden. No announcement. No instructions. Just that sound, and everyone starts moving. Cars are still pulling up, kids hopping out in slow motion, as if time does not apply to them. Loud music from cracked windows, smoke pouring out with them. I don't know where to go, but I don't ask either. I just follow the herd through the front doors like I have done a thousand times.

On the first day of class, I sit down, expecting more of the same awkward silence. Heads down. Everyone is minding their own business, as if they are doing time, not school. But it was not like that. Not here.

These kids were just like me.

Wounded. Wired wrong. Surviving. You could see it in their eyes, tired but alert, like streetlights that never turn off. Once I started talking to them, it was as if I were speaking a language I had forgotten I knew. No fake small talk. No pretending to care about textbooks or test scores. Just realness. And that is rare.

I clicked fast with this one guy, Salvador. He was from New Mexico, had two full tattoo sleeves by the time he was sixteen, all black and gray ink, with bold lines and thick shading that ran from his wrists to his shoulders. Saints, skulls, snakes, the whole story of his life written across his skin. He moved like he had already been through a war and survived it, but barely. We bonded fast. Like brothers in the same trench.

By the second week, we were rolling deep. Not just us. There was a crew. And with the crew came habits. Every morning, before school even started, we were drinking. Smoking in the alley behind the gym. Weed, cigarettes, whatever. Between classes, we would duck behind buildings or slip into bathrooms to light up, sip from whatever bottle someone brought in a backpack. Teachers either did not notice or did not care. Probably both.

Then came the girls.

I started talking to one, quiet at first, but that changed quickly. Then there was another one. Smiles turned into stares, and stares turned into whispers. The kind that echoes and twists. Tensions started to rise. I could feel the heat building every time I walked through the hallway. Guys watching. Girls watching them watch me. Like a storm hanging in the air, just waiting for something to spark it off.

And then it did.

Boom.

A fight. Nothing too wild. Not on school property, which was important. At least in theory. Out on the street, hands thrown. Pride got bruised, not bones. It was over fast, but the tone had shifted. That line you try not to cross. I stepped right over it.

It was at the park with some of the crew. Just trying to cool off, let the smoke clear. Someone knew this kid, a random dude, not from our school. He pulled up with a cheap bottle of vodka and a mouth full of confidence.

We passed the bottle around, half a laugh in the air, the sun dipping low behind the trees. This kid grabbed it, talked all big like he was invincible, then threw his head back and chugged.

We all told him he was wild for that.

"Bro, you're gonna regret that," I said.

Salvador laughed. "Dead man walking."

A few minutes later, he was hunched over. Gagging. At first, we thought he was playing it up, being dramatic. But then he really started puking. Violent. Messy. And then, just like that, he spun toward me and threw up on me.

Not just a little. I am talking all over.

My shirt. My jeans. My shoes.

I froze.

Shock hit first, cold and sudden, like being dunked underwater. I looked down at myself, saw it soaking into my clothes, and smelled the burn of stomach acid and cheap vodka. And something in me snapped.

I blacked out.

The next thing I remember, I hit him. Hard. One shot, maybe two. He stumbled back, hands up, but it was too late. I kept swinging. Over and over. I could not even hear what people were yelling. All I could hear was the roar in my head and the pounding in my chest.

When he hit the ground, I did not stop. Not right away. I kept going until Salvador grabbed my arm and yanked me back.

I stood over him, breathing hard, fists shaking.

And then I just left.

Walked off. Did not say a word. My clothes are still stained, fists still clenched, face tight. I was furious, but not just at him. At everything. The situation. The school. The city. Myself.

The anger followed me home like a shadow. I got home, and the cops showed up. It clung to me so thick, heavy, refusing to let go. No matter how many times I washed my hands, I still saw the blood in the creases. The puke was gone, sure. But the rage? That stuck.

I did not eat that night. Could not. I sat on the edge of my bed in the same clothes, the room dim, the air stale. My knuckles throbbed and cracked when I flexed them, but I welcomed the pain. At least it was real. I kept replaying it in my head. His face. The impact of each hit. How the world around me disappeared. Everyone shouting. That dull, sick sound flesh makes against bones when you stop caring about the consequences. And me, standing there afterward, chest rising and falling like an engine that would not shut off.

Then the knock came.

Hard. Sharp. Final.

Three hits against the front door. Not curious. Not polite. The kind of knock that says we already know who you are.

I looked out my window and saw the squad car, parked crooked across the driveway, lights off but presence loud as hell.

My stomach dropped.

I was downstairs when the knock came. It was heavy, deliberate, the kind that carries consequences behind it. I could not see the door from where I stood, but I heard it loud and clear. Then came the voices. Low. Controlled. Too calm to be casual.

I moved to the top of the stairs and listened. My dad's voice. Then two others, one sharp and the other flat, like he had already said these words ten times tonight. I did not need to see them to know what this was. The pit in my stomach told me before anyone else did.

I turned, walked back to my room, and peeled off the clothes I had been wearing since the park. They were stiff now, reeking of cheap vodka, stomach acid, and violence. My shirt had dried blotches, and my jeans were spotted down the legs. Even my shoes, once clean, were stained with the kind of mess that does not fully wash out.

I stripped everything off and stuffed it into the washer, slamming the lid shut harder than I meant to. I did not bother adding detergent. I just wanted it gone. Like if I scrubbed the clothes clean, the night would disappear with it.

I threw on fresh clothes. Black sweats. A hoodie. Socks. Nothing fancy. Just clean. Neutral. As if I were trying to wipe the slate.

Then came my dad's voice, low and serious, floating up the stairs.

"Gabriel. Come up here."

That tone hit different. Not angry. Not worried. Just done.

I did not answer. Just walked out of my room, down the hall, and toward the stairs. Clean clothes on, but still feeling dirty. Still feeling caught.

And when I reached the bottom and turned the corner, I saw them.

Two cops. One is tall and wide like a vending machine in a bulletproof vest. The other shorter, all sharp features and eyes that did not blink. Their hands rested near their belts. Their faces are blank. Their body language said it all.

They were not here for questions. They were here for me.

They said my name and said I was under arrest, but I shut it out, and I did not hear the rest.

The cold metal bit into my wrists, locking them shut, and left marks on the skin. These cuffs felt familiar, and weird enough, I had always felt like I was walking toward them. It felt like my whole life had been a slow crawl to this exact moment.

They walked me out the front door, past my mom sitting silently on the couch, crying, arms wrapped around herself like she was holding in something that might break her. My dad did not follow. He just stood there, like this was some kind of punishment for him too.

Outside, the night was quiet. No sirens. No yelling. Just the sound of the car door opening, then slamming shut behind me.

I sat in the backseat, hands cuffed, heart numb.

That park. That fight. That kid. One moment of blackout rage, and now I was on my way to being another file in the system. Another number on the docket. Another statistic in a place that is full of them.

And the worst part?

I was not even sorry.

CHAPTER 19: WELCOME TO THE JUNGLE

My parents had bonded me out. A part of me was surprised they did. It was just my mom who came to pick me up. She always came through. Always showed up when it mattered, especially when it was hard. The ride home was quiet, but not cold. She did not press me with questions. She did not say she was disappointed. She did not need to.

I walked into the house with the weight of the world on my shoulders. Everything felt heavier than it did when I left, like even the walls knew. I went straight downstairs to my room, not bothering to turn on the lights. I did not close the door completely. Maybe I did not want to feel completely shut off. I do not know.

A few minutes passed. I sat on the edge of my bed, staring at the floor, quiet and stuck in my head.

Then, I heard her voice.

"Gabe?"

Just one word. My name. In that soft, beautiful, loving voice.

She pushed the door open gently and stepped inside, the hallway light framing her like something out of a memory. I looked up and there she was, my mother. Just her being there felt like oxygen rushing into lungs I did not realize were empty. Her eyes sparkled when she looked at me, not with judgment, but something far worse- love. Unshaken love.

She looked at me the way no one else ever had, like I was still that boy who used to bring her flowers from the backyard, not the kid who just got out of a cell. She smiled, and it was the kind of smile that was warm like a quilt, the kind that felt like forgiveness before a single word was ever spoken. She crossed the room and sat beside me without saying anything. Just her presence was enough to start a quiet ache in my chest, the kind that comes from knowing you have let down someone who would never stop believing in you and only saw the good in you, not the bad.

Her hand found mine, warm and steady.

"I was scared," I whispered, my voice catching. "Not of jail. Not really. Of coming home."

She did not flinch. She did not scold me. She just squeezed my hand gently.

"I'm sorry your dad's like that," she said. "He does love you."

And somehow, it did make me feel a little better.

I looked at her, noticing the few faint silver strands threaded through her hair, the fine lines at the corners of her eyes, the way she still somehow looked the same to me. She was no longer young, but I never saw her as old. I saw her as timeless. The only time I ever saw her furious was when she was defending me against my dad. That kind of love does not come from weakness. It comes from a strength I did not fully understand yet.

"I'm sorry," I said quietly.

She reached up and brushed a hand through my hair, just like she used to when I was little. "I know, Gabe."

And she meant it. She always did.

"Oh, Gabe, when will you learn, when will you grow up?" she said, hugging me tightly.

"I hope soon, Mom," I said. "I hope soon."

And we stayed in each other's arms, crying for a good while.

My father came home from work the next day, but the silence between us was thicker than smoke. We did not exchange a word. Surprisingly, my mom held The Rock back this time, thank God. Still, the weight of my own mistakes was heavy.

I soon had court with charges of assault; probation stamped on my back like a brand. This would forever change my life. Part of that sentence included forty-eight hours of community service, and I had the privilege of choosing where to serve. I chose a local church.

That first Saturday, around 12:30 or 1:00 in the afternoon, I arrived at the old, abandoned Kmart on Circle and Airport, where the church had instructed me to go. The building was hollow, stripped of its past, but on that day, life buzzed inside. A church gathering was being set up, with folding chairs clattering and voices echoing in the empty space.

I stepped in and caught the attention of a man working there. "Sir," I said, "I'm here to start my community service."

He nodded, wiping his hands on his jeans. "Alright. We're having a gathering here tonight. Some folks might throw a party. You can come back later and help with security if you want."

"Just me?" I asked. "Or can I bring a friend?"

The man shrugged, casual. "Doesn't matter."

I was confused, curious about what kind of party would be going on in a gutted Kmart. That curiosity pulled me in a direction I did not yet understand.

That was when I went over to Salvador's house. Salvador lived just a few blocks down, so I made my way to his place and found him in the middle of his usual Saturday grind. I told him about the setup I had stumbled upon earlier: the old Kmart being converted into a church by day and an event center at night. At first, he looked at me like I was joking, but once I threw in the magic words, "might be some females there," that was all it took. He was sold.

By five-thirty that evening, we were rolling back up to the building, curiosity and mischief buzzing between us like static. The place looked different now, transformed into an "event center." Wires snaked across the floor, lights were strung up, and a stage was taking shape at the far end of the court. Emptiness from earlier had been swallowed by energy and anticipation.

"Gabriel!" a voice called out from across the room. It was the same man I had spoken to earlier. He came over, arms wide, grinning like we were old friends. We shook hands.

"How are you guys?" he asked, eyes darting between us.

"We're good," I said. "Just came to help out. This is my friend I told you about, Salvador."

"Pleasure," Salvador said, shaking the man's hand.

I gave Salvador a sideways glance. Pleasure? Really? I bit back a laugh, muttering under my breath, "Pleasure my foot," which only made us both snicker.

The man did not notice or did not care. He handed us each a walkie-talkie and a bright yellow security vest. "You boys will be working the door. I'm counting on you not to let any drugs, weapons, or anything like that inside. Capiche?"

We looked at each other, eyes wide, adrenaline spiking. "Capiche," we echoed, almost in unison.

"Hopefully we find some cool stuff," Salvador whispered with a smirk.

Then the music started. Hard. Pounding. Relentless. Not my scene, not by a long shot. It was different music, heavy bass, sharp synths, the kind of sound that made the walls throb like they had their own heartbeat. That was when it hit me. We were security for a rave. A rave. In an abandoned Kmart. Are you kidding me?

The coordinator clapped his hands and shouted, "Showtime, fellas! Open the doors!"

We turned to see the line. Dozens, then hundreds of people waiting, bodies shifting with restless energy, outfits wild and bright. Salvador took one door, I took the other. We adjusted our vests, clipped on the radios, and braced ourselves.

And then it began.

One after another, they filed in. And with them came the stash: little containers, plastic baggies, bottles, powders, pills. Some I recognized, most I did not. It did not matter. "Nope, that's not getting in," I would say, tossing pills into a growing trash bag. "Marijuana? Sorry, can't have it." Unknown liquids, powders, anything suspicious went straight into the bag. Within an hour, the thing was already a quarter full, and I was starting to realize how insane this night was going to be.

The outfits were another story. Males and females, all dressed or half-dressed in neon, lace, leather, glitter. Boots with fur. Shorts that barely existed. Bras on display. Fishnets stretched across legs like spiderwebs. Hair in every color of the rainbow. Glowing bracelets. Flashing lights wrapped around their bodies like Christmas trees. Two words... Harley Quinn.

I kept staring, shaking my head. Lost. These people were so lost, but at the same time, I couldn't help but notice the confidence and the wildness. It was provocative, intoxicating, and confusing all at once.

By now, my trash bag was heavy with confiscated drugs, a mountain of chemicals and pills that could have fried an army. The crowd kept pouring in, their voices sharp with frustration when I took their stash. Some yelled, some cursed, some just glared. I did not care. I waved them in and kept it moving.

After a while, the line began to thin. I walked over to Salvador, who was patting down a couple of stragglers.

"What's up, fool? You good?" I asked. "You finding any goodies?"

He laughed, that crooked Salvador laugh, and held something up. My eyes went wide.

It was not drugs. It was money. A fat wad of bills, rubber-banded tight.

My jaw dropped. "What in the—how? How did you—?"

He grinned, shoving the cash back in his pocket. "Simple. When I pat them down, I feel the money. I take some, wave 'em in. They don't even notice."

I just stared at him, half shocked, half impressed. Then I laughed, because of course Salvador would figure out a hustle on the very first night. Salvador started breaking it down to me, grinning like he had cracked the code of the streets. I was listening, nodding, but inside I was thinking pure genius. This dude had some big ones, you know? Walking straight into people's pockets, peeling off bills like it was nothing. Why didn't I think of that? My chest tightened with envy and admiration at the same time.

"How much contraband you got?" I asked him, curiously.

He shrugged, casual. "Not much. I've been letting it go. Honestly, I've just been focused on cash."

I laughed, shaking my head.

"And you?" he asked.

He raised his chin at me, waiting. I waved him over to my side of the door, where I had been stockpiling my finds. He saw it, and his eyes went wide. A whole stash. Baggies, pills, powders, rolled joints, bottles. Enough to make a dealer drool. A squirrel collecting nuts for winter, that was what I looked like. Except my nuts were narcotics.

"What is all that?" he asked, stunned. "You took all their stuff?"

I shrugged, almost embarrassed. Truth was, I did not even know what half of it was. But I knew enough to know it wouldn't make it past me. "I don't know what this junk is," I admitted. "But I know this much—they were pissed when I took it."

He just stared at the heap, his mouth hanging open. "Wow."

The crowd outside started to thin, and for the first time, the night eased. I told Salvador, "You good to cover the door?"

He nodded, flashing that cocky grin. "Yeah. Take your time."

So, I walked inside.

The moment I stepped past the threshold, the place hit me like a tidal wave. Lights everywhere, colors swinging back and forth, strobing across the crowd in seizure-bright flashes. The bass pounded through the floor, through my chest, through my skull, until I swore it was rewiring my heartbeat.

People moved like wild animals. Unhinged. Uncontrolled. Sweat was dripping down their bodies until they glistened like they had been hosed down. Their eyes were big, bright, blown wide open. Pupils were so dilated they looked like marbles swallowing the whites. And those eyes did not blink. They just stared, twitched, and glowed in the lights like predator eyes in the dark.

Some of them chewed on pacifiers. Actual baby pacifiers. Gnawing like teething toddlers. Others twirled glow sticks in manic circles, leaving streaks of neon in the air like haunted constellations.

The smell is suffocating. Damp clothes, stale sweat, and something sharp that stings the sinuses. Vicks VapoRub, thick and menthol heavy. It burns my nose, mixes with the reek of bodies, spilled drinks, and something metallic. The air feels wet, heavy, wrong.

I push further in and see some of them on the ground, rolling on the dirty, soaked floor like worms in rain. Eyes rolled back, jaws grinding. Zombies. That is what they look like. Zombies. Walking, dancing, twitching zombies, electrified by whatever they swallowed, smoked, or shot.

A hand slaps my shoulder, and I jolt, spinning around. It is Salvador.

"Hey, bro, you good?"

"Yeah, I'm good," I say, shaking it off. "Just... tripping on these people. You see what they're doing?"

He scans the room, nods slow. "Yeah. This is weird. These people are beyond faded."

"No kidding," I mutter.

Then he leans close, voice low. "Should we take some?"

I look at him, then back at the writhing bodies under the strobes. The thought is tempting, in a reckless, devil-whisper kind of way. But I shake my head. "Nah. We don't even know what we're taking. Let's figure it out first. Then maybe."

"Yeah, you're right."

The event coordinator finds us near the side door, sweat dripping down his temples. He pats our shoulders, smiling like the chaos around us is a well-oiled machine. "We're good for the evening. Can you guys come back tomorrow, same time?"

"Sure," I say, Salvador nodding beside me.

"Of course," Salvador adds, that grin still plastered on his face. "We'll see you then."

We exchanged looks, both of us buzzing. Him from the hustle, me from the sheer insanity of it all. I can already feel it. The hook is in. Tomorrow, we are coming back.

We had stashed everything earlier, just to make sure we could walk away clean if the night got messy. Even now, thinking back, it feels strange, like hiding treasure you did not even know the worth of yet. By the time we left, it was around three-thirty in the morning. The rave was still pulsing behind us, but we were done.

Salvador's place was only a light away, behind the Popeyes on Verde and Circle, just past Fountain. Familiar streets, quiet at that hour, except for the hum of traffic lights blinking red over empty intersections. Once we arrived, I called my boy, Tre.

He was older, sharper, someone who had been in the game a little longer than us. Tre said he would meet us at Salvador's, and he brought a friend of his, a guy named Uso. Someone who, according to Tre, could give us the "proper education" on what we had hauled in.

We got to Salvador's, slipped inside, and locked the door behind us. The place smelled like stale smoke and cheap cologne, a low light buzzing from a lamp in the corner. My heart was racing. Not from fear, but from anticipation.

I pulled out the stash. One by one, I laid everything on Salvador's bed. Bags, pills, powders, weed. It looked surreal, spread out in front of us, like we had robbed a pharmacy and a club dealer all at once.

Uso's eyes widened the second he saw it. He zeroed in on the weed, plucked a bud from the pile, and rolled it between his fingers. Under the lamp, it sparkled. The crystals cling like frost.

"Dang," he muttered, impressed. He pulled out a glass pipe from his jacket pocket like it was always ready, stuffed it with the bud, sparked it, and took a hard drag.

"Cough—cough," he hacked with smoke coming out of his mouth. His eyes watered, but his grin stretched wide. "Man, this is really good. High grade. Stronger than the usual dirt. You can see the crystals."

He passed the pipe. Tre hit it, Salvador hit it and then handed it to me. I hesitated for a second, then took a pull. The smoke scorched my throat, heavy and earthy, before it rolled into my lungs and settled like molten lead. My head buzzed almost instantly.

Uso exhaled, still grinning. "You boys don't know what you've got here. You could sell this quick. People will pay for this, no question."

I nodded, half-listening, half-lost in the shock of it all. I could not believe I was sitting there, staring at a bed piled with contraband like it was a pirate's chest. A greedy thought curled in my head. Maybe I should keep this to myself. I slid a couple of buds back into my pocket while no one was watching, justifying it with a quick lie to myself: finders keepers.

We were mid-laughter, the room hazy with smoke, when it came.

Knock. Knock. Knock.

The sound froze in the air. We all turned toward the door, silent. My buzz snapped clean in half. Salvador's eyes darted to mine. Tre straightened in his chair, tense. Uso just held the pipe, frozen mid-breath.

Three knocks. Heavy. Waiting.

And just like that, the night shifted.

Our eyes went as big as half-dollars. For a minute, the room was all smoke and lamp-glow and the stupid, ridiculous idea that nothing bad could touch us. Salvador threw a blanket over the bed like he was tucking away a treasure map, and the drugs disappeared into shadow. I did not even know how much cash was there yet. We had not counted. And my head was soft from the pipe and the adrenaline. This was too much to take in at three thirty in the morning.

"Hold up," Salvador said, voice low. He moved toward the door with Tre, as if nothing was wrong.

Tre and Salvador opened the door, and the night caught its breath. Tre's sister stood there with a friend, with a sigh of relief, and they slid inside, shoulders hunched like they had been out in the cold.

They all came to explain what we had, and before long, we were crowded. Two sisters, two friends, Uso, Tre, me, Salvador. The room smelled of smoke, cheap perfume, and the wet, leftover stench of the rave.

Uso started talking as if he were reading from an inventory list in some dealer's index, deep within his memory. Everybody leaned in, the darkness leaning with them. He named it fast, almost clinical, and by the time he was done, the list hung heavily in the air. Terrifying and intoxicating at once:

· Special K
· Cocaine
· Marijuana
· Keef
· Ecstasy pills / Molly
· Acid, liquid, and blotter paper
· Shrooms

When Uso said the words, the room tilted. These were not just kids at the party with pocket change and bad decisions. This was inventory. Product. A small black market.

Now, the older people in this room have been on this scene way longer than us, and you could tell by the way their pupils narrowed with business calculation. They knew value when they saw it.

The money? I did not plan on that part, but it was real. Seventeen hundred dollars, split between Salvador and me like a prize from some stupid, very dangerous game. And we won, with eight hundred fifty each.

I still remember the weight of the bills when we divided them, the way the rubber band snapped, the notes lying heavy in my palm.

That cash felt like proof we were winners.

This was our destiny.

CHAPTER 20: C.R.E.A.M

Uso rubbed his hands together. "I know where to move this," he said. His voice was low and slick. "We work tonight; we sell some back to them. We get more when we run the doors. Keep what we want." He did not spell out the details. He did not need to. We all knew enough to feel the promise.

Salvador grinned like he had just found the cheat code to life. We put the treasure chest away and got some rest. The next day, we got ready for round two. It was not a plan, not yet, not the kind with maps and exit strategies. It was a hunger. We mapped the same rhythm in our heads: show up, work, search, seize what we could, resell, repeat. We had already seen how it played out the night before. That was all the rehearsal we needed. The next night could not come fast enough.

Trey decided he wanted in for real. He was older and thought he had nerves. He asked if he could ride. Tre said he wanted to help. I did not promise anything. I was not the boss there.

"Come anyway, see what happens." He swore he would meet us there, and he did.

We showed up early, helped set up lights, hauled cables, and moved boxes. Grunt work that made us look indispensable. The coordinator nodded, as if we were now part of the crew.

"Three are better than two and two's better than one," the coordinator said, half-joking, handing us more vests. "Do the same as last night, okay, guys?"

We saluted him like idiots. Around seven-thirty, the building started to buzz. By eight, the coordinator instructed us to gear up, set up our stations, and check our radios. We checked our belts and each other, our vests tight, our faces blank, our pockets ready. We were nervous and cocky at the same time, the most dangerous combination.

When nine hit, he said, "IT'S SHOWTIME!"

I walked to my door and looked out. The line snaked around the building, longer and hungrier than last night. Bodies pulsed under streetlights, breath of little white ghosts in the cool air. Every head in that line was a bill waiting to be pulled, a pocket to be felt, a secret to be found. All I could see was money. Money in hand is like a promise. I thought of the treasure on the bed back at Salvador's. I thought of the fat stack of cash still warm in my pocket.

The plan was simple, laced with pure greed. Work the door, catch the stash, keep the cash, sell a little back, and come away richer than we were. We told ourselves we were not bad. They told us to do this. We were survivors, opportunists. The truth was simpler and uglier. We were going to get it by whatever means necessary.

Doors opened. The first bodies streamed in. Same as before. We searched, we confiscated, and we tossed it into the bag. Same attitudes, same curse words, same girls with fur boots and eyes like moons. The energy was bigger, wilder. We were ready. We moved in rhythm, practiced now, palms patient, fingers quick.

The greed sat under my skin like a second heartbeat, and I loved it.

People funneled through, as if they had been relieved of gravity, each body a story, a pocket, and a secret. "Sorry, you can't take that in," I said, voice flat, practiced. My hands moved the way they always did. Slip, probe, press. Learning the language of fabric and coin. A hand jerked back when I found pills in a sock. A girl spat curses when I pulled a joint from her ear. "Nope. Can't bring that in." Toss. Next. Repeat.

There was a rhythm to it. My fingers learned the echo of different things: crinkly foil, hard plastic, the soft give of folded bills. Each time something hit the bottom of the bag, it sounded like a tiny bell. The bag swelled, got heavy, and started to sag. It was crazy how quickly my trash bag filled. Tabs, capsules, baggies flecked with dust, a half-smoked blunt twisted into the shape of a lie. The trash can next to me became a graveyard for other people's choices, but by the middle of the night, it looked fuller than it had the night before. Proof the hidden cheat code for life was still activated.

A cold lick kept replaying in my head. The phrase tasted metallic and bright. This was a clean hit. No plan, no fuss, just the night handing you an opportunity and you taking it. Two nights in a row. It felt unreal, like a movie. I caught myself grinning too wide, that guilty spark lighting the back of my throat. Was this really happening again? The bag answered by getting heavier.

Across the glow of the room, I spotted Uso and his crew noodling in line on Salvador's side, easy and slick. Seeing them made my stomach twist. Friends can be anchors or leeches. For a second, the paranoia slid in, thin and cold. Then the bass dropped, and the worry was swallowed by motion. Another body stepped up. Another pocket, just giving me everything.

When the rush slowed and the doors stilled, I stood there with a bag that was almost too full to lift and laughed low and hard to myself. The room hummed with the strobe light, sweat, and the knowledge that we had done it again. We pulled this off, and tonight it felt less like survival and more like a promise. There was more where this came from, if you knew how to take it.

They moved like they owned the light. All girls in neon and lace, hips carving the air, hair whipping in colors that did not belong in daylight. Their bodies glowed under strobes and LEDs. Their movements were a blend of dance and display, a practiced language of provocation. Every twist and arch was a question, every laugh an invitation. Glow sticks traced little comet tails in the smoke-heavy air. It was dazzling and ugly at the same time.

Vicks hung in the room like a second fog, menthol and sweat and something sweet that stuck to your throat. I had seen streets, alleys, and doorways that taught survival in plain terms. This place did not speak that language. It spoke in flashes, in synthetic tempo. For the first time since I could remember, I felt the edge of being a stranger. My teeth found the corner of my lip. One thing I knew for certain was that I was quick to adapt to my surroundings.

Uso found me wedged between bodies, his grin quick as a knife. He leaned in so closely, the bass beat vibrated between us. "Yo," he said, "let me move some of your stuff. I can flip it quick."

The instinct to hoard prickled. This was raw product, and everything in me wanted to guard it at all costs. I thought, looked, and saw that the room was an ocean of customers. Hoarding it would be dumb. Opportunity only worked if you let it flow.

I nodded. "Test the waters," I said. "You move what you can. We split what you make."

He clapped once, gone before the bass dropped hard again.

In the cut of his absence, his sisters drifted toward me like planets pulled into orbit. One of them, brown eyes and a grin edged sharp, stepped in, breath warm with perfume and something bitter. "You got more of what we saw earlier?" she asked.

I kept my voice low. "Yeah. What are you looking for?

She did not hesitate. "Ecstasy. Something to feel good on." Her friends echoed like a chorus. Wanting. Daring. Hungry.

I sifted the memory of the stash in my head, fingertips tracing the shapes I had seen earlier. The stamped pills. Those were the ones. I eased out a handful; palms steady despite the adrenaline and showed them. Under the strobes, the pills looked like tiny suns.

"Want to try with us?" she asked, eyes bright with mischief.

Pause.

The pause hit like a freight train. But pause the story. Think about the position I was in. Do I follow this rabbit down the hole? Or do I take the blue pill and wake back up in my bed, and none of this has really happened? Or do I take the red pill with all these girls in this party and find out just how deep this rabbit hole actually goes? The blue pill was just saying no, and the red pill was to go have fun. Which one would you take?

As for me, I was a risk-taker, and I walked on the wild side. I laughed in the face of danger. My mind was made up. I took a deep breath. I felt the old itch—the one that had led me into alleys and hustles, where not being afraid was the profit margin. I laughed, a short sound that surprised me. Risk was part of the currency I traded in. I had always taken the side roads. Comfort had never been my lane.

"Red pill," I thought, like checking in with a mirror.

I agreed.

Their faces lit up, bright and satisfied. I pulled five pills out of the bag and handed one to each of them. One for you, one for you, one for you, and one for you. The last one stayed in my hand, and Uso's sister grabbed it and put it in my mouth. As soon as she did, she scraped down my lip, my chin, my neck, and down my chest with her nails. Her nails left fire down my skin, and the way she looked at me with pure lust in her eyes, it was not soft, not tender. It was hunger. Pure, uncut hunger. Not the kind that waits or asks. The kind that takes.

Her eyes burned into me, pupils wide as saucers, breathing fast, lips wet like she had already tasted me in her head. Her friends mirrored it, bottom lips caught between teeth, hips shifting like they were already halfway to grinding on me before the music even pulled us in. They did not see me as a person. Not Gabriel. Not Suspect. Not some dude on security. I was meat. Fuel. A live wire with drugs.

When they pulled me to the floor, it was not dancing. It was possession. They pressed close, sweat mixing with sweat, heat off their bodies hitting me like steam. Every brush of skin sparked something animal. They moved like predators, slow but deliberate, arching their backs, rolling their hips, pressing their chests into me. Every move screamed want, screamed take, screamed now.

Lust was not an idea in this place. It was thick in the air, something you could choke on. You could feel it in the way strangers grabbed strangers like they had been waiting their whole lives for this exact song. It was in the way her nails dug deeper into my arms, leaving tracks like proof. In the way their breath grew shallow, quick, hot against my ear. It was overwhelming, raw, relentless. Not love. Not connection. Just bodies chasing the high of touch the same way they chased the high of powder and pills. Lust was not a whisper here. It was a roar.

I got swallowed whole by it. I followed their move. The pill hit slowly at first, like a fuse burning toward dynamite. My tongue tingled, bitter taste fading, and then it crawled through my veins like heat under the skin. Ecstasy did not sneak. It took over. My chest felt wide open, heart thumping in rhythm with the bass, every beat louder than the last. Sweat broke across my forehead, but it did not feel nasty. It felt electric, like my skin itself was buzzing. Colors sharpened, lights smeared into long ribbons that danced even when I closed my eyes. The air itself felt alive, as if I could touch it and bend it.

The touch. That was what got me. Every brush of skin, every graze of a hand, felt like fire and silk all at once. A stranger's fingers on my arm hit harder than a kiss. Nails dragging down my chest did not just sting; they sang. My body was a live wire, and every contact sent sparks racing down to my core. The music was not music anymore. It was inside me. The bass did not just thump. It rewrote my heartbeat, turned me into part of the system. The crowd moved like one, a hive of sweat and lust and glow sticks, and I was in it, drowning in it, loving it, terrified of it.

Ecstasy made everything feel good. Too good. Like the world itself was seductive. Like, even the chaos had arms and was pulling me closer. For the first time in my life, I understood why people chased it. Because at that moment, nothing else mattered. Not probation, not hustling, not even money. Just the height, the touch, the music.

Then it hit me. The danger was not in taking it. The danger was wanting it again, and more of it.

Being there, among them, touching hands, feeling pulse, sharing smoke blurred the lines. The night reframed itself as a possibility. The stash at Salvador's, the split cash in my pocket, the easy angles for a resale. Everything felt louder and softer at the same time. Decisions, once heavy, lightened into momentum.

Uso found me a little later, pockets a little fuller, grin stretched. He threaded back through the crowd to find us laughing, glossy-eyed, the world trimmed in neon and possibility.

"How we looking? Is there anymore? I'm sold out," he said.

I met his gaze and felt the steady, ugly truth hum under the music. We were in too deep to back out clean. The plan had shifted, less about keeping the merchandise and more about moving it, flipping it fast, and using the night's chaos as cover. We would test the market, sell a little, keep a little, and come back for more. The greed sat in my gut like a cold coin.

Everywhere I looked—girls on guys, guys on girls, bodies on bodies, it was the same wild. Everyone drenched in sweat, eyes wide and glassy, chewing pacifiers like their jaws were locked, glow sticks streaking neon across the air like fireflies from hell.

It was Wonderland, but not the kind with rabbits and tea parties. This was Wonderland twisted into something raw and filthy. Wonderland soaked in Vicks, dripping in sweat, lit in strobe lights and sin. Wonderland where people were not people anymore. They were bodies, impulses, animals running loose. And there I was, in the middle of it, heart racing, pupils wide, every nerve lit up like a fuse.

For a moment, I forgot why I was even there. Forgot about Salvador, Trey, Uso, the hustle. Forgot about the trash bag filling with drugs at the door.

Then reality clawed its way back in. I was not here to party. I was not here to get lost. I was supposed to be working the door, watching, pulling in products, running the play we came for. My pulse spiked, panic slicing through the euphoria.

"Wait," I told them, pushing through the press of sweaty arms and sticky skin. "Hold up. I gotta go."

They reached for me, laughing, trying to drag me back, but I broke free, stumbling through the crowd, breathing like I had just outrun something feral. The bass still hammered in my skull, but I forced myself back to my post, back to Salvador, back to Trey, back to the hustle.

I had been gone for what felt like hours but might have only been minutes. Either way, it was too long. I had fallen down the rabbit hole, lost myself in Wonderland, and crawled back out filthily. The rave was chaos. A living, breathing chaos of lust, drugs, and insanity. Somehow, in the middle of it, we were supposed to keep hustling like we were not drowning in the madness ourselves.

I hurried back to the security area, pushed through the thick heat of the crowd, and made my way to the front. The bass still rattled in my chest even after I broke free, like it was stitched into my heartbeat. As soon as I hit the door, I pulled a cigarette from my pocket and sparked it up, trying to steady my nerves. The smoke cut through the sour-sweet stench of sweat, cologne, and Vicks, giving me one small taste of normal in a place that felt anything but.

That was when the coordinator showed. He moved out of the shadows like he owned the night, a fat cigar hanging from his mouth, chewing on it instead of smoking. Chains hung from his neck, heavy silver links stacked one over the other, shining every time the light hit. There were so many I lost count. His grin was wide, gums blackened, teeth stained the color of old yellow tartar. That smile was half-greeting, half-warning, like he was sizing me up and enjoying the process.

"Everything's going good, guys?" he asked, voice gravelly, smoke and liquor wrapped around the words.

I took a drag, kept my cool. "As good as it's gonna get, you know?"

He smirked, eyes narrowing, like he was testing me with the weight of his stare. "I know that's right." He thumbed a cheap lighter, flame catching on the end of his cigar until it burned hot and ugly, smoke curling around his face like a devil's halo. Then, without another word, he adjusted his chain stack, gave a nod. The coordinator chewed on his cigar, smoke curling between his yellowed teeth.

"You guys can take off, or stick around, whatever. Might need you next weekend, but tonight you're good."

He clapped Salvador on the shoulder, eyes cutting over the rest of us like we were tools left on a workbench.

"Okay? Good. Appreciate you. Appreciate you," he said, walking off into the dark.

I caught him before he could leave. "Hold up. What's my hours looking like for community service?"

The coordinator chewed on his cigar, eyes drifting up like the math was written somewhere on the ceiling. He squinted, thought it over, and finally let out a grunt.

"Well... with you and your crew, the time you put in, those two days..." He flicked ash onto the floor. "I'll just call it done. Write you off for the whole thing. I'll tell them you're clear."

The words hit like a reprieve from a sentence I did not know I was still serving.

I nodded, slow. "Appreciate it."

He smirked, teeth the color of tar. "Don't mention it." He disappeared into the darkness, into the sea of people.

I had been around long enough already to know men like him do not just walk off. Every step he took was a move being made for something crooked, something dirty, something I did not need to see but was happening all the same.

From the last two nights here, I already knew this place was not built for the innocent. Deals were going down in corners I had not even found yet.

Girls got swallowed up by shadows and came back different. Money changed hands like cards in a crooked game, and the real power wasn't the music or the crowd; it was the quiet players moving behind it all. Standing there, smoke in my lungs, sweat drying on my shirt, I realized I wasn't just inside a party. I was deep inside a new lifestyle, and once you're in, it doesn't let you walk away clean.

I found Sal, then Trey, and Uso, and together we dragged our take-out back, away from the lights, behind the building where the shadows felt safer. The air stank of wet asphalt and garbage, and our breath hung white in the dark as we laid it all out. What we had was unreal. Piled up in front of us was more than triple what we'd touched yesterday, all the bags, bundles, a dirty glitter of street gold. For free. It didn't feel real, like someone was running a cruel experiment just to see how far we'd take it. They handed us drugs for nothing, and the sick genius was in selling it right back to them. The hustle fed itself.

That night marked the real beginning. Weed had been a side hustle, something to flex on, a way to keep pockets from going empty. But this was a threshold. We stepped through it without even realizing, thinking it was luck, not a trap. The rush was electric, but beneath it I felt the undertow, pulling harder with every breath. I was rising higher than I'd ever dreamed, money, product, status all in reach, but at the same time sinking deeper than I could imagine, like the concrete itself was swallowing me.

It was power before I even knew what power meant. To hold something in your hands that older men whispered about, that kids your age would trade respect for, that twisted me up inside. On the surface, it felt good, almost too good. Money stacking where there'd been nothing, attention from people who never looked twice before, the rush of being needed. Every deal was a secret handshake with danger, and danger was addictive. Underneath the shine, there was a weight. Paranoia in the back of my skull, the constant twitch of eyes scanning corners, wondering if this was the day it all went wrong. The money felt light in my pocket but heavy in my conscience. One second, you're just a kid passing the time, the next you're carrying something that could end you.

The feeling was double-edged, part victory, part curse. It made me walk taller, talk louder, as if I belonged in places I never had. And at the same time, it hollowed me out, like every dollar and every bag carried a piece of me I wouldn't get back.

Selling drugs young was like tasting adulthood too early; it burned going down, but once it was in your system, you couldn't spit it out.

It was intoxicating. It was unstoppable. And it was already too late.

The next morning at school, we couldn't keep our mouths shut. We pulled our close friends aside, told them what went down, what we had stashed. They laughed it off at first, thought we were flexing. But then we emptied our pockets, let the bills spill into our palms, and whispered about the treasure chest back at the house, heavy with narcotics stolen straight from the same people we sold it back to.

Their faces changed. Disbelief turned into silence. Silence turned into envy.

Me? I felt split in half, ashamed but buzzing, guilty but proud. Finders keepers, that's what I told myself. Like it made sense. Like it made it right.

I'd sold weed before, just nickel-and-dime hustles, pocket-change plays. But this was different. This was a machine, and once you stepped into its gears, it didn't stop turning.

Word spread fast. The girls wanted to see it, the guys wanted a piece of it. So, we brought them along. One weekend became two, then three, then routine. Before long, Friday nights weren't optional; they were mandatory. Parties weren't about music anymore. They were about business: get the drugs, sell the drugs, flip the money, and dive back in for more. A cycle that spun until the nights bled together.

We weren't doing security like we were supposed to; we were feeding a hunger that didn't know the word "enough." And in the middle of it all, we learned how to survive that scene: how to talk, how to walk, how to hide the fear behind the swagger. We learned how to move with the rhythm, how to let the music envelop us with breakbeats, pop hooks, and bass that rattle our bones. It wasn't just a party anymore. It was the air we breathed.

We were young, but we were young with stacks of cash, young with more drugs anyone could ever need, young with girls who wanted what we had. There were no ceilings. No limits. Just the feeling that this was the beginning of everything.

Intermission

It was no holds barred. Extreme rules. Everything allowed. That seems to sum it up pretty well. I was never home at this point. Always gone, just doing my own thing. Jumping around from girl to girl. Living my best drug-induced life. I do not think there was a drug I did not try, use, or abuse. If it was on the table, I tried it. If I liked it, I did more. Doubled down.

Looking back now, I am amazed that I could even hold an intelligent conversation or walk and still be alive. Just to be here, breathing, and being able to speak clearly is mind-blowing to me.

I always thought about the rule: think twice, trust no one. People always told me to be careful in what I did. Look ten times before crossing the street, not just both ways. Stay aware of your surroundings. The goal and the rule were simple: do not get high on your own supply. That worked, but the after-parties and the females always got me. The females. I was a sucker for them, but that was between me and myself.

True love should not be hard to find. Pain is love, and love is loyal. The foundation is trust. Once trust is gone, it is done. Zero tolerance for nonsense. Fake friends surrounded me, snakes waiting for the perfect time to strike, waiting for me to slip. Honest words can be painful, even resentful, but they are full of faith. That is why I always kept one hundred. Even when it cut. Even when it burned. Even when I was bleeding from every mistake I had made.

These were the thoughts running through my head. I had to get them off my chest. A multitude of emotions flooded my mind, heart, and soul while writing this book about my life. It feels unreal to think back. I am just talking paper talk to you, and I hope you understand.

During the time of writing, I was filled with a presence that took over me completely. I am not trying to downshift here, not yet. We are just gaining speed, and we are already moving fast. It is about to get better. But know this: God has blessed me and put me here for a reason.

"I shall not die, but live, and declare the works of the Lord."
Psalm 118:17 (KJV)

(You are alive because God preserved you so you can tell your story and glorify Him.)

"For we are God's handiwork, created in Christ Jesus to do good works, which God prepared in advance for us to do."
Ephesians 2:10 (NIV)

(You are not just saved from something, but for something—His work through you.)

"For I know the plans I have for you," declares the Lord, "plans to prosper you and not to harm you, plans to give you hope and a future."
Jeremiah 29:11 (NIV)

(God's saving grace is not random. It is intentional, with a future in mind.)

Sometimes I stop and think about those verses, about the chaos I walked through, the nights I thought would swallow me whole. Every corner I turned, every mistake, every high and every low—somehow, I survived. It was not luck. God saved me for a reason.

Not just to scrape by. Not just to breathe another day. But to live. To tell this story. To show the work He is doing in me.

The streets, the parties, the drugs—they were real, but they did not define me. What defines me is that I am still here. Still standing. Still speaking. Deep down, I know there is a purpose behind it all.

CHAPTER 21: BOMBS AWAY

Buckle your seatbelt. Here we go.

All right. Let me continue. Let me put this into perspective for you for a moment. As I was saying, this party life continued for quite some time. I was seventeen years old, and we were partying all week, fully invested in the scene. By this time, I had been kicked out of every grade from sixth through ninth. Every school was the same story: fights, suspension, walking out before anyone could tell me what to do. I was not just failing the system. I was burning through it.

Each year, another teacher shook their head, another principal threw up their hands. By the time tenth grade rolled around, I was not even in the classrooms anymore.

I was surviving somewhere else, learning lessons the school could not teach. We sold drugs all week and got faded all night.

Thursdays, we met at bars around town for rave nights. It fits the moment. The moment was this, and us. It went hand in hand. It was a time of drugs and guns. I had one of each on me, plus a gun in the trunk and a pocket full of a variety of drugs. You name it, I had it. We had it. We followed the music because of the money.

That Thursday night, we ate four hits of acid each. Everybody around us did the same. The acid hit in waves. First colors, then sounds, the bass vibrating through your chest like it was trying to rearrange your bones. Still, we moved. Sold. Hustled. The party did not stop, and neither did we.

Friday came, and to chase the same trip, you had to double it. Eight hits. Salvador matched me, and the night stretched wide and electric, spinning faster than our minds could follow. New faces crowded in around us, and we handed out hits here and there, just to see the chaos bloom, just to keep the energy raw. All night, we were moving, wheeling and dealing, selling, pocketing. The lines between fun and work dissolved into one blur.

Saturday slowed, only a little. Maybe some weed, smoke drifting in our lungs, but the acid stayed packed away. Still, the selling never stopped. The rave was ours, a machine of strobe lights and sweat, bodies pressing against the floor, the music shaking every nerve. We sold and sold, and the nights bled into each other.

At the end of the party, we headed home. The sun was already creeping over the city. We were not alone. A few girls, caught up in the high, wanted to keep the night alive. We let them come along. By the time we rolled in, it was past seven, maybe seven-thirty in the morning. The city smelled like asphalt and dawn, and the chaos of the night lingered in every corner of the car. Exhausted, wired, alive.

By now, the Saturday party had finally died down. It was early Sunday morning, the city was quiet, but inside our house, the chaos was just shifting gears. The girls wanted to eat some acid, and honestly, so did we. I looked at Salvador, the words heavy in the stale air.

"Dude, we have eaten acid all week," I said. "We are going to have to double it up again."

He raised an eyebrow. "Okay. How much?"

I swallowed, thinking fast. "Sixteen hits, probably."

We froze for a moment, just staring at each other. Sixteen hits. It sounded insane, but that was the point. By now, the people at the house were not just guests. They were part of the life. They trusted us or at least thought they did.

We went for it. Sixteen hits each to start. The girls got their share, too. Then we waited. The room was thick with anticipation, with the faint smell of weed and the scent of sweat-soaked carpet. The acid was already weaving its way through our veins, but we kept busy, breaking up some weed, rolling joints. Not for the high. It was a distraction, a timer, a way to ensure everyone would feel the same way.

The house hummed with nervous energy. Every movement, every laugh, every flicker of the fluorescent light felt magnified, stretched. It was like the walls themselves were breathing, and we were floating inside them, untethered. The night, or maybe the early morning, had become a loop, a living organism, and we were part of it.

In that suspended moment, I realized how far we had gone. How deep the spiral had gotten. The acid was not just a trip anymore. It was a mirror, reflecting every reckless choice, every edge we had danced along, and every risk we were still willing to take.

We were just laughing, talking, passing a joint back and forth, the weed smoke curling like lazy ghosts in the dim light. Then I heard it soft, high-pitched giggles from the girls. They were laughing at nothing, or maybe everything. I leaned toward them.

"Hey, do you guys feel it?"

They looked at me with wide eyes and nodded, still snickering. "Yeah, we feel it."

I glanced at Sal. "You feeling yours?"

He shook his head. "Not yet."

And that was the moment it hit.

My eyes would not stop blinking. Blink, blink, blink, over and over, trying to make sense of what I was seeing. Salvador leaned over.

"Hey, bro, you okay?"

I could not answer. All I saw was color. Not the blur you get after staring at a screen too long. No. This was alive. Red, blue, purple, yellow, orange, green—all melting together, stretching and pulsing. Everything was a rainbow. Everything was wrong.

Panic started to creep in. I thought about the acid, how much we had actually taken. Sixteen hits… no, wait. It was the double-dipped. Thirty-two. My stomach sank. My chest tightened. My head spun like it was about to split open.

The girls noticed. One leaned close, whispering, "He needs air."

The other nodded. "Yeah… he definitely does."

They opened the window. A river of smoke rushed out, thick and heavy, rolling like molten clouds down the Rocky Mountains. It swirled and tangled, thick enough to taste on my tongue, to make my lungs burn and my chest tighten. The room felt both bigger and smaller at the same time. The air was alive, moving, breathing.

I stumbled toward the window, gasping, my heart thudding so hard I could hear it over the pounding bass in my ears. Salvador grabbed my shoulder. "Breathe, bro… just breathe."

I tried. I really tried. But the colors were not stopping. They were everywhere, on everything, inside my head. My body felt weightless but anchored, like I was being dragged through layers of smoke and light, a kaleidoscope I could not escape. And in that moment, I realized just how far we had gone. Just how reckless, just how unstoppable we thought we were.

They kept whispering, voices sharp and thin like glass.

"We need to get him out of here. He's sweating bad. He needs some air."

I could not make sense of their faces, their words. Everything was a smear of color and heat. My shirt clung to my skin like it was melting. My pulse was a jackhammer. The room swayed and breathed. Someone grabbed my arm, trying to steer me toward the door.

"Just keep calm, just keep calm," they kept saying. "You probably ate too much."

I snapped for a moment, just a flicker, back into myself. "Yeah… yeah, you're right…" My voice did not even sound like mine.

Then I saw it. Through the window the sky had gone bright, so bright the sun was blasting like a white fire. It was pouring into the room, crawling over the walls, swallowing shadows. My stomach flipped. I muttered, "That was weird…"

I thought maybe I should go outside and breathe. The second the idea formed in my head, the sky shifted and grew darker than I had ever seen it, like someone had thrown a blanket over it and turned it into night. The shadows thickened. The light disappeared.

"Okay…" I whispered. "Maybe I should stay inside then."

The sun came back instantly, violent and blinding, like it was mocking me. Shining brighter than it ever had before. My breath caught. My hands trembled. Could my thoughts control the weather? Or was the weather trying to tell me something?

Then, through the haze, a voice cut in, shaking.

"Hello, suspect. Hello? Are you there? You're scaring us."

I turned my head. A girl's eyes were wide, glittering with fear.

"You're seriously scaring us," she said.

"What happened?" I asked, my voice low, hollow. "What did you guys do?"

"Nothing," she said. "You keep… you keep going in and out. Looking lost. We keep trying to get your attention, and it's not working."

Their words sounded far away, like they were underwater. My thoughts were louder than their voices. The room was a kaleidoscope, and I was falling through it, my body still there but my mind slipping off the edge.

"It's not working… I don't even know how much I ate…" The words came out broken, my voice echoing against the walls like it did not belong to me.

"Hello, suspect? Listen please. Hello?"

Their voices were muffled now, underwater echoes. My brain tried to grab them, but they slid away. Everything was sliding away.

I heard them saying something about getting me in the shower, calming me down. Feet moving. Water running. Then hands on me—gentle, but too many of them. Clothes peeling off.

"Okay," one of the girls said. "We got you."

Cold tile against my bare feet. Steam curling up from the tub. The hiss of water fills the small space.

And then—snap.

I was back, like someone had ripped a film off my eyes.

"What the hell are you doing?" I shouted. "You think you're slick or something?"

They blinked at me, confused. "We're trying to help—"

I did not hear the rest. Paranoia hit like a punch. My brain spun a new scene with a man crouched under the tub, shotgun loaded, waiting to blow my brains out as soon as I laid down. My heart thundered. Sweat ran down my back.

"Screw that," I growled. "You gotta wake up earlier than that to get the best of me."

I bolted. Naked with just boxers on, wet, adrenaline flooding my veins. Out of the bathroom, down the hall. The carpet felt like it was moving under my feet. The house is like a maze. I skidded into the living room and stopped by a window, chest heaving.

"Suspect, calm down! Please!" one of them shouted from somewhere behind me.

That was all I heard. Just my name—

SUSPECT! SUSPECT!! SUSPECT!!!

Over and over, bouncing off the walls like an accusation.

I stood in the middle of the living room, shaking, every nerve screaming. I could feel eyes on me, invisible crosshairs. "You guys tried to set me up, and I caught you…" Deep down, in the pit of my stomach, I was confused, and I didn't know if it was real or not, but my head didn't care. My head was full of gangster movies I grew up on, every trap, every ambush, every double-cross I had ever watched. All of it folding in on itself now, living and breathing around me. Naked. Cornered. Sweat dripping onto the floor. The room felt like a cage, and I was the only animal inside.

Salvador's mom had been asleep in the back room the whole time. I did not even realize she was there until I heard her voice cutting through chaos like a whip.

"Mijo, what's wrong?" she shouted, bursting into the living room, eyes wide with panic.

Salvador's face drained of color. "Bro… what in the hell are you doing?" he yelled over the noise.

"Mijo, what's wrong?" his mom pleaded, her hands out like she was trying to calm a wild animal.

I was already at the big bay window on the second floor, my chest heaving, sweat stinging my eyes. The room spun around me, faces melting into color, fear leaking into the air. My bare feet gripped the carpet. My knuckles were white against the windowsill.

"Don't take another step," I snarled, voice cracking. "If any of you take another step toward me, I will jump. I don't care. I'll jump. Test me."

One of the girls broke down, her mascara streaking down her cheeks. "No!" she sobbed, reaching a trembling hand toward me.

I looked at her, really looked, and something inside me just went still. My heart was a hammer in my chest. My head felt like it was splitting open.

"Okay," I said. That was it. Just one word. One.

Then I lunged forward. Head first.

Glass shattered around me, exploding into knives of light and color. The sound was deafening, yet muffled, as if I were underwater. For a second, I saw the sun flash off the shards, rainbows dancing midair. Then the world flipped. The air tore past my skin.

A leap to escape. A leap of madness.

Out of the second-story bay window I went, headfirst into nothing.

Time cracked open the second I left the window. The glass gave way with a scream, splintering into a thousand shards that floated around me like frozen fireworks. It was seven a.m. on a Sunday, the kind of morning that should smell like coffee and quiet, but instead I was naked, high out of my mind, plummeting through cold air.

The acid stretched everything. Seconds bled into minutes, minutes into forever. My body tilted forward, head first, arms out like some twisted angel. The sunlight hit the glass shards spinning around me, turning them into rainbows, red, blue, gold, violet, all of it streaking across my vision. I could not tell if I was falling or flying.

The city below looked unreal, a toy town painted in pastel light. Cars crawled by like insects. The streets glistened from the night before. The air whipped against my face, cool and sharp, filling my mouth, my lungs, my skull. It tasted metallic, like blood and static.

Inside my head, the noise was louder than the wind. All the girls, all the parties, all the rules, and all the drugs with a lifetime of chaos flashing in jagged pieces. Somewhere behind me, a girl screamed my name, but it was warped, echoing like a cassette tape dying.

Then it hit me. This was what success felt like. Not good, not bad. Just raw success. The final step off the edge. A leap of faith into whatever came next. I was falling, but my mind was soaring, stretched thin between terror and euphoria. The world spun, the colors smeared, the sky roared. And for a heartbeat, I thought maybe I could stay in the air forever, suspended between the life I had been living and the one waiting for me at the bottom.

You know, thinking back, I always wanted to be a gangster. I always wanted to be the man all the women wanted. Money, power, and respect. I would do whatever it took to get the money. Sometimes, just sometimes, we have a setback.

BAM!

The world did not stop when I hit the glass. It broke around me like ice cracking on a lake, sharp, bright, deafening, but I did not feel a thing. My body went straight through the jeep's windshield, a storm of shattering safety glass and bloodless cuts.

Then I was up. Not crawling. Not stumbling. Up. Moving. Like my body refused to believe physics. Bare feet on pavement, glass biting into my soles, slicing ribbons of red, but my brain did not register pain. I was all adrenaline and acid, lungs sucking in cold morning air like jet fuel. Faster and faster. No hesitation. No pause. No beat skipped.

"Suspect! Wait!" Voices cracked behind me, warped and distant. That was all I could hear—my name—but all they saw were my ankles and elbows, flashing like signals as I bolted out of whatever setup my paranoia swore, they had laid for me. The parking lot blurred into streaks of gray and oil-stain rainbows. Cars became shapes. Shadows became threats. My breath came in hot bursts, heart hammering so loud it drowned the world out.

I reached the edge of the lot, the street yawning wide in front of me. Asphalt. Sunday morning sunlight hitting the cracked road like white fire. Everything slowed for a heartbeat. My muscles coiled.

Just as I stepped off the curb—

Bang.

A car clipped me hard. Metal on flesh. My body spun like a ragdoll, rolling across the blacktop. Asphalt burned my elbows and back, glass and gravel chewing into my skin. I sat up on the curb, head ringing like a church bell, and just stared at the street. Sunday morning, at seven a.m., empty sky. Not a single soul except the driver stepping out, his face white as chalk.

"You okay, man?" he stammered.

I wiped at my mouth, tasting blood, and looked at him like it was nothing. "Yeah, I'm good, bro," I said, voice low and cracked. "You got a cigarette?"

He blinked at me, shook his head, then dug out a pack. Handed me one. Handed me a lighter. My fingers shook, but I lit it anyway, smoke filling my chest like it could stitch me back together.

Then I saw him pull out his phone.

"Who you calling?" I asked, eyes narrowing, voice suddenly sharp.

"Proper authorities," he said, like it was a script.

"Proper authorities..." My head dropped. The words crawled around in my skull. My heartbeat doubled. My breath turned thin.

I stood up before he could say another word and bolted. Fast. My body moved like it belonged to someone else. Bare feet slapping pavement, blood dripping, heart pounding, and my boxers ripped to shreds.

Then—boom.

Another car. Harder this time. My body lifted, slammed, rolled across the concrete like a thrown doll. Sparks of pain burst in my arms and shoulders, but my mind felt numb, detached. "Look both ways," I told myself, rolling. "Look both ways." But I was not looking anywhere. I was gone, darting across the street like a rabbit, all instinct, no thought at all.

Two cars. Two hits and still not out. Acid and adrenaline turned me into something unkillable. Cuts, bruises, blood, none of it mattered. I stopped rolling, sat up on my knees, shaking my head. The world shimmered like heat waves off asphalt. My breath became ragged, but my legs were already under me. I was up before my brain could catch up, running again, faster than before.

To my left, a field opened up, a wide, green stretch of golf course behind Sav-A-Lot on Airport and Circle. It looked unreal, like a painting, grass flickering neon green in my vision.

I did not think. I veered left. Fence ahead. I hit it at full speed and cleared it as if it were nothing, as if it were one big leaf instead of chain-link steel. My body did not even pause. Just over. Into the green.

I hit the grass hard, skin tearing against the wet blades, knees buckling as I fell forward. For a second, I just stayed there, head bowed, palms digging into the earth, breathing like I had swallowed fire. The grass smelled sharp and alive, wet, metallic, almost electric under my nose. My vision pulsed with each heartbeat.

Blink. Blink. Blink. The world flickered like a bad signal.

I lifted my head. Sunday morning sunlight poured over everything like gold, and there they were, golfers, lined up with their clubs, little carts parked neat and clean, shirts tucked in. A perfect picture of suburban calm.

I was not calm at all. I was naked, bloody, barefoot, streaked with glass cuts and dirt, and I could feel my heartbeat in my teeth. My eyes darted back toward the street. The cars that had hit me sat there like metal animals. Any second, I expected red and blue lights, sirens. Any second, they would come for me.

Blink. Blink. Blink. Blink. Blink.

Just like that, in a split second, the golfers were not golfers anymore. Not in my head. They turned into something else—FBI agents. Dark suits, sunglasses, and earpieces glinting. Canine dogs straining at leashes, teeth bared, eyes locked on me.

My heart lurched into my throat. That was what my mind saw. Maybe it wasn't real, but real or not, I wasn't sticking around to find out.

Nope. I spun, the grass slicked under my feet, and bolted back toward the fence. My muscles screamed, but the acid burned hotter, driving me forward.

One more leap like the first time. Over the fence, body flying, knees up, arms pumping, like some feral thing trying to claw its way out of a nightmare. But when I landed on the other side, my stomach dropped.

Cops.

C-S-P-D. Badges, uniforms, boots on pavement. Not one. Not two. Six. Six bodies moving fast. Six sets of eyes on me.

"Oh my God," I muttered. "I'm hit."

One cruiser skidded across the asphalt right in front of me, tires screaming, cutting me off. Another one angled behind. My body went tight, like a trap about to spring.

I had no plans. No way out. Just raw instinct. Acid sweat poured down my face. The whole world is roaring in my ears. I spun on my heels, thinking maybe, just maybe, I would find a hole to slip through. Nope. Two more cops were standing there like walls.

Before I could even think, one lunged, arms wide, trying to wrap me up. His fingers dug into my arm, but he could not get a grip. I twisted, slippery with sweat and blood, too juiced, too wired. He swung me left, then right, trying to drag me down, but my body would not fold.

"Get down and stay down!"

Another one came in from the side. Then another. Hands clawing, radios crackling, boots scraping on pavement. Three—no, four—cops on me now, they are weight like sandbags. They tried to haul me toward a patrol car, one on each limb, like they were wrangling a bull, but I went spread-eagle, stiff as steel, arms and legs locked, refusing the cage. My bare feet scraped the pavement, glass crunching under my heels.

"Sorry," I growled through gritted teeth. "Try again."

Their faces hardened. I could feel the shift in their grip, the change from control to punishment. A split second later came the blow. Not a punch. Not a kick. Something heavier, like the earth itself swung at me. My face slammed into the concrete with a sick, ringing crack.

For a heartbeat, everything went white. Just white. No sound, no color. Like someone cut the power on reality. Then the noise came rushing back. Sirens screaming somewhere behind me. Tires squealing. Radios spitting static. Boots pounding. Voices shouting. Four, maybe five cops were on top of me now, knees in my ribs, hands on my neck, my arms yanked behind me at angles they were not supposed to bend. I could feel my heart hammering like a drum inside a cage. The acid made their voices echo like ghosts.

They rolled me onto a stretcher. Buckles snapped shut across my chest, thighs, and ankles. Restraints clamped tight until I could not move. I was caught. Then the words started spilling out of my mouth, but they were not mine. Not English. Not Spanish. Something else. Tongues. Syllables stacked on top of each other, wild and heavy, like my mouth belonged to someone else.

"What's your name?" a medic barked. "Where do you live?"

I could not answer. Or maybe I did. I do not know what was coming out of my mouth, only that the sounds I was hearing did not belong to me. Everything blurred, melting like wax. The street tilted and spun. Faces bent over me, their eyes sharp as knives.

The world faded, colors draining out, the sirens thinning to a single, high ringing note. I was not on the pavement anymore. I was not in the ambulance. I was sliding out of myself, slipping into somewhere else.

That was when I drifted away.

I awakened in the dream state like a man surfacing from black water, gasping but silent. My eyes snapped open to nothingness. A dark, black cavern. Stone walls slick with moisture and shadows that twitched and squirmed on their own. The air was heavy and wet, thick like oil, and every breath tasted like ash and copper.

Ahead of me, the ground ended. A wide-open, gaping wound in the earth stretched before me with no edges, no bottom. It was like standing at the mouth of something alive, something breathing. The pit exhaled a heat that was not fire but felt like it was burning my skin anyway, like invisible fingers pressing on my face.

"Where am I?" My own voice sounded small, eaten by the echoes.

I started walking forward, my bare feet scraping on cold rock. The darkness moved. Not just shadows but shapes. Shapes like men but not men, flickering and insubstantial, sliding out of the walls, out of the mist. Shadow creatures, tall and bent, their limbs too long, their heads cocked like vultures. Their eyes were not eyes at all but twin hollows, glowing faintly red, like dying embers.

They swarmed around me in silence first. Then the whispers began. My name, they hissed and stretched. Profanities and vile, obscene gestures were yelled and cried at me. It was like hearing every curse word ever spat in a back alley, every insult whispered in a cell block, all at once.

The cavern was filled with their smoke, a choking fog of burned flesh and iron. They reached for me with black fingers like wet rags, tugging at my clothes, clutching my arms.

"Stop," one rasped.

"No," another hissed.

"Stay with us," they cried, their voices overlapping, some harsh as chains dragging, others soft like a lover's breath.

I tried to pull away, but my body kept moving forward. It was not choice. It was compulsion. The pit called me. A voice without words, deeper than thunder, older than stone. Forward. Forward. Forward. I could not help but move forward. My feet carried me right to the cliff's edge.

I looked down and the world tilted. Blackness. Not just dark, but the absence of everything. Like the night sky without stars, without moon, without air. A black so heavy it felt like it was pulling at me, trying to suck me in.

Deep inside that pit, something stirred. I heard it before I saw it. The scratching, like nails dragged slow across a chalkboard, multiplied a thousand times, echoing up from below. The sound slithered into my skull and vibrated my teeth.

Then came the voice. Not a whisper. Not a shout. A sound like stone grinding on stone, deep and old and furious. It was not human. It was not animal. It was ancient.

The smoke at my feet coiled tighter. The shadows clawed harder. The pit breathed out a cold so sharp it felt like it could cut me open.

Something was climbing. Something huge. Something evil. And I knew, without being told, that whatever was coming up from that darkness had been waiting for me all along.

The voice came first, low and crackling, like a record being played backward. "Is he here?" I heard.

"What?" My own voice cracked like glass. I did not even know who I was talking to. The cavern was darker now, if that was possible. A blackness so dense it had weight, pressing against my skin, making my lungs ache. My breath came out in ragged steam that hung in front of me like smoke signals.

Another voice, sharper and malevolent, slid in right after. "This is what you wanted."

"Huh?" My heart tried to crawl out of my chest. The words echoed around me like gunshots ricocheting in a tunnel.

Then I heard, "We summoned him. He's here now."

My body froze. Literally froze. My legs locked up mid-step. My arms stiffened against my sides. It felt like invisible ropes wrapping around me, cinching tighter until I could not even twitch a finger.

Then I saw it, not with my eyes, but in my mind. A straitjacket, pale and filthy, materializing over my skin. My arms pinned. My chest crushed. I was not just being held. I was being claimed.

The smell hit me next. God, the smell. Not like rot. Worse. Like a campfire built from dead trees and burned flesh, mixed with wet mold and sewer water, left to stew under a summer sun until it turned liquid. It poured into my nostrils, heavy and warm, and sat at the back of my throat like a mouthful of spoiled meat.

I tried to scream, but no sound came. It was like my mouth was wired shut, my throat sealed. I tried to swallow, but even that was stolen from me. I could only shake inside my own skin, my body no longer mine.

"Bring him to me," a new voice commanded. It was huge, bigger than the cavern, bigger than the world. It did not make sound. It vibrated. Like the rumble of a freight train in your bones.

"No," I begged inside my head. "Please. Please. I don't—"

Silence. Then I heard, "Too soon," the voice interrupted, almost like it was laughing.

And then, BOOM.

A flash. A sound like every door in the universe slamming shut at once. My vision filled with white light. The smell of rot was replaced by the antiseptic sting of reality.

I woke up gasping, every nerve in my body screaming like I had been dipped in ice water. My heart hammered. My eyes darted around, wild. The dream, or whatever it was, still clung to me like a wet sheet as I came to.

CHAPTER 22: I SEE YOU

I blink, and the world does not move right. My eyelids feel glued shut, my brain full of fog. The light cuts through like a blade. My throat burns like sandpaper, and there is this high-pitched ringing in my ears, like a bad trip that never ended. When I finally pry my eyes open, everything is wrong. The ceiling above me is a dull, gray tile grid, and something is beeping beside me—steady, mechanical, cold.

I try to move, but my arms feel like they belong to somebody else. Heavy. Numb. A dead weight strapped to this hospital bed. I happen to look out the door and see the words on the wall: "Intensive Care Unit."

My fingers twitch, and I feel plastic. Tubes. Wires. Tape pulling at my skin. Something stuck in my arm. Another thing in my chest. My breath catches fast, and panic sets in before my brain can even find words for it.

What the...? What happened? Where am I?

My mouth is dry as chalk. I try to talk, but it comes out as a whisper, like I am speaking through sand.

A nurse walks in, eyes wide. She freezes, drops her clipboard, then spins and bolts out of the room, yelling for the doctor. I just lie there in confusion, half-conscious, staring at the IV bag dripping its slow poison into my veins. My body feels hollowed out, like something got taken from me.

A few minutes later, but I could not tell exactly how long, the door swings open. A man walks in wearing that doctor face. Calm. Fake sympathy. White coat. Stethoscope hanging like authority around his neck.

"Well, well, well," he says, voice low but smug. "Look who's awake."

His shoes click against the tile as he steps up to my bedside. He looks at me like I am some science project that just started moving again.

"Who's the president, son?"

My mind scrambles. Everything is blurry, a half-memory of news channels and old conversations. "Bush?" I say under my breath.

He raises an eyebrow. "What year is it?"

"Two thousand one?" I say, unsure, voice cracking.

The doctor studied me for a moment, his light moving left to right from one eye to the other. Then his pen stops moving. He sighs, like he has been through this kind of miracle before.

"Alright, son. Do you remember what happened? Why you're here?"

I stared at the wall. My head is pounding like a drum. "No, sir," I say. "I don't know why."

He nods slowly. "I bet you're confused. Anyone would be after what you've been through. See, the thing is, when you came in, you weren't in much shape to explain anything. You were long gone on LSD. And not just that. You had everything in your system that I could think of. And I mean everything, son. LSD, methamphetamine, cocaine, alcohol, God knows what else. You were out there talking to shadows, covered in mud, naked from the waist up with shreds of underwear just hanging on from the waist down. Screaming at the sky like it had answers."

"The EMTs said you tried to fight them off. As well as the police. Told them you were being hunted by demons."

I blink, trying to piece together flashes. Blue lights. Sirens. Somebody shouted my name. Then darkness.

He keeps going, voice steady, like he is reading off a report. "They had to sedate you. You went into cardiac arrest on the way to the hospital. We put you under. Medically induced coma. To save what was left of your brain. It's been a month, son. We didn't know if you'd ever wake up. Or if you did, whether you'd still be... you."

He hands me a stack of papers. Three pages stapled together. "Here," he says. "That's everything we found in your system. Your tox screen."

I stared at it. Names. Numbers. Chemical words I can't even pronounce. Three pages of poison. Written proof that I tried to kill myself without meaning to.

"You're lucky, son," he says, and it sounds like both insult and mercy. "Lucky you're not brain-dead. Lucky you woke up at all. Let's try to make some better choices, shall we?"

I swallow hard. My chest feels heavy. My ribs ache. My throat tightens around the word "lucky."

He turns toward the door. "I'm calling your family. They'll want to know you're awake."

Then he is gone. Just like that. Like I am a box he has checked off his list.

The room goes quiet, except for the steady beep of the monitor and the sound of my own breathing. Slow. Shaky. Mechanical.

I look down at the paper again. My vision is still blurry, but I can make out one word at the top: LSD —positive.

Another line says cocaine — detected. Another says methamphetamines — confirmed.

The list keeps going. I do not even recognize half the chemicals written there.

It's like someone took a piece of my soul, tore it open, and spilled out every bad decision I ever made. I close my eyes. Try to remember something. Anything. But it's all noise—flashes of color, the smell of smoke, a streetlight flickering over wet pavement. Someone laughing. Maybe me. Maybe not. I don't know.

The weight of the world presses down. Guilt, shame, confusion—all boiling up like hot water on the stove. I think of my father. The Rock. The man everyone respected and feared. The one who would tell me I was better than this, even when I never believed him.

If that doctor only knew who my dad was. If he knew where I came from. The man built walls around his pain so thick you could hear the echoes when he spoke. If he only knew what it took to survive this far in life—the fights, the pain, the nights that never ended.

He walked out like he just did me a favor. I stare at the ceiling, heart pounding, trying to process it all.

The clock ticks. The monitor beeps. The world moves on, and I just lie there, half-alive, half-dead, wondering what it's going to take to crawl out of this hole. Because right now, with these tubes, monitors, and a body that doesn't even feel like mine, this paper full of poison in front of me, laying in the ICU—ugh.

Maybe that's the real curse here. Waking up and not knowing if you deserve to.

They say life's about choices, but where I come from, you don't get choices. You get conditions. Born into a house that was more battlefield than home.

My father. The Rock. The name fit him too well. Hard. Cold. Unbreakable on the outside, but sharp enough to cut you just by standing too close. He wasn't a man who talked about love. He talked with fists, with silence, with the sound of a belt sliding through the loops of his jeans.

When I cried, he would say, "Man up. You want to cry? I'll give you something to cry about." When I bled, he said it built character. He said pain was only weakness leaving your body.

I believed him for a long time, until I realized he was just trying to pass down his own poison.

So, I learned early that love hurts, trust kills, and home isn't always safe. I used to dream about running away, but you can't outrun blood. So, I ran to the only thing that felt stronger than fear, and that was the streets.

Out there, the rules were simple.

Money. Respect. Reputation.

You get all three, you live. You lose one, you die.

One thing was certain—I was good at surviving.

Fast learner. Quick with my hands. Even faster on my feet.

Did what I had to do.

The gang, they weren't friends. They were my brothers, forged in brokenness.

Each one of us running from something.

Drugs. Poverty. Abuse. Shame. Fighting different demons. Same darkness.

We didn't talk about pain. We masked it.

We made money. Got high. Threw fists. Acted like kings when really we were just scared little boys pretending the world couldn't touch us.

I told myself the drugs were just business at first.

Then they became my escape.

One line for the pain in my head.

One pill for the echoes of my father's voice.

One bottle for the face of every brother I buried.

Cocaine. Meth. Ketamine. Ecstasy.

The list grew longer as the years passed.

Every time I swore I would stop, I found myself back in it, chasing the same numbness. Because sober meant feeling and feeling meant remembering. And I didn't want to remember.

I remember the night that led to what almost ended.

The room is spinning. Lights fading.

My crew is laughing in the background. Bottles clinking. Bass shaking the floor.

Someone yelled my name. Or maybe it was a warning.

Then silence.

Then darkness.

Next thing I know, I'm waking up in a hospital bed. Tubes in my body. The doctor is tells me it's a miracle that I'm alive.

He shows me a list.

Half the names I can't pronounce.

Half the memories I can't face.

They said I had been out for a month.

A medically induced coma.

Guess that's what it takes to shut a man up who's been running his whole life.

I lay there thinking about my family. How much of a disappointment I am.

How they probably call me weak for ending up here.

How he would say, "You made your bed. Now lie in it."

Maybe watching me self-destruct was the only way he knew how to relate.

Then it hit me harder than a lock in a sock.

I had spent my whole life trying to be tougher than the man who broke me.

And I didn't realize I became him.

CHAPTER 23: SOARING EAGLE

My parents were there to pick me up. No hugs. No smiles. No small talk. Just the sound of the car door slamming shut. The silence between us was thicker than the air outside. You could taste the disappointment, heavy and metallic, like blood.

Nobody said a word the whole ride home. My mom kept her eyes on the road. My dad gripped the wheel like it might run away if he didn't. The radio stayed off. Just the hum of the tires and the faint buzz of tension filling the car.

Days passed. Next thing I knew, I was in front of a judge again. Probation violations. They sent me off to boot camp, a three-month program. Just another part of my sentence, they said. Just another "lesson."

Boot camp was not what I expected. It was discipline and distance. Exactly what I didn't know I needed. No drugs. No crew. No noise from the block. Just dirt, sweat, and rules.

For once, I had structure. And in a strange way, I liked it. I woke up early, did my drills, and stayed focused. I pushed myself harder than I ever had on the outside. Maybe it was the fresh air. Maybe it was the quiet. Or maybe it was just being away from all the chaos.

Out there in the middle of nowhere, I wasn't the drug dealer, the addict, the troublemaker, or the screw-up everyone had given up on. I became a leader. The drill instructors saw something in me, some kind of grit, maybe, or just the hunger to be better than what I was.

Boot camp made me think of my dad. How he wasn't just a father. He was a drill sergeant without the uniform, and he carried that same authority into our house. Every command, every word, every look was like a loaded gun.

He didn't raise his voice for attention. He raised it to dominate, to break you down, to prove he was always in control. At home, it wasn't discipline. It was survival.

Growing up under him, you learned fast. One wrong move and you were getting knocked down, not just emotionally but physically. I didn't just fear him. I defied him.

With that being said, boot camp hit you the same way. Like a freight train, the second you stepped through the gates. Pants too big and baggy. They took your belt.

The air smelled like sweat, gunpowder, and discipline. The first thing you noticed was the uniformed men moving like clockwork, eyes sharp, voices like whips cracking over your head.

You weren't a kid here anymore. You were raw material, and they were building you into a soldier. Rough edges that needed grinding down. And they weren't gentle about it.

Every morning started before dawn. The sun hadn't even cracked the sky when we were shoved out of our bunks. Shoes laced. Uniforms crisp.

The whistle screamed across the yard, echoing off the walls, and you ran like your life depended on it, because in a way, it did.

Push-ups. Sit-ups. Drills. Formations. The physical punishment until you threw up. It was endless. Each repetition a test of endurance and ego.

If you slowed, the trainers pounced, yelling your failures like daggers.

It wasn't just the body they worked. They went after your mind. They broke you down, forcing you to confront laziness, fear, and excuses.

You learned rules fast. You will respect commands. You will follow protocol. Trust no one outside your lane. Sleep was brief. Food was basic. Mistakes had consequences, sometimes public, sometimes personal, always humiliating.

Yet in the midst of all that chaos, there was structure. You could measure your own progress, the sore muscles, the blisters, the moments when you pushed past every limit you thought you had.

For the first time in a long time, you felt capable. Focused. Accountable.

Boot camp was not for the faint-hearted. It chewed up your weaknesses, spit out grit, and forced you to reckon with yourself.

For a kid used to surviving the streets, it was brutal. But in that intensity, you found a strange kind of freedom.

It was a clear lane to prove you could be more than the world told you. More than your past mistakes. More than the broken home you came from.

So, after some time, it felt like the natural extension of my life at home.

I walked into those gates with every bit of anger, every bit of defiance, still simmering from years of living under my father's shadow.

The whistle screamed. The drill instructors barked. And I snapped into attention, not because I respected them, not yet, but because I recognized the pattern.

The yelling. The intimidation. The power.

Boot camp didn't just train bodies. It trained me to take my anger, my defiance, and turn it into focus.

For the first time in my life, I wasn't just surviving my dad's shadow. I was learning how to step out of it.

They let me design a mural for our class wall. I remember the smell of that paint, so sharp and so clean, cutting through the sweat and dust.

I poured everything I had into it. Every mistake I made. Every loss I took. Every apology I never said.

It reshaped me into this:

A soldier of 1st Platoon. The Mighty Eagles.

By the time I was done, that wall told my story without saying a word. I was proud of what I accomplished.

For three months, I was somebody. For three months, I felt peace.

Then, like all good things in my life, it ended.

CHAPTER 24: MONTEBELLO

I got out, and the world kept spinning without me. My family had moved while I was gone. We used to live in K-Land off Fountain and Circle. It was the edge, the outskirts, but that was where everybody knew my name, for better or worse. That was home. My block. My dirt. My ghosts.

Now we were in the Parkside, over on Shenandoah and Capulin. It was just three lights away from my old life, but it might as well have been another planet. Different crowd. Different rhythm. A different kind of danger. K-Land was raw and ghetto, kids with torn sneakers and pocketknives, fighting over pride. Parkside was full of new faces, new drama, new hustlers. People pretending they had it together while still bleeding on the inside. New levels bring different devils.

When I first arrived, I didn't really fit in. My boys were scattered all over town. Salvador was lost in thought, caught up in something heavy. Isaac, too, was still running the streets, I did not even recognize him anymore. Everything I knew had shifted while I was gone.

And me? I was trying to figure out who I was supposed to be now. The old me wanted to go back and chase that rush, to feel alive again. The new me, the one they tried to build in boot camp, wanted to stay clean. Stay focused. Be better.

I learned this one the hard way. The streets do not care about your good intentions. They do not care that you changed. They just wait patiently, silently, knowing that sooner or later, you will come back home, where you will feel like yourself again.

The Streets. You do not see a physical form in robes or horns. He wears asphalt and neon lights, smog and sirens. He whispers promises from every cracked sidewalk, every flickering streetlight. Lust coils around him like smoke from a tire fire. Drugs drip from his fingertips, candy for the desperate, poison for the greedy. Money rains in his presence, but it is never free. It is always soaked in sweat, betrayal, or blood.

He smiles in the faces of everyone who has ever wanted something they should not. Like the glittering windows of corner stores, only what you find there is pills, powder, lust, and cash exchanged freely for you to take. He laughs in the echo of gunfire down empty alleys, in the screams of those who wanted too much too fast. The Streets do not care if you are strong or weak. They do not care if you have a plan, a heart, or a family waiting.

They promise everything: love, power, respect, even fame. The thing is, they even deliver, but it is never clean. Every gift comes wrapped in pain, betrayal, or grief. Every high has a low waiting behind it. Every corner turned secretly into a trap. Sometimes, when you chase him long enough, when you think you have tamed him, he gives you the ultimate gift: a grave. Silent. Cold. Final. The Streets are beauty and death wrapped in one.

The Streets wait patiently, silently, knowing that sooner or later, you will come back home, where you will feel like yourself again.

We moved into this decent house in the Parkside. It was bigger than our old house and nicer too. I was lost on that side of town, and that's where I messed up. I got bored. Then I met the guy next door. He had that same look in his eyes I used to see in the mirror. Empty. Restless. Hungry. Trying to play it cool but ready to burn the world down for a little excitement.

We clicked fast. Talked about music, girls, and money. Before I knew it, we started hanging around again and again. Just to talk. Just to chill. The thing about "just chilling" is that it always leads somewhere. It is how every story like mine starts.

A whole neighborhood away from my past, and I could already feel it catching up. My neighbor, we will just call him B, had this cousin named Red. Red was about my age, but B was a few years older, the type that already carried that calm danger about him. He did not talk much. He did not have to. When he looked at you, it felt like he was reading your soul, checking if you had the stomach for what was coming.

We started chilling heavily, hitting parties every weekend. I was around eighteen or nineteen at the time. Old enough to know better. Young enough not to care. The kind of age where you think you can outrun karma if you move fast enough.

It started with little things. A few grams here, a few there. Then it turned into ounces. Cocaine. Meth. Weed. Whatever the streets wanted, we supplied it.

Money started stacking faster than I could count it. Nights blurred into mornings, and mornings into more deals. That was when I had to reach out to a few old connects. There was Lungs, this guy I had grown up with. He got his name from the way he hit a blunt like he was trying to kill it. Then there was Ray-Ray, a wild one. Always laughing, always loud, but never the one to cross.

They had a five-bedroom spot on the north side, over on Montebello, tucked deep enough that cops did not come sniffing unless someone called them. When I pulled up to their place the first time, I knew this was not small-time anymore.

You could smell the hustle before you even hit the door. Expensive cologne and weed smoke. Empty baggies on the counter. A scale sitting like a crown. Music thumping low. Cash rubber-banded in stacks thick enough to choke a man.

They had been pushing small, some weed, a little powder, nothing major. Just enough to live, not enough to shine. I was no longer about living small. Boot camp had sharpened me, but it had not killed that hunger. I wanted more. I knew how to make it happen. So, I started putting the pieces together, my team.

Lungs, Red, Trey, B, Ray-Ray, and me. That was the lineup. Six of us, each one is good at something. Lungs could move weight quietly, no trail. Ray-Ray had the talk, the kind of mouth that could turn a skeptic into a buyer in sixty seconds. Trey had people and plugs, and he did not blink when things got sideways. B knew the scene, and Red had connections with the younger crowd that wanted to prove themselves.

And me? I was the one pulling strings. The one who saw the whole map while everyone else was focused on the next move.

I was nervous at first. I had always kept my worlds separate, never mixed friends with friends. Too many stories ended badly that way. Somebody always got greedy, jealous, or sloppy. But this time, I broke my own rule, and I did not care.

We met up at Montebello that first night, all six of us. The house smelled like fresh paint and paranoia. Everyone was sizing each other up. Lungs cracked jokes to ease the tension. Ray-Ray poured shots. Trey leaned against the wall, quiet, watching. When the money hit the table and that first big drop landed, it was like the air changed.

We were not kids anymore.

We were businessmen.

Criminals, sure, but with ambition.

I laid it out clean.

"We do this smart. We stay low. Nothing flashy. No bringing heat to the spot. Everybody plays their lane."

Heads nodded.

But deep down, I knew how this life worked. Loyalty lasts until the money gets too big. Trust holds until someone feels left out. Still, in that moment, sitting in that Montebello house with a crew I built from the ground up, surrounded by the smell of dope and ambition, I felt untouchable. We were building an empire, but in reality, we were lighting a fuse.

Trey and I went way back before all this, before the dirt and the deals, before the blood on the money. We used to hit the rave scene hard, chasing lights and bass drops like they could drown out our demons. Back then, we thought we were just living fast. We did not know we were training for something darker.

Trey was always by my side. My right hand. We had been drinking for months, those wild nights that turned into long mornings. His people had the coke plug locked down, solid and steady. No middlemen. Straight fire, straight from Mexico.

Then there was Red, quiet but dangerous, his veins running with meth money from his side of town.

When I look back now, it almost felt magical, the way we all got drawn together, like gravity pulling broken pieces into one orbit.

Different gangs. Different neighborhoods. Different hustles. Same hunger. I took the risk and introduced everyone. Something I swore I would never do, but at that moment, it just felt right.

So, I loaded the car with Trey, Red, B, and me. We rolled up north toward Montebello, to Lung's spot. That house sat at the end of a quiet cul-de-sac, five bedrooms deep, two stories with curtains always half-drawn.

It was clean too, for the kind of dirt we were about to do. The neighbors were military families and retired couples who waved at you when you drove by. Nobody ever suspected that behind that front door, the next small empire was being drawn up.

We sat in the living room, the blinds slanted just enough for the evening light to hit the smoke floating through the air. Everybody offered up what they could bring to the table.

Trey brought coke.

Red brought meth.

Lungs had the weed plug, dirt cheap, steady supply, Colorado green straight from the source.

And me, I had the drive. The plan. The mind for it.

Ray-Ray, depending on who you asked, was sitting off to the side, spinning a lighter between his fingers. He had not been pushing much lately, just coasting. I could see something in his eyes, that hunger, that need to prove himself.

So, I asked him straight up, "Alright, bro. What lane you trying to run? What you bringing in?"

He thought for a minute, looked around the room like he was sizing us all up. Then he said, "Crack."

The room went quiet. You could have heard a dollar drop. I did not expect that one. Not from him. Crack was for the old heads, the kind of hustle that built legends and buried them in the same breath.

Trey raised his brow. Red grinned. Me, I just nodded slow.

"You sure about that?" I asked.

He looked me dead in the eye and said, "Yeah. I know people who still want it. They don't care what year it is. They just want the rock."

No one laughed. No one doubted him. We just looked at each other, all of us, six men, six hustles, and right then, it felt like we were all writing our own street commandments.

We agreed we would start small. A few ounces. Test the waters. Ray-Ray said he could get it off quick, no problem. So, we would buy the coke and make it hard ourselves, kitchen chemistry, old-school style.

The next morning, with the sun barely came up, we were already moving. Pagers beeping. Cars gassed up. We hit the north side and met up with a connect Trey's people vouched for, a heavyset dude with a scar down his jaw and a stare that said he had seen too many people lose their souls to fast money.

He went by Ghost. Ghost did not smile, did not talk much. He was the type who let silence do the business for him. We met in an alley behind a beat-up strip mall, cold wind blowing dust across the cracked pavement. The smell of grease and exhaust hung thick. He opened the trunk of a faded gray Tahoe.

Inside: vacuum-sealed bricks, double-wrapped. The real deal.

Trey looked at me, waiting for the nod. I gave it. We counted out the cash, stacked, banded, and sweated in my hands. It felt like trading a piece of my soul for something I could not stop chasing. Ghost closed the trunk, looked at me for a long second, then said,

"Don't get greedy, kid. This game don't love nobody."

I did not say anything. Just nodded.

We drove back to Montebello, the weight in the trunk heavier than just drugs. It was everything—the risk, the money, the addiction to danger. As the city lights faded behind us, I swear I felt it, that shift.

We were not just hustling anymore.

We were becoming something else.

Something darker.

Something we could not turn off.

I had never actually made crack from coke. This would be my first time. I learned the chemistry, watched hands move like surgeons in a kitchen, saw the glassware and the makeshift burners, smelled the acid and the rubber, but I was not the one running the pot.

We cooked up a couple of batches and handed the finished product off to Ray-Ray. Not everything. We kept most back, a gamble, a way to test him, to see if he could really move weight like he said he could. Maybe a quarter of the load was his to flip. The rest was ours to hold until trust and profits lined up.

You do not know how hungry you are until you taste the money. You do not know what you will do until you do it. So, I cleaned up the rest of my act for a minute. Stopped the nonsense. Stopped bouncing between highs. Because when you want to convince a plug you are reliable, you show up steady. You show up sober. You show up early.

Ghost was the kind of man who made you feel the cold in your bones. He moved slowly, measured, like he was always calculating what the next five years looked like for you, and whether you would fold under pressure. Trey introduced me, vouched for me, and for a second, it felt like I leveled up.

When I called Ghost the next day for the re-up, my palms were sweating so hard the house phone was slick in my grip. I told him I was ready. He sounded surprised, like he had not expected anyone from our side to have the discipline to answer that way.

"That was quick. Meet me," he said.

His house smelled different than Montebello. Less smoke, more paperwork. A place where business was done without music, without jokes. The kid from the block does not fit in places like that, but I sat at his table and stared at the laminate briefly, trying not to let the floor show the way my knees wanted to give.

Ghost slid the price across the table like a dealer sliding a wad, only a pinch thinner than the night before. He cut me a better rate. A discount on trust. A lower number meant he saw something in me, or at least something worth testing.

I paid him cash, feeling the bills pass from my hand into his like a promise. He did not say much.

"Hit me up if you need more. I got you."

Then a nod, and the door closed behind me.

That nod was legit approval in our world. It was a green light to take the rest of the city for as much as we could handle. Back in the car, the product felt warm. My mind was already doing the math. We had the Montebello buyers and, down south, the neighborhood kids hungry for anything with spark.

We moved quick. By midnight I was back at Montebello with my pockets full, and I thought of Ghost's nod earlier. He had tested me, and I had passed.

MISSION COMPLETE.

I went back for more, because you do not let a plug with a good rate think you are a one-hit wonder. You return, you buy bigger, you demonstrate appetite. We picked up again, more cash, more risk, and each pickup felt like stepping a little farther, a little closer to the man who could disappear if the wrong person learned his name.

There were moments in those nights between the drops when the city opened up like a wound. The air tasted like burnt rubber and leftover celebrations. Each exchange left a residue on me. I started sleeping like a man who had stolen peace, half at a time, never whole. Always one eye open.

The enterprise grew because we fed it oxygen: discipline, muscle, variety, and a willingness to lie to ourselves. Lungs kept the green flowing. Trey kept the snow falling. Ray-Ray turned his hustle into cash. B and Red focused on the meth. Me? I stitched the seam together. I negotiated. I bought. I sold. I kept my face calm when people got loud. I learned to read the small things: a hand in a jacket, a cough that meant a phone call was coming, a car idling too long that meant trouble.

By now, we were living life with no jobs and no paychecks. No nine-to-five, no timecards, no bosses. Just product, profit, and paranoia. We slept through the day, moved through the night, hustled like it was religion. Every morning the blinds stayed drawn, the house silent except for the low hum of the fridge and the occasional clink of a scale on the counter.

That Montebello house had its own heartbeat. Each of us was a pulse inside it: Trey, Red, Lungs, Ray-Ray, and me. Five of us living in the same rhythm, breathing the same smoke, dreaming the same dangerous dream.

We did not just hustle. We lived it. We were it. We knew the neighborhood was watching. Retired couples. Military families. The kind of people who call the cops if your grass gets too long. So, we played the part. Every day, at the same time, the same car leaves the driveway. We would roll out at eight in the morning like we had real jobs, disappear into the city, and come back late like men working overtime for the American dream.

If the neighbors looked out their windows, they saw discipline. Routine. They did not see the duffel bags in the trunk. They did not smell the residue on our clothes or notice the small rotation of cars that parked three blocks away and walked up the hill after midnight.

We were the perfect lie. Quiet, polite, and predictable. We did not bring people over. No parties. No visitors. The house was our vault, our temple. We did dirt everywhere except there. If we wanted to celebrate, we drove across town, hit clubs under fake names, and ordered bottles we did not finish. If we crashed, it would be a hard crash. All day. Blackout sleep. Curtains drawn. The house phone is unplugged from the wall.

When we woke, hunger returned. And it always came back.

Six months passed like pressing fast forward on life. Ghost and me? We got tight. Real tight. He stopped being just a plug. He became a mentor, always showing me the game.

Now see, he did not know about Montebello. He did not know the crew except Tre, but I was always going to him solo. We would ride around together in his Tahoe, windows cracked, music low, always talking business. He would point at random buildings and say, "That's money, kid. Just sitting there. Waiting for someone with guts to go get it."

Sometimes we made trips to Vegas, Cali, back and forth like it was nothing. He had connects out there, heavy hitters, people who did not speak unless they were counting, and eyes were always watching. I would sit shotgun, watching the desert blur past, feeling like I was gradually passing missions into another level of the game.

Making sure every note hit right. If a problem came up, we handled it. No fear, no hesitation. Sometimes that meant words. Sometimes that meant fists. And sometimes it meant people got handled.

Ghost used to say, "The streets don't respect words, only results." We lived by that. We were not social workers. We were not playing Robin Hood. We were not saving souls. We were in it to win it, and in our world, winning meant surviving.

The more we made, the colder we got. Money stopped feeling like money. It was just paper, just numbers. But power, that was what hooked us. The control. The speed. The fear in people's eyes when they realized we were not bluffing.

We would sit around the kitchen table at night counting stacks, the sound of rubber bands snapping echoing through the house. That sound was our lullaby. We thought we had time. We thought the world could not touch us.

Ghost always said it best:

"...time's a fuse. You light it the day you start hustling, and every deal, every trip, every lie, every kick door burns it shorter..."

At the time, though, we could not see it. We were alive. We were untouchable. We were kings hiding in plain sight, five men living in a dream made of power and paranoia. We were running out of both.

By the time I met Natalie, I was knee-deep in the life. Natalie was Mexican, the kind of girl whose presence could silence a room without a word. Her skin had that warm, sun-kissed glow, the kind you could stare at and get lost in without realizing it. Long brown hair cascaded down her back like silk, catching the light in soft waves whenever she moved. It framed her face perfectly, a little wild yet gentle, always brushing against her shoulders or falling over her eyes when she laughed.

Her eyes were brown, deep, endless, the kind that made you feel like she could see every secret you thought you hid. They were not sharp or judgmental. They were patient, like a quiet river that understood pain and joy equally. When she looked at you, it was like she was weighing every piece of you—the truth, the lies, the hustle, the broken edges—and still deciding you were worth the time.

No tattoos. No piercings. No flashy distractions. Just her. Simple and dangerous in a quiet way, because she could take your heart and hold it without trying. Natalie was not flashy. She was not loud. She did not need to be. She had this rare kind of beauty and calm confidence that made you want to protect her, impress her, and, if you were lucky, earn the right to be part of her world.

In a life built of chaos, she was the quiet you never realized you were craving. Soft, steady, unforgettable.

Trips to Cali. Money on the table. Phone calls at three in the morning that could not wait. But whenever I had a sliver of free time, I was at her apartment, a small two-bedroom on the west side with lemon-colored walls and the faint smell of vanilla candles. It was the only place I felt like I could breathe without looking over my shoulder.

I would walk in from a run, dust still on my clothes, and she would be waiting on the couch with her legs tucked under her, TV low. Her smile was small, almost shy, but it hit me like a punch every time.

One day, a few days after I came back from California, we celebrated quietly. Me laying out pieces of the story without ever naming the hustle, her listening with those big, curious eyes. She confused me. One minute she said all she wanted was to be happy. The next she was pressed against my shoulder, whispering how she liked the danger in me.

Sometimes she was so sweet it almost hurt. Sometimes she would look up at me from the couch, and I would swear I could make her mine with one sentence. She blushed easily, cheeks red like roses when I teased her. She would call me enough; tell me I was already good enough.

I would laugh, tell her I was just a "cash type," chasing the fast life. She would nod like she understood, even though I knew she did not.

I came from a broken home. A father who raised his hands before his voice. A mother who was protective of me but turned her face instead of fighting back. I never learned how to stay long enough.

Natalie said she understood all that too. Said she could wait a hundred times if she had to. She did not know she had me wrapped around her finger already. But the game had its hooks on me, deep.

I had to play it cool. Always.

My pager buzzed on the coffee table. It's Ghost, I have to call him.

"Yo," I said.

"Bro, we gotta hit Cali. You ready?"

"I stay ready," I told him, and hung up.

I stood, grabbing my hoodie from the back of her chair.

"I gotta get my stuff together," I told her.

She reached for my hand. Her fingers were small and warm. She pressed my knuckles to her lips. "Baby," She said, voice soft but steady, "no matter what you're into, you don't have to say it. Just... be careful and come back to me, please." She kissed my hand again, holding it tight. I looked down into her eyes. They weren't scared, just deep like she could see right through the armor. In that moment, she was the only thing real in my world. No one else I could open up to. No one else I wanted to.

But I couldn't stay. Not yet.

"I got you," I said.

I leaned down, kissed her goodbye. She smelled like jasmine and soap. Then I turned, walked out into the early morning, the cool air hitting my face like a warning. My heart was still in that apartment, but my body was back on the clock. I slid into my car, started the engine. The bass kicked in low.

Bags to pack.

Ghost to meet.

Another run.

As the city blurred past my window, I caught myself thinking...

Me and her? We were a good pair, but me and the street? We were married long before she came around.

I shifted gears and eyes on the road, and drove toward the life I couldn't put down.

CHAPTER 25: THE TASTE OF ME

The road to California felt endless, just a blur of headlights, cigarette smoke, and static-filled radio. Ghost sat behind the wheel, calm and focused, the kind of quiet that made you wonder what he was really thinking. The rental was clean, no plates that screamed attention. His boy from the dealership hooked it up with dealer tags, tinted windows, nothing that would get pulled on the highway. Smart, I thought when he told me. Ghost was always thinking three moves ahead.

Somewhere past Vegas, my eyes got heavy again. I drifted in and out of sleep, my head leaning against the glass, the hum of the tires lulling me into a dream that was neither peaceful nor restful, but rather numb. Every time I cracked my eyes open, the sky had changed from black to gray, then orange and pink bleeding across the horizon. California was waking up.

When I finally came to, the sign read Santa Monica, with the sunlight bouncing off the ocean like a thousand shards of glass. Palms stood tall like soldiers, and the air had that salty bite that only the coast could give. The streets shimmered with life, with joggers, beach bums, the smell of grilled fish, and diesel mixing in the breeze. Expensive cars rolled past, their engines purring, music thumping through tinted glass. Everything looked rich, polished, perfect, but under it all, I could still feel that same grime from back home. Just dres sed up better.

We parked the rental in the garage. They had it open, just waiting on us. Concrete walls echoed every sound. The moment I stepped out, my body felt heavy, like the sleep, the ride, the whole trip had pressed me into the ground. Ghost led the way, the air still smelling faintly of the sea.

We got inside, and the house was spotless. Modern furniture. Big windows looking out toward the coast. His people greeted us like family, hugs here and there, a few nods, a couple of firm handshakes, that unspoken respect of men who live by the same code. They told me I could shower, and I agreed. They guided me in the right direction.

I hit the shower, let the hot water burn the road off my skin. Dinner came easily—beer bottles clinking, laughter cutting through low music. The kind of calm that comes before things get serious. Out there, the ocean crashed against the pier like it had secrets. Inside, we pretended everything was smooth, but I could sense something brewing beneath the surface.

Nothing ever stayed calm for long. Not in this life. Not with Ghost.

We packed up before the sun could even climb in the sky. Ghost said we could not stay long. Business was done, and lingering meant trouble. I tossed my duffel into the trunk, slammed it shut, and felt that familiar itch in my veins. The road was calling.

He tossed me the keys halfway down the hallway and said, "You drive, I'm beat."

By the time we hit the desert, it was close to eleven. The world outside was nothing but black dunes, wind, and stars. The kind of dark that made the highway look endless, like it was swallowing us whole. The headlights carved two thin lines through the dust as night fell, and I kept my foot down, pushing the Dodge to its limit, the engine growling like it had something to prove.

The silence between us was heavy. Only the hum of the tires, the dry rattle of air through the vents. Four or five hours in, somewhere in Nevada, I broke it.

"Where's all the dope, bro? I didn't see anything."

Ghost did not even look up from rolling his joint.

"That's your concern?" he said.

"I'm just saying... we picked up, right?"

He smirked slowly. "We picked up, all right. We're stuffed like a piñata."

I froze.

"Door panels, roof, under the seats, damn near everywhere," he added, exhaling smoke.

"So, chill out, keep your hands steady, and don't drive like you got the devil himself in the trunk."

Too late for that. My foot eased up off the gas, heart started to pound now that I knew we were rolling hot. That was when I saw it, a flash of white and blue off to the shoulder. A state trooper, sitting dead still under a flickering speed sign.

"Ghost," I muttered.

"I see him," he said, leaning forward, eyes narrow.

"What do I do?"

"You ain't stopping. That's what you do."

I stared at him. "You willing to chance that?"

He did not answer with words. Just pulled his snub-nose from his waistband, metal glinting under the dashboard light. That was answer enough. My throat went dry. I gripped the wheel tighter and kept my foot down. The Dodge roared forward, desert wind screaming past us. In the mirror, the red and blue exploded behind us.

"NO WAY!" I shouted.

"Go!" Ghost barked.

I slammed the pedal. The speedometer climbed—ninety, one hundred, one hundred ten. The whole car shook, loose gravel spitting up behind us. The siren's scream started to fade behind the growl of the engine. A hill was coming up fast, a long black rise cutting across the desert.

"What's the plan?" Ghost yelled.

"Hold on," I snapped.

"Hold on!"

We hit the top of the hill, and I could see everything: the valley below, black and endless. I dropped my foot and let gravity take over. The car screamed downhill, engine redlining. The siren and lights disappeared behind the roar of the wind as we descended. At the bottom, I yanked the wheel hard left, off the asphalt, and straight into the dirt. The tires bit into the sand, kicking up clouds thick enough to swallow the headlights.

We were in an open desert now, filled with cactus fields, dry brush, and jagged rocks. The car bounced and screamed, but I did not stop. Finally, I killed the lights and spun out as I slammed the brakes. The engine sputtered once, then went silent. We sat in the dark, lungs burning, hearts banging like drums in our chests. I could still taste the fear in my mouth.

"Don't move," I whispered. "He won't see us."

Ghost did not respond. He was shaking, his pistol still in his hand, finger twitching on the trigger. I lit a cigarette, the tip glowing bright in the dark. It was the only light for miles. Then we saw it—headlights cresting the hill. The trooper. The beam swept across the valley like a lighthouse.

We held our breath. His car slowed, engine whining. He stopped right in front of us for a brief second.

Please keep going, please keep going...

Ghost was whispering it like a prayer. I was saying it too, but only in my head. My whole body felt locked, frozen in that second between life and death, knowing Ghost would use the pistol if need be.

And then, the trooper's lights moved on. He kept driving.

I exhaled, shaky. Ghost dropped the gun and leaned back, eyes wet, face pale. For a man who had seen everything, he looked like a ghost himself. I had never seen him like that—the big-time hustler, the fearless shot-caller—looking small under the weight of what almost was.

The desert swallowed the sound of the cruiser fading away, and in the silence, I realized something. No matter how fast we drove, how much money we made, or how deep we hid, the Streets were still right there, grinning in the dark, waiting to collect.

I still cannot believe that cop kept driving. The sound of the sirens sticks to my bones, that sharp wail cutting through the night like lightning splitting the sky. Every echo felt closer, like the desert itself was breathing heavy, waiting to see who would live and who would not.

We had made it out, somehow, and now we sat there. Still. Silent. Hidden. For hours. Not a word, not a move. The engine was dead, the metal hot from the chase, ticking softly as it cooled. The smell of relief hung in the air, stealing our breath and refusing to leave. The moonlight threw a thin white glow across the sand.

I finally whispered, "We should get behind that rock."

Ghost did not say anything. He just nodded, jaw tight, sweat glistening on his forehead. No lights. No sirens. Nothing but the sound of our own heartbeat.

Two hours passed like that, just waiting, listening, dying inside every second that felt like a lifetime. My nerves were shot. My fingers trembled when I reached for the keys again.

"I'm moving," I finally said.

Ghost flinched like he had been slapped. "What are you doing?"

"Leaving," I said, rolling the car forward, lights still off.

"Leaving?" he said, confused, until he saw what I was doing. I angled the car behind a boulder near the road, the kind of move only someone paranoid enough to live could think of.

"Oh," he said, letting out a breath. "Good idea."

The silence after that was worse than the gunfire. There was no music, no talking, just the desert breathing around us. I could hear the tick of the cooling metal, Ghost's breathing, and my own pulse pounding in my ears. Every distant shadow looked like flashing lights.

Hours passed, and still nothing. No cops. No headlights. No sound. Just emptiness.

Finally, I turned the key again. The Dodge coughed, growled back to life. I took a deep breath, eased back onto the road. The tires hummed softly over the asphalt. I kept it steady this time, lights on, doing the speed limit. The adrenaline had burned out, leaving nothing but hollow silence and exhaustion.

I glanced over at Ghost. He looked wrecked, eyes wide, face pale, sweat dripping down his temples. He was staring out the window like the darkness was whispering to him. His hand still trembled on his knee. The man who had laughed in the face of danger now looked like he had been carved out by fear.

"Breathe," I told him. "We're good."

He did not answer. Did not even blink. Just kept looking out into nothing. Mile after mile, the desert slowly gave way to faint lights on the horizon. The sky started to turn gray with dawn, the air cooling. Each sign we passed took a little weight off my chest.

Hours later, maybe eleven or twelve hours, there it was:

Welcome to Colorado Springs.

The letters glowed under the morning sky, and for the first time all night, I let out a long, shaking breath. My hands were stiff around the wheel. I had been gripping it so hard my knuckles were white.

Ghost finally looked up, eyes red and wet. "We made it," he said.

"Yeah," I replied, staring straight ahead. "But I don't think we ever left."

The truth was, the desert, the chase, the getaway, it was still in us. Still running through our blood. And deep down, I knew the streets never let you go. They just let you drive long enough to think you have escaped.

The closer we got to the Springs, the quieter Ghost became. His mind was not on the road anymore. I could feel it, that heaviness he carried leaking through the silence. He was slouched in the seat, elbow propped on the door, cigarette burning low between his fingers. Every now and then, he would drag hard, exhale slow, like he was trying to breathe something out that kept clawing at him from the inside.

I glanced over. "You good, my boy?"

He did not answer right away. He just stared out the window, jaw tight, smoke rolling past his face like ghosts of bad decisions.

"Yeah," he finally muttered. "Kind of, bro. I'm just thinkin' about my chick, you know?"

The way he said it was low and tiring, and it told me everything. Whatever it was, it was eating him alive.

"She trippin'? About the trip or what's up?" I asked, keeping one hand on the wheel, eyes flicking between the road and his reflection in the glass.

He sighed, rubbed his forehead. "It's this other chick, bro. She's messin' everything up. My girl's pissed. She won't leave me alone. I'm caught up in some dumb drama, and it's killin' me!"

I laughed under my breath. "Man, ain't that always the problem? Always a female, bro. Always."

But he did not laugh. He turned toward me, eyes serious. "Nah, for real, bro. I need your help."

"Talk to me, brother."

He leaned back, staring at the roof. "I need you to take this girl off my hands. For real. She's bad news. She won't stop callin', won't stop comin' by my crib. I can't go back to my girl like this. It's too much heat... for real."

"Off your hands? Who is she?" I asked.

"Her name's Felicia," he said, shaking his head. "She's cool, but she's gone crazy over me. Keeps paging me, showin' up uninvited. At first, I was just sellin' to her, you know? But then one night, we hooked up... and now she thinks we're something."

He rubbed his face again, frustrated. "I ain't gonna lie, I messed up. It was when my girl and I broke up, but now that she knows what I do, she won't leave me alone. She's pullin' up to my house, startin' fights. My girl almost threw hands with her twice already. I can't live like this."

The air inside the car got thick. The road stretched on, miles of nothing but headlights and quiet breathing. I looked at him, shook my head slowly. "Bro, if she's already sprung like that, that's gonna be a mission."

He cut me off, eyes wild, voice sharp. "Nah, you got this. I know you can handle it."

I stared at him, the desperation in his tone throwing me off. Ghost was not the type to ask for help, not like this.

"All right," I said finally, nodding. "All right, bro. I got you."

He relaxed, barely, leaning back in the seat like he had just put a mountain down. We rolled into the Springs with that unspoken tension between us, two men who had been through hell and back, but still could not outrun the drama the streets always threw at us.

"Let's hit the Montebello house," I said. "We'll unload, get settled. I'll introduce you to some of the people, show you what we got goin' on."

He nodded, a slow smirk crawling onto his face again, like he was trying to shake the weight of it off. As we turned off the highway, the city lights rising up in front of us, I could not shake that feeling. The kind that creeps up before something goes bad. The kind that whispers this is not over. Because in the game we played, women were not just temptation, they were landmines. Ghost had already stepped on one.

We pulled into a gas station just outside of town, the heat from the drive still clinging to our skin. I filled the tank while Ghost leaned on the hood. He went to use the pay phone, low voice trying to calm whatever storm he had left behind. I heard him give her the address to the Montebello house, told her we would be there soon, that everything was cool. His tone said otherwise.

We got back on the road. Afternoon light was bleeding gold across the sky when the street signs for Montebello came up. It was around nine-thirty or ten in the morning. We were fresh off the California trip, all tired, dirty, and restless. I was beat, ready to drop everything off and breathe for a second. Let me tell you, peace never lasts.

As we rounded the last corner, I saw them before the car even stopped. Two women in the front yard, hair flying, voices tearing through the quiet block. Felicia and Ghost's girl, face-to-face at the doorway, screaming names that would burn paint off a wall. Cuss words, threats, tears—the whole neighborhood watching from behind blinds.

Ghost jumped out before I could even park. He ran up, shouting, trying to pull his girl off Felicia, but the two of them were locked in—wild, clawing, pure rage. He finally grabbed his girl, dragged her inside, yelling for me to handle it.

"Here you go, bro," he said, breathing hard. "This your chance."

Felicia turned on me, still screaming, eyes red and glassy. Before she could swing, I stepped forward, wrapped my arms around her waist, and lifted her clean off the ground. She kicked and thrashed, fists slamming into my back.

"Let me go! Put me down!" she screamed, her voice cracking.

"Listen," I said, breath tight, trying to keep my calm. "We can't be doin' that here. Not this house. You hear me? You're gonna get the cops called. You need to chill."

She kept fighting, tears streaking her makeup, until I got her to the curb. "That your black car?" I asked, pointing.

She nodded between gasps. "Why?"

I opened the door and guided her in. I knew it was hers. Her hand was still on her shoulder. She was shaking, angry, and embarrassed, fixing her hair, brushing dirt off her jeans.

"Just stay here, all right? Cool off," I said, my voice low, steady. "You keep goin' like this, someone's callin' the police. Nobody needs that."

She did not say a word, just looked at herself in the side mirror, adjusting her top, trying to pull herself together.

I walked back toward the house, but Ghost's girl was inside now, yelling from the doorway, saying she followed her here, that he left his truck back at her place. It was chaos. I could hear Ghost's voice trying to calm her down, but it was useless.

So, I turned back to Felicia's car. She was still there, eyes dark, chest rising and falling fast. I walked back to the car and opened the passenger door.

"Come on," I said quietly. "Let's take a drive. Get you outta here for a bit."

She hesitated, then nodded. "Where we goin'?"

"Somewhere chill. You smoke?"

"Yeah," she said, staring out the windshield. "I need somethin' to take this edge off."

We drove south, the streets blurring by the tension fading just enough to breathe again. She started talking quickly about everything that had happened, sharing her side of the story. Different from Ghost's version. Way different. But I let her talk. I was not here to take sides. I was just keeping the peace.

When she finished, she sighed. "You got somethin'? Anything?"

I nodded. "Yeah, I got some stuff on me. We can stop somewhere, chill out."

She agreed, rubbing her arms and eyes red but softer now.

We pulled up at her friend's house, a small single-story spot on the south side. Screen door hanging crooked, paint peeling, smell of beer and smoke leaking out. She went in first, came back out, then waved me inside.

Inside, it was dim. Shades drawn, fan buzzing, a few people lounging on a sagging couch. I handed them a little something, and within minutes, they were ready, lighting up, chasing the high. I rolled up a blunt while someone passed me a Corona.

Felicia sat across from me, legs crossed, watching me through the haze.

CHAPTER 26: 6.5.4

Some time passed, and now I was on the run, ducking the law everywhere I went. Missing court for driving with no license. Catching shadows instead of rest. Months went by like smoke. Felicia was now two or three months pregnant. Every time I closed my eyes, I saw her belly starting to round, getting bigger, and it hit me hard. That was my child in there. My daughter. My blood.

I knew right then I could not keep running forever. I had to make a choice: man up or die hiding. I told myself that if I ever wanted to be part of my daughter's life, I had to face this head-on; otherwise, it would only get worse. I had accumulated four driving without a license tickets in a month. They rolled all the cases into one, and I missed it. The judge was already mad, but now he was going to be furious.

So, I decided. I was turning myself in. Doing my time like a man. Maybe, just maybe, I would make it out in time to hold her when she was born.

The night before, the crew threw me a little sendoff. Smoke thick in the air, bottles clinking, laughter trying to drown out the silence sitting in the back of my head. Everybody pretended it was all good, but I knew tomorrow was not a party. Tomorrow was the reckoning.

When morning came, I got up slowly, the weight of it all pressing down on my chest. I moved through the motions—shower, clothes, shoes—same as always. But when I looked in the mirror, I did not see the same man. I saw a version of me stripped down. Tired. Scarred. Uncertain of the future, but ready. Ready to stop running.

My mind drifted back to everything—the streets, the fights, the pain. To Natalie. I had never even called her after I came back from Cali. I wondered if she still thought about me, or if she had learned to forget, like I had. I had been used, abused, recycled, and put back on the shelf for resale too many times to count. This time it felt different. I had something to lose now.

When I pulled up to Felicia's, she was glowing, that kind of glow only a woman carrying life can have. She was beautiful in a way I had never noticed before. I told her I was turning myself in, and the tears started rolling before I could even finish the sentence. She grabbed my hands and said, "No matter what happens, you don't know what you mean to me." That broke me a little inside.

I told her, "You can always count on me being there for our daughter. No matter where I'm at." Then I wiped her tears away, trying not to let her see my own. At first, she and I felt forced, like I was just doing the right thing, doing what Ghost would expect of me. But somewhere along the line, something shifted. It stopped being an obligation. It started feeling real.

When I found out she was pregnant, I thought I had to pretend to be in love. But looking at her that day, standing there with our unborn child, I realized that somewhere between the lies, the chaos, and the running, I had become what I was pretending to be.

Felicia's eyes were already red when I told her. She tried to hold it in, but her lips trembled. "Gabriel," she said, her voice cracking like glass, "I do love you. All I think about is you. I know we never took nothin' slow... but just come back to me. Come back to me and our baby."

Those words hit harder than any bullet. I could feel the pain in her voice, heavy, desperate, shaking. She looked like she wanted to fight fate itself just to keep me there one more day. But I was tired. Not the kind of tired that sleep fixes. No, the kind that sinks into your bones. The kind that makes you want to stop running from yourself.

"I'm just sick and tired of worrying," I told her, staring at the floor because I could not face her eyes. "I need to get this done. I can't live like this anymore. Once it's over, I'll be able to breathe again. I gotta do this... for me and for our baby."

The silence between us was louder than any siren I had heard in months. Then I reached out, brushed my hand along her cheek, and kissed her slow, like I was trying to remember the taste for later. When I pulled back, she covered her face with both hands, hiding her tears, but I could still hear them breaking through her fingers. She turned away before I did, as if maybe if she didn't see me leave, it wouldn't be real.

I stood there for a second, just watching her. Her small frame trembling, the soft light from the window outlining her silhouette. My chest felt hollow, but my decision was made.

I walked out the door without looking back. Outside, the air was cold and dry. The streets were quiet, like even the world knew something was ending. I slid into the driver's seat, turned the key, and just sat there with my hands on the wheel, staring out into nothing.

Then I drove. The tires hummed against the cracked asphalt as I made my way to my parents' house. The city passed by like memories once lived—blurred streetlights, boarded-up corners, every block reminding me of something I had done or someone I had lost.

It was early morning, one of those mornings where the sky looks bruised, heavy with thunder. The wipers struggled to keep up, smearing the water across the glass like tears. When I stepped out, the smell of wet dirt and asphalt filled the air. I could see the light on in the front window, same as always when they were waiting on me.

Inside, my mom was sitting at the kitchen table, her hands wrapped around a cup of cold coffee. My dad stood behind her, quiet, arms crossed, eyes hard but tired. They did not yell. They did not even look surprised. The warmth inside hit me with the smell of coffee, old furniture, and the life I once knew. It felt strange. The house was clean, and the house was still.

I looked around and thought this might be the last normal moment I would have had for a while. When I finally sat down, head in my hands, I was not thinking about the time I was about to serve. I was thinking about Felicia's tears, and the tiny heartbeat inside her that I would one day call my daughter.

They said they would take me down to CJC themselves. They already knew everything. They knew Felicia was pregnant. They knew I had been out there selling. They knew I was running from the law. They knew everything.

I sat down across from them. The clock ticked loud, like each second was a countdown to something I could not stop. My mom finally spoke, her voice trembling slightly.

"Boy, we can't change what's done," she said. "But you can change what's next."

My dad just nodded, slowly. "You're doing the right thing, son."

However, the truth was that I did not feel like I was doing the right thing. I felt like I was walking into my own grave.

The ride to CJC was silent. The rain hit the windshield so hard it sounded like static. My thoughts were louder than the storm. Every red light felt like a chance to turn back, every corner a fork in the road between freedom and responsibility.

Maybe I should just dip, I thought. Maybe just one more run, one more hustle, one more bag. But deep down, I knew that "one more" never ends.

My mom reached over and put her hand on my arm. "You're doing the right thing," she whispered.

I nodded, but I could not speak. My throat was dry, my chest tight.

When we pulled up to the El Paso County Criminal Justice Center, the lights from the building glared through the rain. Harsh. White. Sterile. I stepped out into the downpour, water soaking through my hoodie, my jeans heavy. The smell of wet concrete and diesel filled my nose.

That was when it hit me. This was real. No turning back.

I walked inside, dripping, and told the deputy my name. He did not flinch. He ran my name and nodded, more with acceptance than judgment. Just nodded and said, "Have a seat, an officer will be right out."

Then I saw him. The cop.

He came out of the glass doors slowly, calmly, like he had been expecting me all along. His badge caught the glow from the lights above, reflecting it right into my eyes. He had that look—not mean, not kind, just official and proud. The look of a man who had seen too many young fools like me walk right into their own endings. His hand rested lazily on his belt, but his eyes... his eyes were sharp. Scanning me. Sizing me up. He did not even need to ask my name. He knew.

I swallowed hard. My feet felt like cement. My mind flashed through everything: Felicia's tears, my unborn daughter, the streets, the nights I terrorized the city. It all hit me at once.

"You, Gabriel Hinojosa?" he asked, voice steady.

I nodded. "Yep, I am."

He nodded back, subtle, almost respectful. "You ready?"

That word—ready—cut deep. Was I?

I took one last look at the morning sky, dark and soaked and endless. The streets behind me, but at the same time, the same ones that raised me, broke me, and bled me. They were quiet now.

"Yeah," I finally said, voice low. "I'm ready."

He stepped closer. I could smell the leather of his gloves. The metallic click of the cuffs was louder than thunder in my ears. He turned me around, cold steel against my wrists...

...and just like that, it was over.

Cold cuffs wrapped around my wrists. The sound of metal locking shut echoed in my head. I could feel my pulse thumping against the steel. I knew I was facing time. I did not know how much, and I no longer cared. I just wanted to stop running.

When the time came and I finally stood before the judge, he looked me over like he had seen a thousand versions of me before. He did not see a monster. He saw just another lost kid.

"Nine months," he said, flat and final.

That was it. No drama. No emotion. Just a number and a gavel.

That was not bad. I thought it would be worse. Come to find out, I would get good time too. I had been arrested plenty of times—in and out, in and out.

Inside, it was different. CJC had its own heartbeat—cold and full of regret. The moment the doors slammed behind me, the world shifted. The air was thick, not just with sweat, but with desperation, fear, and the chemical haze of whatever people had managed to sneak in. Every breath smelled hot and sour. Every sound was amplified keys rattling, shouts echoing off concrete, the slap of shoes on cold floors.

The people around me were a mix of anger, madness, and survival. Some paced the cells, eyes darting, muttering to themselves like they were keeping secrets only they could understand. Others leaned against the walls, staring blankly, lost somewhere deep inside their own heads. There were fights over nothing—over air, over space, over pride. When someone snapped, the chaos came fast with punches, screams, the smell of blood mingling with the stench of unwashed bodies.

Drugs were everywhere—whispered deals, hidden packets, eyes rolling back from what I hoped was oblivion. Everyone had a story, and most were looking to erase theirs. Cigarettes and dip were currency. Weed was currency. Pills were currency. All traded for food, commissaries, and soups.

Mental states ranged from numb to explosive. Some men laughed at nothing, bouncing off the walls, while others sat in corners rocking back and forth, muttering prayers no one could hear. Fear was constant. Anger was constant. The walls absorbed it all and threw it back louder, harder, like a warning.

I learned quickly: stay quiet, watch, protect your head, and don't get caught slipping. Every glance could be a challenge. Every conversation could be a setup. Every smile could be a lie.

Through it all, the clock did not move for anyone. Minutes stretched like hours, days blended into nights, and you counted everything time, mistakes, and losses because that was all you had. Jail did not just take freedom. It took your rhythm, your patience, your soul. And if you let it, it reshaped you. Some men left broken. Some men left hardened. Some never left at all.

The floors smelled like bleach, the walls like sweat and disappointment. Nights were long, mornings came early. I started working in the kitchen cutting, cleaning, serving trays to faces that all looked like mine in some way: tired, hungry, searching for something. I stayed out of the mix for the most part. Stayed focused.

Time moved slowly inside, but Felicia kept me alive in there. Her letters came every few weeks, her handwriting neat but shaky, like she was fighting back tears with every word. She told me how the baby was growing, how she could feel her kick, how she wished I was there to see it.

Sometimes she came to visit, belly round, glowing under those harsh fluorescent lights. I would watch her walk through the visiting room, her face lighting up when she saw me, and for a second the fences, the guards, all of it disappeared. It was just her and me, talking through glass, dreaming about a future that did not feel real yet.

We already knew it was a girl. She told me she had been thinking of names.

"I like the name Nevaeh," she said, smiling. "N-E-V-A-E-H—heaven spelled backwards."

I thought about that name for days, even wrote it on paper over and over until it started to feel like it belonged to me, to us. When she told me she wanted me to pick the middle name, I sat up all night on my bunk, thinking. I wanted something that sounded soft but strong, like her.

Then it came to me:

Nevaeh Alisianna Hinojosa.

It was perfect. Just like she would be. It sounded like hope. Like a new beginning.

It was strange, but that place, that cell, those routines became a kind of peace. For the first time in years, I was not looking over my shoulder. I was not hustling. I was not running. I was thinking. I started to see things different. Started asking myself questions I had never had time to ask out there. Who I was. Who I wanted to be when I got out.

With that, the nine months went to six with good time. Those six months did not break me. They helped me. Piece by piece.

When I walked out, the world felt new. So did I. I felt like I was walking out of a fog. The air hit different—lighter, sharper, cleaner. I remember walking straight to Felicia's mom's house, heart pounding like a drum. When I showed up, everyone froze. Eyes wide, jaws dropping. I did not even have to say a word. Felicia screamed when she saw me, ran straight into my arms, belly and all.

That night, we partied not with Felicia, but with her three sisters, countless cousins, and friends, everyone who came around as if nothing else mattered. Bottles popping, smoke thick in the air, music loud enough to drown out all the noise inside my head. I was free, alive, and back where I belonged.

A few days passed. Felicia's belly looked stretched to the max, skintight and glowing under the low light. She moved slowly, one hand on her back, wincing every few steps.

I cannot remember exactly where we were, maybe near the park, maybe at her house, maybe in the car. I do not know. But I will never forget the sound. Felicia gasped, froze, and then whoosh. Her water broke, running down her legs, soaking the ground beneath her.

We rushed to the hospital, hearts racing, only for the doctor to tell us it was a false alarm. "Walk," he said. "Keep her moving. Help her dilate." So, we left, walking the block, rain misting the air, the streetlights bouncing off the wet pavement. I held her hand, steadying her every few steps. We laughed, cursed, and prayed all at once.

The next morning, it happened for real.

She grabbed my arm, breathing fast. "Gabriel," she said, voice trembling, "it's time."

And it was.

We jumped in the car, flying down the road like the world was ending. Every red light turned green just for us, my heart thumping so hard I could feel it in my ears. When we hit the hospital, everything turned into chaos. Nurses rushing, doctors barking orders, the air is thick with tension. Felicia was screaming, clutching my hand so tight it felt like bone on bone.

The doctor's face went pale as he checked her. "She's past dilated," he muttered, then louder, "We need to get this baby out—NOW!"

He called for a gurney, his voice breaking the calm like a siren. "Emergency C-section!" he shouted. It all blurred together—alarms, footsteps, Felicia crying out, the cold swing of double doors. I tried to follow, but a nurse held me back. "You can't come in, sir! Not yet!"

I stood there, frozen, watching the doors close. My reflection stared back at me in the little glass window. I felt helpless, scared, and praying under my breath. All I could hear was the sound of machines, voices yelling orders, and my own heartbeat pounding in my ears.

Minutes felt like hours. Then silence.

I pressed my forehead against the wall, whispering her name. Please, God, not like this. Everything was happening too fast.

One second, the nurse was telling me to suit up, and the next thing I knew, the whole room was a storm. My hands were shaking so badly that I couldn't get the scrubs on right—strings tangled, sleeves backward, mask half on. My heart was racing like I was back on the block, running from sirens.

Inside that room, it was not just noise. It was panic wearing a white coat. The doctor's voice cut through the air. "We need to move faster!"

I had never heard fear in a doctor's voice before.

When I finally got inside, the smell of antiseptic hit me like a wall. Bright lights burned down from every direction, turning the room into a stage where life and death were fighting for the same spotlight. Felicia was on the table, her body trembling, reacting to things neither of us could control. The machines were beeping faster and faster, and I swear the sound drilled straight through my chest.

"Felicia!" I called out, my voice breaking. "You don't feel that?"

She turned her head toward me, her eyes wide and glassy. I did not know what to say. I was standing there in a place where no street rules applied, no quick fix could help. I just reached for her hand, cold and trembling, and held it tight.

The doctors moved around us in a blur, talking fast, metal clattering, footsteps shuffling. I could not see everything, but I saw enough to know it was not good. The sheet was high, blocking her view, but I could see past it. Just flashes of motion, gloves, instruments, and tension that filled the air like smoke before a fire.

"Stay with me, stay with me," I said, my voice low, trying to sound strong even though my insides were unraveling. She looked up at me, eyes full of fear, and whispered, "Don't let go."

I didn't. Not once.

In that moment, all the noise faded. It was just her hand in mine, her breath shallow, and my heart praying harder than it ever had in its life. I looked at the doctor, then back at her, then at the doctor again. Back and forth. Back and forth. If I stopped watching either one of them, I would lose both.

And then, for a split second, the world went quiet. No sound. No motion. Just the stillness before something changes forever.

The panic came at me in a rush. The baby's heart was pounding out of rhythm, too fast, too faint. "If it drops again, we lose her," one of the nurses snapped, and that line hit me harder than any cell door ever did.

I was shaking, fumbling with the scrubs like a rookie on his first day out. The ties would not knot, the sleeves twisted up, and my fingers felt like they belonged to someone else. My heart was sprinting, and my mind was on fire, flashing every worst case I could think of.

"Think faster," the doctor barked, eyes sharp behind his fogged-up goggles. His tone was not asking. It was begging the universe to cooperate.

I stumbled toward Felicia, and the air hit me. It smelled like cold steel and panic. She was still not. Her body was trembling in a way that did not look human. She was losing color, her lips fading like the last bit of sunset over a cracked street. The monitors screamed. Nurses rushed around her, voices clipped, movements mechanical. Nobody was breathing right.

"Felicia," I said, trying to sound calm, but my voice cracked halfway through. "You don't feel that?"

She looked at me, her eyes wide, lost, and for a second, it was as if she were underwater, seeing me through glass. "No," she said. "What's going on? Am I okay?"

Her voice shook. I could hear the fear, and it ripped through me. Her hand was in mine, slick and cold. I squeezed harder, trying to keep her here, trying to give her something real to hold onto.

The doctor looked up for a split second, his eyes darting to me, then back down. I could read everything in that look. It was bad. Real bad. I did not need words.

The beeping started to slow, stretch out, and echo. Every sound felt heavier than the last. I whispered her name again, softer this time, as if saying it might bring her back to me, to the world, to our baby, the one we already named, the one that was fighting to breathe.

For a second, time folded in on itself. It was just me, her, and that fragile heartbeat echoing through the room, the sound of life trying to survive in the middle of a storm.

Every second was a gamble. Then...

"Sir," the doctor said, his voice steady but edged with panic. "The umbilical cord is wrapped severely. We are running out of time. You have to choose between your baby and the baby's mother.

Please tell me. **Time is of the essence**."

For a second, everything stopped. The buzzing machines, the nurses shouting orders, it all faded. The words hit me like a stray bullet straight to the chest.

CHOOSE?

I just stared at him. I did not even blink. My mouth opened, but nothing came out. My mind was blank and loud at the same time, like static, like the inside of a hurricane. I looked at Felicia. Her face was pale, wet with sweat, her hair stuck to her forehead. She was trying to talk, her body convulsing. The sheet was still up, and all I could see were her eyes, wide, scared, searching for me. My heart broke open right there.

"I... I can't..." I choked out, my throat locked up.

The doctor stepped closer. "We don't have time," he said, almost yelling now. "I need an answer!"

And that was when it hit me. I dropped my head into my hands. My fingers dug into my skin, my palms wet with tears before I even realized I was crying. My shoulders shook, hard, like something inside me was collapsing. I hit my face with my hands again and again, like I was trying to wake up from this nightmare. My breath turned into gasps, sharp and ugly. My knees gave out, and I dropped right there on the tile floor. Cold. Hard. Tile. I could taste salt and sweat. My tears fell fast, hitting the floor like rain. I was shaking, whispering prayers that no longer sounded like prayers, just broken pieces of words.

I heard the doctor calling my name, but it was far away. Everything was spinning. The smell of antiseptic, the sound of heart monitors, the hum of lights overhead. I was stuck in this moment; torn between the woman I loved and the life we made together. Right then, I swear it felt like the whole world was watching me crumble, waiting for me to decide which piece of my soul I was willing to live without. On my knees. I could not make a decision. How could I? Who would I choose?

PAUSE

Let's stop right here. Think about it. They wanted me to choose between the woman I love and the daughter I had not even held yet. Between the heartbeat that was fading and the one that was just beginning. Choose? Seriously?

Tell me, what would you do? Could you pick? Could you stand there, hearing monitors scream and nurses yelling and blood soaking through the sheets, and actually make that call? Would you save the one new to this world, a new life, or the one who helped create it?

It sounds simple when it is someone else's story, doesn't it? But when it is you, when it is your life on that tile floor, when the air feels thick with decisions and the smell of metal, fear, and blood, all of a sudden time does not move right. You cannot think straight. You just shake, and you break, and the only sound that comes out is a prayer that does not even sound like one.

Could you do it? On the drop of a dime? No time to think, no time to breathe, just pick one and live with it forever. Makes you think, doesn't it?

UNPAUSE

The noise came back all at once. The beeping, the shouting, the clatter of metal trays. My head was still bowed, but I heard chaos spinning around me. I felt the floor vibrating under my palms. My breath was ragged, my throat dry. I could hear it: the panic, desperation. I wanted to scream, to fight, to take her pain, but I was frozen. My body would not move. My heart was a war drum, slamming in my chest, and all I could do was whisper His name. God... please...

The room spun, bright white lights flickering like lightning. The smell of iron, blood, and bleach filled the air, heavy enough to taste. I lifted my head, and what I saw next changed me forever.

My chest felt like it was splitting open, heart breaking, full of everything I had carried all these years, all at once. The chaos, the running, the fear all stopped.

And then... silence. Complete, deafening silence.

And through it, I heard it. A baby crying.

I pulled my head up, gasping, and the world rushed back. Doctors shouting, machines beeping, the smell of antiseptic and sweat thick in the air. A nurse grabbed Felicia, saying, "We need to move her to the ER immediately!" and suddenly it was all motion, all panic again. But in the middle of it, I locked eyes with her.

They had made the decision for me.

I stood up, and she reached out. One hand, trembling, almost touching me, like she was begging me to stay, to hold on, to be there. I stretched my arms toward her, palms open, feeling her desperate need for me, and in that moment, it hit me. My daughter was here.

"Oh my God," I whispered to only myself. "My daughter... she's here..."

A doctor handed me the scissors. The umbilical cord had already been cut from Felicia, but he wanted me to do it to mark this moment. My hands were shaking, but I took them, and I did it. Careful. Deliberate. And then… they handed her to me.

Nevaeh Alisianna Hinojosa.

My baby girl was born June 5, 2004, at 4:20 a.m. She was eight pounds, three ounces of pure perfection. She was so beautiful. My heart skipped a beat the moment I laid eyes on her. Her skin was soft, warm, and alive. She fit into my arms like she was always meant to, like every scar, every mistake, every fight I had ever had had led me to hold this tiny human being in my hands.

She was quiet now, swallowing, snug against me, and I could not breathe fast enough. She was mine. She was part of me. I was part of her. I looked down at her, and something inside me shattered and rebuilt at the same time.

I will never forget her tiny fists curling, the way her eyes fluttered open, the little rise and fall of her chest. This moment is eternal. My daughter. My Nevaeh. My perfect baby girl.

I will protect her, love her, and carry this moment in me forever. Every street I walked, every run I made, every mistake—it all ended here, in the quiet heartbeat of my child, in my arms.

CHAPTER 27: FAMILY AFFAIR

Have you ever danced with the devil under the pale moonlight? Well, I have, and I have got some great advice for you. Listen up. Hear this. Do not miss it. Do not ever dance with the devil, because that dance might last forever, and you will not even know it until it is too late.

Felicia pulled through. She did not die. She came out of that surgery sore, stitched, but alive, and for a while that was enough to make me believe everything was going to be okay. She healed quick, smiled a little, held the baby like she had been born to do it. I swear to you, I loved that woman with everything I had in me. My heart, my soul, my breath. All of it.

Let me say this now, loud and clear. The Felicia that came home from that hospital was not the same Felicia I fell in love with. Whoever they released from that ER, she had the same face, the same voice, but her spirit, her heart, was gone. Cold. Something inside her had flipped. She looked at me like I was a stranger who had overstayed his welcome. Her words cut different now—sharp, mean, meant to bruise. She did not just stop loving me. She started hating me, and I could not tell you why.

I tried, man. I tried hard. Got me a job doing landscaping, busting my back under the sun, hands raw, skin burnt, sweat dripping into my eyes. I was trying to build something for us, a life, stability, whatever you want to call it. But no matter what I did, I was wrong. Always. End of story.

Day in, day out, it was arguments. About money. About time. About nothing. Every word turned into a fight. Every silence turned into distance. And when I looked at her—really looked at her—I could see it in her eyes. She was done with me long before she ever said it out loud. It was like she was trying to push me out, testing how far I would go before I finally broke.

Do not get me wrong, we had moments. Tiny ones, but they were moments. Maybe five percent of the time we would laugh, maybe touch, maybe remember what love used to feel like. Five percent of one hundred does not keep a family together.

Now, remember I told you Felicia had sisters? Yeah, well... that is where things start to twist. This may hurt your brain, so take it slow. Let me break this down for you real quick, because this part right here is important if you are going to understand the chaos that came after.

Felicia had three sisters: Amber, Pearl, and Candace. Trust me when I say, every single one of them had their own flavor of drama.

I met this dude named Paul. Solid guy. He was younger, but cool, the kind that knew the streets but still had a little bit of heart left. Over time, he became like my brother. Real talk, blood could not have made us tighter.

Paul got with Amber, Felicia's sister. So yeah, that made him kind of my brother-in-law.

Now Paul had a brother named Luke. Luke was slick, a smooth talker, always running game like he was born for it. He got with Candace, the other sister. Candace had this best friend named Carol, and Luke, being who he was, could not keep it zipped up. He ended up with Carol too.

Then there was Pearl, the wild one. No shame in her walk, no fear in her tone. She would flirt with the wind if it whistled right. Promiscuous, yeah, that is the polite word for it. Eventually, she settled down with a dude named John. Shocking, I know.

Now here is where it gets sideways. Carol—the same Carol Luke slid in with after Candace—had a mom named Stephanie. And Stephanie? She started seeing Beatrice, who just so happened to be Felicia's mom. You following?

So now we had:

- Me and Felicia had a baby.
- Paul and Amber had a baby.
- Luke and Candace had a baby.
- Luke and Carol had a baby.
- John and Pearl did not have a baby.

And if Stephanie and Beatrice could have, they would have. Given the fact they were together, it probably would not work. Did not stop them from trying though.

That is what it turned into—one big, tangled-up, love-drunk, backstabbing, chaotic mess living in a trailer park with a double wide. It was like everyone was connected somehow through blood, lust, or both. Thanksgiving dinners? Forget it. Family functions felt more like parole check-ins. You never knew who would show up angry, high, pregnant, or heartbroken.

Okay, that was a lot. Do not get frustrated. I know that was a lot, but that genealogy is important. Then I had my boy Aiden living directly across the street. He drove a blue '92 Chevy Camaro RS drop top. He would come close, kick it with all of us, and start talking to Candace. With all that being said, it was Paul, Aiden, and myself. Hell, the Three Amigos with no direction, chasing noise instead of purpose.

We worked all week, sun-up to sun-down labor, sweat, dirt under the nails. But come Friday? We turned all that exhaustion into chaos. I still sold drugs on the side—that never stopped—but I actually had a real nine-to-five. Around that time, I was about twenty-three, twenty-four. Still young, still stupid, still full of fire and liquor.

The sisters—Felicia, Amber, Pearl, and Candace—they would always find something to argue about. Maybe it was on purpose, maybe they just wanted to be left alone so they could do them. But now that I look back on it, we were not couples. Nah. They were not our girls anymore. Never were. They were just our baby mamas. The love had turned into obligation, and the obligation into noise.

So, we made our own escape: keg parties. Big ones. Double kegs, triple kegs. We would line them up like trophies, fill the coolers with ice, blast the music until the bass shook the dirt off the floorboards. Those nights? Man, they were madness. We had the kind of parties that made the cops circle the block before deciding it was not worth it.

People packed in shoulder to shoulder, smoke hanging low like fog, beer sloshing over red cups, girls laughing in the hallways. Arguments turned into fights, fights turned into brawls, and by the end of it, the house looked like a warzone. Drywall cracked, beer soaking in the carpet, blood on the back porch, a few lost shoes scattered in the yard. Uncensored. Violent. X-rated parties. That is what it was. Period.

When the smoke cleared, I would sit out back with a half-warm beer and think about Felicia and Nevaeh. How it could have been. How it should have been. She never really believed me when I told her I loved her. Perhaps I didn't believe myself either. I tried to bring the best out of her. Sad to say, but I guess I was not influential enough for her. It is what it is. Maybe I was not good enough, or maybe the streets had already claimed too much for both of us. It is sad when you realize love cannot breathe where violence sleeps.

So, I leaned into it full force. The streets never left me alone. I was going to stick to this violence I knew. The parties. The fights. The madness. The girls and the drugs. If the streets wanted me, then the streets would have me. I was living proof it worked—or at least, that it had not killed me yet.

Month after month, party after party, we burned through every house we could find. Nobody wanted to host us anymore. We would roll up with kegs in the bed of the truck, bass rattling the windows, and a line of cars behind us like it was a Chick-fil-A drive-thru. Lights flashing, people yelling, cops cruising by pretending not to see it. Pure insanity.

Then one night, it hit me. If we could not party in the city, then we would take it to the mountains.

I sent the word out.

By sundown, we had a caravan of cars heading into the dark, headlights cutting through the pines, music shaking the hills. It was not just a party anymore. It was an escape. A declaration. A bunch of lost souls looking for freedom under the cover of night. And as we climbed higher, into the black sky and cold air, I swear I could feel something waiting up there for us. Something big. Something that was going to change everything.

The town. The town would talk.

Oh, believe me, word got around fast. You could not walk into a gas station, a liquor store, or even the laundromat without someone whispering about our parties. They said we were out of control, that we were wild, reckless, and dangerous. They said we were going to end up in jail, or dead, or both. But all that talk just added fuel to the fire.

Girls came and went like smoke through the night. Here for the thrill, gone by sunrise. Different faces, same stories. They would show up in tight jeans, cheap perfume, and that same hungry look, the kind that says, I just want to feel alive for a minute. And we gave them that. The music, the chaos, the lights cutting through the dark. It was a scene built to make you forget who you were.

Nights blurred together until the weekends no longer meant anything. Monday felt like Saturday, and Saturday felt like forever. Every hangover just blended into the next. We were living in slow motion, but it all moved too fast.

The sisters—oh, the sisters—they hated it. The baby mamas, the ones who used to ride for us, they saw it firsthand. All the pictures, heard all the stories, felt the distance. Every time we threw another party, it was like we were spitting on whatever was left of the love we once had. They would call, yell, cry, and threaten to leave. But by then, we were already two beers deep and halfway gone.

It was toxic, yeah.

But it was ours.

That wild, lawless stretch of time where nothing mattered but the music, the liquor, the women, and the night. The world could have burned down around us, and we would not have noticed. And if we did, we would have added more fuel.

We were too busy chasing the noise.

CHAPTER 28: RUMORS

By this time, I was staying up in this little one-bedroom apartment in a run-down complex off Carmel, the kind of place where the walls whispered at night and every hallway light flickered like it was afraid of the dark. The carpet was stained, the paint was peeling, and the air always smelled like a mix of fried food, weed smoke, and regret. But it was mine. My own space. My own mess.

I could not stay with my parents. That chapter was closed. Too much tension, too much past that could not be scrubbed clean. So, I made my own spot. A one-bedroom, barely holding together, but enough to crash, think, and hustle out of when I needed to. Funny thing was, even though I had moved out, I had not really gone far. My whole family was stacked in that same complex.

My sister Bernadette lived downstairs on the first floor. She got with this guy. He was wild, loud, never could stay still, always working on lowriders, and before long they had a couple of kids running around with sticky hands and messy hair, chasing each other up and down the stairs.

My brother, Chris, lived there too, in the same building, just a few floors below me. Chris had found himself a girl, got her pregnant, and they tried to playhouse as we all did. He was different than me. He was into sports, worked, and stayed in school. He was trying to make ends meet, trying to make sense of everything going on around all of us. My sister and brother were definitely raised different than me. They both stayed in school.

Now, in the other building across the lot, that was where my parents stayed. My dad was the maintenance man for the whole complex. He walked around with this little dog and key rings louder than his work boots, fixing leaks, unclogging drains, patching up other people's problems while trying not to deal with his own. He had that old-school pride about him. He did not talk much. He would smile more now, but you could tell he was watching me, just waiting for me to fall or finally figure it out. We never talked about the past, about the abuse, the silence, the pain we swept under the rug. That stuff stayed buried. He knew. I knew. We just did not speak it.

As I grew older, things between my old man and me started to change. We were not enemies anymore. We were not friends either, but something shifted. He knew I sold weed. Hell, he even came to me for some. I would see him knock on my door, eyes tired but calm, and he would say, "You got a little something?" I would hook him up.

We would stand outside by the dumpster or sit on the tailgate of his old truck, passing a joint back and forth while the streetlights buzzed above us. For the first time in years, it felt like we understood each other. Two men trying to survive the hand they were dealt.

Right there in that same building, because life likes to keep things messy, was Felicia's mom, Beatrice, and her sisters. I swear, everywhere I turned, that family was right there, in my face. Like I could not escape them if I tried. Even though I wanted to be close to my daughter, I did not want to stay too close to Felicia. She was wild, unpredictable, and very toxic. One minute she would love me, the next she would be swinging on me, screaming, locking me out of their apartment like I was nothing. It was chaos.

I would try to talk to her, try to reason, but it always ended in shouting matches and slammed doors. I loved her, I really did, but if that was love, it didn't mean you stayed around. Sometimes, it was just another battlefield. How much are you willing to endure? I was close enough to see my daughter when I could, when Felicia would let me, but far enough to breathe when I needed to.

Every night, sitting by that cracked window, watching the parking lot glow under the orange streetlight, I would wonder how life ended up circling back to this. My family, Felicia's family, and I were all trapped in the same broken concrete cage, trying to act as if it were home.

I was still selling. Still moving weight on the low, just enough to keep money in my pocket and food on the table. I had a legit job too, working, trying to look like I stayed clean. But the streets do not just let go of you because you say you are done. They cling to you, like smoke in your clothes. I was right in the middle of it. Ground zero.

I was selling more than I probably should have been. Mostly weed, but I would move coke too when it came around. Sometimes pills, sometimes whatever somebody needed. If I could get my hands on it, I would flip it.

But weed? That was my bread and butter. Always had it. Always. Pockets full, car smelling like it, fingertips sticky from breaking down buds. That was just how I lived.

One night after work, I decided it was time to step out. Had to clean up first. I could not be out there looking like a bum. That was not me. I had to be G'd up from my feet up, clean fade, fresh kicks, shirt crisp. It was not just about looking good, dressing to impress. It was about walking like I owned the night. That was my armor. I learned that at an early age.

I hit up Aiden and Paul, told them what was up, told them the plan. We had been through a lot together, so I did not have to explain much. They already knew the vibe. They both said, "Bet. Let's get it."

That night came quickly, like time knew what we were up to and wanted to hurry us into it. Everything started smoothly. For once, everybody was getting along. Paul was good with his baby mama, Amber. No yelling, no drama for once. Aiden and Candace were on chill terms too, laughing, holding hands like they had finally remembered why they started talking in the first place. And me? I was talking to Felicia again, and we were actually good. No fighting, no screaming. It felt weird, like the calm before something you do not see coming.

We partied that night like the world was not broken. Bottles popped. Blunts burned slow. Music loud enough to shake the walls and drown out the thoughts we did not want to deal with. We laughed, smoked, and drank. I passed out where I sat in my apartment, and for the first time in a long time, it felt like old times. Nobody was beefing, nobody was locked up, and nobody had tears in their eyes.

But that night ended good. Maybe too good.

Next thing I knew, I was waking up to Felicia pounding on my door like the cops. My head was spinning, my mouth was dry, and my heart was pounding. I could not even remember what time it was, and daylight was bleeding through the blinds like a warning. I stumbled up, eyes burning, trying to make sense of where I was. The apartment looked like a bomb had gone off.

Empty bottles everywhere. Ashtrays overflowing. Half-smoked blunts stuck to the floor. Trash was knocked over. The smell hit first—stale beer, spilled liquor, weed smoke that had soaked into everything. It smelled like sweat, sin, and last night's bad choices.

Felicia was still at the door, yelling my name, something about watching Nevaeh and why I was not answering the phone. Her voice was sharp enough to cut through the hangover. Like, come on now, you were here too last night while your mom watched our baby, and you wake me up like this, screaming at me. You do not know how to talk without being crazy all the time. I could not. I just could not with her.

I did not even know what happened between when I passed out and now. The whole night was a blur. Flashes of laughter. Someone dropping a bottle. Music thumping. Smoke hanging thick in the air like fog. Now, standing in that mess, looking around at the wreckage, I felt sick. Not just from the smell or the hangover, but from what it all meant. This was what my "normal" looked like. And as I think of it now, it makes me sicker.

Parties that ended in chaos.

Love that came with bruises.

Money that disappeared faster than it came.

And for the first time, I started to feel it—that quiet pull in my chest telling me this life was not going anywhere good. But back then, I was not ready to listen.

By this point, I was moving weight to anyone and everyone who had the cash. Did not matter who they were. Old heads. College kids. Dudes from the block. Even soccer moms trying to hide their stress behind a joint. If you needed it, I had it. Weed was my main hustle, but if you wanted something harder, I could make a call, make it happen.

That was how I met Vanessa.

She was a regular. Always needed something rolled up, always came through smiling. And man, she was bad. About five-five, smooth brown skin that glowed under the light, long dark hair that changed colors every time I saw her. Sometimes auburn, sometimes highlighted with honey streaks that caught the light just right. Her hair ran down her back like silk. Her eyes were deep brown, but not just brown. They had that kind of warmth that made you forget what you were saying mid-sentence.

Yeah, she took my breath away every time. But I never acted on it. Never made a move.

She knew I liked her, I am sure she did, but I kept it cool, kept it business. Still, she had that way of getting free smoke out of me. I knew it, and she knew I knew it. Did not matter though. I would still hook her up every time. That was just how it was.

One night, Vanessa hit me up and said she wanted to come through and bring her cousin and a couple of friends. Said they wanted to chill, listen to some music, smoke, maybe drink a little. I was already faded with Paul and Aiden—the fearsome threesome, same old crew, same routine. We had been drinking, smoking, laughing, talking loud. We blew off the sisters to hang with these other girls.

The room was hazy, thick with blunt smoke and cheap liquor. The girls showed up looking good. Loud laughter, perfume in the air, tight jeans as if they were painted on, lip gloss shining in the low light. Music thumping through the walls, bass shaking the floorboards. Everyone vibing, dancing, flirting, getting comfortable.

I remember Paul ending up hugged up with some chick, grinning like he had already won the night. Everything was smooth, easy. The kind of night where nothing mattered.

A few hours in, I started realizing I could not see Vanessa's cousin anymore.

She was there one second, gone the next. I glance around, no Paul either. My gut tightens a little. "ight, whatever," I tell myself, trying to play it cool. Keep the music up, take another swig of my beer.

Then I hear , knock, knock, knock.

Hard.

I freeze for a second.

Who the that? I thought,

I yell, "Who is it?"

Nothing.

I try again. "Yo, who's there?"

Still no answer. Just silence behind that door.

And that's when it hits me, not too many people even know where I moved. My stomach drops, heartbeat starts thudding in my ears.

Knock. Knock. Knock. Knock.

Faster this time. Harder.

I walk slowly to the door, eyes darting around, trying to think who it could be. I peek through the peephole, can't see much, just a shadow. I hesitate, then I unlatch the lock, turn the knob. As soon as I open it, the door flies open and boom! The door hits the wall, nearly knocking me off my feet. I stumble back, my mind racing. The door explodes open, and a stampede pours through. It's Amber, Felicia, Candace, and a few other girls, like a wave crashing into my living room. Screams, curses, and shoes slapping the floor. The music cuts off mid-beat, and everything snaps to a new, ugly focus.

I caught Paul cornered at the bathroom door, his back to the sink, one arm tangled with the cousin who came with Vanessa. The cousin's face goes white when she sees the mob. She didn't expect this. Nobody did. For a second, everything moves in slow, cruel frames. Amber moves like rage fuels up and ignites bones, no hesitation, no warning, no fear. One second, she's standing there, the next she's a blur of fury, flying across the room so fast it feels like the air itself splits open. The bathroom door bursts inward with a hollow crack that echoes through the apartment. Then comes the sound I'll never forget, a raw, chaotic, sickening sound. A crash of a porcelain toilet. Someone slams something heavy against the porcelain, the toilet clangs, the sound echoing like metal on bone. The cousin gets pinned, trapped between the tub and the rim, fighting air and panic.

Girls are screaming, the bathroom door slams, and then the whole room goes mad, fists, frantic yanking, the sick, hollow sound of someone being restrained. I hear the cousin scream like someone's ripping the light out of her throat. It's raw, it's ugly. Amber keeps her in there and slams the door shut, leaving no room for anyone to exit or anyone to enter... terrifying minutes pass... all I hear is muffled screaming and a frantic, stern, angry voice cussing with each blow through the wood. People pound and threaten at the door, voices like broken glass. Then the girls get it open.

Amber stops.

A thud echoes in the room as she releases that girl's head, and it hits the floor. It's over.

Everyone pauses, faces wet with emotion, wild expressions with something that's not even anger anymore, it's business.

Someone yells. Someone else gasps. Amber starts again just keeps on punishing her face as she lays there limp.

That was when I could not stand it anymore. I moved through the mess, past overturned chairs and tables with beer bottles, and toward the bathroom. Pushing past the girls, I threw my weight into Amber and pried her off the cousin's lifeless shoulders. She looked at me like a deer in headlights. For a second, we locked eyes. Amber's pupils were pinpoints, rage burning in her stare like a furnace. She was soaked in sweat and blood, her breath ragged, chest heaving. There was no pleading there, no shame, just fire.

For a wild second, she looked like she could tear the world in half. Then she recognized me. Whatever she was ready to do fractured when my face landed in her line of sight. Something unreadable flashed in her eyes. Maybe reality hit. Maybe fear of what she had just done.

I looked down. Amber was staring at her hands. I saw them too covered in blood, rings on every finger. She broke. Amber shoved free from me and bolted, sprinting through the crowd and out the door, leaving a trail of blood behind her. Her sisters and the other girls followed, talking trash, throwing bottles, screaming profanity as they left.

Then, just like that, everything stopped. The silence that followed was not peace. It was heavy, like the room itself was holding its breath, waiting to see if this was real, waiting to see if the body left for dead would move again.

The cousin struggled, desperate to get up, her cries tearing through the walls. The sisters had come, they had seen, they had conquered. Vanessa and her crew stood still, like hunters who had just become the hunted. For a moment, the room was a courtroom. Girls yelling accusations. Paul and Aiden backing up, hands raised as if to show they had done nothing.

Vanessa's cousin stumbled out, arms wrapped around herself, eyes wide with fear. Vanessa rushed to help her. People shouted names, called each other liars, wagging fingers and throwing threats. The accusation landed heavy. They thought we had set them up. They thought we had played them, lured them over for this to happen.

I glanced at Vanessa. She gave me a slow, deliberate look, devilish and hateful all at once. How dare you. That was what her eyes said. She could not believe what had just happened, and even if she could, she would never let me forget. With that look, I saw the distance grow between us. If there had ever been a chance with her, it evaporated right there.

The room was a hurricane of shouting. So, I did what I had always done when things got too heavy. I took control the only way I knew how.

"Y'all gotta go," I said, my voice flat, heavy.

I pointed toward the door and kept saying it until bodies moved. I kicked people out, one by one, shoving them into the hallway, and slammed the door shut.

I waited a few minutes, then walked back out to the parking lot. They were piling into cars, doors slamming, voices still screaming. "Watch your back. We'll be back!" they shouted. Vanessa drove off as I stepped outside, her car pulling away slowly, her silhouette vanishing into the night. If there had ever been a chance with her, it left on her taillights.

I knew the fallout from this was just beginning. The bathroom door stood open like a wound. Paul's face was gray. He would not meet my eyes. Aiden sat there, drinking again, not saying a word. I swept the wrecked apartment with my gaze. Cups toppled. A lamp cracked. A smear of blood on the wall where things had gone too far. My bathroom looked like a crime scene.

The chill hit me. This was too much. Too many lines crossed. This had been a planned hit. They had seen the girls come in, and they came to collect—in blood.

I could not make this up if I tried. When the smoke finally cleared, the sisters had stormed out, the girls were gone, and the night had gone dead quiet. It was around 1:30, maybe 2 a.m. Aiden, Paul, and I were just sitting there, the last men standing, passing the bottle back and forth, trying to laugh off the madness that had just gone down. The air was thick with the smell of weed smoke, cheap beer, and burnt plastic from whatever was in the ashtray.

We were half gone, half numb, just talking nonsense when—

Knock. Knock. Knock.

I froze mid-sentence. Looked at Paul.

He looked back at me.

"Who the hell could that be now?" I mumbled, standing up slowly, feeling the buzz in my legs.

I walked over, peeked through the peephole, and saw nothing but darkness.

"Hello?" I called out, pulling the door open an inch.

BOOM!

A fist rocketed through the crack and smacked me dead in the jaw. My whole head snapped sideways, stars exploding in my vision.

"What the—?!" I could not even finish before another hit landed, then another. My body went on with instinct. Hands up, trying to block, trying to shove the door closed at the same time. Whoever it was, they were pushing back hard. There was weight behind that door. Big weight.

I caught a glimpse through the gap. It was not just one or two.

No. It was a whole herd. A crew of women. And not just any women. Big, grown, furious women. Fifteen deep, easy. Every one of them looked like they had come straight from the club to throw hands.

I could smell them—their lotion, perfume, sweat, liquor, rage.

They were shouting over each other.

"Gabe! Come out here now! We gon' mess you up!"

I was trying to hold the door, my feet sliding on the tile.

"Paul! Aiden! Yo, help me!"

They rushed over, and we were all braced against the door, shoulder to shoulder, struggling. The hinges screamed, the wood bowed, and they were pounding and pushing and then—

BAM!

The whole thing blasted open like an explosion.

They poured in. Hands, feet, yelling, chaos. I was catching slaps, scratches, and wild punches from every direction. Somebody pulled my shirt, and another grabbed my hair. I could not even tell who was hitting me anymore, just flashes of faces, flashes of gold hoop earrings, nails, lipstick, fury.

"Aiden! Paul! Hold the damn door!" I yelled, stumbling backward.

My mind was racing. I could not fight them all. I needed to get them out.

So, I did the most brilliant, yet most foolish thing I could think of. I shoved the door open wide and pushed through the crowd, trying to lead them out into the hallway, away from the apartment. It was obvious this was for me and me alone.

It was like getting caught in a stampede with a herd of buffalo. Hands grabbing. Nails scraping. Hits landing left and right.

Pop. Pop. Boom. Bam.

I stumbled down the narrow hallway, sneakers sliding on the floor, their voices echoing off the walls.

"Hold the door! Hold it shut!" I yelled back.

Paul and Aiden slammed it behind me, locking themselves inside. I was outside now, in the middle of the storm. They were all around me, coming down like rain. Slaps. Punches. Shoves. They screamed my name like banshees, voices sharp enough to cut glass.

I pushed through, trying to get to the stairs, backing up fast, blood on my lip, sweat stinging my eyes. My chest was heaving, and all I could think was, this is insane.

Then I heard it.

A voice.

Deep. Familiar.

"Hey, boy!"

Everything stopped for a second.

I turned my head, breathing hard, and there he was—my dad. Standing at the bottom of the stairs, flashlight in one hand, leash in the other. The maintenance man. The unofficial security of the whole complex. Out walking his dog, just doing his nightly rounds, and now he was standing there, looking up at his son, bruised and surrounded by twenty furious women throwing punches like it was Judgment Day.

For a split second, nobody moved. Just the echo of our breathing, the smell of perfume and sweat hanging heavily in the air.

Then my dad started running toward me, the dog barking, the flashlight swinging like a cop's baton. I knew right then this night was not over. This was just the next round.

Punch after punch after punch. Fists pounding against skin. Nails raking. A heel caught my shin. I was moving backward like a man dragged by a tide, feet slipping on the linoleum, breath burning in my chest.

"Hey, boy!" he yelled again, voice cracking the air like a warning.

"What the heck's going on here?" he shouted.

"I don't know!" I shouted back, mind fogged from hits and adrenaline. I was still trying to block every blow, still trying to breathe. Someone grabbed my arm and twisted. I yanked away, tasting blood in my mouth.

"Boy, swing back!" he yelled again.

In the chaos, his command cut through the noise cleanly. He was coming up the stairs, boots slapping, clearing a path like a man done with the world's nonsense.

Boom. Boom. Boom.

He moved through the crowd, and I watched women fall one after the other.

He was right. These girls were not playing. They had come to hurt me. I did not even know who they were, but they knew me, and somewhere down the line I had pissed them off.

Something in me snapped loose. I closed my eyes, closed my fist, and let every ugly feeling I had been carrying—anger, fear, shame, aggression—turn into one single, desperate motion. I started swinging.

My fist connected. Hard. One of them crumpled. Another staggered back and fell. That blow broke the spell.

My dad was working his way toward me from the rear. My dad and I moved together. What had been twenty, then fifteen, then ten, finally split down to five as the crowd shifted into retreat mode. Hands up. Pushing. Shouting. Driving the last of them down the steps as they picked each other up.

They backed up, cursed, and started running to their cars. Heels pounding. Jackets flapping. Hair messed up. Spitting into the night toward parked cars.

They shouted back-

"We got you! Watch your back! Gabe! We'll be back!"

The names came like bullets, every insult they could pull from their chests, names meant to bruise. They called me every name under the sun. I barely heard them. My ears rang. I took one long, shuddering breath. I bent over, hands on my knees, lunging for air. My shirt was torn at the sleeve, my knuckles stung, and my face was hot. I looked up through the stale, smoke-hung air and took in the wreckage.

Windows were spider-webbed, shattered glass glittering like confetti in the light of the main corridor. The entrance door was hanging, and a smear of something dark tracked across the linoleum like a road map to the night's violence. The smell of spilled beer, weed, and sweat hung thick, sour, and heavy. People shouted from behind doors. A dog barked somewhere far off. Moonlight sliced through the broken windows and made the whole place look wrecked, destroyed.

My dad stood there breathing hard, shoulders broad, the flashlight sweating in his hand. He looked at me like he was seeing every choice I had ever made rolled up into one bruised body. No words. Just that look—a mix of anger, exhaustion, and something like grief.

Around us, the complex hummed back to life in little bursts. Neighbors peeking out. A car engine revving. Someone calling the cops. But for those few seconds, it was just me, my father, and the echo of a night that blew up loud enough to leave a mark.

I pulled myself together the best I could, tried to fix my stretched-out, ripped shirt with trembling hands, trying to hold my pride shut with it. My chest still heaved, my face stung, and the night air burned in my lungs. That was when it sank in harder—the streets do not care who you are or what you have done. One wrong move, one bad mix of people, and everything flips.

The line between running the game and getting trampled by it is not even a line. It is a thread. And I just felt it snap.

I stopped in the middle of the wreckage and thought, this could have been no one else. It had Vanessa's family written all over it. Her aunties came deep, furious, and heavy, with that kind of old-school vengeance passed down from generation to generation. They did not come to talk. They came to handle what Vanessa and her crew could not.

They came to kill, steal, and destroy.

I took a deep breath, slow and burning, like I was trying to inhale the truth and choke it down. It did not even matter what really happened, because now, in her eyes, I was the villain. Whatever chance I had with Vanessa was gone. Vanished in the blood.

The worst part? I wanted to talk to her. Really talk to her. I wanted to tell her I did not set her cousin up, that I did not know a damn thing about the sisters showing up. That it was chaos, wrong place, wrong time, and it blew up bigger than any of us could control. I wanted to tell her that when I looked at her after all this happened, before she left. But she will never hear that now, because instead of words, she got war. Instead of love, she got chaos. And now the message is written in broken glass, busted windows, and blood. Blood everywhere.

Like I said before, do not dance with the devil under the pale moonlight.

I know the streets well enough to know how this goes. You pay for other people's sins. You carry the blame even when you were just standing too close to the blast. Vanessa got pushed away by other people's actions, and I got accused of those actions. That is how this life goes. One wrong night, one wrong look, and your world burns down faster than you can put the fire out.

I got to my apartment. The guys left. The sun started to rise, bleeding through the blinds. My face still stung where one of those aunties had landed a clean shot, scratches burning across my skin.

The air smelled like dust, beer, and bad decisions. My hands were swollen, my heart heavier than a hangover, and my head kept replaying her face—those brown eyes that used to make me feel like maybe there was more to life than survival.

The next day could not come fast enough. Not because I wanted to move on, but because I needed the night behind me. Needed to breathe again without tasting guilt and regret in every inhale.

As I sat there, half broken, half still buzzing with leftover adrenaline, I realized something cold and permanent. This life, this street life, takes more than it ever gives back.

And last night, it took the one thing I did not even get the chance to hold.

I had just gotten off work, still tripping about the chaos from the night before—the broken windows, the blood, the yelling that echoed in my head like a siren that would not stop. My shirt still smelled like sweat and smoke. I told myself I would help clean up the mess later, but first I had to handle business.

So, I clocked out from my nine-to-five, lit a cigarette, and drove across town to my plug's spot. No words exchanged. No smiles. Just that unspoken understanding. I grabbed a few bricks, tucked them tight in my backpack, and I was out. Quick. Clean. Quiet.

By the time I pulled up to my complex, the sun was dipping low, that orange haze crawling up the spider-webbed glass in the hallway like a cold reminder from last night.

There were still little pieces on the ground left over, and with every crunch under my shoes the sound was louder than it should have been. I climbed the stairs, bag on my back, the weight pressing on my shoulders like I was carrying more than product. To anyone watching, I was just a man with groceries. A couple of Walmart bags, double wrapped, clinking softly as I shifted my grip. But between those thin layers of plastic, the streets were hiding within, cold, heavy, and worth every risk I was stupid enough to take.

I slid my key in, pushed the door open, dropped the bags on the couch, and exhaled. The apartment was quiet now. Too quiet. It smelled like cheap liquor and Lysol. I shook my head. "Man, it's been a wild week."

Ring, ring, ring.

"Yo."

"Hey, what's up? Can I come by?"

"Yeah, yeah, pull up."

"Alright, on the way." Click.

I hung up and started getting things ready, heart ticking faster with every sound.

Before I could even sit down—ring, ring, ring again.

"Yo."

"Bro, what's good? You around? I'm ready."

"Yeah, yeah. Slide through."

I ended the call, looked around the room—busted blinds, crooked lamp, product on the table—and thought to myself...

This ain't living. This is surviving.

My phone would not stop going off, like a leaf shaking in the wind. Calls, texts, the little green bubbles piling up until I had nowhere to ignore them. I rinsed quick in the shower like a man waiting to go somewhere or waiting for someone to show up. The hot water was so hot it scoured last night off my skin, but not the taste of it from my mouth.

Dressed clean with a fresh tee, hoodie zipped just right, jeans not too baggy. I slapped a beat on and let the music ride loud enough to make the floor hum. By the time I hit the couch, the night was on fast-forward. I poured a shot. I rolled up.

People pulled up, and I ran out. Deals moved slick and easy—fast hands, fast cash, the small quiet rituals of the trade. A stack of bills slid into my pocket; another face left with a grin and a pocket full of green. I counted, pocketed, and for a minute it felt like the old power, like the world still owed me something.

I got back upstairs...

Then—**knock, knock, knock**.

Now I wondered who this was. Too many people knew where I was living, given the past few nights. They knew the complex, sure, but there were four different floors, maybe eighty apartments. I looked out the peephole. My mom and my sister stood there. Bernadette's hair pulled back, one hand on her hip. Mom with her coat unbuttoned and heavy, the worry already stitched into her face. They had come to check on me.

I let them in. The apartment smelled clean, like a mixture of Clorox and Pine-Sol. I had to get the house back in order, especially after all the blood I had scrubbed to get a hold on the place. Never know.

I had bricks laid out on the kitchen counter, neat rows of green-wrapped plastic. They caught me in the middle of weighing it out. I had been triple-checking, moving money around, stashing cash here and there, just in case. My sister's eyes went straight to the counter. Mom's mouth fell open a fraction. For one second, the music did not matter, the cash did not matter, only the kitchen and that stack on the laminate did.

"Boy," my mom said softly, one syllable that held a mountain. It got my attention. Then she said, "You'd better be careful."

"I will," I lied easily, brushing my hand over a brick like it was nothing more than a loaf of bread. "If the cops come, I'll just throw it out the window or something. I don't know." I tried a shrug, a grin. Bad jokes meant to lighten a load that would not lift.

Mom did not laugh. She cocked her head, eyes narrowed. "Yeah, yeah, that's what you say now."

I folded my arms, feeling defensive. "If it doesn't make dollars, it doesn't make sense," I told her with a shrug that was half bravado, half pleading. I could feel the truth in the room like cold air. I had been doing this for years.

I knew patterns. I knew faces. I knew how to move quietly. But tonight, the weight felt different, like the glass of the broken windows had started to sink into everything.

They sat for a minute, watching me as if they could see right through me. I tried to play it off, poured another shot, told a dumb joke to pull the edge off. They talked about groceries, about some neighbor's dog, small-town gossip, and the way people use small talk to cover big fears.

Bernadette stepped closer and crossed her arms. "What about last night?" she asked. Her voice was sharp, but under it was the tremor I heard in Mom.

"Big old misunderstanding," I said, quick with it. The words tasted like ash. I'd said them before. I'd say them again. I watched their faces with a crack of doubt. Mom let out a sound that wasn't a laugh, more of a weary exhale. "Yeah, right," she said, but there was no heat in it. It was worry boxed in with that long, tired acceptance only parents get. She crossed the room and hugged me quickly, the kind of hug that smelled like laundry soap and warnings.

"I love you guys. Be safe," I said. The words felt thin, but I meant them, all of them.

"You too, boy. We love you," Mom answered, pressing her forehead to mine for a beat. Bernadette half-hugged, half-smirked, half-everything, the ritual of family that always comes wrapped in worry. When they left, it was with more hugs and more warnings — "Call me when you get in," "Don't let people set you up," and the impossible promise, "We're here for you." I watched them go down the hall, watched Mom straighten her coat, and Bernadette tug Mom's sleeve like she wanted to linger. I shut the door and leaned against it, the apartment suddenly hollow like a drum. I thumbed the lighter, took a long drag on the blunt I'd rolled earlier, and then let out a breath that tasted like compromise. The music kicked back in, louder this time to replace the quiet. I cracked a beer, lined the bills up again, and the phone started to light up all over.

Business as usual, I told myself. Keep moving. Keep your head down. I picked up the phone, answered another call, took another deal. The night went on, the music played, and for a little while, I let the money and the noise drown out everything else. I must've blacked out somewhere between the last shot and the last song. The room spun itself to sleep around me, smoke hanging thick in the air like bad memories that refused to leave. My body ached from every angle, sore knuckles, bruised ribs, headache pounding like bass through drywall. I put all the weed and scales in the drawer under the stove. East access for later if someone calls. I kept drinking until I couldn't. I didn't even remember hitting the bed. When I came to, the world was blurred at the edges. My mouth tasted like yesterday's decisions. Then a shadow leaned over me, a figure I knew by the weight of his silence before my eyes even cleared.

"Boy," my dad's voice. Low. Hard. Not angry, but close.

He had the spare keys, always did; he was the maintenance person. I blinked, trying to focus. The light behind him cut through the fog in my head, and that's when I saw what he saw, sprawling across the bed, one gun in each hand. My .38 snub nose in my right, my .357 in my left, both locked cock, ready to rock and roll. For a second, I didn't even breathe. I didn't remember grabbing them. Didn't remember falling asleep with death sitting that close on my palms. Dad's jaw was locked tight. "You outta your mind, boy," he said, his voice cracked between fear and fury. He didn't wait for me to answer. He just took them, fast, quiet, the way you take a snake out of a kid's hand.

"I ain't lettin' you do nothin' stupid," he said. "Not you. Not after all this."

I wanted to talk, but my tongue was heavy. The room drifted again, his voice turned to echo, his outline fading. Then nothing. Just black. I don't know how much time passed after that. Could've been minutes. It could've been hours, but the next thing I knew, I was shot awake by the sound of the door being assaulted.

DOO DOO DOO DOO DOO DOO DOO DOO DOO DOO DOO.

Each knock hit like gunfire. Fast. Aggressive.

My eyes snapped open, heart racing like I'd been dropped in the middle of a war.

"Who the hell—?" I mumbled, wiping drool off my cheek. I stumbled up, still foggy, half-drunk, half-dead. The knocking didn't stop.

DOO DOO DOO DOO DOO DOO DOO DOO.

It echoed through the small apartment, vibrating the windows and shaking the lingering smoke from the night before.

I staggered toward the door. "Yo! Who is it?"

Nothing.

"Hello?" I said again, leaning closer. "You guys gonna answer me or what?"

Silence.

I pressed my eye to the peephole; I squinted, but all I saw was darkness. Nothing. No movement. Just the hollow shadow of a hallway that felt like it was holding its breath.

For a second, I thought maybe I was still dreaming. But then came one last knock, slower this time, deliberate. **DOO... DOO... DOO.**

It crawled down my spine like a warning.

The hallway outside was dead quiet, but I swear I could feel somebody out there. Waiting. I bet you it's Felicia.

Can't even see her short self through the peephole. Figures.

I twist the knob and barely get the door cracked when...

BOOM!

The whole thing exploded inward, slamming me flat on my back. The wood bit into my shoulder as boots rushed in like thunder.

"Suspect, put your hands up! Put 'em up now!"

"What—what the—are you serious right now?" I was confused, blinking, the room spinning.

"On your knees! Don't try nothin' stupid!"

And just like that, it hit me. I was surrounded. Flashlights in my face, the smell of gun oil and cold steel. They had me boxed in like a caged animal.

I never thought I would see this day. Me? Getting raided? Huh? Never that. Whenever you saw me, you saw the player. The money. The women. The swagger that came with it. But right there, my knees on that dirty floor, wrists behind my back, I was not any of that. I was just caught.

Been here only a couple of months. Already stirring up heat. Somebody out there was mad, real mad. You would think people would be proud to see me making moves, stacking, shining. Nah. They just called me crazy for thinking I could win.

"Sir, please stand up," one said, his tone flat, professional, like I was just another number. They yanked me to my feet, cuffed tight, and dragged me to the living room, sitting me on the couch. Two others went straight to the back, to my bedroom.

One cop leaned in close, smirking.

"Sir, or Gabriel... or suspect, whichever you prefer, where's it at?"

I blinked, buying time.

"Where's what?"

"The dope."

"Dope? Man, please. I ain't got no dope."

He snorted, leaning back. "Don't play dumb. We've been watching you come in and out all day. Selling. Dropping. Moving weight. All day."

That was when my stomach dropped, because I knew exactly what they were talking about. I had just finished weighing out sacks in the kitchen. Put everything under the drawer beneath the stove. And now these fools were standing right there.

I could hear drawers sliding, hangers clattering from my bedroom. Nothing in there. Keep searching.

"Sir, make it easy on yourself," the interrogator said. "Tell me where it is."

"I don't know nothin'," I said, staring straight ahead.

"Come on, suspect," he said. "Don't make me dig for it."

Then the cops left my bedroom and headed toward the kitchen. And I thought, they're in the kitchen... oh my God, they're in the kitchen.

I swallowed hard, looked him dead in the eye.

"I can tell you this," I said.

He tilted his head, half-smirking, half-curious. "Yeah? What's that?"

"Lawyer."

Silence. Heavy. Thick. Then a voice from the kitchen cut through it like a blade—

One cop bent over and pulled out the drawer underneath the stove. Then I heard...

"Bingo!"

My heart sank.

The cop crouched by the stove held up a Walmart bag, double-knotted, full of my work. Bricks wrapped tight.

The interrogator looked down, grinning.

"Didn't you just say you didn't have nothin', huh?"

He leaned close enough for me to smell his breath.

"Someone once told me," he said, "the streets don't lie. But you just did."

As they escorted me out of the apartment, down the stairs, and outside to their patrol car, all I could think was how fast everything flips in the blink of a knock. Who was it? Who ran their mouth? It could have been any one of the females that were mad at me.

You know, someone wise once told me...

"You keep playing in the kitchen, sooner or later the grease is gonna pop. That's just how it goes. Don't cry when you get burned."

That stuck with me more than ever.

CHAPTER 29: CRUCIAL CONFLICT

The cops found my stash. I still do not know if they found my money. They never said anything about the money, just gave me that look like they already knew everything but wanted me to sweat it out. As they walked me out of my apartment, hands cuffed behind my back, I thought, Good thing Pops took those pistols. I can still see him last night, moving quietly through my room, eyes heavy like he already knew this day was coming. I did not think much of it then, but now? Yeah. That was real. The cops did not grab any guns, so my dad did what he had to do. He was my saving grace. Probably saved me from twenty years. I just wonder what else he took when he came through. Either way, he was looking out, always was, just in his own diabolical, sinister, despicable sort of way, I guess.

Like I said before, my folks had stopped fighting over who I was. They accepted it. The streets had raised me more than they ever could. They knew I was not trying to be anybody else. I wasn't chasing a dream job, nor was I looking for a white picket fence. I was chasing money. Power. Respect. A name that made people think twice before crossing me. That was my calling. That was my pride. I was what I always wanted to be—a gangster. Point blank. Period. End of story. I was Suspect, and I owned that.

My name rang bells in corners most people feared walking. I earned that. I did not take anything from anybody unless they had it coming. I was a force. People called me a suspect, as if it were a bad thing. I turned it into a brand. I was the dude your momma warned you about. The one the block could not forget.

Sitting in the back of that squad car, I started to feel something different. Cold seat under me, wrists burning from the cuffs, I could hear my heartbeat louder than the siren. That was not fear. That was a realization.

For the first time, I was not fighting the world. I was fighting myself. All that pain I buried under reputation, all that hate I carried like armor, it was breaking through. I had to face it now. The betrayal. The envy. The setup. Somebody out there had hated me enough to want me gone. Maybe it was jealousy. Maybe revenge. Did not matter. The pain hit different when it comes from one of your own.

As the cruiser pulled away, lights bouncing off every dark window on the block, I realized something… They did not just arrest me for what I did. They arrested the man I became.

I now realize, looking back, that some of us become addicted to chaos, just as we are to oxygen. We breathe it in. Live off it. Without it, we do not even feel alive. The madness becomes our comfort zone, the yelling, the sirens, the street noise, the constant edge of something about to go down. We call it life, but really, it is survival in disguise. We get used to waking up in the middle of storms, used to drama so thick we cannot tell peace from boredom. The calm feels too quiet, too strange. We do not know what to do when everything is not falling apart. And when that peace finally shows up, we do not trust it. It feels suspicious, so we sabotage it just to feel normal again.

Darkness? That was my best friend. It kept my secrets. It covered my sins. When the night fell, I felt free to move, to scheme, to be whoever I wanted. However, the thing about darkness is that it does not stay loyal. It hides you only long enough to blind you. Then one day, you realize you can no longer see yourself.

Light? That was what I was really running from. Because light exposes things. Light shows what is broken. It does not lie. But the truth is, you need that light when you are tired of tripping over the same mistakes. When you are done stumbling through life with your eyes closed, pretending you have control.

If only I had known back, then what I know now. Maybe I would have stopped fighting the light sooner. Maybe I would have faced the pain before it turned me cold.

All these thoughts started flooding my mind as the patrol car rocked over potholes. My reflection stared back at me from the glass, just tired eyes, cuffed hands, but a heart that was trying to wake up.

We pulled up to the infamous CJC, the Criminal Justice Center. Everybody talks about the place, but nobody wants to see for themselves. Its gray walls rose up like judgment, swallowing hope whole. The air got thicker as the door opened, and as those cuffs tightened one last time, I finally thought I understood. Sometimes God has to take you to the darkest place so you will finally start looking for the light.

The cops found my stash. I still do not know if they found my money. They never said anything about the money, just gave me that look like they already knew everything but wanted me to sweat it out. As they walked me out of my apartment, hands cuffed behind my back, I thought, Good thing Pops took those pistols. I can still see him last night, moving quietly through my room, eyes heavy like he already knew this day was coming. I did not think much of it then, but now? Yeah. That was real. The cops did not grab any guns, so my dad did what he had to do. He was my saving grace. Probably saved me from twenty years. I just wonder what else he took when he came through. Either way, he was looking out, always was, just in his own diabolical, sinister, despicable sort of way, I guess.

Like I said before, my folks had stopped fighting who I was. They accepted it. The streets had raised me more than they ever could. They knew I was not trying to be anybody else. I wasn't chasing a dream job, nor was I looking for a white picket fence. I was chasing money. Power. Respect. A name that made people think twice before crossing me. That was my calling. That was my pride. I was what I always wanted to be, a gangster. Point blank. Period. End of story. I was Suspect, and I owned that.

My name rang bells in corners most people feared to walk. I earned that. I did not take anything from anybody unless they had it coming. I was a force. People called me "Suspect" as if it were a bad thing. I turned it into a brand. I was the dude your momma warned you about. The one the block could not forget.

Sitting in the back of that squad car, I started to feel something different. Cold seat under me, wrists burning from the cuffs, I could hear my heartbeat louder than the siren. That was not fear. That was a realization.

For the first time, I was not fighting the world. I was fighting myself. All that pain I buried under reputation, all that hate I carried like armor, it was breaking through. I had to face it now. The betrayal. The envy. The setup. Somebody out there had hated me enough to want me gone. Maybe it was jealousy. Maybe revenge. Did not matter. The pain hit different when it comes from one of your own.

As the cruiser pulled away, lights bouncing off every dark window on the block, I realized something. They did not just arrest me for what I did. They arrested the man I became.

I know now, looking back, that some of us get addicted to chaos like it is oxygen. We breathe it in. Live off it. Without it, we do not even feel alive. The madness becomes our comfort zone, the yelling, the sirens, the street noise, the constant edge of something about to go down. We call it life, but really, it is survival in disguise. We get used to waking up in the middle of storms, used to drama so thick we cannot tell peace from boredom. The calm feels too quiet, too strange. We do not know what to do when everything is not falling apart. And when that peace finally shows up, we do not trust it. It feels suspicious, so we sabotage it just to feel normal again.

Darkness was my best friend. It kept my secrets. It covered my sins. When the night fell, I felt free to move, to scheme, to be whoever I wanted. But the thing about darkness, it does not stay loyal. It hides you only long enough to blind you. Then one day, you realize you cannot even see yourself anymore.

Light was what I was really running from. Because light exposes things. Light shows what is broken. It does not lie. But the truth is, you need that light when you are tired of tripping over the same mistakes. When you are done stumbling through life with your eyes closed, pretending you have control.

If only I had known back then what I know now. Maybe I would have stopped fighting the light sooner. Maybe I would have faced the pain before it turned me cold.

All these thoughts started flooding my mind as the patrol car rocked over potholes. My reflection stared back at me from the glass, just tired eyes, cuffed hands, but a heart that was trying to wake up.

We pulled up to the infamous CJC, the Criminal Justice Center. The place everybody talks about but nobody wants to see for themselves. Its gray walls rose up like judgment, swallowing hope whole. The air got thicker as the door opened, and as those cuffs tightened one last time, I finally thought I understood. Sometimes God has to take you to the darkest place so you will finally start looking for the light.

Handcuffed, wrists biting, I knew right then I had finally met my match. The metal dug into my skin like a reminder that the game always catches up. Could have been worse, I guess. Could have been shot or left face down in some alley. Right? But this was my new reality.

Still, the question burned in my head. Who dropped the dime on me? Felicia's mom? It would not surprise me. She hated me from day one, said I was not good enough the moment she met me. But once that dope sack came out and I fixed her addiction, I was her best friend. Or maybe one of her sisters? Those eyes always followed me, judging, whispering.

Then again, maybe it was Vanessa. Or her people. Yeah, that made sense too. Vanessa and her family were tight with each other, and her cousin, the one who got caught slipping in the bathroom at my place, her family would never let that go. Some street grudges do not fade. They ferment, grow bitter, and stink of revenge. That was all it could be, honestly.

I made my way into booking and the room smelled like bleach. Cold tile floors, buzzing fluorescent lights, that faint echo of somebody crying in another cell. Deputies moved around like clockwork. They looked bored, but it was routine. To them, I was just another file, another number in a long line of bad decisions.

They stripped you down to nothing in county. No pride, no jewelry, no underwear. Just a felony orange jumpsuit and sandals. The smell of bleach was overpowering, mixed with sweat and body odor and stories nobody wanted to tell. My old clothes gone, my name reduced to a booking number. That was how fast the streets forget you.

"Name?" the officer asked, monotone, fingers tapping the keyboard.

"Gabriel Hinojosa," I said, voice flat but heavy.

"Age?"

"Twenty-four."

"Race?"

"Hispanic."

He did not even look up. "Sir, do you know why you are here?"

"Yeah," I said, eyes on the floor.

"Sir, you are being charged with felony marijuana with intent to distribute."

The words hit like a slow punch. Felony marijuana. It sounded heavier out loud. Like a weight you could not shake. He kept typing. "Your bond is fifty thousand dollars. If you do not bond out, you will have court tomorrow morning. You can use the phone over there on the wall."

I nodded, jaw tight. "Okay."

He gestured with his chin. "That is all, sir."

I turned toward the phone on the wall. Same dirty receiver, same fake freedom. Every inmate in the room watched like they had seen this a hundred times.

"This is crazy," I muttered under my breath, pressing the receiver to my ear.

A robotic voice cut through the silence:

"Please enter your eight-digit account number."

"Ugh, I hate this," I thought to myself.

"Press one for English or press two for Spanish."

Beep.

"Press zero for collect call."

Beep.

My finger hesitated, then hit the button.

"After the beep, say 'With Global Tel Link, your voice is your password.'"

Beep.

I took a breath, throat dry.

"With Global Tel Link, my voice is my password."

The machine hummed, cold and heartless.

"Enter the number and area code first…"

I punched it in, the keypad sticky under my fingertips.

"Thank you. Please hold."

Silence. Every second stretched. My reflection stared back at me in the scratched-up metal of the phone box.

Finally, a voice.

"Hello? … You have a collect call from an inmate at the El Paso County Jail… From Gabriel Hinojosa… Press one to connect."

Beep.

"You are now connected."

It was shaky, like they already knew who it was. Like they had been waiting on this call but dreading it all the same. My throat tightened.

"Hello?"

"Hello?"

"Dad?"

"Boy, what happened?" His voice sounded tired, like he had aged ten years in one breath.

"They kicked my door," I said, glancing at the deputy posted at his desk.

"No."

"Yeah... Look, Dad, there's no time."

"What you mean no time? What's going on? It's eight a.m."

He exhaled, long and heavy. "Boy..."

"Listen to me. Go to my apartment. Right now. You hear me?"

"Go to your apartment? For what?"

"Just listen. When you get there, go straight to my room. In the closet. Clothes hanging up. Jeans, jackets, all that. Search every pocket. Shirt pockets too."

He paused, suspicion in his tone. "For real, why?"

"Yes, for real," I said, almost snapping. My eyes darted to the deputy again. "There's way more than enough bail money in there. Enough to get me out. And check the TV. Inside the TV too."

For a moment, neither of us said a word. Just that cold silence between collect call beeps. I knew he was trying to process what I was saying. Then his voice softened.

"I'm going now, boy."

"Okay. Hurry up, please," I whispered. "Thank you, Dad. For real."

"See you soon. And be careful, boy."

"I will."

"Love you."

"Love you too."

Click.

The line died. The phone hummed, that empty tone echoing in my ear like a heartbeat that would not quit. I hung up slowly, staring at my reflection in the scratched-up glass. Orange jumpsuit. Dead eyes. Everything I built on the streets now sitting in my dad's hands.

The guard waved me off. Somewhere out there, my pops was digging through my closet, not for memories, but for money. Trying to save the same son he once prayed and wished would make it out of this life before it came to this.

My dad came through. Always did when it mattered most. Good thing I still had that money. If the cops had found it, they would have bagged it up and called it evidence. But my dad knew where to look. That man is closed off and sticks to himself nowadays from what I see, but he is solid. Street-smart in his own old-school way. He does not say much, but when he moves, he moves with purpose.

I sat holding the walls with the color of cigarette ash, the hum of flickering lights drilling into my skull. Time moves weird in jail. Minutes feel like hours. Hours feel like forever.

All I could do was wait. Waiting to hear my name. Wait for a bed. Wait so I could rest my head and get some rest. Wait to breathe air that did not smell like bleach and bad decisions.

Hours passed. I had been sitting there for a while. I got arrested last night. Now it was five p.m. the next day.

Finally, a deputy called out, "Hinojosa."

A bed, I thought, as I stood up and gave a final stretch. I stood slow, joints stiff from sitting too long.

"This way, sir. You're getting processed for release."

Those words hit different. Like a small crack of light in a tunnel that never ends. I follow him down a corridor that smells like sweat, rubber, and disinfectant. I wait and give them my name. They hand me a plastic bag with my street clothes. My old life folded up inside. The jeans still smell faintly like smoke and cologne, the same ones I wore when the cops slammed me against the wall and kicked my door open.

"Sign here, sir. Make sure all your belongings are there before you sign."

As I change, I catch my reflection in the mirror above the bench. I look older. Harder. Like someone who has seen too much and learned very little.

Then comes the waiting again. Release paperwork. The deputies moving slow, typing one key at a time like they have all the hours in the world. Oh yeah, they get paid by the hour.

"Okay, sir. Come with me," the deputy says, voice flat.

I follow her to the release desk. My file slides across the counter like the last page of a bad chapter.

"Okay, here's your court date," she says. "Sign here."

I sign.

"Can't possess any firearms. Sign here."

I sign again.

"Can't leave the county. Sign here."

Another signature. Another chain, invisible but tight around my neck.

"Do you agree to all these terms?"

"Yeah."

"Sign here."

"Do you agree you'll appear in court?"

"Yeah."

"Sign here."

Each signature feels heavier than the one before it. Like I'm writing my name into a promise I'm not sure I can keep.

Finally, she stamps the paper. The sound echoes through the room like a gavel.

"That's it," she says. "You're free to go."

Free.

That word does not even feel real.

"Oh yeah, let me see your wrist. You can't take your bracelet with you. It's the county's."

As she escorts me to the exit, her tone softens.

"Make better choices," she says, holding the door open. "And have a better day, sir."

I nodded, stepping out into the daylight. The sun burns my eyes, sharp and blinding after all that time in the dark. For a second, I just stand there, breathing it in. The freedom mixed with guilt and confusion. The streets stretch out in front of me, same as before, but something in me feels different. Maybe it is not the system that is holding me down anymore.

Maybe it is me.

I was not far from my apartment, but I figured I might as well walk. The night air hit differently. It was cool, quiet, and heavy with everything I had just been through. It had to be pushing eight thirty p.m., maybe closer to nine. Streets are half-empty, just the sound of distant bass from someone's car and the hiss of streetlights that never quite shut up. No phone. No numbers. No ride. Just me and my thoughts.

My parents were probably asleep by now. Mom is still praying that I will wake up one day and change. So yeah, walking it is. Long walk, too. Plenty of time to replay the day over and over like a broken record.

I could not believe someone snitched. It was wild. I kept thinking, who would have done it? My stomach twisted. Betrayal always hits harder when it comes from close to home.

When I finally got near the complex, I heard it before I saw it. Laughter. Loud music. A thick smell of smoke and cheap liquor hanging in the air. Figures. It looked like a party at my baby mama's place. Nothing had changed or skipped a beat. Same cars out front. The same fools are still inside, acting loud for no reason.

I shook my head, kept walking past to my apartment like a ghost. I knew my boys, Paul and Aiden, were up there too. Up the stairs I went. Down the hallway until I reached my door.

The key slid in the lock. My apartment was quiet, dark, and smelled stale, as if the air had not moved since the police left. I flicked on the light. Everything looked untouched, but I could feel where they had been. Drawers cracked open. Stuff shifted just enough to let me know they were digging.

I stripped down and hit the shower. The water ran hot, almost too hot, burning away the stink of holding cells and county soap. I felt like I was washing off more than dirt. I felt like I was trying to wash off the day itself.

When I stepped out, I threw on clean clothes. Jeans. White tee. Fresh socks. Turned my phone on, and instantly it lit up like fireworks on the Fourth of July. Missed calls. Messages. Over and over.

The streets do not sleep, even when you do.

I cracked open a beer, that first sip hitting bitter and cold. I looked around, scanning the room like I was casing my own spot. I looked at a few places, then I grinned.

The fools did not find all the weed.

"Ha," I said under my breath, shaking my head. "Suckers."

The phone rang, loud, cutting through the silence.

Ring. Ring. Ring.

I glanced at the screen. Vanessa.

I hesitated, then answered. "Hello?"

"Hey," she said, voice soft but slick, like she already knew what she wanted.

"Hey."

"You good?"

"Yeah. What's up?"

"Can I come grab a half? It's just me."

I paused, looking around my apartment, half-smiling. The streets do not ever change. They just circle back.

"Yeah," I said finally. "Come through. Don't come up though. Call once you are close."

"Okay."

Click.

I hung up and took another sip.

If she ran her mouth about me, I did not think she would be calling for some work. Right?

I leaned back in the chair, staring at the ceiling.

Fresh out, and already back in the game.

I finished getting the weed together for Vanessa, tucked it in my pocket, and off I went. I headed across to Felicia's. Same walkway. Same busted stairwell. Same people partying on the inside.

The apartment was loud, a mess of cheap liquor, cigarette smoke, and weed. Laughter cut through the room like a knife. Nobody was sober. Nobody was looking for trouble, except trouble always found me.

I slid through the crowd, acting casual because that was half the game. I did not tell anybody about the raid. That kind of talk draws attention and raises questions, and questions turn into fingers pointing. I had to play this smooth.

Instead, I pulled Paul aside. Paul was steady, the kind of guy you could whisper a plan to and trust he would not blab. Aiden had dipped out earlier. Someone told me when I asked around. Probably smart for once.

"Hey fool," I said to Paul, loud enough for him to hear.

"Huh?" Paul blinked, beer in his hand, slow to register but most likely stuck in his own head.

"Come here," I said.

"I got raided last night."

"Shut up," he said, like it was a joke. Like I was lying.

"You know why," I kept it low and calm.

"What? What?" He leaned closer, suddenly awake.

"I know someone ran their mouth on me," I told him.

"No way. That's crazy."

"Don't say anything. Not yet."

My phone started buzzing in my pocket.

Ring. Ring. Ring.

I checked the screen. My cousin.

I lifted my head. "Hold up, bro," I told Paul. "Hold up a second."

I answered, voice softer on the line. "Hello?"

"Cousin..." she said, sniffles breaking through. Her voice cracked like it had been pushed to the limit with fear. Tears tore through her words.

"Hey cuzo, this fool just kidnapped me. He will not let me go home. I am scared, cuz." She whispered.

My chest went cold and hot at the same time.

Adrenaline is not subtle. It slammed through me like a runaway train.

"Are you kidding me? Tell whoever you are with to bring you to me right now."

I stood, turning quickly to the corner, trying to hide so no one at the party heard me before the words finished.

Silence. She covered the phone so I couldn't hear him. Then,

She came back. "I told him. He will not. He said he will not let me get out," she said, crying her eyes out.

Background noise was muffled. I heard shouting. A man's voice, rough and possessive, slid in and out of the call.

"Alright." I was already calculating. Routes. Names. Faces.

"Where are you? Who are you with? Lena, tell me something!" I yelled.

I could hear this fool in the background.

"You called Suspect? Where is he? Tell me. On Monterey?"

She came back again.

"He is saying he will be outside in five minutes. He is coming to Monterey."

My jaw set.

Monterey was a block with no witnesses. A place where things go quiet fast and stay quiet.

I could hear my cousin's fear like gravel in my mouth as I clenched my teeth.

I overheard him say,

"Tell him he is done for. And be outside if he is a real man."

There was movement in the background. Maybe her kidnapper trying to snatch the phone. I did not know. She gasped.

"He's saying he's gonna show me who's what. Spider, stop already!"

Click. The line dropped.

Silence settled around me for a second, heavier than the smoke. People around me were watching now, the party vibrating with new, thin electricity. Paul's eyes locked on mine, steady and dangerous. He looked like he wanted to run and pick a fight at the same time.

"What the... what was all that about?" Paul asked, voice low, eyes scanning the room.

I took a deep breath in and out, letting it slow my pulse.

"Look, bruh." I squeezed my jaw. "Spider."

"Spider?" Paul repeated this, his expression shifting to one of confusion. "Which Spider?"

"He just kidnapped Lena," I told him, staring out the window.

"Lena?" Paul's face changed like someone flicked a switch. "Your cousin Lena?"

"Yeah," I said. "He wasn't trying to bring her back home. And when he knew I was on the phone and freaked out, he said he's headed this way. Let's go outside. He should be pulling up."

I took another breath, slow and deep, letting the air fill my lungs like a car submerged underwater, finally cracking open the door to escape. The weed in my pocket felt light. The beer in my hand tasted like nothing as I took a sip.

The room sharpened, the bass, the laughter, the light, and everything focused into a single point. Outside. My cousin. A man who thought he could take anything he wanted, even women, by force.

"Listen," I said, voice low enough for only Paul to hear. "We handle this clean. No extra noise. No stupid moves. We get her out. We do it right."

Paul nodded, rolling his shoulders, ready.

I thought to myself, I did not have any of my pistols. No time to run to my dad's house.

I noticed the drunk crowd trying to cling to what I was saying, and the music trying to drown us out. But I was already moving out the door, down the steps, heart hammering like it was trying to break out of my chest.

Tonight was not about the stash, or the cops, or who snitched. Tonight was about family. And any fool who made that the line they crossed was about to learn the price and pay it.

One thing I could say about Paul—he always had my back. Always down for whatever. My ride-or-die. No talk, just action.

We moved like a pair, slipping past the drunk, the loud, and the smoke. Heads turned. Someone shouted. We did not answer. Energy followed us out, a rippling tide of voices trailing behind like a shadow.

The stairwell breathed stale beer, sweat, and dirt. The building's back exit, half-entrance, half-alleyway, opened to the parking lot.

Outside, the night was colder. Sharp like sharpened metal.

I saw Vanessa first, to my right, as she pulled up. She made eye contact with me, and I hustled over. She did not ask questions. Her hand went to her pocket, palms rough.

I showed her the small packet I had folded earlier with what she wanted. She did not hesitate and slid a wad into my hand. Thin bills folded tight.

"Don't lose it," she said, low. Her lips trembled, like she was holding back more than tears and wanted to say something.

I tucked the money away without even looking at it. No time to be sentimental.

Behind me, I felt the weight of people moving too. I looked back, and a crowd was flowing out. The entire party followed—curious heads, a few fools itching for drama. They must have overheard. I did not mean for the whole party to follow me, but whatever. The more eyes, the more witnesses. That meant more chaos.

Vanessa noticed the crowd and said, "What's going on?"

At the far side of the lot, the night fractured and tires screamed. A car came flying around the corner, headlights slicing the darkness like knives.

"Hold on," I said, locking eyes with the car and starting to walk that way.

The vehicle skidded, a bad angel of a coupe, and the passenger door jerked open. My chest dropped into my stomach, not knowing what to expect.

My cousin Lena leapt out before the car finished moving, feet hitting gravel and dirt. She ran straight for me, tears making tracks down her cheeks, hair a mess. I threw my arms out and pulled her in, half-hug, half-push. Protect her. Get her behind me.

Her body squeezed into mine, small and shaking. Her breath was hot against my neck. She buried her face in her palms and started bawling, the kind of cry that was all jagged edges and nothing pretty.

"Get out of here," I told her, and she ran off, disappearing into the crowd.

Then the driver's door swung fully open, and he stepped out.

Spider.

He stepped out like the night made him; all shadow and menace stitched into a man's shape. The streetlight caught on his coat, long and heavy, its hem frayed like it had been dragged through every alley in the city.

The leather creaked when he moved, slow and deliberate, like each step was a decision and he had already judged you and you were guilty. His boots hit the concrete with that dull, heavy thud, the kind that said he was not here to talk.

His face looked like it had been through wars that nobody had written down. A scar sliced from the corner of his lip to his ear, old and pale, like a grin someone carved there and forgot to finish. His nose sat crooked, healed wrong, as if he had not bothered to fix it after the last time someone tried to help him.

His eyes, man, those eyes—dead gray, flat as gunmetal, but always calculating. They did not blink much, and when they did, it was like shutters snapping closed on a storm. He was the type that stared too long, and when he did, you felt like he was already picturing how you would bleed.

There was something wrong. Maybe fear. Maybe the kind of crazy that comes from mixing paranoia with liquid courage. You could smell it on him as he got closer. That bitter-sweet smoke and liquor. Not just any liquor. Whiskey. The scent of a man who had slept in his sins too long.

Spider was the kind of man who did not talk threats. He was one. Even silence bent around him.

The crowd felt it. They backed up without meaning to. Nobody breathed too loudly.

He grinned again, lips cracked, showing a flash of a gold tooth and old blood. His grin stretched like a dare.

"Hey, you think you can just kidnap my cousin or what?"

His laugh was short, nasty bark.

Before my mouth could form the right kind of curse, his hand slid into his waistband and pulled out a sawed-off shotgun. Oak and iron, scuffed raw, smelling of old smoke and cheap oil.

The barrel pointed at my face, and the world narrowed to metal and breath.

Time mutated. It was as if someone had poured syrup into the air.

I saw the muzzle in perfect, terrible detail. The rough seam where the metal met the wood. A ring of soot inside the barrel. The tiny fleck of dried powder was like a dead star.

My lungs slow down by accident. All the other noise—the music, voices, the slap of feet on gravel—muffles into the thud of my own heart. I hear my pulse in my teeth.

"What now?" he asks, continuing with his grin.

I plant my feet in the gravel, keep my shoulders low, my voice flat and even.

"Pull it," I say. "Do me a favor. Pull it. What you scared of, Spider?"

Saying it calms me, like saying his name might tame him. Maybe it does. Or maybe it makes him angrier.

He slams his thumb to the trigger.

Click.

The sound is small and hollow, like a door stuck on its latch. He tries again.

Click. Click.

The shotgun coughs but will not speak. With each dead pull, the grin thins, then cracks. Confusion slides over his face like fog. His hands—previously confident—start to fidget, working the stock, checking the breach, fingers slapping metal like a man trying to wake something that will not wake.

While he is distracted, toying with his own arrogance, shaking the weapon to force it to work, it betrays him.

A single, violent boom detonates.

Not from where it had been steady-pointed in my face, but from the arc of his fumble as he lifted it and it pointed in the air. The blast rips the night open. It punches a cone of sound into the parking lot, a jagged, hot noise that vibrates the teeth and throws dust off the cinderblocks.

The air fills with the raw smell of burnt powder and hot metal. It stings my throat. The shotgun kicks and locks up.

It jammed.

Spider stands there, half-frozen and suddenly very small. The laugh drains from his face, replaced with that stunned blankness you see in men who thought they controlled the script and just watched the pen explode.

He stares at the gun like it is a mirror showing him his own bluff. For the first time, the angle of his jaw does not cut fear. It shows disbelief.

He shoves the weapon away from his hands like a piece of trash. Panicked, he bolts for his car.

People scatter like a flock. Shouts shred into the night.

My knees go weak, then steady. Adrenaline slams through me like a second heartbeat. I do not move. I am still trying to process what just happened.

Spider slams his car door. The engine skips a beat, then starts to peel away.

For a moment, I am caught in the aftershock. I stand there, chest heaving, hands numb—not from the cold, but from the shock that something that should have ended us instead ended in a misfire.

Everything spikes into motion. My legs finally catch up with my brain.

I shout, "He's leaving!" but the night has already spilled into chaos.

People scatter like scared birds. The party crowd that followed us breaks off into small packs, scattering down alleys and into cars.

I fully turn around. I only see Paul. He is the only one to stay by my side, the only one who did not run. His face is pale but steady, eyes hard as stone.

We do not waste words. I take off running and Paul follows.

"Where we running to?" Paul yells.

"Vanessa's car!"

We sprint past smashed bottles and trash thrown everywhere on the ground, lungs burning, shoes pounding the asphalt.

Adrenaline punches hard. It makes you fast when time is running out.

Vanessa's door flies open when we get there. She is shaking, hands trembling, but her eyes are focused.

"What was that about?" she asks, trying to fold terror into composure.

"Just drive. Now."

I toss the packet of cash to her and it lands like truth on her lap.

Just then, as we start to go, we see Aiden walking up.

"Aiden, get in!" I shout with a roar.

He jumps in the back with Paul. I tell Vanessa, "Let's go. Do not let him get away."

She grinds the engine to life, tires howling, and we peel out, rocks spitting everywhere behind us.

I slam my palm against the dash for balance, pulse hammering.

I see Spider's busted car ahead, fumbling, trying to get traction and get away.

Vanessa guns it toward Hancock.

Inside the car, the world is all motion and noise. No radio. Heavy breathing. The city flicking by like a film strip.

We give chase recklessly. We are flying.

Spider is going to get his. That is all I could think.

That moment—caught in headlights, shotgun pointed in my face, gunpowder taste in my mouth—changed something.

I am no longer just surviving the street's laws.

I am defending family. Answering the only code I know.

Street code.

Out here, it is simple. Listen up. You either ride hard or you do not ride at all. Go hard or go home.

There is no half-stepping. No second chances.

The streets owe you nothing, especially not respect. You earn it with every move, every look, every breath you take.

The code is clear. Loyalty first. Survival always.

Keep your circle tight. Talk is cheap. Actions speak louder than words.

If you say you are down, you'd better be ready to prove it.

Hesitation gets you killed. Fear is not an option. Courage is the only ticket out alive. Remember the names of those who never made it. Their mistakes are your lessons. Their loss is your warning. Live fast. Move smarter. Every sunrise is borrowed time. Every night is a test. And remember this most of all—the streets do not sleep. They do not forgive. They do not love. You either stand by the code, or the code stands by itself and you will not be standing. Do or die. No excuses. No regrets. That is the street's law. Period.

Vanessa slides the car into a safer lane, voice low as gravel. We are all breathing like we ran a mile. Vanessa's foot is mashed to the floor, tires screaming, her hands ghost white on the wheel.

"I thought he was gonna shoot you in the face," she keeps saying, voice stuck between panic and anger.

"Me too," I say, throat raw. "He definitely tried and kept pulling the trigger. It just kept clicking. Then it went boom when he moved it away."

"What? It went off?" she breathes.

"It did. Once he moved it."

"Oh my God. Are you serious?" she cries.

"Hurry. He turned on Hancock. He is gonna get away," I say.

"We got him," Paul snaps, voice like steel. "We are gonna catch him."

She floors it. The city blurs. I notice Aiden's hands flying across his phone—calling, texting, cussing. Paul keeps throwing looks out the window. This packet of cash burns in my jacket pocket, proof that the night is still two layers deep: money and blood.

Then the hum above us was a low, mechanical growl that eats street noise. I look up and my stomach drops. Ghetto Bird. The CSPD helicopter with searchlight splits the sky, the eye in the sky. It tracks us and keeps its spotlight on us.

"We got company, guys," Paul says, voice tight. "The chopper's on us."

"They are following the wrong people. We are the victims here."

The turn onto Circle Drive feels unreal. We are blocked in ahead, like a curtain closing. Two all-black Navigators, black on black, dark tinted windows, engines idling. Men in black gear step out—tactical. AR-15s hang from their shoulders like iron promises. They are not city cops in shiny uniforms. They are something else—federal, private, or the kind of crew that makes you rethink every split-second decision. They point, and the world freezes to muzzles and fingers on triggers.

One car angles to block our path. The other squares off to cover. A voice booms from a megaphone.

"Pull over now! Keep your hands visible!"

That voice is not asking. We freeze. Vanessa's knuckles whiten on the wheel. The seat vibrates under my knees. My mind races. If we do not stop, they will light us up. If we do stop, what the hell are we walking into? I picture Spider's car—gun jammed, fleeing the scene, running away—and it hits me. He slipped away from this net and these men here.

Vanessa eases the car to the side of the road, heart in her throat. Engines idle.

"If you guys got anything, give it to me now," Vanessa gasps, voice surprisingly steady, looking directly at us. "Hurry."

Her hand hovers in front of the dash like a judge waiting for testimony.

The men in black fan out, rifles leveled, boots crunching over gravel. One of them pans a flashlight through the car like he is scanning the future. Another barks over a radio. For one breath, we are actors on a stage where the director is a loaded gun. Outside, the men in black are breathing engines and authority. The chopper light swings again, lighting our faces in a cold, surgical glow.

"Hands where I can see 'em!" someone yells.

Vanessa slides cash and cigarettes across the dash fast, like trading a life for a second. The money lands with a soft slap, an offering to the night. For a second, everything shows itself— the money, the chopper's beam, the black rifles, the echo of Spider's shotgun jam. This is the street's courtroom with no judge, only consequences.

They yank us out like we are luggage unwanted on a cheap flight. One officer hauls Vanessa out the driver door. Another levels his AR and tells us all to get out, shoving us to the curb. The barrel irons my spine. The world tilts to the rhythm of boots and commands. The chopper's beam paints everything white and mean. For a second, I swear you could hear the air breathe.

The other cop, lean and brisk, goes to work on the car. Palms crawl through upholstery, pulling floor mats and peering under seats like he is looking for secrets. Gravel digs into my knees as we are forced down, hands curled into the curb, face lit by the sick light of a spotlight.

"Where are the guns at?" one of them says.

"You totally got the wrong car, idiot. They tried to shoot us and we were chasing them," Vanessa says.

They come up short. No stash slipping out the back door. No weapon tucked under a seat. The hidden pockets and careful folds do what they always do when you have learned the game—disappear.

"You guys are good to go," the searching cop finally says, voice flat and tilted toward boredom. Like that seals it. Like the night's verdict just got handed to us wrapped in a badge.

I spit the sentence back out into the cold.

"We told you. We were victims. The guy shot at us."

My voice is rough. It hangs there between the hum of the chopper and the static in my ears.

Vanessa climbs back into the car, hands shaking, the seatbelt a lifeline she pulls across her chest like armor. Luckily, she had her driver's license, and we did not have any real drugs on us—just enough for Vanessa to shove in her bra.

"Now what?" she asks, eyes still wide.

"I guess take us back," I tell her. I do not know where Spider went. He could be anywhere.

"Who knows where that fool went now?"

That was wild, I think. The city's teeth flashed out at us and then retreated. We played our part and lived to tell it. Someone had called it in. That chopper and the all-black SWAT team could not have just appeared out of nowhere. The party must have screamed like a signal somebody above picked up on. Or maybe fate's favor swings randomly like a drunk driver. I do not know.

The ride back is quiet in the way that comes after a storm. Vanessa drives like she is steering a coffin—careful, slow, hands gripping the wheel. The streets slide by, familiar and alien under the chopper's fading light.

We get dropped off at my spot like survivors getting left at the dock of the world. I want to thank Vanessa, and I mean it. She smiles, small and tight, like a woman who has been spared and wants to pretend it is all casual.

"Anytime," she says, but the word breaks a little at the edges.

We headed upstairs. Drained. The apartment still smells of stale smoke, spilled beer, and the faint perfume of regret. My boys sit back in the living room. We pass the blunt around, inhaling slowly. Voices get low. Stories loop. Who screamed, who ran, who did not, who froze. Paul's eyes are bright and hard. Aiden is mad; he missed out.

We smoke and talk like men trying to put the night into words that make sense. But sense is not what this city deals with. It trades in moments that are shallow, sharp, and finished before you can swallow.

After a few hours, the bottles are lighter, but the eyes are heavier. I can feel the adrenaline finally unhooking from my ribs and leaving a bruise. My boys leave.

I stare into the dark window, seeing my own face abstracted in the glass, tired, young, something brewing under the surface. The city keeps breathing. Its lights blink like accusations. The world did not stop because a shotgun misfired. It moved on.

Tonight, I survived. Tomorrow, the streets will ask for their fair share in return.

The next day always came too fast, like time was running a hustle on me. I had about twelve grand tucked away in my "just in case" stash. Thought it would last me a minute, but getting out of jail ate five right off the top. Just like that, gone.

That left me with a little over six, but I needed a lawyer and quick. Could not afford to play the public defender game. I started calling around, chasing names through whispers and favors. Finally, I found a lawyer who seemed to know his way around my kind of trouble. He did not smile much, just held out his hand and said,

"Two thousand five-hundred-dollar retainer."

No payment plans. No mercy. I had to pay for that.

That is when it hit me. I was running out of runway. Money is drying up faster than I could think. Every dollar had a heartbeat, and I could hear it fading.

So, I did what I knew. Took what was left, hit the block, and picked up some more. Had to get the bag moving again. Get my money right before everything collapsed.

I called the plug. Told him what happened the cops, the bail, the lawyer. He was not happy. Said I was hot now. That heat was on me.

I told him I would move carefully. He just said, "Be safe, bro." But his tone said he was already second-guessing me.

We both knew what that meant. The streets do not give do-overs. You either bounce back fast or you get swallowed whole.

I pulled up to my parents' place, trying to keep it cool, but my mind was racing. Pops was outside, leaning against his car like he had been waiting for me. He nodded once, slowly.

"I got a surprise for you," he said.

I raised an eyebrow. "Yeah? What's that?"

"Just watch."

We walked across the lot, toward the other apartment complex. He took the back way—the kind of route people who have seen too much always use. No cameras. No questions. We reached the back stairwell, and the air grew colder, heavier with the smell of concrete and metal.

Halfway up, he stopped, pulled out a key, and held it up between his fingers.

I smirked. "You serious?"

He grinned, that half-smile that said he was proud but did not want to admit it. Then he pressed the key into my palm.

"Here. Your new spot."

I looked at it; it was silver, fresh-cut, still sharp on the edges. "Nice," I said, pocketing it. But then he reached into his other pocket and pulled out a second key.

"And this one," he said, "is across the hall. It is usually for storage or maintenance." He looked me dead in the eye. "Keep all your stuff in there. You hear me? Do not keep anything at your house."

We stepped inside that room—empty, but not really. An old fridge hums in the corner, its shelves scattered with tools and paint cans, the air filled with the smell of dust and oil. He walked around like he had been there before.

"There's power. There's space. You can stash whatever you got here. Toys, goodies, whatever you got going on. Everything stays in here. Not where you sleep. You understand? Do not tell anybody either."

I nodded. No words needed.

That was when it hit me. My dad, The Rock, was a gangster too. Not the kind that bragged or flashed it, but the kind that carried it quietly, like a second skin. He had walked that same road I was on, only his was paved roughly, more darkly. He had spent years trying to beat that life out of me, warning me how it ends and how cold the streets are—hard times filled with no peace. He wanted better for me, even when I could not see it.

When he realized I was not stopping, not by a long shot, he stopped fighting me. He just adjusted. That is what real ones do, right? They love you through the mess. He knew the signs—the late calls, the fast cash, the tired eyes.

I thought deep down that he was no longer angry. Just content with it all. Because he knew exactly what it cost to live like that. Saw me paying the same price. This time, instead of lectures, he handed me tools in the form of keys and silence.

That silence meant more than words ever could. It was him saying, I see you. I know what you are doing. Just do not get caught.

For the first time, I saw him not as the one who tried to change me, but as the one who never left me. Out there under the same streetlight that once watched us drift apart, we found a little peace with each other—not perfect, but real. My father's love.

Yeah, my dad also loved his weed. Always did. He just did not hide it now. It was his peace, the same way the streets were mine. So, if I had it, he had it too. I would roll through, drop him something nice, no questions asked.So, if I had it, he had it too. I would roll through, drop him something nice, no questions, no thanks, just that nod we both understood. That was when I learned something real. Sometimes you just have to accept it—the life, the choices, the bloodline that comes with it. You can fight it all you want, but some things are already written. You have to pay the cost to be the boss, and lately, that cost was getting higher.

Now, I am not saying I was a drug lord or anything, but I was making moves. I was my own supply chain, bought bulk with my own money at cost, and sold at retail.

I got sloppy. Too many eyes, too many mouths knowing too much. I knew better. I knew never to keep weight where you sleep, but I let comfort fool me.

Lesson learned.

In this life, awareness is not optional. It is survival. And I was done slipping. I kept stacking. Working. Living. Doing my best to move like everything was cool, like the walls were not closing in a little more every day.

My time was split between working my nine-to-five, the streets, hustling, and my daughter, Nevaeh. She was my peace in the chaos. Just hearing her laugh made the noise fade, even for a minute.

Deep down, I knew what was coming. I could feel it creeping closer, like a shadow that never left. Prison. I would have to sit down for a while.

Months passed. I was making money, staying busy, trying not to think about the case hanging over my head. Then one afternoon, my phone rang. I already knew who it was before I answered.

"Hello?" I said.

"Hello, Mr. Hinojosa?"

"Yeah, speaking."

"Hey, this is your lawyer. Got a few updates for you."

My stomach tightened. "Alright, what's the word?"

He took a breath, that slow kind that tells you it is not good.

"I have good news and bad news, okay?"

I leaned back, eyes on the ceiling. "Hit me."

"You are looking at four years DOC..."

"DOC?" I interrupted.

"Department of Corrections. Prison."

The word prison hit like a punch, even though I had been expecting it.

He kept going. "But there is another option—COMCOR."

"What is COMCOR?"

"It is Community Corrections. Basically, a halfway house. You apply, and if they accept you, you live there instead of going to prison. You get a job, go to work, check in, check out. More freedom, but still under DOC."

For a moment, I couldn't say anything. Then I said, "Alright. Apply me."

"Okay," he replied, papers shuffling on the other end. "I will submit an application. Someone might contact you to do a PSI."

"What is a PSI?"

"Pre-Sentence Investigation. They dig into your background, family, work history, everything. That is how they decide if you qualify."

"Alright," I said. "That is what I want. Go ahead."

"Will do. Stay out of trouble, alright?"

"Yeah," I said quietly. "Will do."

"Okay, goodbye."

"Goodbye."

Click.

The line went dead. I just sat there, phone still to my ear, listening to the silence that came after. Four years DOC, or maybe a halfway house if I got lucky. Either way, the clock was ticking.

I looked around my place—half-clean, half-chaos. Smoke hanging in the air. The city moving outside my window like it did not care who was free and who was not.

That was when I told myself: keep working, keep stacking, keep breathing. Until they put cuffs on me again, I was still out there. Still living.

CHAPTER 30: LET IT BURN

I had been trying hard to make it work between me and Felicia, especially for our daughter, Nevaeh. I ended up getting a two-bedroom apartment away from everything and everyone, with our own rhythm. Just the three of us, trying to build something that almost looked like a family up on Fillmore Street. For a while, I thought maybe things were finally looking up. Even with all the chaos, all the yelling, all the bruises, all the police calls—I kept trying. I wanted that picture, that family. I wanted Nevaeh to grow up seeing her parents together. Not because my parents weren't together, because they still were, but because all the people around me had broken families.

Unfortunately, Felicia had her demons and I had mine. There were nights filled with arguments that turned into something else. Words turned sharp, hands flew, and the air filled with that bitter mix of love and hate that only comes when two broken people won't let go. There were multiple domestic violence cases reported, filled with all that noise. I never hit her back, not once. Only guarded and protected my face from getting hit. No matter how hard she came at me, I just took it. She would end up in jail, then out, and then right back in my arms. Same cycle, different day.

Still, I kept hustling. Selling weed on the side, doing landscaping jobs, anything to keep money coming in. When I caught that case, I thought I was gone for real this time—thought I was going to prison, four years DOC. Finally, I heard from my lawyer and I lucked out. They sent me to Comcor instead, Community Corrections. A halfway house. I did my time, stayed at the apartment, sold drugs during the day, worked here and there, and slept at the halfway house. I handled my business and even got off paper two years early.

But the streets don't let go that easy, and neither did she.

My parents moved closer to me not long after that. They actually got into a house just across the street from my apartment on Fillmore. Ten minutes away if you were walking. It felt good knowing they were close. Like a safety net I would never admit I needed. Time rolled on, and so did the arguments with Felicia. Same old story, day in, day out. I started thinking maybe she picked fights just to get away, to have an excuse to leave and do her own thing. Maybe I was wrong, maybe I was right. Maybe I just didn't want to see the actual truth.

When she was gone, I stayed home. Me and my baby girl would chill, watch cartoons, eat whatever we could throw together—eggs, noodles, cereal for dinner. Didn't matter. Those were the best moments. Just me and Nevaeh, quiet, warm, safe. I will always cherish those moments.

Even when Felicia's mom started wilding out on me—and believe me, there's more to that story—I still tried to keep it together. Tried to keep that family picture taped together, even when the corners kept tearing off. But the fights… they never stopped. I would hear her voice rise, feel my heart sink. After a while, it just got old. Same pain, same pattern, different day.

That was when it hit me. I wasn't staying for love anymore. I was staying for duty. For my daughter. That realization hurt more than anything she had ever done to me. I tried, man. I really did. Bit my tongue until it bled. Swallowed my pride, my anger, my peace—all of it. But I couldn't do it anymore. By then, Nevaeh was six, maybe seven. Old enough to see things she shouldn't. Old enough to ask questions I couldn't answer.

And that was my breaking point.

Finally, I couldn't take the fighting anymore. It wasn't love anymore, it was just noise. The same words, the same pain, looping like a bad song. It got to the point where even silence felt heavy.

One night after work, I sat in the room by myself for a while, sitting on the edge of the bed, just breathing and crying. I had already called my parents, told them what was up—the yelling, the abuse continuing, the nights that turned ugly for no reason. My mom stayed quiet. My dad just said, "Do what you gotta do, son," and that was enough for me.

The apartment was empty. No yelling. No footsteps. Just quiet—the kind of quiet that feels strange at first but peaceful after a while. I looked around and the place still smelled like her perfume and smoke. Nevaeh's toys were scattered on the floor. A half-finished coloring book sat on the coffee table. That hit me.

I packed my clothes, just the essentials. Left everything else behind. The TV, the furniture, the kitchen stuff of it. It was hers now. Or better yet, it was for Nevaeh. She deserved to keep her world as normal as possible, even if mine was falling apart.

As I zipped my bag, I felt that mix of relief and heartbreak. Felicia had turned mean, cruel even. Not just angry but pure cold. I don't know if it was the streets, the stress, or just who she really was. But whatever the case may be, I was done. Emotionally tapped out.

I walked out, closed the door behind me, and didn't look back.

A few days passed and the emptiness started settling in. Nights felt longer. I kept hearing her voice in my head sometimes angry, sometimes soft. I knew I had to drown it out before it ate me alive. So, I remembered something I once told one of my boys:

"Best way to get over a girl is to get under another one."

Those words seemed cold but real in that moment. I moved into my parents' basement. Started talking to new women. Different faces, same game. Nothing serious, just company, just noise to fill the quiet. Still selling. Still doing me. Just trying to find a rhythm again, figure life out one day at a time. Freedom felt good, but it was lonely too. I had traded one kind of pain for another, but at least now I could breathe.

Even after all that chaos, Felicia still found her way back. Uninvited. I would be at my parents' house, downstairs in the basement, trying to keep low, keep quiet, just breathe for a minute. Somehow, she would show up like smoke through a crack. Every time there was a girl over, she would come storming in like she owned the place, bright-eyed, ready to throw hands. It did not matter who it was. She did not care. She would fight anybody.

I would stand there watching it go down, thinking, What the hell happened to us? You fought with me about everything, pushed me away. Now you could go do whatever, have whoever... and you were mad because I was talking to someone else? You did not want me then.

It got so bad, these girls were trying to kill each other—real blood, not just words. I remember feeling trapped, embarrassed even, but mostly tired. I could not believe how far gone she was. I just wished she would let it go, move on, like I was trying to. It was so obvious we could not be around each other. We were not even together anymore. We had called it quits. There was no reason for it, no logic, just that same storm she carried everywhere she went.

Around that same time, I picked up a job at a small-time marketing research firm, one of those call centers tucked inside a strip mall. They did surveys over the phone. It was not glamorous, but I needed something different, something clean.

The interview was nothing—a room full of fluorescent lights, stale coffee, and people who looked just as lost as me. They handed me a script and instructed me to read it. I read it cleanly, steadily, as if I had been doing it for years.

Passed the script test.

Then they put me in front of a computer to check if I could type and navigate.

Passed that too.

"You're hired," the manager said, barely looking up from his papers.

That was it. A small win, but it felt bigger than it was. I remember walking out into the parking lot afterwards, the air cold and heavy, thinking maybe—just maybe—this was the start of something new. A door is cracking open. A way out from under Felicia's madness, from under my own past.

I did not know where it would lead, but for the first time in a long while, I felt like I was walking toward something instead of running from it. And maybe, just maybe, I would finally get away from Felicia's path.

CHAPTER 31: TURN DOWN FOR WHAT?

I started working at that call center six, sometimes seven days a week, thinking I was finally pulling my life together. What I did not realize then was that place was not just a job. It was the spot. The underground heartbeat of the city hiding behind cubicles and headsets.

I learned quickly that everybody there was chasing something other than a paycheck, and it was not coffee or energy drinks. That was not what kept them up through those long shifts. No. It was something darker. You could smell it before you even sat down—tired eyes, desperation, burnt foil, chemical sweat. The grind did not just live on the phones. It ran through veins, and it was an itch.

At first, I played it cool. I brought my little bag of weed, nothing heavy. Just enough to get through the hours of calling strangers who hung up before you even said your name. The more I stayed, the more I saw. The look in people's eyes during breaks. The quiet deals in the rear parking lot. The whispers that came with a folded twenty.

It did not take long before I leveled up and took over.

Pills.

Crystal.

Cocaine.

And of course, weed—whatever moved fast.

Soon enough, I was running it all. My backpack turned into a mobile pharmacy with the extras—blunt sticks, joint papers, foil, and straws. I kept it clean and organized like a pro. Everyone knew who to come to. It did not matter what shift they were on. I was there. Even if I was not scheduled to work that day, I was there.

That place never slept. The schedule was split into projects, people coming and going every hour.

2–6 p.m.

3–7 p.m.

4–8 p.m.

5–9 p.m.

6–10 p.m.

People were coming and going all day long, a nonstop shuffle of faces. I could have someone pull up, make a pickup, and nobody would even blink. Constant rotation. You would look up and the whole room would be different—new voices, new eyes, same hunger. Phones ringing nonstop. Voices echoing off the cheap walls. Keyboards clacking like teeth in the cold. The hum of the fluorescent lights never stopped either, a low, dirty buzz that felt like it was watching me, judging me.

In the middle of all that chaos, I was moving product right under their noses, right there in the mix, hidden in plain sight. Nobody questioned anything. Too much traffic. Too much chaos. It was a cold lick, fast money, no stress. And for a while, it felt like I had found my own kind of success. Deep down, I knew when things come easy like that, there is always a price waiting to get paid.

Back then, I was still living in my parents' basement. It had its own bathroom and shower, two bedrooms, a huge living area, low ceiling, and just enough space to breathe between the noise upstairs and the demons downstairs. What started small turned wild fast. The call center money was coming in steady, and the crowd I ran with—including Paul, Aiden, and whoever else drifted through—we kept the party alive almost every night.

The basement had turned into a whole different world at night. Dim lights bleeding through clouds of smoke so thick you could taste it in the back of your throat. Music rattled the walls, bass heavy enough to shake the bottles lining the floor. Ashtrays overflowed, the air stale with burnt paper and spilled liquor. Laughter mixed with shouting, arguments breaking out and fading just as fast. The hum of cell phones buzzed across the table with calls, deals, messages, everyone chasing something.

Every night bled into the next, a haze of smoke, bass, and restless energy. Faces blurred, slipping in and out like ghosts, each chasing the same escape, the same deadened edge that kept them moving.

The call center crew showed up like clockwork, fresh from the fluorescent grind, sweat mingled with cheap cologne, eyes already half-distant from the day. They clocked out from dialing strangers and clocked right in down here—scripts traded for smoke; survey sheets swapped for rolled bills and lines cut across mirrored surfaces.

Nobody spoke of tomorrow. Down there, tomorrow did not exist. There was only the drumbeat of music vibrating through the floor, the taste of smoke in your mouth. A sense of untouchable power draped over the room for a few hours. We thought we were larger than life, invisible to consequences, untethered from the streets and jobs that ruled us the rest of the day.

In the quiet moments between laughter and chaos, when the smoke thinned and the bass dropped low, the emptiness seeped in. That feeling of being untouchable? It was temporary, and we all knew it, even if we never said it aloud.

Vanessa started coming around more, too, always rolling through with money, buying weed, drinking, just being part of the mix. Felicia couldn't stand it. Even before all this, she swore something was going on between Vanessa and me—but there wasn't. Vanessa was cool. She knew the game, knew where I stood. Still, that tension was there every time she showed up. Unspoken. Heavy. Like the calm before a storm.

I tried not to think too much about it. I was making money, stacking paper, keeping the parties lit. Every night was another excuse to stay numb, to not deal with what was waiting for me when the music stopped. Down there in that basement, it felt like my own world. My rules. My rhythm. My grind. Even then, deep inside, I knew what every real one knows—when the party's that loud, it's only because you're trying to drown something out.

Time moved differently. Days bled into nights, and nights turned into stories I barely remembered but everybody else did. The streets started whispering my name—Suspect. It wasn't just a name anymore. It was a whole identity I had built from smoke and survival.

At that time, I was in an '82 Monte Carlo, midnight blue with chrome flakes that caught the streetlights like sparks off a fuse. Thirteen-inch chrome rims. Windows tinted so dark you couldn't tell if anyone was inside. She purred low and mean, looked like the car from Training Day—just a few years off, with the same attitude, the same danger. When I pulled up, people noticed. That ride said everything I didn't have to.

I was in the middle of building something, a name, a legend, a persona. Suspect. That was who I was becoming more and more. I wasn't chasing women anymore. They were chasing me. And me? I was chasing status. Paper. Power. I had already tasted enough love to know it didn't last. But money—that had a different kind of loyalty.

Yeah, the women still came and left just as quick. I didn't care if they had a man or not. That was their business, not mine. I was Suspect, and I always got what I wanted. Period. Cold heart. Clear mission. Steal your love and leave. That was the code.

Women felt that energy before I even said a word. They could smell the fast life on me—the money in the air, danger in my walk. Some wanted to save me. Others just wanted to taste the flame. Either way, they came. But I wasn't looking for love. I had traded that in a long time ago for control, attention, and respect. All the things the streets tell you are worth more than peace.

I had mastered the art of being wanted but never reachable. Behind closed doors, though, there was silence. The kind that hums. The kind that makes you think about what it costs to be that person. But I had trained myself to drown it out—another call, another face, another deal.

I told myself I was proud of who I had become. I believed it too. Suspect didn't break. Didn't love. Didn't lose. He just moved. Cold. Calculated. Focused. Somewhere underneath all that, buried deep, the real me—the one who used to care—was still breathing. Barely. Watching it all happen from the inside, too afraid to speak up.

You could ask about me. Yeah, the stories were out there. I wore my reputation like a crown, and at that time, I took pride in it. It didn't matter who got hurt, who got left behind. All I saw was the grind, the glory, and my reflection in it.

I wasn't living for love. I was living for the fame—for my name.

The call center had become more than a job, it was an ecosystem, a city within walls and I was climbing it fast. What started as just answering phones turned into something bigger. I got close with the higher-ups, the ones who ran things, both legit and off the books. We leaned on each other, partied together, moved weight together. Late nights, strip clubs, cash flashing under neon lights. Loyalty built in smoke-filled backrooms and lines cut across tabletops. It didn't take long before they pulled me from the phones.

The first promotion was to Coach. I was the one guiding the interviewers, showing them how to talk smoothly, keep people on the line, and fake the smile that made the surveys sound real. Then I climbed higher, they called it The Point. That title meant something. I was the one everybody went through. Coaches, interviewers, project scripts — all of it ran across my desk. The "point of contact," yeah, but really, I was the heartbeat of that building, and I ran it clean.

Professional by day, dealer by night, but honestly, those lines blurred a long time ago. By then, I was both. Eventually, I was bumped again — to Scheduling Manager. Real title, real power. Nine-to-five office keys, my name on paperwork. I was the one putting hundreds of people on the schedule, with three or four hundred voices a day working under me. If someone misses a shift, I put them on probation. Three strikes — fired. Just like that. I was handing out paychecks and pink slips while still running my own hustle behind the scenes.

There I was sitting in a real office, writing names on spreadsheets with one hand, and bagging up with the other. Still selling. Still partying. Still keeping both worlds spinning. It was all working, or at least I thought it was.

After a stretch of months and climbing the ranks, with promotions stacking up, the side hustle is still moving forward. I finally had enough to step out on my own. Got a townhouse not far from work, two stories, three bedrooms, a fireplace that looked too nice for the streets I'd just crawled out of. A solid spot, clean lines, the kind of place that made you feel like maybe you'd arrived somewhere. Five minutes from the call center, quick enough to handle whatever came my way, whether it was work, money or business that couldn't be handled over the phone.

It was different, having my own personal space. Nobody was going to know where I slept, not a single person. No basement walls closing in, no neighbors watching me like a zoo exhibit. Just me, my hustle, and room enough to breathe. I set it up just right, planning for Nevaeh when she came over, making it feel like a real home instead of just another stops on the grind. A couple of weeks passed, and a routine in full swing, working both jobs, when my phone rang. The screen lit up, and as I looked at the screen, I noticed it was Vanessa, a familiar voice on the other end...

"Hey..." I answer.

"Hey, you got any trees?"

"Of course. Always. I'll bring it by." I said.

She started showing up more, every day, every night. Drinks became a ritual, bottles cracked, laughter spilling over the rims, smoke curling in the corners. We'd been around each other for years now, always close but never serious. Flirting here and there, teasing, testing but never crossing the line... but with that one simple call came a small spark in that quiet townhouse, away from the chaos of the basement and the constant grind of the call center, that little spark felt like a fuse lighting in the dark and I knew whatever came next, it wasn't just a delivery. It was a reminder that the streets didn't care where I lived. They always found me. That little spark would light the fuse on everything that came next.

CHAPTER 32: BEWARE OF THE SERPENT'S KISS

"A trusted figure delivers betrayal with a kiss, venomous, calculated and cloaked in charm. The devil's wrath isn't loud. It's intimate. Payback brews beneath the surface, ready to strike."

"Okay, see you soon," Vanessa said, like the night already belonged to her. She would call her homegirls over, and I would bring my boys, Paul and Aiden—my day ones, my ride-or-dies. The crews mixed like sparks in gasoline, energy bouncing off the walls, music pulsing, the streets watching through windows tinted with smoke and neon reflection.

Vanessa had brothers, Steven and Anthony. They were solid, protective, but solid in a way that made sure nobody crossed her line. She stayed at Anthony's house off Union, and that became our spot. Her brothers and I hadn't gotten along in school growing up. We were raised on different sides of the tracks. A similar life, just in different neighborhoods. It was iffy at first with them coming around, but I knew Vanessa told them to chill. Nights there were exciting and thrilling—bottles, bass, cigarette smoke, whispers, secrets traded in glances.

Then it happened. Slowly, almost without noticing, the friendship shifted. The teasing, the late-night laughter, the shared silences, it all turned into something bigger. Something real. Our connection bloomed and blossomed like fire in the night, hot and unstoppable. My feelings for Vanessa ran deep, carved into me, and were impossible to ignore. Love snuck in through the cracks of chaos, and for once, the streets couldn't touch it.

One summer night, the kind that sticks to your skin, we were all drinking like usual, bottles clinking, laughter bouncing off the walls, the air thick with smoke and heat. Time didn't exist in those moments, just the blur of the night. That night, Paul was ready to leave somewhere, and I had been picked up by him earlier. I needed a ride back to my Monte Carlo. I didn't want to be stranded at Vanessa's, stumbling through the streets half-drunk back home.

Paul agreed to give me a ride, and Vanessa insisted on coming too. She could drive us both back to her house because I was completely trashed and had been gone. If I was that gone, I could only imagine how trashed Paul was—but he insisted he wasn't.

We stepped out into the warm, humid air, exiting Vanessa's house, the streetlights painting long, lazy shadows. Paul's ride was waiting—a 1999 Cadillac, four-door, rims shining faintly under the dim glow of the streetlamps. Sleek, heavy, the kind of car that looks suspicious. We all slid in. Paul behind the wheel, me in the passenger seat, Vanessa jumping in the back.

Paul flicked the lighter, the small flame dancing before catching the tip of the cigarette he put to his lips. Sparks flew like tiny fireflies in the dark, the metallic click echoing softly through the Cadillac. He drew the first inhale deep, smoke filling his lungs, and exhaled slowly, the glowing ember bright in the dark like a heartbeat. The sharp scent of tobacco mixed with the tang of spilled liquor and worn leather, curling through the Cadillac, heavy and thick.

He let the cigarette rest between his fingers for a second, then slammed it into the ashtray with a practiced flick. Sparks scattered, a tiny flash that lingered before fading into shadow. The motion was casual but precisely quiet warning, a mark of control. Every move in that car had rhythm.

Then the music hits, bass rolling through the frame like a living spirit, rattling every nerve in my body. Paul shifted smoothly into gear, cracked open the sunroof, and let the smoke bellow out. Tires ready to go against the asphalt with a steady pulse, syncing to the heartbeat of the city itself.

The streets blurred streetlights stretched into long gold streaks, neon signs bleeding color across the wet pavement like distant fireworks frozen in motion. Paul slid into the left lane, handing me the cigarette as we eased onto Fillmore. The clock read two, maybe two-thirty in the morning. The streets were quiet, city lights glowing faintly in the distance, the kind of hour that makes you feel like the world is yours.

We were heading west, mountains rising in the distance, silhouettes cutting across the horizon. The bass thumped through the car, a steady heartbeat, keeping time with the hum of the tires on asphalt. Paul grinned, and I could feel the tension coiled in him, ready to snap. He floored the engine just a little, letting the Cadillac growl under us, and I laughed, leaning back.

"What?" he asked, voice low, amused but curious.

"This car ain't fast, bro," I said, flicking ashes out the window. "Cool it already."

He shot me a look so foul, sharp—the kind of glare that made the back of your neck prickle. "You don't think so?" he asked, voice tight with challenge.

I shrugged, smirked. "Don't think so."

Paul's eyes narrowed. Then a grin cracked across his face, the kind that promised trouble. "Okay," he said. "Watch this."

With that, the tires bit harder into the asphalt, the engine roaring like it had been waiting for this moment the entire time. The street blurred beneath us, lights stretching into lines of fire, the night rushing past—alive, untouchable, dangerous—and we were right in the middle of it, spinning toward whatever came next. Smoke spiraled upward through the sunroof, mixing with the sharp tang of alcohol and leather, filling the inside of the Cadillac with a weight that pressed against our skin.

Outside, the city moved faster than life itself. Shadows danced in alleyways, windows glimmered with unknown stories, and for a moment, the streets belonged to us. That tiny flick of a cigarette, a spark in the dark, felt like a signal, the heartbeat of the night. In that instant, everything was sharp, alive, ours. Real.

I thought, Oh man, Paul's stupid. And before I could even blink, he floored it again. The Cadillac roared through the red lights at Nevada and Fillmore, tires screaming against asphalt, adrenaline hitting me like a punch. Down the hill we flew past the next set of lights at Cascade and Fillmore. I grabbed the handle like it was the only thing keeping me alive.

"Okay, Paul. Okay, Paul. Slow down!" I yelled, gripping tight.

Vanessa was in the backseat, screaming, "Slow down! Slow down!"

"I got you," Paul said, calm as ice, his foot buried in the gas.

The Cadillac soared over the uneven asphalt, up and down, like a rollercoaster engineered by chaos. The air shocks absorbed the jumps, letting the car float, glide, almost defy gravity. Paul was ten toes down on the pedal, eyes locked ahead, a statement burning in every motion. This wasn't just driving. This was a message, and we were all living it.

Faster and faster, we barreled past the Dairy Queen, the lights flashing past like strobe signals in a nightmare. Around the bend we went, the wheel jerking under his hands, the car still airborne for a split second, suspending us between earth and sky. Every nerve in my body screamed, heart hammering against my ribs.

Then—**skrrrrrrrt**—we landed and slid.

BOOM! We crashed.

The Cadillac slammed into the guardrail with full force, metal screaming, tires skidding, the smell of burnt rubber rattling our bones, shaking us like ragdolls. Vanessa screamed again, but this time it was a different kind of sound, it cut through the chaos like glass. Everything slowed, each second stretching like taffy. The Cadillac shuddered. In that moment, I realized something I should have known all along: in Paul's world, control was an illusion, and danger was just part of the ride.

As soon as we hit the first guardrail, we didn't stop. Paul yanked the wheel hard left and we flew in the other direction.

BOOM!

The Cadillac slammed into the guardrail on the opposite side of the street, metal screaming, sparks flying like firecrackers in the dark. The second impact stole my breath and shoved me into Paul. The car didn't stop. It couldn't. Momentum carried us like a freight train on wheels.

The tires skidded, scraping, grinding against metal as we rode the guardrail with sparks and smoke trailing behind us. The road blurred beneath us—streetlights stretching into jagged streaks, neon signs flashing warped colors across shattered mirrors of the car.

For what felt like forever—maybe a block, maybe half a block—the Cadillac rode the rail, bouncing, jerking, tilting. Every jolt was a hammer to my chest, every turn a gamble with gravity. Air shocks slammed, suspending us just enough to keep flying, keep floating over disaster.

The roar of metal on metal filled my ears and drowned out everything else, the bass from the stereo, our screams, the world itself.

Then, finally... we hit a streetlight.

Airbags exploded, knocking me out. And everything went black.

BLACKOUT.

I wake up. I don't know how long I've been out, seconds? Minutes? The world is still shaking. The first thing I hear is the horn, a long, endless BEEEEEEEEEEEEEEEP, drilling straight into my skull. My ears ring, my chest feels crushed. Smoke curls up from the dash, thick and gray, the taste of burnt oil and metal filling my mouth. I blink hard. Everything's blurry, flashing broken streetlight, broken glass scattered across the seats, blood on my forearm I don't remember getting.

Then I look down.

The engine's sitting in my lap. Steam hisses from somewhere deep under the hood, the heat pushing through my jeans. I can smell it, that scorched metal, hot rubber, and something sweet and sick like antifreeze or maybe blood. I don't even know.

I turn my head. Paul slumped over the wheel, motionless, smoke rising around him like a ghost.

"Paul!" I shouted, voice cracking. Nothing. "Paul! Wake up!"

I reached over and slapped his shoulder hard. Once. Twice. The horn keeps screaming, one long death cry in the dark. I hit him again, "Paul, wake up!" The sound tears out of me.

Then, finally, movement. His hand twitches. His head lifts slowly, like it weighs a hundred pounds, eyes glassy and lost. The horn dies mid-note with that ugly beep, leaving behind a silence that feels heavier than the sound. He blinks at me, dazed, blood trickling from his eyebrow.

"What... what happened?" he says, voice small, broken.

I stare at him, disbelief cutting through the adrenaline.

"What do you mean? What happened? You already know what happened, dummy." My voice shakes, half rage, half relief.

I push against the crumpled metal, my legs pinned under the twisted frame. I shove, grunt, and twist my body free. Pain shoots through my ribs, but I don't care; I just need to get out. I glance down and my stomach drops straight through my shoes. The engine shoved up against my thighs, wires and steam spitting between my knees. I'm wedged, folded like some cheap piece of furniture shoved into a trunk.

The door's half-bent, groaning when I force it open. Smoke pours out like it's been waiting to escape. I stumble out the car into the cold night, air hitting my face, lungs dragging in oxygen that tastes like fire and fear.

In front of me, the Cadillac hisses and ticks, the once-beautiful ride now a crushed animal breathing its last breath. The street's empty. No sirens yet. Just silence, broken glass, and the faint hum of what's left of our night.

He looks at me, and for a second, it's just two guys in a car and the whole world is thin glass between us and the sky.

"What... what happened?" he says, voice small, somewhere between apology and shock.

"You don't have to tell me anything," I spit, half laughing, half sobbing. My ribs scream every time I move. The car is a coffin, and it tried hard to end us.

I stagger up, one hand on the mangled door for balance, and look into the back seat.

"Vanessa?" My voice cracks.

The seat's empty with glass everywhere, the smell of gas thick and sour. Just her Nikes on the floorboard, one upright, one on its side like she'd been ripped right out of them. My stomach drops.

"Paul," I shout, turning toward him. His face is pale, streaked with blood and confusion.

"Where's Vanessa?"

He blinks, slow, like the question's coming from another planet.

"Wait... what?"

"She's not in there, bro! Where's Vanessa?"

His eyes dart around, wide now, panicked.

"She was just—"

"VANESSA!" I screamed into the night, voice tearing out of me.

The sound echoes down Fillmore, bouncing off the mangled car and the empty street. Silence answers first, heavy and cruel.

174

Then, faint, from somewhere beyond my sight, I hear…

"…help…"

It's small, faint, barely there but it's there. It has to be her. My heart kicks hard against my ribs. I spin toward the sound, scanning the dark. Smoke rolls past my legs, the engine still ticking hot behind me. The smell of burnt rubber and blood fills my nose.

"Hold on!" I yell, stumbling toward the voice. My shoes slip on the oil-slick pavement. "I'm coming, Vanessa!" The streetlight buzzes above, casting a sickly yellow glow over everything: the twisted metal, the shattered glass, and the faint trail leading off the road. The world feels quiet except for my heartbeat and the whisper of her voice, faint and desperate, bleeding through the night.

I hear her voice again, fainter, more broken, cutting through the ringing in my ears like a whisper through static.

"Help…"

It's far off, somewhere in the dark. I try to run, but pain rips through my chest, sharp and deep, like my ribs are splintered glass. Every breath feels wrong. Still, I push forward, dragging my feet through gravel and glass.

Then I see her, barely sprawled out on the cold asphalt, the glow of a broken streetlight brushing her body in flashes. She's on her stomach, one arm outstretched, fingers trembling in my direction, reaching.

"Vanessa!" I choke out. My voice sounds strange, hollow, like it's coming from somewhere else, like it's not mine. I limp closer, every step fight against the pain in my ribs. The smell of burnt metal and gasoline stings my nose.

When I finally reach her, I drop to my knees beside her, hands shaking as I roll her gently.

"Are you okay?" I ask, but my voice is already trembling.

Her eyes flutter open, glassy but alive. "Yeah," she whispers, "I'm all right… but I'm bleeding." She tries to sit up. I grabbed her under the arms, lifting her slowly, steadily. My palms come away wet and warm. I look down, and my stomach twists. Blood. A lot of blood.

"Oh my God," I say under my breath, staring at my hands, at her hair clumped with red.

"Oh my God."

She looks at me, dazed, confused. "What? What is it?"

"You're bleeding badly. Like, really bad."

She shakes her head, stubbornly, still half in shock. "No… you're lying. You're the one…"

"Vanessa, your bad and my bad are probably way different… and this is really bad. Trust me."

Her eyes go wide. "Oh my God…" Blood pours down the front of her face. I rip my shirt off, press it against her head to stop the bleeding. My hands won't stop shaking. "Hold it there," I tell her.

Paul's footsteps crunch up behind us, uneven, panicked. He looks wrecked, blood on his face too, eyes huge, chest heaving. When he sees Vanessa, he freezes.

"Oh my God… Vanessa, I'm so sorry," he says, voice breaking, like he's seeing what he did for the first time.

"It's okay," she whispers, weak but steady.

Vanessa's head is split right down the middle from the back to the front of her forehead, her face covered in blood. Her hair is matted, dripping down her cheeks and neck. Her hands shake as she tries to hold the shirt in place. I can see the panic in Paul's face, his guilt, his fear. We all feel it.

The street is quiet except for the ticking of the busted engine cooling behind us. Smoke floats over the wreck like a ghost. The night that started with music and laughter now smells like blood and burnt oil.

There we are three broken souls standing in the middle of Fillmore with our choices bleeding out right there on the pavement.

Paul's eyes are wide as floodlights, unblinking, wild, bouncing between her and me like he can't process what he's seeing. Her head. My face. Her head again. His mouth is stuck open, but no words come out. Just that blank, haunted stare that says it all—we messed up. Bad.

The air is thick with smoke and fear. Every breath hurts. Vanessa's blood drips through my fingers, warm and slick, running down my arm. I press the torn shirt tighter against her head, but it won't stop. She trembles, her knees threatening to give out, but she keeps saying, "I'm okay… I'm okay," over and over, like if she says it enough, it will make it true.

"We gotta get her home," I say. My voice cracks. Her parents live just a few blocks down, off the same street. "She's losing too much blood."

Paul nods fast, too fast, eyes still darting. "Yeah. Yeah, come on. We'll take her. Just—just hold her up."

Vanessa hooks her right arm around my shoulders, her left around Paul's. We lift her together, step by step, her feet dragging, the sound of gravel crunching under us loud in the quiet. Her body is heavy from the weight of what just happened. She can barely walk. Each step hurts. My ribs scream.

The night is still except for our breathing, ragged, uneven, the sound of three people hanging on by threads. The streetlight flickers behind us, throwing our shadows long and broken.

We make the left, cutting through the bushes toward the shortcut that leads straight to her block. Just a few more feet, I tell myself. Just a few more, even though it isn't.

There is a creek bed running right beneath us, a dark cut through the earth I hadn't even noticed until it was too late. The street we had flown down and crashed, that's why those guardrails were there in the first place. It was a bridge. Those guardrails were there to prevent people from falling off into the creek.

We move slowly, half-blind through the night. The bushes scratch at our legs, branches snapping underfoot. The air is thick with the smell of dirt, metal, and blood—Vanessa's blood. Her arm hangs heavy over my shoulder, and I can feel her whole body trembling. Every few steps, she stumbles, whispering something I can't catch. My ribs ache like fire, but I hold her tighter.

Paul is on the other side, holding her other arm, breathing hard, mumbling curses under his breath. None of us can see where we're stepping. The only light comes from the broken glow of the streetlight, where the Cadillac still smokes faintly behind us, smoke curling into the night like a warning.

We can hear sirens now in the distance.

Then it happened.

There was this crack, the sound of branches breaking under pressure, and suddenly Paul screamed.

"Ahhhhhhhhhh!"

I looked to my left and Paul was gone. Just gone. The air sucked him right into thin air. Disappeared. Gone. Then came a loud thud and a splash from below.

"Paul!" I yelled, spinning toward the sound.

From the darkness, his voice shot back, panicked, echoing up from the ravine.

"HEY! I CAN'T GET UP! MY ANKLES ARE BROKEN BRO!"

I edged closer to the drop near the cliff, heart pounding, one arm still holding Vanessa upright. The night swallowed everything. No streetlights. No sound but the shallow trickle of water below and Paul's ragged breathing. I couldn't even see him, just the faint rustle of movement somewhere in the blackness.

"Paul!" I shouted again, desperate. "Hang on! Just don't move, bro!"

"I CAN'T MOVE!" he yelled back, voice breaking on the last word.

I looked down at Vanessa, her blood still seeping through the shirt wrapped around her head. She was barely standing now, leaning all her weight on me. Her lips were pale, eyes glassy. She was whispering something, maybe praying, maybe just breathing.

"Bro," I said, voice trembling, "I can't carry both of you. I can't."

There was silence for a second. Then Paul yelled back, "Go! Take her! I'm good! Just come back, man. Come back for me."

"I'll be back!" I shouted, gripping Vanessa tighter, the words burning my throat.

I turned away from the edge, half-carrying, half-dragging her through the brush. My chest felt like it was caving in. Every step away from that drop felt wrong, like leaving a piece of myself behind. Behind us, sirens reached the crash, and Paul's voice was silent now, just the sound of the creek below as we tried to hurry.

I kept walking. I had to. The sound of him kept playing in my head, the pain, the fear, the way his voice cracked. It stuck in my mind like shrapnel. The night closed in around us, thick and merciless, and I knew, deep down, that even if I made it back, nothing was ever going to be the same after this.

What were the chances of this even happening? Paul falling to his doom and snapping both ankles right after we had just crawled out of a wreck. Vanessa thrown from the car, through the sunroof, head split open. Me crawling out with smoke in my lungs and fire on my hands. What were the odds? Slim to none.

But then again, what were the odds of me still being here to even tell the story after everything I endured? When I thought about it like that, yeah, it blew my mind. Because if something could go wrong, it would, and it would find me directly in its path. Every time. Like it was personal. Like life had my name scribbled at the top of its hit list.

The night around me was dead quiet now, the kind of silence that only comes after chaos. Vanessa leaned heavy on me, blood streaked down her face like war paint. Her breath came in shallow pulls. She tried to talk, but nothing came out, just a whimper and the sound of air leaking from her lungs.

What were the chances of any of this?

But here I was, dragging what was left of my people through the dark, hands shaking, adrenaline burned out. Every step I took felt borrowed, like the ground could open up next and it would be my turn to fall.

See, some people get lucky breaks. Me? I get the kind that breaks you.

And the truth is, I wouldn't expect anything less. Because if something wild, unreal, or impossible was going to happen, you best believe it was going to happen to me. That's just my kind of luck. The cursed kind. The kind that doesn't run out. It just keeps cashing in.

Knock. Knock. Knock.

I finally reached the house. I pounded on the door. The lights turned on. I hit the door like my knuckles might break. The sound echoed through the quiet street, hollow, desperate. Lights flickered on inside. Curtains shifted. A shadow moved. Then the door swung open so hard it banged the wall.

"Oh my God... Vanessa!" her mom screamed.

She didn't hesitate. She ripped Vanessa straight out of my arms, pulling her into the light. Blood stained her hands instantly, but she didn't care. She was crying, calling for her husband, voice cracking under the weight of panic.

Her dad rushed out from the back, eyes wide, shirt half-buttoned. He froze for a second when he saw his daughter, then everything kicked in. He scooped her up, shouting orders like a soldier.

"Get the keys! Now!"

Her mom doesn't even look at me. I don't blame her. Vanessa's older brother comes out next, still in his boxers, and stares at me like I'm poison.

"Take off," he says, voice low, cold. "We got it from here."

I just stand there, chest heaving, hands trembling, blood half hers and half mine drying on my skin. Then they rush out of the house, fly past me, pile into the truck, throw it in reverse down the driveway, gravel spitting, and disappear into the dark.

And just like that, it's quiet again.

I stood there for a second, the night pressing down on me, my shirt gone, skin freezing under the streetlight. I can still smell the smoke on me. Still taste metal and fear in the back of my throat.

Then it hits me. Paul.

I turn and start running back toward the crash site, every breath cutting deeper than the last. My ribs scream, but I don't stop. The sirens are far now, like they belong to someone else's story.

When I reach the spot, nothing. No Paul. No sound. He's nowhere to be found. Just the twisted rail up top, the dented asphalt, and the black void of that creek below. My phone is broken.

Gone. Just like that.

The night feels heavier now, like it's holding a secret it doesn't plan to give back.

I barely slept that night, if you could call it sleep. Every time I closed my eyes, I saw headlights, smoke, and blood on my hands. I heard that horn. Heard Vanessa screaming. Then silence. By the time the sun came up, my body felt like it had been dragged through hell. My ribs screamed every time I moved, my knuckles still raw, my head pounding like a drum. But my mind? It was on her.

Paul didn't break his ankles. He got hold of me, got away, and was lying low from the police. Vanessa. I kept replaying everything—her mom's scream, her brother's cold eyes, the truck disappearing into the night. I knew they blamed me. Hell, I might've blamed myself too if I were them. But I wasn't driving. And I brought her home. I didn't think twice. I just knew we were around the corner from her house and didn't want to wait for the police. Granted, I wouldn't have gone to jail. She wouldn't have either. Paul might have. I didn't just bounce out and leave her to die.

Still, guilt has a way of finding a seat and staying for a while.

By early afternoon, I was done pacing. I got up, showered, patched myself up with medical tape tight around my ribs, a fresh shirt over bruises that looked like spilled ink. In the mirror, I looked like someone who had just crawled out of a car crash and tried to convince himself he was fine.

I wasn't.

But I knew what I had to do.

I grabbed my keys, stepped outside, and the October air hit me sharp and cold. My Monte sat at the curb, deep midnight blue, chrome flakes dull under the daylight. I slid in, the seat squeaking, and turned the key. The engine coughed, then roared alive, a sound I had always loved.

I stopped by Safeway or King Soopers, and bought a bunch of flowers but nothing fancy, just what I could grab. The cashier looked at me twice, probably wondering why a dude with busted knuckles and bandaged ribs was buying roses.

Didn't matter.

As I pulled up to Vanessa's house, my stomach tightened. Their truck wasn't there. The blinds were half-drawn. The whole block felt still, too quiet, like the calm after a fight. I sat in the car a minute, hands on the wheel, breathing through it. I didn't know what was waiting for me. Maybe her brothers. Maybe her dad. Maybe worse.

But I wasn't turning back.

I killed the engine, stepped out, and looked at the house. Same porch light. Same cracked walkway. Same front door I had pounded on last night.

I gripped the flowers tighter. My ribs ached with every step.

What would they do? Fight me? Yell? Spit in my face?

Wouldn't be the first.

Didn't matter.

I was here because she mattered to me.

Knock. Knock. Knock.

I stand there, flowers clutched tight in my hands, feeling the weight of every step that led me here. The porch beneath my shoes creaks, the air thin and tense around me. I can't breathe right. Expecting the worst, hoping for the best. The curtains twitch, a shadow passes, then stillness. I knock again, louder this time.

Knock. Knock. Knock.

The sound cuts sharp against the quiet street. The door creaks open, and I'm met with her mom's eyes, sharp, filled with a mix of anger and hatred. I start to read her expression.

"Hi, ma'am," I begin, voice tight, hands gripping the bouquet like a lifeline. "I know you don't know me, but my name is Gabriel. I... I'd like to give these flowers to your daughter, if—if there's any way possible. I'm truly sorry about what happened last night, and... I'd like to see if she's okay, please."

Her eyes scan me from head to toe, taking in the blood stains still on my shirt, the cuts on my knuckles, the way I'm holding my chest like every breath hurts. She says nothing, then closes the door.

The world slows. My chest pounds in the silence of the porch. Every second stretches into a lifetime. I shift the flowers in my hands, from one to the other, sweat dripping down my temples. My stomach is a tight knot. My ribs ache. I feel like I'm walking a tightrope over fire.

Then, finally, the door swings open again.

"You know, Gabriel," her mom says, voice low but firm, eyes piercing directly through me, "you must be either real brave... or completely stupid. I haven't decided yet." She pauses, scanning me like she's weighing the outcome of every choice I've ever made. "Her brothers... they're pissed. Real pissed."

My stomach twists, but I nod.

"Well," she continues, voice softening a fraction, "I told her you were here. She said... to let you in."

She gestures toward her bedroom where Vanessa is laying down. Oh my God. Access granted. Seriously? It worked, I thought. In that moment, every nerve in me is alive—full of fear, guilt, hope, and something else I can't name, all tangled together. The night is gone, but the scars remain, and standing there on the edge of her world, I know I'm not walking away from this. Not now.

"Thank you," I say, voice barely more than a whisper. "I... I'm truly sorry about all this, ma'am. I really am."

I push the door open, heart hammering so loud I swear she can hear it. The room is quiet, but it carries the faint smell of antiseptic mixed with her perfume, the glow of a single lamp casting everything in a golden hue. She's lying there, still pale, bandages peeking out from under her hair. Her eyes meet mine, and for a moment, the world tilts. My chest tightens so bad it's hard to breathe.

"Hey," I say, voice tight, rough around the edges.

"Hi," she says, and for a second her smile hits me like sunlight through smoke. Fragile, tentative, but it's there.

"I'm... I've been so worried about you," I tell her, the words tasting raw in my mouth.

"Thank you for taking care of me and... bringing me home," she whispers.

"You're welcome," I say, though it feels crazy to think about everything we went through.

I stay with her for the night. Sit beside her, make sure she has water, hold her steady while she breathes. I listen when she talks, follow what she says.

"What you need," I tell her. "Let me know. I'm here to help. Okay?"

She smiles again, small but honest. "Okay," she says. "I'd like that."

I stay there, keeping her company, guarding her like a wounded soldier against the night. Exhaustion comes for me, but I don't leave. I fall asleep in the same room, her breathing slow and steady, her hand brushing mine by accident—and I don't move it.

Morning comes too soon. I wake up knowing I have to go to work, but my first thought is her. I'll be back after my shift. I'll be there again, tending to her needs, helping her walk back to normalcy piece by piece. Every little thing—water, medicine, comfort, laughter, silence, I'll be there. Wholehearted. No half-measures.

The fear, the guilt, the adrenaline, the love, it's all tangled inside me like a storm. But deep down, I know something I can't hide anymore or deny I love her. I always have.

With that, I suppressed Suspect. Kept him locked up. Kept the part of me that flirted with danger, risk, the heartless persona I worked so hard to build. I suppressed him. I let emotion show, just enough to be human. Just enough to love her. And it grew.

The world outside is chaotic, unforgiving, cruel. But in that room, for a little while, there's a chance to breathe. To care. To love. And I hold onto it like it's the only thing worth surviving for.

The months rolled on, and for the first time in a long time, life felt steady—like I could breathe without expecting the world to crash down on me. I spent every moment I could with her, every second stitched together with a care I hadn't known I could give. My nights weren't about flashing lights, parties, or fleeting highs anymore. They were about Vanessa. About helping her put the pieces of herself back together.

I got her a job at my workplace, something steady, something normal, something that would anchor her. Watching her walk into that office on her first day, nervous but holding her head high, I felt this protective heat in my chest. Like I'd built a little corner of the world just for her, and she belonged there.

Vanessa had a son, Derek. A little dude with eyes sharp as mine and a mouth full of attitude. I took him in as my own, like blood didn't matter as long as care did. We were a small, messy family, stitched together out of survival and love and a past that had almost broken us.

And me? I was still dealing. Street hustle never fully leaves. But around that time, it became legal in Colorado. Just another twist in the chaos I'd been living. I was around 29, working steady, climbing at the call center. I became a project manager. Keys to the building. Responsibilities stacked on me, running projects and data reports, client files flowing across my desk like evidence of a life that was changing.

I had one foot in the street and one foot in something else—stability, responsibility, even hope. But that other foot kept me sharp, kept me alive.

I knew life didn't just hand you chances like this. You had to survive to deserve them. And I wasn't about to let go. We were making it work. Broken pieces, stitched hearts, bruised bodies—but still breathing, still moving forward. For the first time, I could say, maybe, just maybe, this life… this mess, this chaos… could mean something real.

The afternoons on my days off started slow. My dad would show up, no warning, just him—jeans pulled up too high, shirt tucked in, old flannel buttoned up, baseball hat forward and straight as can be. The smell of his cologne mixed with cigarettes and weed drifted through the doorway.

I'd be in the living room, football game on, blunt burning low in the ashtray.

"Thought I'd stop by," he'd say, taking off his jacket.

We'd sit on the couch, side by side, football on the screen but rarely our focus. Dad would crack a joke about a player's haircut and I'd laugh harder than I had in months—the kind of laugh that makes your chest hurt and your shoulders loosen, the kind that reminds you there's still life outside the chaos.

Sometimes we'd crack open a beer, sometimes a joint, sometimes both. Smoke curling up to the ceiling, sweating beer on the side table. The room would fill with warmth, the hum of the TV blending with our conversation, our teasing, the sound of us just being.

I noticed things I'd never paid attention to before, the way his hands moved when he gestured, the way his laugh sounded different when he was actually at ease, the way he'd glance at me like he'd been waiting for this moment for years.

We'd argue about the game, trash talk players, but it was playful. A battle of wits and pride. And when the game ended, the quiet wouldn't feel heavy. It would feel full, peaceful, with understanding, connection, and respect.

Those afternoons, those small ordinary moments, stitched us closer together. I started seeing him not just as my dad, the man who warned me, yelled at me, tried to keep me straight—but as a person. A real man. Flawed, stubborn, alive.

This man wasn't only my father now. No. He was my friend, and I loved him. And me? I finally felt like I belonged somewhere, like I was part of something bigger than just survival, money, or the streets. For a few hours, just a few, the world outside could burn down and I wouldn't care. We had this room, this bond, this life—and it was enough. I finally had my dad.

Vanessa and I… we fell back into it. The partying, the drinking, the smoking, the streets buzzing around us like electricity. Life felt easy for a while—work, kids, friends, chaos—all spinning together. I thought it was perfect. I thought we had it all figured out. But I knew, deep down, nothing that felt good could last forever.

By the time I hit 30, it seemed like life had finally let me breathe. The kids were okay, work was steady, and the streets were familiar. But that calm… it was fragile, like something could happen at any moment.

I let go of the townhouse, sold the Monte, and picked up a new ride. My escape. My statement. An '82 Cadillac Coupe DeVille. Blue, sitting high on 20-inch rims when I first got it—but that wasn't enough. I had to make it mine.

Dropped it down to 13s. Painted it cocaine white, with blue and chrome flakes catching the sun like shards of glass. The top is wrapped in blue vinyl, interior stitched with cocaine-white leather, blue piping, and matching buttons. Even the floor mats had their own detail. Windows are tinted at 2% all the way around. Man, that car shined under the sunlight. The spokes dipped in white to match. Three 12-inch speakers thumped in the trunk, bass so heavy you could feel it in your chest—and that was just the start.

This car wasn't just transportation. It was a declaration. Every inch, every detail screamed status, hustle, survival. The streets saw it. The neighbors saw it. And inside, when I rolled up with Vanessa by my side, music booming, leather warm under our hands… it felt like we were untouchable. Like we owned every corner of the city. Maybe we did, in our own heads, for a little while. But I knew better than anyone—the higher you climb, the harder the fall. Still, I didn't care. Not yet. Not while the car gleamed, the bass shook the pavement, and life, messy, chaotic, intoxicating, was ours to drive.

Vanessa loved that car. Loved it like it was hers, sliding behind the wheel. Then, of all coincidences, my parents moved. From Fillmore, they ended up one house over from Vanessa's parents. Neither of them knew until it happened. In a strange, messed-up way, it made life easier—family gatherings, holidays, birthdays. Everything was convenient, even if the streets around us stayed chaotic.

I'd walk back and forth between the houses, lighting blunts along the way, letting smoke curl into the night. Life was still the same—hitting corners, lowriders shining under streetlights, deals, hustle. I tried hard to gather enough to pull myself and my family out of the hood. Had to keep moving. The streets had a way of keeping you close, like a lover who didn't care if you were happy. Love and hate tangled tightly and I understood that. I got it. Every corner, every late-night drive, every deal, I knew the rhythm, the danger, and the reward.

By then, Derek and Nevaeh were getting older, and they were ours in the ways that mattered. Vanessa and I were learning each other, learning the kids as they grew, figuring out what family meant to us with our lifestyle.

The townhouse we had. It wasn't enough. Space was tight. The kids needed room. The lowrider was cramped.

So, I moved us. Bigger. Better. On the West Side. A townhouse that could breathe. More room for life, for the chaos, for all of us—me, Vanessa, the kids. A place where we could exist without feeling crushed by the streets.

It wasn't perfect. Hell, perfection didn't exist where we lived. But for a little while, it felt like ours. A space that could hold all the noise, all the laughter, all the love—and maybe, just maybe, keep the darkness at the door.

CHAPTER 33: THE DEVOURER ARRIVES

"He don't negotiate, he don't warn, you don't even see him coming. But once he's here, it's already too late."

The house was full of perfume and laughter. Vanessa and her friends had the kind of energy that shook walls—music low, heels tapping, hair dryers humming, the sight of too much make-up. The smell of cocoa butter and cheap wine floated through the place. I sat back on the couch, half-watching the news, half-watching her moving around like she owned every inch of light in the room.

She looked over, smiling that sideways smile.

"Hey."

"Yeah?"

"I'm gonna go out tonight with my homegirls. That cool?"

"Yeah, that's fine. You wanna go?"

She laughed, flipping her hair. "Nah, I think you need time with your friends. It's cool."

My head had been packed tight lately—job stress, calls, meetings, deadlines. Thirty-two, assistant project manager at a small marketing research firm. Not bad money, but too many people talking at once. I was drained. And the second job of supply and demand never stopped. Plus, I didn't like her friends anyway. I'd rather stay home in peace. Our kids were good, bills paid. Me and Vanessa were solid. Everything felt golden. Still, I was tired. Tired of holding it all together.

Vanessa said she would take Derek to her mom's. They left in a cloud of laughter and perfume, the front door slamming behind them, car lights flooding the room as they pulled away. Then silence. Just me and the sound of the clock ticking on the wall, the TV rambling on about something.

That's when my phone rang.

Ring. Ring. Ring.

Mom.

I picked up. "Yeah, Mom? What's up?"

Her voice cracked a little. "Boy… you might wanna come over."

My stomach tightened. "What's going on?"

"It's your dad. I don't think he's doing good."

"What you mean not doing good?"

A pause. That kind of silence that drips heavy.

"Just come over, please."

"Okay, I'm on the way. I love you."

Click.

I stood there, staring at the phone, as if it had said something different. My chest felt heavy. Then everything started moving at once. Keys. Wallet. Door. The air outside hit cold, like cold metal against skin. I jumped in the '82 and fired it up. The engine roared, and I took off. Streetlights stretched long across the windshield, rain misting down like the sky was sweating. Tires hissed over wet pavement. The night was quiet, too quiet, the kind of quiet where your thoughts start talking too loudly.

Every block I passed, something old from the park where we all gathered for Nevaeh's birthday would pull me in, with us tossing the football around and barbecuing. At the liquor store, he'd wait outside while I ran in. That corner where he once told me, "Don't let this world break you, boy. Stand on something."

Now, I was praying I'd get to hear him say anything again.

When I turned onto their street, my stomach dropped hard. The world got quiet, just the hum of the tires over wet asphalt and the steady slap of rain on the windshield. The porch light was on, throwing a dull yellow glow over the yard, cutting through the mist like it didn't want to.

I saw my mom outside, standing under that light, one arm wrapped around herself, the other holding a cigarette like it was the only thing keeping her steady. The smoke curled up into the rain, twisting slowly before the drizzle broke it apart. Her jacket clung to her, damp at the edges. She dragged from the cigarette deeply, eyes half-closed, chest rising like she was trying to breathe through the weight sitting on her.

I pulled up, killed the engine. Suddenly, silence roared in my ears. No radio. No motor. Just the soft crackle of rain hitting metal and the faint hiss of her cigarette burning down.

My door creaked open. My shoes sank into the mud, that wet, sticky kind with no grass to hold it. The smell of earth and rain mixed with the bitter smoke she exhaled. My steps felt heavy, slower than normal, like each one was trying to prepare me for what was waiting inside.

My mom's eyes caught mine.

She didn't say a word. Her lips trembled and that cigarette shook between her fingers, ashes clinging to the tip before falling into the puddles below.

Her eyes already said it. Something inside that house wasn't right.

The night I thought would bring me peace ended up being the one that broke it forever.

"Your dad... I don't think he's doing good."

"What do you mean by not doing well?"

Something told me tonight was about to change everything.

When the door opened, Mom's face told me everything before she spoke. Eyes swollen, mouth trembling, one hand clutching her elbow like she needed something to hold her up.

"He's inside," she whispered.

The air in the house was heavy, smelled like Vicks, old wood, and slow sadness. The TV was on low, showing an old western, but nobody was watching it. My dad sat on the couch, that same beat-up couch he'd had since forever. His eyes were on the floor, elbows resting on his knees, hands clapping like he had been praying.

He looked up when he heard my footsteps.

"Hey, son."

His voice cracked on the word.

"Hey, Dad. What's wrong?"

He exhaled slowly, like he was letting go of something he had been holding too long. The kind of breath that carries more than air carries truth.

"Doctor called today," he said quietly. "Said I got cirrhosis of the liver... and cancer."

He said it calmly, steadily, like he had already been sitting with the news, turning it over, looking for the silver lining buried somewhere in the wreckage. His eyes didn't flinch; they just drifted, searching for the room for meaning that wasn't there. The air went thin. The clock ticked once, then nothing. I just stood there, staring at him, trying to pull together words that wouldn't come. His face was still, the kind of calm that doesn't come from acceptance but from exhaustion. His hands trembled just a little, that quiet, honest shake of a man holding back everything he was too proud to let out.

"Are you—" I swallowed hard. "Are you serious?"

He looked at me, straight in the eyes. "Yeah, son. It's bad. They just found it today."

The TV crowd roared in the background, a fake celebration cutting through the silence. My throat tightened. My eyes burned. I blinked hard, fighting it, but the tears pushed through anyway. I turned away before he could see.

"I'll be right back," I said, voice rough.

I stepped out the front door, and the night hit me cold. Rain fell harder now, slow and steady, like the sky was crying for me. I walked around the corner of the house and just stood.

The world blurred.

I leaned against the house, chest heaving, hands becoming fists. I wanted to scream. I wanted to punch something. Mostly, I just wanted to rewind time back to when he was healthy, back to when I still called him "old man" with a smile instead of fear. We had just gotten good. After all the years, I thought he didn't care and fought with each other. After all the time I spent gone from home, caught up in my own demons, I left myself to figure life out alone. Then out of nowhere, he came back.

We rebuilt. Brick by brick.

Now I could feel that time slipping.

Tears cut through the rain on my face. I tried to wipe them, but more came. I bent forward, hands on my knees, breath coming out shaky. That deep, ugly cry you can't hide.

Then I heard the screen door squeak open.

I turned around.

It was him. My father. Standing there in the rain, seeing me wrecked, moving slow but moving. His steps were heavy, yet he still carried strength. My dad stepped out with a gray shirt, old pajama pants, and slippers. His shoulders hunched like he was carrying the weight of the world, but he still moved like a man trying to protect his last bit of pride.

"Don't cry for me, son," he said quietly, voice shaking but proud. "We finally got it right. That's all that matters."

I couldn't even speak. My lip trembled. I just nodded, looking down, rain dripping off my chin. We stood there in silence, two men, father and son, both broken, both trying to be strong for the other. The world around us disappeared.

"What's wrong, boy?"

I tried to speak, but my throat locked up. My face twisted, eyes blurring. Finally, it broke through. Tears came uncontrollably.

"I don't wanna lose you, Dad! Not now!"

It came out soft but hit like thunder. I started crying; there was no stopping it. Tears mixed with the rain falling fast. He stepped closer, his eyes shining wet too, voice softer now, that deep tone that used to make me listen even when I didn't want to.

"Listen," he said, "I love you, son. You hear me? I love you and I'm proud of you. Proud of the man you became. Proud of the man you are today."

"I love you too, Dad. I'm sorry for everything I did growing up."

He paused, rain dripping off his head. "And I'm sorry. I'm sorry for everything I did to you. For the way I was towards you, growing. For not being there when you needed me."

Then he pulled me in, arms heavy, strong, trembling a little. That embrace hit differently. Not like a handshake, not like a shoulder tap. It was deep, all those years of distance, all those lost words, finally crushed out in silence. And at that moment, for the first time ever, my father embraced me with his everlasting love.

My father. The rock.

Or as he would say, "Big Bad Daddy Dave."

We cried for a little bit, and he told me it would be okay. I had to pull myself together. The rain fell harder, soaking through our clothes, but we didn't move. I felt his heart against mine, slow and uneven but still fighting. I smelled the faint trace of smoke and aftershave on his shirt. My hands gripped his back, afraid to let go. After a while, he leaned back, hands still resting on my arms, looking me in the eyes like he was memorizing my face.

"It's gonna be okay," he said, voice rough but full of that same old strength.

I nodded, even though I didn't believe it. His body was fading. His health was bad. I could see it in the color of his skin, the tiredness in his eyes. Still, in that moment, in that darkness, on that wet street, we weren't broken anymore.

We were whole for the time being.

He told me the doctor's words hit like a hammer to the chest.

Six months to a year.

That's what he said, flat voice, eyes tired like he had said it too many times before.

I couldn't even look at my dad at that moment. Just stared at the mud as the rain fell, listening to the hum of the streetlights and the ticking clock in my head like it was counting down something sacred.

Six months. Maybe a year.

That's not the time. That's a sentence.

I said my good-byes for the night and headed home. When I walked through the door, Vanessa was there. She saw it on me right away—the heaviness, the red eyes, the kind of silence that hangs between every word.

"What happened?" she asked softly.

I sat down, rubbed my face, and said it plain. "My dad is dying. The doctor said six months to a year. He is sick."

Her eyes dropped. She didn't know what to say either. She just came over and wrapped her arms around me. For a moment, I let it all go—all the pride, all the weight. Just rested my head against her and cried.

I spent the next few days with him, trying to act normally. We'd sit on the couch and watch TV in silence. Sometimes he'd talk about football or the past like everything was fine, like nothing inside him was dying. Other times, he just stared off, lost in his thoughts, eyes glassy and distant. I tried to hold it together. I tried to keep my face calm. But inside, it was chaos. It was grief clawing at the edges of my chest.

Eventually, I had to go home, get my head straight.

After that, it became a routine. Every day after work, I'd drive over to my parents' house. Same road, same rain-stained drive, same porch light buzzing weak. I'd sit with him. Talk. Watch TV. We would eat together. Sometimes he'd laugh, sometimes he'd forget what we were talking about halfway through.

Two weeks in, everything changed.

I walked in one afternoon and found him sitting on the couch, eyes cloudy, staring past me.

"Hey, Dad," I said.

He looked up, blinked slowly, confusion crossing his face. "Who… who are you again?"

My heart stopped cold.

"It's me, Dad. It's your son."

He nodded faintly, like the name was familiar but far away, somewhere deep he couldn't reach anymore.

That broke something in me I didn't know could break.

I turned toward Mom. She was in the kitchen, wiping her eyes with the edge of a dish towel, trying to stay strong, but you could see she was failing miserably. The sound of her sobbing filled the house, small and soft at first, then deeper, the kind of crying that comes from the soul. I walked over, put my arm around her. She leaned into me, shaking.

"I can't lose him," she whispered, voice cracking. "Not like this."

I didn't know what to say. There weren't words for that kind of pain. All I could do was hold her, feeling her body tremble against mine, smelling the salt of her tears and the faint scent of coffee that clung to her clothes. I looked back at Dad. He was still in his chair, eyes blank, somewhere far from us already. That's when it hit me—this was the cruelest kind of loss. Watching someone fade while they're still breathing. You think you're ready for it, but you're not. You can't be.

I saw my mom overwhelmed in tears, heartbroken, crying and crying. I tried to comfort her but I couldn't. I was at a loss for words, too. I couldn't possibly imagine her pain, or even start to feel how she felt. To lose someone like that, to see them fade away before your eyes and forget you. Because the moment you start to feel that pain, to see the life slip from their eyes day by day, you realize death isn't the part that hurts.

It's the waiting.

The next day came fast. The ringing of the phone cut through the noise at work.

Ring. Ring. Ring.

I grabbed it, dreading the call I was about to get. "Hello?"

It was my mom. Her voice cracked before the words even came out.

"Boy… the nurse said you should come and say your goodbyes."

For a second, everything went quietly. Just static on the line and the thump of my own heartbeat in my ears. She didn't even wait for me to respond. "You need to come now," she said, and then the line went dead.

I sat there frozen; phone still pressed to my ear. Then I moved—fast. Called work. "I'm not coming in. Family emergency." No explanations. Just that. Next thing I knew, I was in the car, tearing through red lights, the city spinning around me. My hands were shaking on the wheel, knuckles white with pressure, eyes burning. The radio was off. All I could hear was the hum of the engine and my own breath, sharp and uneven.

When I pulled up to the house, the street was full of cars I didn't recognize, faces I hadn't seen in years. I jumped out before the car even stopped rolling, hit the porch two steps at a time, and pushed through the door.

The smell hit first—that sterile, hospital-clean smell that doesn't belong in a home. The air was thick with prayer and grief. My mom was standing by the bed, hands over her mouth, tears streaking her face. My sister Bernadette was on her knees, praying under her breath, voice trembling. A few family members huddled in the corners, whispering, crying, waiting for the inevitable.

And there he was. My dad.

Lying there, sunken in, face pale and still. His breathing was ragged, shallow. His eyes open, staring at nothing, somewhere between this world and the next.

"Dad," I said, stepping closer. "Dad, it's me. Gabe."

No response.

"Gabriel," I said louder, leaning over him, my voice cracking. "It's your son, Dad."

His eyes were barely flickered. His lips moved slowly, like dragging words out of deep water.

"My... sonny boy."

That's what he used to call me sometimes when I was a kid.

Hearing it again broke something loose inside me.

"Yeah, Dad," I whispered, gripping his hand tight. "I'm here. I love you."

He blinked once, still staring into space. "I... I love you," he whispered, voice barely there.

The nurse looked up from the other side of the bed, quiet, calm, but her eyes told me everything. "He's in and out," she said softly. "He doesn't really know where he is anymore."

I nodded, but I wasn't hearing her. All I could do was watch him breathe—slower, slower—until the space between breaths stretched too long. Then came the silence. A silence that swallowed the whole room.

The nurse reached forward, touched his wrist, then looked at me. Her voice dropped to a whisper.

"He's gone."

Everything in me snapped.

I stumbled back, fists balled, chest tight. I turned and slammed my fist into the wall, once, twice, until the drywall cracked and the skin on my knuckles split. I didn't even feel it. All I could feel was the ache. The emptiness. The sound of my mother wailing behind me, a sound I'll never forget. My sister's prayers turned into cries. The whole room collapsing under the weight of loss.

I couldn't breathe. Couldn't think. I looked at my dad one last time, still peaceful now, and I had to get out. I pushed past the people, past the tears and whispers, out the front door into the cold air. The sun was gone; the darkness filled the sky. The world kept going like nothing happened. Cars passed. Birds chirped. Somewhere, a dog barked. But mine had just stopped.

And standing there, fists bleeding, eyes burning, I realized the strongest man I ever knew was gone.

My dad passed away May 18th, 2014.

"Today is the first day of the rest of your life." I'll always remember that.

Rest in Peace, David Robert Hinojosa—my father.

The two weeks off work felt like a lifetime compressed into heartbreak. Funeral, cremation, family, condolences. Everyone came to pay their respects. Even Felicia and her family showed up, nodding, murmuring, offering hugs that felt heavy with sympathy. I let it all wash over me, but inside, the ache never eased.

A few days later, I felt it—the emptiness. My dad wasn't here anymore. Gone like the wind. And the rhythm of life I thought I had, the one where Sundays were football and backyard barbecues, it was over.

Vanessa wanted to go paint the town red with her friends again. Thursday night, ladies' night. I wasn't feeling it, so I told her to just go ahead. Morning came and she didn't. I looked around and she never came home.

I called her.

Ring. Ring. Ring. Nothing.

Ring. Ring. Ring. Still nothing.

Ring. Ring. Ring. Over and over, my voice grew harsher, more desperate.

Finally, she answered the phone.

"Hello?" I said.

"Vanessa, what's going on?"

Silence. Then finally, cold, clipped.

"Listen, I need some time to figure things out."

"Figure things out? Like what?"

"Just things. I'll call you later."

Click.

The line went dead. My hand shook as I gripped the phone, staring at it as if it had betrayed me. My mind spun into circles. Everything had been fine. No fights. No warning. And now, out of nowhere, she was gone.

I exhaled slowly and sank onto the couch. The house felt hollow, walls echoing, empty rooms staring back at me. I lay there, staring at the ceiling, wondering what the hell she was doing, why she wouldn't come home.

The next few weeks blurred together. Work became unbearable. Every meeting, every email, every simple task felt impossible. I couldn't focus. My mind was a battlefield of grief and confusion. My dad's death, Vanessa disappearing, the weight of loss pressing down like bricks.

I reached out to her friends. Nobody would tell me where she was. I drove all night, the streets slick with rain, my headlights cutting through darkness, the city lights smeared into streaks. Nothing. Empty roads, empty gas stations, the world moving on while I was stuck.

It felt like a bad country song, you hear how they lost the girl, the house, everything, even the dog. But in mine, there wasn't even a dog. Just me, and everything I had lost.

Then it all came crashing down. The office called me in. They'd noticed. The mistakes, the missed deadlines, the empty eyes. They said it was best if they let me go.

And just like that, in two short weeks, I lost it all.

- · lost my dad to cancer and cirrhosis.
- · lost my girl to... I don't even know what. Just gone.
- · I lost my job, my career.
- · I was about to lose my house.

Drugs became my temporary refuge, burning down the edge of my pain for a while. I tried to drink and brought bottles to flood my emotions, but the taste of alcohol was gone. One sip and it was immediately gross.

I was alone. Completely alone.

Driving all night, windows down, cold rain on my face, city streets melting into neon puddles, I couldn't stop thinking: how did it all fall apart so fast? Where did I go wrong? What did I miss?

The world was moving around me, indifferent to me. And at that moment, I realized—I had nothing. Nothing left but the aching echo of everything I'd lost.

I was angry. Furious at life itself. I wanted to scream, to make the world feel the weight pressing down on me. I needed a release. My mind was spinning wildly, and I knew I wasn't in a sane place. I thought maybe I needed to check in somewhere, because the way I was thinking wasn't safe.

CHAPTER 34: SUSPECT LIVES

"Evil is the deliberate choice to do harm, inflict suffering, or act with malicious intent toward others. It is the active or passive presence of harm, corruption, or malice, a force or choice that causes suffering, injustice, or moral decay."

I couldn't get past all this. It really was a bad country song, the kind you'd laugh at if it wasn't your life burning in the lyrics. My dad was gone, my girl vanished, my job was down the drain, and then to top it off, the drugs. They made everything louder, meaner. Every hit pulled me a little further from who I was and a little closer to something I didn't even recognize.

The pills came first just to take the edge off. Then the meth, sharp and bright, like fire in my veins. I'd tell myself I could handle it, that I was in control, but the truth was, control had packed up and left weeks ago. Between my thoughts and my actions, it was chaos, pure insanity wearing my face.

I'd wake up and not know what day it was. Nights bled into mornings, and the mirror began to show someone else. Eyes are too wide. Skin too tight. Jaws grinding through the silence. I was chasing the numb, but all I found was noise. Sober didn't exist anymore. I couldn't even imagine it. Sobriety felt like a fairytale for people who hadn't been broken this way. I told myself if I ever got clean, it'd be because I was in a casket.

So, I kept running. Higher. Harder. Deeper into the streets where light didn't reach. I was a ghost with a heartbeat fueled by chemicals, hate, and hurt. I didn't have plans anymore, just impulses. Rage was easier than grief. Anger was cleaner than pain. And somewhere in the middle of all that chaos, her name kept echoing, Vanessa. The way she left, the way it didn't make sense. That silence started to eat at me. I couldn't find her, but I knew where to start.

Her friends. So, I hit the streets again, eyes burning, heart hollow, fists tight in my jacket. The city hummed with danger, and I walked straight into it, headfirst. I tried to suppress suspect, but SUSPECT still lives. I was an empty soul, full of rage and revenge. No sad faces. No more tears. I'd have to pull this off legit. Time to try and start to master this art.

Perception.

Even though I was heartbroken and torn to shreds inside, I could never show it, especially around these girls. I know where I messed up, and it was giving Vanessa 100% of my heart. When she left, I was devastated and lost and ill-minded. I couldn't even think at all. I was like a lost puppy, but all that was going to change.

I knew where some of her friends lived. That was the dangerous part, just knowing. Knowledge is a kind of weapon on the streets. You point it out and something gives. Tonight, it pointed me at Rosanna's complex, a bunch of beat-down bricks with a tired light on the west side where the halls always smelled like old cooking oil and somebody else's regret.

I walked up to her door and knocked like I'd rehearsed it a dozen times in my head, steady, loud enough to force an answer but not so loud it sounded desperate. The door cracked open. Rosanna's face floated there for a second, sleepy and suspicious, and then she made the little gesture with her finger to come in but be quiet.

Inside, the living room was a war zone. Clothes thrown everywhere on the floor and the chairs, cigarette butts in an ashtray like little fallen soldiers, a TV glowing with something meaningless. Someone laying on the floor, someone else was there too, a shadow on the stairs. Looked like Lucy. Two birds with one stone, I thought, and my heartbeat put a beat on that idea.

Rosanna started right away. "Vanessa?" she said, like Vanessa was a rumor no one believed anymore. She moved her hands while she talked, eyes searching for the right pieces. "She been acting crazy. I haven't seen her. I don't understand why she'd do what she did."

All the words rolled over me like cheap rain. Blah, blah, blah. Blah, blah, blah. Blah, blah, blah. Blah, blah, blah. Blah, blah, blah. Just noise in my ear. It wasn't that I didn't care about what they thought, it was that their guesses didn't reach the place where the knife went. The place that kept replaying her leaving and not returning. The look on her face the last time I saw her. Everything else dissolved into white static. I just wanted to know, and no one would tell me.

Then I tried to flirt with her, but she wasn't having it.

"Look, suspect," she said. "You're doing this out of spite. I see right through you, friend."

"You're right. You're right. I apologize," I said.

I headed to the bathroom. In the narrow hallway I bumped into Lucy. Her eyes were the color of storm drains, dark, reflective, bottomless.

"What you up to tonight?" I asked.

Her answer was a shrug that tasted like an invitation and a lie.

"Nothing," she said. "Why not?"

It was automatic, a reflex built from years of practice.

"You gonna be around later?" I said, smiling like I wanted to sell her something she didn't need.

She shrugged me off with a confused smile. "Suspect," she said, then laughed. "You've always been a little loud for trouble."

I took it as a challenge. I left my number with her, as if I were offering friendship and maybe something more.

"Call me," I said, and she watched the way I left, like I was keeping a secret for myself.

That small, useless exchange lit something that had been coiled in my chest for weeks. I told them to keep me out of Vanessa's business, but of course, I hadn't come to beg. I left the apartment, and the cold air outside snapped at my face like a reminder. I got into my car, and the engine coughed awake.

Time to start over, I thought. Time to get my mind right. My head filled with plans for the night: steal some cars, run into some garages, pull some kick doors —the kind of talk that sounds like thunder but is really just someone yelling into a storm.

I would go ahead a couple more spots, circling the city like a predator marking territory I knew I'd soon lose. My house was on borrowed time, and every step I took away from it felt like practice for the inevitable collapse.

I hit the houses like clockwork. Get high over here, kick it with a friend over there, slide down to the lake over there, catch another high somewhere else. Every stop was a ritual, a small attempt to keep myself stitched together while the edges of my life frayed.

After a while, people began to notice. They could see it in the way my hands moved, how my eyes shifted, how my voice had this low edge, a knife tucked in between the syllables. Some of them didn't ask questions. They just paid me. Paid me to handle things. Handle collections, handle threats, handle the aggression that bubbled in me like red-hot magma.

I became a tool, a weapon, a delivery system for somebody else's pain, and it didn't matter. It was survival. It was what you did when the world had already dealt you a losing hand.

The aggression didn't leave. It followed me home, like a dog with broken teeth, gnawing at the edges of my mind. I didn't fight it. I leaned into it. I knew it would serve me, and I knew that one day, I'd have to pay it back. One day.

I got a call from Lucy. She asked me to come over. I told her to send the address, and I hopped on I-25, phone tucked under my chin like it was the only lifeline I had. The highway ate the miles in a smear of lights, the engine steady, my hands steady, but something underneath me was cautious.

Halfway there, she texted, "Gabriel, where are you at?"

I typed back, "Close."

She shot back, "Okay, well, can we go somewhere else because I don't want you here. They're tripping on me about bringing someone."

She sounded nervous. IDK.

My phone said seven minutes away. I told her, "Okay, I'm coming out." I kept driving. The plan was carved out and simple. Do not ask about Vanessa. Don't pry. Don't beg for explanations. I had already decided what I was going to do. Plain and ugly. Something Vanessa could never get back. Her friendship.

I was going to sleep with her best friend. Period.

I ran through it like a checklist in my head. Don't make it about mercy. Don't make it about love.

By the time I pulled up, I could feel the heat in my jaw, the petty, steady anger that labeled everything I touched. I texted that I was here and waited for whatever came next.

I was a man who had already done the math in the dark and decided the only payment that counted was the one he could take with his own two hands.

Deep breath. Always something. I got nothing to lose, but we can't just sit in the car. I guess I'll get a hotel, since she can't be over here. That's the plan then. When Vanessa finds this out, because females talk, she gonna be so mad, but I don't care. Oh well. This is it. This is my revenge.

I'm a wine-and-dine friend. Seduce her. Professional at the small, quiet manipulations that make people lean in. Hopefully she doesn't fall in love or do anything crazy. Doesn't matter. Tonight's about a single line, the goal. She gets in the car and she's going along with me. I don't know if it's personal vengeance on her side, if she's playing it off to the T and doesn't care about her friend, or if she's really into me. She keeps it subtle, teasing, making me chase her attention. Either way, I'm in it to win it. Almost feels like I'm getting played, but I don't care. I know the rules of the streets. Sometimes you get taken, sometimes you take.

We pull up to the hotel, the kind with flickering neon that smells like cigarettes and bleach. I park, run inside, slide to the front desk, ask for a room like it's nothing. She follows, quiet but confident, leaning into the rhythm I set. Inside, the room is a thin-skulled space of beige walls and cheap carpet, smells of old perfume and stale smoke. I don't think. I just move.

We end up sleeping together. No poetry. No attachment. Just the heat of the moment and the quiet click of doors closing behind us. Nothing special. Morning comes soft and gray, light spilling under the blinds. I get up, slide into my jacket, and head out before the city fully wakes. No words. No promises. We separate paths and go back to our own lives.

At this moment, I've completed one of my goals. A small victory, a line crossed, and I gotta get going. Streets wait for no one, and I've got my next move burning in the back of my mind. I get going, jump in the car, and take off like a man with fire under his feet.

I pull up to a gas station, kill the engine, check my pockets. All my money, gone. Every bill, every card, everything, all my dope, gone. Oh man. Oh hell no. This girl just jacked me. My hands go cold. I fly back to the hotel like a bat out of hell. The door's ajar. The room's empty. She's gone. My head spins. She had the audacity. She set me up while I was setting her up.

UGHHHHHHH, I think, straight up, completely. How did I miss it? She acted like everything was okay, like I was the only player on the board. Wow.

Then she calls me later that night. Her voice is light, like nothing happened.

"What are you doing?" she asks. I say, "What do you think I'm doing? You jacked me."

She shrugs it off through the line. "Why are you bringing up old stuff? That was earlier today." The calm in her voice is a blade.

I tell her, "Watch. I got you. You're dead."

Click. The line goes dead, and the silence tastes like iron.

I'm feeling everything at once:

Confused, how did this even happen?

Tested, did I misread everything?

Angry, pure hot anger that burns my chest.

Upset, the small quiet kind that hollows you out.

Distraught, the world tilting under me.

Disturbed by how easily I was played.

Vengeful, the thought of paying her back like currency.

Rage, a low animal noise behind my teeth.

Frustrated with myself and the idiots who I let orbit me.

Emotional, weird, raw, exposed.

Unhinged, the edges of me are burned.

Determined, the part that knots up and says, not this time.

I sit in my car with the engine off and let the city piss and hum around me and just pound my fist into the steering wheel. Over and over again. The money's gone, but the sting's worse. Trust. Ego. The little illusion that I was still calling the shots. She smiled while she cut me out of my plans. She laughed while she emptied my pockets.

Now the math's simple. I was the easy mark, and she made a clean job of it. Revenge wants a shape. Rage needs a plan. Determination tightens around my ribs like a rope. I'm not sleeping on this. The city is full of exits and entrances, and I'm already thinking about which doors I'll burn to make sure she remembers the man she thought she could rob.

All these feelings roll through me like a freight train, through my mind, down my bones, into my gut. It isn't accidental anymore. It's surgical. She set me up the way I'd planned to set her up, and that neat symmetry warps something inside me. I can feel the blueprint of the betrayal like a map burned into my skin.

The devil perches on my shoulder like he never left, small, calm, and smiling with teeth carved from memory. He hums low, a tune that sounds like temptation, like something older than language. His whispers slide through me, soft, sharp, and familiar, the kind of words that promise satisfaction wrapped in ruin. They sink deep. The talk of hurt. The call for payback. Each word lights up in my blood, fire chasing through my veins faster than reason can keep up. Heat climbs my arms, fills my chest, burns behind my eyes until all I see is red and memory of what was.

Whatever holiness I ever had melts away, thin as candle wax under a steady flame. Righteousness drips down to the floor, leaving me stripped bare, just flesh, breath, and anger. I taste it, that torque of rage turning inside me, the engine of vengeance grinding to life. It hums in my ribs, mechanical and merciless, demanding movement, demanding consequence. The thought of making them feel what they made me feel becomes a language my bones suddenly understand.

"I want blood."

The words aren't spoken. They're breathed. They're felt. They're real. They drum through my throat in time with my heartbeat, a rhythm older than mercy. And for a moment, the devil doesn't whisper anymore. He just smiles because he knows I see what he sees. It's a world painted in black and white with pure clarity, where pain is power and the only truth left is the one written in fury.

I continue on this destructive path for a few months. I end up selling the '82 for drugs and money. Stealing whatever I could to get high. Destroying whatever to get high. There was no limit or cap. I was blinded with anger and emotion and fueled with drugs.

As time passed, I found out. Vanessa, get this. Vanessa got so drunk at the bar that night and ended up going home with some guy. She woke up in his bed and she slept with him. She didn't have the courage to come home and look me in the face. So she stayed away. Nobody would tell me anything because they were afraid of what I would do, what I was capable of doing. Everyone hid her for her safety. That's what I found out. Can you believe that? And she tried to flip it on me, like I did something wrong.

I lift my head to the pale moonlight and its cold shine cuts across my face like a blade. In that reflection, I barely recognize the man staring back. He's not who he once was. He's something broken, rebuilt, and dangerous in a quiet way. The kind of dangerous that doesn't need to prove itself anymore. Who I am checks in like a stranger at the door, bruised by time, shaped by survival. I don't brace myself with courage or pride, just with the steady inhale of someone who understands that the world has shifted and there's no turning it back.

Tonight isn't about plans. It isn't about talk. It's about acceptance of what I've done, what I've lost, what I've become.

The devil comes and I don't run. I take his hand. We dance.

Months would pass, and eventually, one night led to the night that unfolded the beginning of this story I've been telling you, no detours, no metaphors. It started with a stolen truck filled with packages, porch lights, quick hands, snatch and go, the small clink of other people's lives dropping into my bag. Everything was motion. Everything was a transaction.

Pills and meth rode with me in my pocket and in my head, eating the edges of hesitation until the city was only lanes and targets. Speed pulled me further. I pressed the pedal and the road opened, bright lines racing past. Cops turned into noise behind me, then closer, so I pushed harder. I cut through neighborhoods like a man bent on erasing the world behind him. I drove right through the house, metal screaming, my tires spitting rubber and sparks, and felt the pure, stupid rush of getting away.

They kept breathing down my neck. The famous blue and red cherry lights braided the night, and every turn felt narrower. I ducked into side streets, bounced curbs, slipped through gaps people left in the city when they thought no one was watching.

Eventually, it all came to a screeching halt. I hid for hours in trash bags. I woke up, felt out of pure exhaustion, and pretty much belly crawled to Allison's house. The cops took the truck and trailer. Pills and meth kept me going for months.

Now I'm sitting in a cell, where we began, and the story is blunt and far from finished. Back to the whys and what's.

CHAPTER 35: ALL CAUGHT UP

I had been sitting in the El Paso County Jail for months, counting the days by the shift changes and the echoes of metal doors clanging shut. Four, maybe five months had gone by since the night I got arrested for felony eluding, substantial risk of causing death, and possession of a stolen vehicle.

Time moved differently in there. The lights never went off, and the smell of bleach and sweat hung in the air like fog that never cleared.

The guard's voice echoed through the ward.

"Hinojosa! You got a visit!"

My stomach twisted. I didn't know who'd even bother coming to see me. I'd been down four, maybe five months, staring at the same gray walls, breathing the same recycled air, counting the same minutes that felt like years. Visits weren't something I expected anymore.

The guard cuffed me up, and I followed him down the hall. The smell of bleach and sweat filled the narrow corridor. The hum of fluorescent lights buzzed above my head, matching the pounding in my chest. My sandals scraped against the cold concrete. The closer we got to visitation, the more I felt like I was walking into something I couldn't dodge.

They sat me in a cubicle-sized room behind glass. The metal stool was cold. I could see my reflection faintly in the glass—tired eyes, jailhouse skin, hair grown out uneven.

A few minutes passed before the door on the other side opened and a woman stepped in. She wasn't dressed like a cop. No uniform. A clipboard, yes, but not of judgment. She had that social worker look—all neat, polite, calm, but with eyes that had seen too much.

She sat down and lifted the phone to her ear. I did the same.

"Mr. Hinojosa," she began softly, her tone professional but heavy.

"Yes," I said, confused.

"So, I'm just going to be as frank as I possibly can with you, and long story short... we had a girl come into the hospital."

I didn't say anything. Just watched her mouth move.

"She was pregnant. The girl was high on drugs and intoxicated by alcohol. During the pregnancy, the baby struggled severely. Afterwards..." She hesitated for a moment. "...Afterwards, she named you as the father."

She said it with the most stern and serious expression on her face. The words hit like a slow-moving car crash. My throat tightened, but I stayed quiet, now even more confused.

"She left right after delivering the baby," the woman paused, then continued. "Walked out of the emergency room before we could even discharge her. We don't know where she went. She had active warrants, so we assume she was scared of getting locked up. The baby is still in our care. A baby boy."

She let that last word hang there. Boy.

It buzzed in my head like an alarm I didn't know how to shut off. She leaned closer to the glass.

"My whole conversation with you, sir, is leading up to this..."

"We'd like to know if you'd like to pursue paternity, to see if this is your son."

For a second, all the noise in my head went quiet. The fights. The memories. The chaos. Just silence. Then the weight of it all hit at once. The glass between us blurred as my eyes watered, and I hated that she could see that. My hand trembled slightly as I gripped the phone tighter.

"My son?" I finally asked, voice low and cracked.

"Yes," she said, eyes soft but unflinching. "Your son, well, potentially."

The guard behind me shifted. The fluorescent lights flickered. Somewhere down the hall, someone was yelling, but all I could think about was that one word echoing over and over. Son.

The woman on the other side of the glass looked like she carried a thousand sad stories in her clipboard, but this one belonged to me. I shifted on the cold metal stool, heartbeat pounding through my ribs. My throat was dry as desert sand.

"Can I ask you the woman's name, please?" I finally said.

She looked down at her notes, then back up at me. "Of course. Her name is Lucy. Does that ring a bell?"

The name hit me like a punch. My jaw tightened, and I let out a shaky breath.

"Lucy…" I said, almost to myself. "Yeah. I know her."

The woman's eyebrows lifted slightly. "You do?"

I nodded. My mind started spinning flashes of nights that blurred together—smoke-filled rooms, motel lights humming through dirty curtains. I could see Lucy laughing with that wild look in her eyes. Lucy, the one that jacked me. The way she lived like she was larger than life.

"Yeah," I said again, voice low, gritty. "I know her."

She gave a small nod, pen tapping against her notepad. "Alright. So, Mr. Hinojosa, would you like to pursue paternity? We can set up a DNA test to determine if he's your son."

I swallowed hard. For a second, the jail faded away—the glass, the noise, the weight of my charges. All I could picture was a small baby somewhere out there, struggling to breathe, born into chaos, maybe with my blood running through him.

"Yeah," I said, steady this time. "I'll do whatever we have to do. If he's my son… I need to know."

She smiled faintly, that practiced, professional kind of smile, the kind that hides the ache behind her eyes. "Alright. Perfect. I'll be in touch in the next couple days. We'll get everything arranged for the test." She paused, her voice softening. "Until then, sir, just try to behave. We'll talk soon. Have a good day."

She hung up the phone and stood. The line went dead as I continued to hold the phone in disbelief about what just happened. Her reflection faded as she walked away. I just sat there, staring at the empty chair through the glass. The guard behind me said something, but I didn't catch it. My thoughts were somewhere else, with a name and a maybe.

Lucy, are you serious?

A baby?

My son?

Two kids now?

I leaned forward, forehead against the cold glass, whispering to no one. "Wow… I might have a son too now."

The words felt unreal in my mouth. The walls seemed to close in tighter, the hum of the lights louder, the air heavier. Somewhere deep inside, something cracked open, something I thought had died long ago.

Weeks rolled by like smoke. The days in jail bled into each other, gray on gray, time stretching and folding until you forgot what real air smelled like. Then, one morning, the guard called my name again.

"Hinojosa, you got a visit."

I knew before I even walked in who it was. Same woman. Same calm face that carried weight behind her eyes. She didn't waste time with small talk. She just opened the folder and looked up at me through the glass.

"It's confirmed," she said. "He's your son."

For a second, I couldn't breathe. The noise from the pod, the shouting, the metal clanging, the smell of disinfectant—all went silent. My chest felt hollow, like my heart had been scooped out and set somewhere I couldn't reach.

I leaned closer to the glass. "What's his name?"

"Ezekiel, born November 9th, 2015," she said. "He's living in Pueblo right now. With Lucy's mom's… ummm partner." She hesitated a little. "Her mom's long-time lover or something like that. Yeah, that's who's been taking care of him."

Ezekiel.

The name burned through me. It sounded too clean, too holy, for a world like mine. A name like that didn't belong in the same sentence as my life, but it was mine now. My blood. My boy.

She went on, her tone softer now. "Lucy's gone. We don't know where she is. The caregiver wants what's best for Ezekiel."

"We'd like to know if you're willing to be involved in the DHS case. Parenting classes. Meetings. Anything that shows you're serious about being his father."

I nodded slowly. "Yeah," I said, the word heavy in my mouth. "Yeah, I'll do whatever I have to do. He's my son."

She studied me a moment. "Are you going to prison?"

I looked down, rubbing my cuffed hands together. "I don't know. I'm still waiting to get sentenced. Could go either way."

"Well," she said, closing the folder, "if you agree to do the parenting and show the court you're serious, I'll speak to the judge myself."

Her voice carried something almost like hope, something I hadn't heard directed at me in a long time.

Days later, when sentencing came, I stood there in that cold courtroom, hands cuffed, chains around my ankles, family gone, friends gone, everything stripped down to truth. I waited for the gavel to fall, expecting the worst. But the judge looked over the paperwork, looked at me, and said the words that changed everything.

"Five years. Halfway house."

I didn't move at first. Didn't blink. The sound barely made sense. Halfway house? Not prison? Freedom on a leash, but freedom still. She did it. She pulled her strings.

When I arrived at Comcor, that smell of outside air hit me like a memory I forgot I missed. The night was cool, the sky bruised with purple clouds, and for the first time in almost a year, I looked up and saw the stars not through a window behind bars. Somewhere out there my kids, my daughter Nevaeh, my son Ezekiel, were breathing the same air as me. I didn't just want to survive. I wanted to be the man my kids could call "Dad." Nevaeh's mom and I always beefed, and she would keep her away. Plus, I wasn't the best father figure either.

Comcor wasn't freedom. It was a tighter kind of cage, a place where the walls breathed down your neck and the rules never slept. The day I got there, the air smelled like clean from the rain. My head was heavy from court, my heart even heavier. I had a five-year sentence hanging over me, waiting to snap shut if I so much as blinked wrong. If I messed up this program, I'd be going to prison. No appeal. No questions. Straight to prison.

So, I walked through those doors like a man walking a balance beam between hell and redemption.

Comcor was built on order. Four levels: Level One to Level Four. Each one is like a rung on a ladder to freedom. You earned your way up through sobriety, work hours, classes, and behavior. After completion of Level Four, you could finally move into your own place, your own roof, your own rules. Until then, you were owned.

They wanted accountability for everything. Random UAs. Curfews that hit like sirens. You had to call before leaving, call when you arrived, and call when you returned. Sleep there every night. No exceptions. One slip and you were done, back to jail.

But the halfway house wasn't the only storm I was caught in. I had my DHS case running side by side with therapy, parenting classes, drug and alcohol counseling, meetings, and random UAs with this place, too. Visits with my son down in Pueblo. Every week, the same long ride. A couple of hours there, a couple of hours back. Don't forget the forty-plus hours of work on top of all that.

Here's the kicker. Do you want to know the catch to all this? I wasn't even allowed to drive. Even if you had a driver's license, you could not drive until Level Four.

So, I had to hustle rides, beg for favors, catch buses when I could. Anything to see my boy, Ezekiel. The reason I couldn't mess up.

His mom wasn't nowhere around and depended on me to show up. Nevaeh had her mom, they had their ups and downs too. Nevaeh loved her grandparents. She was always with them. It killed Nevaeh when my dad died. They were best friends. Now, Nevaeh leans on my mom a lot. They are really close too. At least Nevaeh had them. Ezekiel didn't have that, and I wanted him to have that. A family with us.

Mornings started before dawn. 4:30 a.m. actually, if you wanted to eat breakfast. I'd wake up to the buzz of alarms, six to eight men shuffling in one room, sharing one bathroom, the smell of burnt coffee and sweat. I'd lace up my boots.

One day I met a guy named Kevin. He was the owner of a local landscaping company. He was looking for workers, and I was knowledgeable in that field—pretty much all I ever did, other than the call center thing and selling drugs. Kevin was built like a man who'd carried too many years on his back and refused to let any of them break him. Broad shoulders. Hands rough as concrete. Eyes that looked like they'd seen everything twice, once when it happened and again in his sleep. He had that stillness about him, the kind that comes from doing real time, from learning when to talk and when to just watch.

He'd done twelve years straight behind bars. Twelve birthdays behind steel and echoes.

But when he came out, he didn't carry the bitterness most men did. He carried purpose. He was sharp, focused, clean. He built his own business from the ground up, piece by piece, like he was rebuilding himself along with it. Nothing fancy, just honest work. And at the end of the day, it was his.

Kevin was the kind of man who didn't have to say much to be respected. His presence spoke louder than any speech. But I'm not going to lie—he loved giving speeches too. He moved with a slow certainty, every step measured, every word deliberate. There was something in his voice, something like authority mixed with calm, that could settle a whole room.

We got along from day one. There was no judgment in him, just understanding. He saw me where I was at—thrown in the halfway house, DHS case, ankle-deep in responsibility— and didn't flinch. He showed up when others didn't. Made sure I made it to every class, every therapy session, every UA. If I had somewhere to be, he made it work. Already in the truck waiting, engine running, music loud. He'd pick me up before work and drop me off after. No complaints. No lectures. Just respect. A dependable rhythm that kept me from slipping.

Sometimes we'd ride in silence, just the hum of the road between us. Other times we'd share stories, bits of prison and wisdom, coded in patience and survival. He'd talk about how you can lose your mind if you stop believing you've got a reason to get up in the morning.

Kevin was more than a boss. He was solid. One of those rare ones you could lean on without fear of them folding. Kevin turned into family right away and was one of the only actual people in my life I could call my brother. I don't know what I would've done if he hadn't been there. In a time when I was balancing everything—court, classes, visits, sobriety, Kevin was the gravity that kept my world from spinning apart.

Afternoons were stacked with classes. Anger management. Substance abuse. Relapse prevention. Therapy, one-on-ones and groups. Words on words on words, all the things I used to ignore, now being hammered into my skull. By the time I got back to the halfway house, I was running on fumes.

Then there were the nights I'd lie on that thin mattress, staring at the ceiling, phone in hand, thinking about my kids. How now it was time to show up. Now.

I had a lot on my plate. Felt like too much for one man, maybe. But I knew what the stakes were. One wrong move, one dirty test, one missed call, and everything I was fighting for would disappear.

Comcor taught me discipline through fear. DHS taught me responsibility through guilt. But my kids… they were teaching me purpose.

CHAPTER 36: CRAVING CHAOS

I was living in all this chaos, the kind that never really leaves you, it just gets quieter when you're too tired to fight it. Every day was about discipline, structure, trying to keep my mind straight and my body clean. I was doing everything I had to do—all the classes, therapy, U.A.s, meetings, working—just to prove I wasn't that same reckless man anymore. The truth was, I was still walking a fine line between survival and relapse. One slip, one wrong move, and everything I worked for could vanish in the blink of an eye.

Comcor was supposed to be a fresh start, a second chance, an alternative to prison. Still, it was a concrete box where broken people tried to glue themselves back together under fluorescent lights and group schedules. The walls had this tired yellow tint, like they'd soaked up every tear and argument that ever happened inside. Every face there told a story filled with addiction, loss, pain, and second chances. You could feel it in the air—it was heavy, desperate, and hungry for being human again.

That's where I met Christina.

She was Native, with strong cheekbones, dark hair that fell over her shoulders, and eyes that could cut right through the armor I wore. She had this fire in her, like someone who'd been through the storm and learned how to stand still in the middle of it. The first time we talked, it was during a smoke break after group. The sky was gray, the kind that made everything feel colder than it was. We stood outside, sharing a lighter, talking about nothing and everything all at once. Stories of where we came from, who we lost, what we wanted out of life if we ever made it past this halfway point.

After that, it became routine. Late-night talks after curfew checks on the phone. She lived in a different building down the street where they housed the females. Segregation, rules, cameras—but none of that stopped us. We found ways. Notes slipped in the chow hall. Quick glances during breakfast. Long looks that said everything without saying a word.

It started as comfort. Attention. Two broken people trying to hold on to something that felt human, that felt like the normalcy of life beyond this place. But temptation doesn't care about recovery or reintegration. It waits for you when you're lonely. It finds you when your guard's down. And one night, we indulged. We crossed the line.

It wasn't planned. It never is. It happened in the shadows, in that reckless way that always feels like love when it's happening and guilt the second it's done. Her skin was soft, her heartbeat was loud, and for a moment, I forgot about the rules, the staff, the programming of it. For a few stolen minutes, I wasn't an addict or a convict or a case file. I was just a man feeling alive again.

Come to find out, the world doesn't give out blessings for free.

A few weeks later, Christina came to me. Her face pale, her hands shaking, her voice barely above a whisper.

"I'm pregnant."

I didn't say anything at first. I just stood there, feeling the air leave my lungs. Pregnant? That one word hit me harder than any judge's sentence. We were both still in the halfway house. Still trying to earn trust back. I was still learning how to live a clean life. I didn't even have a place of my own yet, just a bunk bed and a binder full of relapse prevention worksheets.

I sat on the edge of my bed that night, staring at the cracked paint on the wall. My mind was spinning with thoughts and emotions—fear, guilt, pride, confusion—all tangled together. I wanted to do the right thing, but what was the right thing? I wasn't ready. She definitely wasn't ready. Maybe this was the moment I'd been running from—the one that forced me to grow up, to stop being greedy for all the wrong things and start being greedy for life.

Christina cried that night. She said she didn't know what to do. I told her the truth—that neither did I. We'd figure it out together. We had to. Because for the first time, it wasn't just about me anymore. It wasn't about staying sober for the courts or for the program, or for appearances. It was about a life, one that didn't even ask to be part of our mess but was coming anyway.

I already had two kids; one I barely found out about and who lived in a whole different city.

The next few weeks were a blur. Rumors started spreading through the facility. Staff got suspicious. People whispered, pointed, and judged. The tension was thick. Every time I saw her, I could see she wanted to run to me, but she couldn't. All we had were brief moments and short conversations before the cameras caught on. Still, there was something powerful in it, like we were building our own small world in the middle of that chaos. Even if it was messy. Even if it was wrong. Even if it costs us everything.

Time kept moving, even when I wished it would stop. The days inside Comcor started to blend together, the same routine on repeat, like a scratched record that wouldn't quit skipping.

Christina had started pulling away from me, getting distant. I could feel it long before I could admit it. It was in the way she spoke, short and clipped, like every word she gave me cost her something. It was in her eyes too. Those same eyes that used to light up when she saw me now looked past me, as if she was already gone.

I tried to fight it. I tried to hold on. Every part of me wanted to make it work. I told myself I'd been here before and messed it up before, and I wasn't about to do it again. I had already failed twice with both of my kids in my life. When it came to love and family, I swore I wouldn't fail a third time. I didn't want to. Not this time. Not with her. Not with the baby.

Sometimes I'd see her walking across the street. The light would hit her just right, outlining her growing stomach as she held it with one hand. She moved slower than before. She didn't laugh anymore. She didn't stop to talk. She'd just walk right past me, hoodie zipped up, eyes on the ground. I'd stand there, pretending not to care, pretending it didn't hurt, but inside I was breaking a little more each day.

She stopped answering the phone. When I was alone in my room, everything hit harder. The air felt heavy. The walls seemed closer. I'd sit on the edge of my bunk, elbows on my knees, staring at the cracked tile floor. The hum of the pipes above my head was the only sound, steady and cold. I thought about everything that had brought me there—the bad choices, the street life, the lies I told myself just to get through another night. I thought about her too. About the first time we talked, the first time she laughed, the way she made me forget for a second that I was still stuck in that place.

Was it love? I couldn't say yes or no. Maybe it was just comfort. Maybe it was two broken people trying to fill the empty spaces inside each other. I don't know. But whatever it was, it felt real when it happened. And now, even though it was falling apart, I still wanted to believe in it. I wanted to believe that I could be the man who stayed this time. That I could show up. That I could be there for my children no matter what.

Even in a place like that, love was dangerous. It had its own rules. It was greedy, hungry, selfish. It took what it wanted and left scars behind. I was covered in them, inside and out. I knew I couldn't escape that truth. I knew this was only the beginning of something bigger than either of us could handle.

Time passed, and she continued to grow. One day, I saw her walking to a bus stop and ran to talk to her. She was sitting on a concrete bench by a fence, her hands resting on her stomach, eyes lost somewhere in the distance. The wind was cold, and the air smelled like wet concrete and cigarette smoke.

I walked over, slow, careful not to scare her off. She didn't look up right away. I sat next to her, leaving just enough space for her to breathe. For a while, neither of us said a word. When I finally spoke, my voice cracked a little. I told her I didn't know how to fix things, but I wanted to be there for the baby. That was all I knew. I wanted to show up, no matter what it took.

She didn't say much, just nodded, her eyes glassy with emotion she was trying to hold back.

In that moment, I realized it wasn't about being perfect or proving anything. It was about being present. It was about owning up to what I started and not running this time. The silence between us said everything. The chaos around us didn't stop, the rules didn't change, but for that brief moment under the gray sky, something inside me did.

Finally, after what felt like weeks of circling the same conversations with Christina—about us, about the baby, about what we wanted our lives to look like—I made a decision. I was tired of talking about what could be. I wanted to make something real. Every time we spoke, I could feel her slipping further away, like trying to hold water in my hands. I knew she was losing faith in me. Maybe she already had. But I couldn't let her walk away, not with my child, and disappear. I wanted her to see that I could be the man I kept promising I'd become.

We stood outside the chow hall one morning, where we met for breakfast, our voices low, the air between us thick with tension and quiet hope. She looked tired, not just physically but in her soul—the kind of tired you get from years of disappointment. Still, there was something in her eyes, something soft that told me there was a chance left, if I moved now.

So, I told her, 'What if we got married?' Crazy, I know. I continued to say… right then. Not someday. Not when I got out. Now.

She looked at me like she didn't know whether to laugh or cry. There was this long silence where I could feel her weighing all the lies, I'd told against the man I was trying to be. I told her I meant it, that I wanted to be her husband, that I wanted our child to know their father didn't run this time.

To my surprise, she agreed. Part of me thought she would play this out to see if I was serious, to see if I'd go all the way through with this and actually do it.

We made a plan, and a few days later, we went down to the DMV downtown. It wasn't anything like the weddings people dream about. No music. No family. No friends. Just two people who had been through hell, standing at a counter, signing a piece of paper that meant something much bigger than it looked.

I still had to check in at the halfway house every night, still had curfews and rules, still had the weight of my past chained to me. But in that moment, for once, I felt like I was doing something right. I wanted to be there for my daughter.

She wore a simple outfit—jeans and a white shirt, her hair pulled back like she didn't want to make a big deal out of it. To me, she looked beautiful. Not in the way people mean when they talk about beauty, but in the way someone looks when you realize they're giving you one last chance to prove yourself.

I wore my best clothes, which wasn't saying much, a hoodie and jeans. Nothing special.

When the clerk handed us the paperwork, my hands shook. Signing my name felt heavier than any sentence I'd ever done. It was just a piece of paper. It wasn't spiritual. It wasn't romantic. For me, it was a promise I'd be there. Who knows what it was to her. She couldn't even change her last name because she didn't want parole to know.

When it was done, we stood outside the DMV, just looking at each other. Cars honked, people passed by, and life went on around us like nothing happened. I honestly couldn't believe this happened. I think we both thought each other would back down and we were calling each other's bluff to the very end, and to my surprise, neither of us folded. I remember afterwards, it was quiet, reaching for her hand and she didn't pull away. That small gesture meant she was willing to stay and try.

We didn't celebrate, didn't go out to eat or take pictures. We just walked to the bus stop, rode the bus back to the halfway house, and we kissed and said goodbye. That night, lying in my narrow bed under the buzz of the ceiling light, I felt something I hadn't felt in a long time, and that was hope. It wasn't loud or dramatic. It was quiet and fragile, so fragile it felt like it could be broken easily. Even though part of me knew the road ahead would be hard, I believed, for that brief moment, that maybe, just maybe, we could make it work.

Nobody in my family knew about the marriage. Not my mom, not my sister, not a single soul. I kept it to myself, holding it like a fragile secret, I wasn't ready to let the world judge. It wasn't about shame; it was about protection. I didn't want to hear the disappointment in their voices or see it in their eyes. I wanted to hold on to that one piece of hope I had, untouched by doubt or criticism.

When I finally told them, everything changed. My mom froze, the kind of stillness that speaks louder than words. My sister's eyes went wide and then she looked away, shaking her head slowly as if she'd already seen this ending before it even began. The silence felt thick, like the air was trying to swallow me whole, and then came the questions, one after another. Why didn't you tell us? Why her? What are you thinking?

Their words cut deep, not because they were cruel but because they were scared for me. My mom said I should have waited, that love doesn't fix broken things, it just makes you forget they're broken for a while. My sister said I needed to find myself before I tried to build something with someone else. I heard them, I really did, but my heart wasn't listening. I believed in what I was doing. I believed in the chance to build something new, something better than what my past had to offer.

So I went back to my routine. Work, classes, therapy, U.A.s, all of it. Every day was another step away from the man I used to be. The structure kept me sane. I poured myself into it like it was the only thing holding me together, and in a way, it was. I reached Level Four, full completion. That moment was more than just a milestone. It was a message to myself that I could start over, that I could see something through to the end without destroying it.

On weekends, I got to see Ezekiel. Those moments were sacred. When I'd hold him, his tiny hand gripping my finger, the world felt smaller and safer. His laugh had a way of breaking through everything that was heavy in me. Sometimes my mom would bring Nevaeh to visit me with my sister Bernadette. One time we all went together to visit Ezekiel in Pueblo, and watching Nevaeh with her little brother brought a peace I hadn't felt in years. He was still a baby, and seeing her hold him, everyone's laughter echoing, I would just stand there quietly, trying to take in every second before it slipped away.

Eventually, I saved enough to get a house. Not just a room, not a shared space, but a real home. A three-bedroom house. I still remember unlocking that door for the first time. The smell of fresh paint mixed with dust, the sound of my footsteps echoing against bare walls. It was empty, but it was freedom. Each room represented something. One for me. One for my kids. I told my mom about the house and asked her if she wanted to move in. She agreed.

Before going to the non-residential program with Comcor, I had to get a house phone. It sounded small, but to me, it was a symbol of achievement. They needed to reach me anytime randomly after curfew, to make sure I stayed accountable. Also, a reminder that I was still moving forward. I went out and bought a cheap corded phone, the kind most people don't even use anymore. Plugging it into the wall felt strange, but it grounded me. It was a connection to something steady, something real.

Finally, I would get the approval to live in the new house. Now I had to wait for Christina to get parole, and she would move in. She went to prison and came to the halfway house after prison. I was a direct sentence to the halfway house, and we were on two different programs.

My first night in the new house, after work and meetings, my mom moved in and had a room. It was amazing having my mom around. At night, I would sit alone in the living room. No furniture, just a steel chair to sit on. In my bedroom I had nothing, just a few blankets and a pillow and the floor for a bed. The house was quiet except for the hum of the refrigerator and the occasional car passing outside. Sometimes I would just stare at the walls, thinking about how far I had come. From cells to halfway houses to this. A place I could finally call my own again.

There was pride in that silence. Not loud or boastful, but deep and still. I had made it here, one step at a time, through everything that tried to break me. My family still didn't understand, and maybe they never would, but I did. I understood what it took to hold on when everything in your past told you to let go.

That house wasn't just shelter. It was proof that I was still fighting for something better, even when the world doubted me. It was proof that hard work doesn't pay off all at once. It comes quietly, through effort, through hope that refuses to die, one day at a time.

CHAPTER 37: COME TO COLLECT

I finally saved up enough money to buy a 1998 Jeep Grand Cherokee. It wasn't much by most standards, but to me, it was freedom on four wheels, and it was mine. The paint was faded in some spots, a dark blue that caught the light in streaks, and the engine had that rough growl that told you it had seen better days. It ran strong. I washed it every weekend, Armor All on the tires, vacuumed the inside until it smelled like fresh cloth and hope. It was the first car I had bought with my own money after years of losing everything, and sitting behind that wheel made me feel like I was finally steering my life somewhere new.

Not long after, Christina got parole. When I heard the news, I felt a rush of emotions full of excitement, relief, and anxiety all tangled up together. She didn't parole to me though. She went to a friend's house on the other side of town. I understood why. I was still getting settled, still proving I could keep things stable. We talked every day though and I saw her when I could. I wanted to make sure everything would be ready when she and the baby could come home.

Those weeks felt long. I worked during the day and spent my nights getting the house together piece by piece. A donated couch, a secondhand dining table, a few beds I bought off Craigslist. Every little thing felt like a victory. I'd stand in the empty rooms, imagining where the crib would go, how it would feel to finally have my family under one roof. There was a quiet kind of pride in that, the kind that doesn't need to be spoken, just felt.

Then one night, everything changed. I was at Christina's friend's house, just visiting, helping her carry a few things in from the car. It was late, one of those calm nights when the city feels like it's taking a breath. She had been feeling off all day, her hand occasionally resting on her belly, her face tense but trying to hide it. I remember the way she moved, slow and careful, like she was already bracing herself for what was coming.

We were sitting in the living room, the television playing low in the background, when she suddenly grabbed my arm. Her breath hitched, and her face twisted in pain. I froze for a second, my heart jumping into my throat. She said it was time. The baby was coming, and when she said that fear, worry, and concern were written all over her face.

Everything after that felt like a blur and a movie at the same time. I helped her to the Jeep, my hands shaking, adrenaline flooding through me. She was breathing heavy, trying to stay calm, and I kept telling her it was going to be okay, even though I was barely holding it together myself. The drive to the hospital felt endless. The sound of the tires on the pavement, the streetlights flashing over us, the smell of the cold night air coming in through the cracked window, every detail burned into my mind.

Inside, I was praying. Not out loud, but in my heart. Praying that this birth would be different from the last one. The last time still haunted me, the panic, the fear, the blood, the feeling of helplessness as everything went wrong. I remember standing there, watching doctors rush around, hearing machines beep, feeling like the world was falling apart right in front of me. That memory had scarred me deeper than I ever admitted.

This time, I told myself, it would be different. This time, I'd be ready.

When we reached the hospital, I parked crooked across two spaces and ran inside. Nurses came rushing with a wheelchair while Christina clung to my arm, her face pale, her body trembling through contractions. They moved quickly, guiding her through double doors and down bright, white hallways that smelled of sanitizer and adrenaline. My heart was pounding so hard I could feel it in my throat.

The delivery room felt frozen in time, even though everything was happening at breakneck speed. Nurses moved around us like a blur, snapping on gloves, adjusting machines, calling out numbers I couldn't process. Christina's hand gripped mine tighter than ever, her eyes wide open with pain, sweat rolling down her forehead. I kept telling her, "You got this, baby, you got this," even though my voice was shaking.

The doctor's voice cut through the noise, calm but commanding. "One more push. You're right there."

Then it happened. A cry. Sharp, raw, real. It cut through everything, the fear, the chaos, the noise. It was the most beautiful sound I'd ever heard. For a second, I forgot to breathe. I just stood there staring as the nurse lifted this tiny, wrinkled, perfect little life into the air. My child.

They placed the baby on Christina's chest, and I swear time stopped. Her tears mixed with the baby's cries, and I could feel something inside me break. All the pain, all the years, all the mistakes, it all led to this single moment of grace. The baby's little fingers wrapped around one of mine, barely strong enough to hold but still holding on, and I realized right then this wasn't just a new life coming into the world. It was another chance for me, too.

Then, in a rush of light and sound. It was over in an instant and she came...

Aiyannauh Bernadette Hinojosa
Born November 4th, 2017, 7 pounds 1 ounce, 6:44 a.m.

Tears ran before I could stop them. I didn't even try. I just held her, whispering promises I wasn't gonna break this time. I told her I'd be there, not just in the easy moments but in the hard ones. That I'd fight for her. That I'd never let her grow up wondering if her daddy loved her.

The hospital days felt like a blur wrapped in exhaustion. Machines humming, nurses coming in and out, Christina's tired eyes fading in and out of sleep. I'd sit there in that hard plastic chair, staring at my beautiful daughter in that clear crib beside her bed, tiny, healthy, and oh so perfect, breathing soft. Every rise and fall of her chest felt like a second chance being written in front of me.

When the nurses came in with discharge papers, something in me tightened. I helped Christina pack her things, held the baby bag like it was made of gold. We walked out slow, her leaning on me, both of us quiet. Outside, the world looked different. Even the sky felt heavier, brighter, like God himself was watching to see what I'd do next.

Christina went back to her friend's house, the same place she paroled to. I watched her walk up those steps holding our baby girl and I stood there a minute before I drove off. I didn't say it out loud, but I promised myself right then I'd make sure that baby never grew up the way I did.

The house I'd been fixing up was finally starting to feel like something worth fighting for. It smelled like new paint and laundry detergent. I'd been piecing it together with secondhand furniture and pride, just waiting for the moment. I got a crib built by hand—I don't know who made it but that's what they told me—blankets folded, bottles lined up by the sink like trophies. Every nail I drove, every board I fixed, felt like I was patching something inside me too.

When Christina finally called to transfer her parole to my address, it felt like a door opening, not just for her, but for all of us. Around the same time is when DHS started showing up. They came with their clipboards, with their polished shoes and rehearsed concern, walking through my living room like detectives. I didn't care. I had nothing to hide. No more smoke in the air, no more chaos, no more ghosts. Just me, trying to do it right this time.

Court became my second home. The smell of paper, the sound of names being called, that feeling of sitting on the edge of everything. Every hearing, I showed up dressed clean, sober, ready. I kept my head up and my eyes forward. No excuses. Just proof.

Eventually, they found Lucy. She came in looking like she'd been running from herself for years. When the judge asked if she wanted to keep her parental rights, she didn't even look at me. She just said,

"Can I just go? I don't even want to be here."

You could see it in her eyes. She didn't care about life, didn't care about consequences, didn't care about anyone but herself and that next fix. It hit me in a way I hadn't expected. I didn't feel anger, not really. I felt this cold, heavy sadness that settled in my chest, the kind that makes your hands go numb and your mind rewind through every broken choice you've ever seen.

It was like watching someone hand over the last piece of hope they ever had and walk away without a second thought. My son needed more than sorrow or resentment. He needed a father who would show up, who would fight even when the world had already turned its back. So I swallowed the hurt, pushed the bitterness down deep, and focused on him. Everything else could wait.

Months rolled by. I did everything—the classes, the therapy, the home visits, the U.A.s, the sleepless nights wondering if it was all enough. Slowly, the doubt started to fade. I started to feel something I hadn't in years... peace.

Then one morning, they called my name in court for the final hearing. I stood there, palms sweating, heart pounding. The judge looked down at me through those glasses and smiled.

She said, "Mr. Hinojosa, you've completed every requirement and demonstrated what it means to be a responsible, loving parent. I'm proud to grant you full custody of your son, Ezekiel."

For a second, I couldn't breathe. The room faded out, and all I could see was that little boy's face. My eyes burned, my throat tightened, but I didn't cry. Not in front of them. I just nodded, holding that plaque they handed me. "Recognized as a fit parent," it said, but to me, it wasn't a plaque. It was a success. I did it.

That night, when I finally brought Ezekiel home, the sun was setting, that deep orange glow bleeding through the blinds. I carried him through the doorway and stood in the middle of the living room, the same one I made a home, piece by piece. The house was quiet, but it felt alive.

I held him against my chest, his small heartbeat thumping against mine, and whispered, "We made it, Zeke. You ain't ever gonna live the way I did. I promise."

He blinked up at me, half asleep, and I swear it felt like the world had stopped spinning for a second. All the pain, the years in chains, the losses, the regrets all melted into that one moment. For the first time in my life, I was on the right track, and I was proud of it. I was standing exactly where I was meant to be.

For the first time, life didn't feel like it was just taking from me. The house had sound again, real sound, messy and alive, full of little voices that needed me, eyes that looked to me for safety. Ezekiel crawled across the floor with sticky little fingers, reaching for me, laughing before he even fully understood why. His birth had been rough, and due to his birth mother Lucy using during her pregnancy, he was smaller than most kids his age. He was delayed in more ways than one, but let me tell you, that little boy is something else. He's amazing. He's precious. He's mine. I love that little guy like nothing else in the world.

I woke before the sun just to watch him breathe, just to make sure he was okay, that he was alive, that I was still there. That I was still capable of holding something pure in a world that had only ever given me pain, a world that had trained me to survive but never to care. Every breath he took reminded me that I could care that I could protect, that I could build something worth holding onto.

Christina was holding herself together, finally. Clean, steady, working, being compliant with parole, her eyes carrying something I hadn't seen in a while. It wasn't a street fire or the sharp edge of survival rage. It was something quieter, stronger. It was acceptance, a willingness to live and to heal. Then she started talking about her daughters in Arizona. Two little girls who had grown up in someone else's hands, surviving in ways no child should. She wanted to bring them home.

I didn't hesitate. I could feel it in my chest, in the part of me that still remembered what it was to feel invisible. I told her, "Bring them home. Let's do it right."

The house got louder almost overnight. At first, the girls moved through the rooms like shadows, careful and quiet, watching everything, measuring the air like it might crush them if they mis stepped. But day by day, the walls started to echo with their laughter. They began to relax, leaning into the rhythm of this place, learning that it could be a safe space, that I could be someone they could lean on.

Then trouble hit closer than I ever expected. Felicia and my daughter Nevaeh were spiraling fast, out of control in ways that made my chest tighten. Nevaeh ran. She showed up at my door, trembling, eyes wide, carrying herself like she'd been holding the weight of the world on her small shoulders for far too long. She didn't cry at first. She just stood there, shaking, staring at me like she had nowhere else to go. I pulled her inside and didn't let her go.

A fire erupted inside me, hot and relentless, the same fire that had kept me alive in the streets, the same fire that had dragged me back from every edge I had ever faced. I held her tight and promised her she wouldn't have to fight alone anymore. I reminded her that she had me. I would be her shield, her anchor. I told her that this was her home now.

DHS got involved and called me, setting up a court date. Court became the next battlefield. I walked in steady, but inside I felt every memory of failure, every time I'd been told I wasn't enough. I told them everything. The sleepless nights, the counseling, the classes, the home visits. I told them about the plaque they had given me for Ezekiel and how it wasn't just recognition. It was proof that a man could change. I told them my house was no longer a place to survive. It was a home. It was a family.

The judge looked down at me and said words that shook me to my core. "Mr. Hinojosa, you have proven yourself through and through. Temporary full custody of your daughter, Nevaeh, is granted."

My chest felt like it was going to explode. I couldn't even think about breathing. I walked out of that courtroom holding the papers like they were lifelines, carrying a second chance I wasn't going to waste.

When we got home, Nevaeh buried her face in my chest, and I held her like I would never let go. Christina held Aiyannauh while Ezekiel was starting to walk around. The girls from Arizona ran through the house, laughing as if the world had finally given them something they deserved. My mom helped with what she could. Five kids now, with six lives depending on me and my mom.

What started as two, just me and Christina scraping by, fighting for a chance, had grown into a tribe. The house was loud and full of life. Laughter collided with tears. Toys littered the floor like battlefield remnants; proof of lives being rebuilt. It was a mess, exhausting, overwhelming, and challenging, but it was ours. It was life. It was love. Now, I was building something real, something unbreakable.

Late at night, when the noise faded and the city outside was silent, I'd sit in the living room, the plaque glowing faintly on the wall, and think about the streets I'd walked, people I robbed, the nights I had nowhere to go. Now I was the one holding five kids safe from the chaos I had once called home. From chaos to creation. From chains to fatherhood. This time, I was not running from life. I was building one.

There were days when life felt almost normal again. The house smelled like barbecue smoke and charcoal, the kind of smell that clung to your clothes and reminded you that, at least for a moment, you were home. I'd fire up the grill in the backyard, that old metal drum Kevin helped me fix, and the sizzle of meat hitting the grates was like a soundtrack to something I didn't think I'd ever have again... peace.

Family started showing up more often. My sister, her husband, and their kids ran wild through the yard with my kids, jumping on the trampoline, chasing each other with water balloons and sticky popsicle hands. My brother and his wife would pull up with their kids, and before long, the laughter and noise filled every corner of the place. e'd drag out the folding tables, throw on mismatched tablecloths, and pile them high with potato salad, chips, ribs, burgers, corn on the cob—all the backyard classics. Somebody always brought soda, someone else showed up late with ice, and it didn't even matter. We were together. That was the point.

As the sun dipped low, the sky would fade from gold to orange to that deep desert blue that makes the stars look closer than they should. The kids would run around together shouting and laughing, and for a few hours, life felt full again. I started getting closer to everyone—my sister, my brother, my nephews, my nieces. There was something about the laughter, the shared stories, the teasing that came with love. We'd talk about old times, the dumb things we used to do as kids, the fights that didn't matter anymore.

It wasn't perfect. It wasn't easy. But it was real.

Those barbecues became something sacred. Not because of the food or the music, but because of what they represented.

Rebuilding.

Belonging.

A reminder that even after all the chaos, all the brokenness, there were still people who showed up, who stayed, who cared.

And for a man who'd spent too many years trying to survive alone, that meant everything.

CHAPTER 38: A BITTER AWAKENING

I was still working for Kevin. Long days under that blistering hot sun, the smell of diesel, dirt, and sweat soaked into my clothes. Landscaping wasn't glamorous, but it was honest, and that felt good. Bills were getting paid. The kids were in daycare, the older ones in school. Life was steady, at least for a while.

Sometimes, life doesn't crash all at once, it leaks. Little by little. One lie at a time. One missed call. One strange look. Christina had been working here and there, cleaning jobs, gas stations, whatever she could get, but something started feeling off. Her eyes stopped meeting mine. She was always tired, always gone, always with a reason that didn't sound right. I wanted to believe her, I really did. I wanted to believe that the woman who came home from prison was still fighting for that new start. Then the truth came crawling out. She was still using. Still chasing that high that ruins everything it touches. I tried not to let it show, but inside, it tore me apart. I'd seen that look before because I had it—the guilt, the distance, the silence that comes before everything falls apart.

Then the call came.

Her parole officer said she had been charged with theft. Just a small case, but enough. Parole was revoked. They were sending her back to prison. She had to turn herself in at El Paso County Jail. She told me this when I was at work. I sat there in the car after work, just staring at the steering wheel. My hands felt heavy, as if I were holding the whole world in my palms. I didn't even know what to say when I walked in the house. The kids were watching TV. Christina was sitting at the table with Ezekiel and Aiyannauh, feeding them but quiet.

"I gotta go back," she said, voice low.

I nodded, trying to swallow the lump in my throat. "Yeah," I said. "I know."

The next morning came heavy. The kind of morning where even the sun feels tired. We didn't say much about getting ready, just quiet movements, the sound of drawers closing, the kids still asleep in their beds, unaware that everything was about to change again. Christina moved slowly, like every step hurt. She stood in the doorway for a long time, watching the house, watching the space she was about to leave behind.

Then we got in the Jeep.

The road to the CJC, the Criminal Justice Center, was straight and quiet. The kind of road where silence has its own voice. The hum of the tires was steady, hypnotic, and almost peaceful if it didn't hurt so bad. Outside, all you see are the mountains. They stretched wide, big, and blue. Heat shimmering above the asphalt. The sun was rising low and red, bleeding through the windshield, painting her face in this strange morning light. She sat in the passenger seat, hands folded in her lap, eyes locked on the horizon.

I kept glancing over at her, at the woman who once made me believe in hope. The woman who carried my child. But sitting there now, she looked far away, like something inside her had already started fading. Every few miles, I wanted to say something. Anything. Tell her I forgave her. Tell her we'd get through this. But the words stayed stuck somewhere between my chest and my throat.

When we arrived at the CJC, I pulled into the lot and shut off the engine. The air went still. For a moment, neither of us moved. She just stared at the building—gray concrete walls, metal doors, barbed wire cutting through the sky like it was dividing heaven from earth.

She took a deep breath and finally spoke.

"Please take care of the kids."

Her voice cracked halfway through, soft and trembling.

"I got 'em," I said. My own voice broke too, rough and unsteady.

She turned to me then, and for a second, it felt like time froze. She didn't look at me like a wife, or a mother, or even the woman I fell for. She looked at me like someone who finally saw the wreckage she couldn't fix. The pain she couldn't undo.

"I'm sorry," she whispered.

I swallowed hard. "I know."

And that was it.

Her parole officer was already waiting outside. Clipboard in hand. Sunglasses hiding whatever pity might've been there. Christina opened the door slowly, her hands shaking, and stepped out. I watched as he cuffed her. The sound of the metal clicking shut felt louder than it should've been. She didn't fight it. Didn't even flinch.

She just kept her head down and started walking. The sun hit her back as she moved toward those heavy steel doors. Every step echoed through me. I just sat there, frozen, watching the woman I loved disappear into a system that never showed mercy.

The doors opened. She walked through.

They shut behind her with a thud that sounded like finality and then it was just me again. Sitting in that old Jeep. Hands gripping the steering wheel so tight my knuckles turned white. The engine off. The world quiet. For a long time, I didn't move. Just stared at the building, waiting for something, anything to change, but nothing did. The only thing that moved was the wind, brushing sand across the pavement, whispering through the silence like a ghost. I closed my eyes and thought it was all on me. The kids, the house, the life we were trying to build.

As I sat there under that morning sun, I realized something. Sometimes, love doesn't get to save the person, and sometimes, it just has to carry what's left behind.

The same sun that once felt warm now felt cold. Life just went on. Bills still needed paying. Kids still needed feeding. And me... well, I just kept going, even when my heart felt like it was dragging behind me. That's what you do when you've lived through the streets, through jail, through loss. You keep moving, even when the people you love can't.

I kept thinking of the night before. Before she left, Christina called the kids into the living room. Her voice was soft, like she was trying to hold something fragile inside. The kids came running in, laughing, thinking maybe it was snack time or movie time. But when they saw her face, the room went still. They saw Christina's tears. She knelt down on the floor, hugged each one of them, kissed their cheeks. Told them she loved them, that she'd see them soon. The little ones didn't understand, not really. They just knew something didn't feel right. The older ones, they felt it. They knew.

For me... what did I do? I just stood there, watching her, trying to hold myself together. Because when she kissed them goodbye, she broke them a little, but she broke me worse. That hurt stayed with me. The hurt was seeing the kids cry. Now she was gone.

I drove back home from County Jail, the seat next to me empty. I went to work, and later that night the kids asked questions I didn't have answers to.

"Where's Mom?"

"Did she really leave?"

"When's she coming home?"

"Did she have to go to work?"

I forced a smile that didn't belong on my face and said, "She's gotta take care of some things, then come home, guys. She'll be okay..." But deep down, I knew it was gonna be a long time.

The days that followed turned into routine. Just me, the kids, and the grind. I'd get up before the sun, drop the little ones at daycare, get the older ones ready for school, make sure they had lunch, clean clothes, brushed hair. Then I'd clock in with Kevin, sun beating down on my neck, dirt under my nails, sweat burning my eyes. Come home, cook dinner, do laundry, check homework, pack lunches for tomorrow.

My mom helped where she could. She worked a full-time job, but most of it was on me. I'm not going to lie, it was a lot. Kids of all ages and girls' hair... ponytails... I got good. I got good real quick. That was okay though. I didn't complain. For the first time in my life, I had a reason to stay steady.

Months went by like that. Quiet grind. Long days. Empty bed. The ache never really left, it just learned to live beside me. Christina called maybe once a month. Every time I got paid, so did she. I made sure she had money on her books.

Then one morning, it was July 4th, 2019. My dad had been gone for five years. My dad's birthday. This year, we'd been invited to my cousin's house. Big family get-together. I loaded the kids in the Jeep, their faces pressed to the windows, fireworks already going off somewhere in the distance. The sun hot as ever. No clouds, just a big blue sky. I could smell the charcoal and hear the music long before we got there.

Our family was everywhere. My sister and her family. My brother and his family. Older cousins, aunties, and uncles filled the yard with laughter, stories, kids running barefoot through the grass. My mom and aunties were smiling when they saw us pull up. They all hugged me like they knew I was tired, like they could feel how much I'd been carrying. Everyone was drinking, just having a good time.

For a moment, it felt good. Felt normal, almost. The kids were laughing, chasing each other, faces sticky from melted popsicles. I stood off to the side, watching them, listening to the hum of family and fireworks mixing in the air.

Right there, under the crack of fireworks and the smell of smoke and burgers, I felt it— that ache again. My dad. Not the sharp kind this time. The quiet kind. The kind that comes when you realize you've made it through another storm, but the person you used to be was changing again.

Still, I was proud. I'd stepped up. I'd done what I had to do. Maybe that's what freedom really looked like for me that year. Not fireworks. Not flags. But learning how to keep going when everything around you gets harder.

Night was falling, painting the sky in deep purples and inky blues. The smell of barbecue smoke and charred burgers lingered in the air. Laughter bounced off the walls of the backyard, punctuated by the sharp crackle of fireworks. Kids were running around, sparklers in hand. Adults were drinking, faces lit with excitement, their shadows dancing across the grass.

I saw one of the little ones struggling with a mortar, one of those big tube fireworks. His foot pressed down on it at the wrong angle, sparks flying dangerously close. Without thinking, I ran over. Adrenaline surged and I grabbed the tube, holding it straight in the air like I'd done this a hundred times before. My brother was standing a few feet away, shouting something I didn't hear.

The first boom hit.

Not up. Not into the sky. Into the bottom of the tube, right in my hand. My eyes went wide with confusion. Pain exploded instantly, sharp and unrelenting, burning through my fingers and wrist. I barely had time to react before the second boom hit, louder than anything I'd ever felt.

The world went white.

White.

Everything else disappeared. The screams, the fireworks, the laughter—all gone. My ears rang with a high-pitched screech. The heat burned across my chest and face, and the smell of gunpowder filled my lungs. My hand felt like it wasn't mine anymore, skin screaming from where it had been torn and burned. I stumbled backward, barely aware of the ground beneath me. The night, once alive with color and sound, now felt like a frozen nightmare. Shadows twisted, sparks floated like ghosts in the air, and all I could see was that blinding white light. Somewhere in the distance, my brother's voice broke through the haze, sharp and panicked.

"Gabe! Are you okay?!"

But for a moment, I wasn't sure I even existed. The world was white, hot, and quiet in a way that screamed louder than anything I'd ever heard.

Then everything came back like reality had been slammed into fast-forward.

The white haze faded and the world hit me all at once. The laughter, the music, the sparks in the night—all gone. Replaced by screams, shouts, chaos, and a high-pitched ringing that drilled through my skull like fire. I was still standing, but it felt like my body wasn't mine. My heart pounded in my throat. My legs shook but refused to buckle.

I looked down and saw my hand. It wasn't a hand anymore. It was inside out. Mangled, twisted, unrecognizable. My palm was torn, bones barely holding together, dark red streaked with ash and smoke. The smell hit me like a freight train—burnt flesh, gunpowder, charred metal. My stomach twisted. My mind froze. Nothing made sense. My body was there, but my soul hadn't caught up.

Shock spread through me like electricity. I couldn't feel pain yet, just a buzzing, pulsing numbness running up my arm and through the ear-drilling ringing. My brother's face flickered in the chaos, lips moving, yelling, but his words didn't reach me.

I stared at the blood dripping from my mangled fingers, seeping into the asphalt, puddling fast, mixing with car grease and spent fireworks. Sparks from the scattered mortar tubes floated in the air like little fireflies, but I barely noticed. My brain was screaming for action, my body moving on instinct.

I grabbed my shirt with my good hand and wrapped the shredded remains of my hand tight. "I need to go to the hospital NOW!" I shouted.

My brother froze, then a friend yelled for help, for keys, for anything, and took off running. The kids were screaming, crying, chaos reflected in their little faces. My mom's hands shook as she stared at me, her face pale, eyes wide. Everything felt distant, like I was watching through glass. Nobody knew what to do. Neighbors were still lighting fireworks. Cars tried to drive by but couldn't because of the side street on the 4th of July. Only the people in direct view knew what happened.

The night that had been alive with fireworks and laughter was gone. It had turned into a nightmare, thick and heavy, burning into my memory. Every sound was sharp, every smell twisted, every heartbeat a hammer. I wasn't just hurt. I was alive in a way I'd never been before, staring at my own mistake, staring death in the face, and somehow still standing.

Headlights cut through the smoke and haze. My boy came flying up, tires screaming, gravel spitting. The truck slid sideways and stopped in front of me, his face pure panic, eyes wide like he was staring at death itself. The door flew open. I looked down. I was covered in blood. It was everywhere. On my jeans, my shoes, my chest. My shirt was soaked, sticking to me like wet paper. My hand was wrapped up in what used to be my shirt, blood leaking through it, dripping onto the ground in thick drops. It looked like a bomb went off.

I climbed in the truck, barely thinking, barely breathing. The world was spinning, but I was locked in. My ears were still ringing. My heartbeat was louder than anything. He was yelling, panicking, hands shaking on the wheel.

His words blur together. I can't exactly remember, something about being drunk, something about not believing what he is seeing. I don't even know if I responded. My voice feels trapped somewhere deep in my chest.

He slams the gas. The tires spin out and we shoot down the street. The neighborhood looks like a war zone. Fireworks explode in every direction, lighting up the sky in reds, blues, and greens, flashes of chaos reflecting off the windshield. Smoke fills the air, thick and choking. Kids are screaming. Dogs are barking. The night sounds like gunfire. We are flying down the block, weaving through it all. Fireworks shoot across the street, popping under the tires. Sparks explode against the side of the truck. It feels like we are dodging bombs. Every flash lights up the blood on my arm, the smoke curling off the bandage. I can smell the gunpowder, the sweat, and the copper of my own blood. My friend grips the wheel tighter, eyes darting, his breathing loud and heavy.

A mortar explodes ahead, bright white, and he swerves. The tires screech, almost losing control. The truck fishtails, but he catches it and keeps going. We drive over spent fireworks and they crack and pop under us like the ground is alive. Every second feels like it could be the last. I'm losing a lot of blood. My vision blurs. The world tunnels. I can taste metal in my mouth. The ringing will not stop. The streetlights stretch and bend like we are moving through some fever dream. He keeps yelling my name, keeps saying stay with me, stay with me, but I can feel the darkness crawling up the edges of my mind. Then silence hits for a moment right before another explosion lights up the sky behind us. I realize how close death feels. Not the idea of it, not the word, but the real thing. Through all that chaos, I remember thinking that this could be it. Right here. This could be the last ride.

My mind snaps back for a second. Through the ringing in my ears, I grab my phone with my good hand and scroll with blood-slick fingers. I hit Kevin's name. It feels like the longest ring of my life. He picks up and I can barely get the words out.

"Kev..."

"Yeah..."

"I blew my hand up, bro. I'm going to the hospital. I can't make it to work tomorrow."

There is silence, then his voice explodes through the speaker. "What? WHAT HAPPENED?"

"I blew my hand up..."

"Which hospital?"

"In Fountain," I manage to say. "On the mesa."

"I'm on the way," he says without hesitation, voice tight and serious.

Click.

The world feels like it is closing in. My friend's knuckles are white on the steering wheel. We pull into the hospital parking lot so fast the tires squeal. He parks right at the entrance, half on the curb, and jumps out before the truck even stops. I'm still sitting there, light-headed, staring at the blood running down my arm, dripping onto the floor mat, making small red puddles that look almost black in the dashboard light.

He bursts through the sliding doors and yells something. I can see people turning their heads. Then he comes running back with a wheelchair, moving fast, adrenaline in his steps. He swings the door open and I climb out. My legs feel weak, like I am walking through water. My ears are ringing. My hand is wrapped up tight, pulsing, hot. I can feel my heartbeat inside the wound. He pushes me through the automatic doors and into the emergency room. The smell of antiseptic hits me like a wall. Cold air, bright lights, and chaos. The nurses look up and freeze for a second. Then everything goes into motion.

They rush toward me, shouting to each other, eyes locked on my arm. One of them says, "He's been shot!" Another grabs the wheelchair and starts moving me before I can say anything. I try to explain, words coming out slow and slurred. "No... I blew my hand up... fireworks... not a gun." But they do not hear me. Or they don't believe me. Another one of them says, "He's been shot!"

I'm surrounded. Bright lights. Gloves snapping. Someone cutting my shirt. Blood everywhere. A nurse's hand presses on my arm, and I flinch, not from pain but from the shock of it all. They keep asking questions, but I can't answer fast enough. My vision blurs. The room spins.

I catch flashes of faces. A doctor shouting for gauze. A nurse calling for trauma. Someone saying, "He's losing a lot of blood." The world fades in and out like bad TV reception. My head tilts back. The ceiling lights stretch and warp into streaks. I hear the faint sound of fireworks outside, muffled through the walls. Each one sounds like another heartbeat trying to escape my chest.

Someone yells something. They move me fast, wheels squeaking, voices echoing. I can feel my body getting lighter, like gravity is slipping away. My friend's voice is somewhere behind me, shouting my name, but it sounds far off, like he's at the end of a tunnel. I look down one last time at what's left of my right hand. Wrapped tight. Blood seeping through. My own shirt tied around it. The sight doesn't even look real anymore.

Then the light swallows everything and I close my eyes.

I come to in a blur, floating somewhere between dream and reality. The room is cold, humming with machines, the air thick with antiseptic and electricity. My arm is stretched out on a table, my hand submerged in a stainless-steel pan filled with water that's gone cloudy pink from blood. I blink, trying to remember where I am. The last thing I remember is fireworks, noise, and running lights.

A nurse leans over me, saying something calm but distant. Her lips move slower than her words reach me. She adjusts a needle in my arm, and my body sinks deeper into the bed. The pain is gone, completely gone. For the first time since the explosion, I feel nothing but the weight of silence pressing on my chest. I glance down again. My hand is still there. It doesn't even look real, like something sculpted out of wax, pale and swollen, my palm inside out.

A doctor appears beside me, checking the wound. His gloves are red from cleaning, his eyes sharp and focused. He says they stopped the bleeding. They're numbing it more. I can feel the cold creeping up my arm, but my mind is too far away to care.

The door opens. Footsteps echo across the tile. It's Kevin. He walks in slowly, like he's not sure he's supposed to be there. His face tells it all—shock, relief, disbelief, all tangled together. He stops at the end of the bed, looking down at me, then at my hand, then back at me again.

"I thought you blew your hand clean off," he says, eyes wide, voice breaking somewhere between fear and laughter. Then he grins, shaking his head. "Bro, it's still there. You big dummy."

He starts laughing, that nervous kind of laugh people do when they're unsure whether to cry instead. I can't help it. I laugh too. It hurts when I do, but it feels good not to be dead. Like air finally coming back into my lungs. The room softens around us, the chaos fading into background noise. Nurses move around, checking monitors, whispering, but all I see is Kevin standing there, smiling like he just saw a ghost come back to life.

For a second, I realize how close it really was. How thin the line is between being here and not. Between laughing with your brother and being zipped up in a bag. And as Kevin keeps talking, trying to make light of it all, I stare at my hand soaking in that pink water, still breathing, still here, and somewhere deep down I think, how am I going to work or pay these bills.

The door swings open again, and a rush of movement fills the room. Voices overlap, calm but urgent. A doctor leans over me, talking fast, words coming out clipped and heavy. Something about surgery. Something about time. The nurses move around me with practiced speed, snapping gloves, unhooking cords, rewrapping the bandages tighter. The bleeding's stopped for now, but it won't hold. They say I have to go into emergency surgery.

The reality hits like a wave. My heart starts pounding harder than it should. I can feel it in my throat, in my ears, in the space where the pain used to be. Kevin's still standing there, hands shoved in his pockets, eyes locked on me. He looks like he's trying to hold everything in place, but the worry's written all over his face.

They're getting the stretcher ready. The nurse is calling for transport. I know what's happening, but my mind feels a step behind. I turn my head toward Kevin. My voice comes out low and tired. "Kev... they're moving me. I'll call you once I can."

He nods, forcing a grin, the kind you make when you don't know what else to do. "Don't worry about work tomorrow," he says, trying to keep it light. "But I'll see you bright and early Monday morning." He lets out a small laugh as he steps back.

Behind him, I hear the doctor quietly say, "He's not working for a while."

Kevin glances over his shoulder and just shakes his head. "I know," he says softly, and the door closes behind him.

The noise drops away. The nurse's voice blends into the sound of wheels and machines. They unhook my IV from the wall and clip it to the stretcher. Cold air hits me as they roll me toward the hallway. The fluorescent lights pass overhead in a blur, one after another, each one flashing across my face like camera flashes at a crime scene.

The double doors open and the night air hits differently outside. It smells like rain, asphalt, and smoke from leftover fireworks. They loaded me into the ambulance. The inside is glowing white, everything sterile and humming. I stared up at the ceiling lights and heard the paramedic talking to the hospital through the radio. I don't really hear the words, just the rhythm of them.

We started moving. The sirens kick in. Red and blue lights flicker across the windows. My thoughts start looping, like a broken record. I can't believe this. I can't believe this happened. I can't believe I'm here. I can't believe how fast everything changed.

My chest feels tight. My eyes burn. The city lights start to blur together as we speed through the streets. Somewhere between the flashing lights and the siren's scream, it hit me how close I came to losing everything. I close my eyes, still whispering the same thing in my head over and over.

I can't believe this.

I can't.

The ambulance doors fly open, and the cold night rushes in. The lights from the hospital spill across the pavement, bright and harsh, painting everything red and blue. They wheel me out fast, tires bumping over the curb, the stretcher rattling under me. The paramedic's voice is loud, calling out numbers, blood pressure, and vitals, as well as something about the hand. My eyes drift to the sky for just a second. It's black and endless, no stars, just smoke from the fireworks still hanging in the air.

They push me through another set of glass doors and into Memorial Central. The smell hits me first. Disinfectant, metal, and the faint trace of burnt powder still cling to me. Everything moves fast. Voices blur together. The fluorescent lights flicker overhead, cold and unfeeling. I can feel the rush of the gurney wheels as they move me through narrow hallways lined with stainless steel and white tile. Nurses appear and disappear, gloved hands tugging at IV lines, checking monitors, adjusting oxygen.

Then I heard it. "We're taking him in now."

They push me into a bright room that feels more like an operating stage than anything human. A doctor leans over me. His eyes are calm but sharp. He tells me they're going to put me under. It's time. I nodded, barely. My throat is dry. The mask comes down over my face, and I feel the cool sting of anesthesia moving through my veins. My body feels heavy. My heartbeat slows. The world begins to melt at the edges, colors fading into white.

And then nothing.

Just silence.

When I open my eyes again, it's morning. The light coming through the window is soft, gray, and empty. The room is still. Machines hum quietly beside me. My arm feels heavy, wrapped in thick white bandages, suspended slightly above the bed by a sling. For a second, I don't know where I am. I blink hard, trying to piece it together. It feels like a dream, or like I'm watching someone else's life from a distance.

Then it hits me. The explosion. The blood. The ride. The hospital.

I look around the room. The reality starts to settle like dust after a storm. My body feels drained, my mouth is dry, and my thoughts are slow. I stare at my arm again. It's still there. Beaten, broken, stitched, but there. I whisper under my breath, "Thank you, God."

The silence feels thick. No nurses, no voices. Just the faint beep of the monitor kept in rhythm with my heart.

Then the next thought hits me. The kids.

I close my eyes, sinking into the pillow. I'm still in the non-residential program at Comcor. I can't believe this. I have to call them and let them know I'm in the hospital. I hope the kids are okay. I hope they're safe. But as I start to think of everything, I know my family has them. I know they're taken care of.

I let out a long breath and stare up at the ceiling, feeling the weight of everything all at once. The pain. The relief. The guilt. It all crashes down in that quiet hospital room.

Somewhere deep inside, I know this isn't the end of something. It's the beginning of something new.

The hospital days crawl. Every hour feels like a stretch of forever. I lie there staring at the ceiling, counting the tiny holes in the tiles, listening to the soft hiss of the oxygen vents. My arm feels heavy, thick with pain, bandaged so tight it almost hums. Nurses come and go. They check my pulse, swap the IV bags, and ask if I need more meds. I tell them yes, but the truth is the ache never leaves. It just hides.

When the release papers finally come, it doesn't feel real. The nurse brings a wheelchair and tells me to take it slow. Then I see him—Kevin. Leaning against the wall near the sliding doors, head down, phone in his hand. When he looks up, he grins, shaking his head like he can't believe what he's seeing.

"Man," he says, walking over, "you're something else. You actually did it. You really blew your hand up."

I laugh a little, weak, half-dazed from the painkillers. "Yeah," I say. "Guess I did."

He takes the bag from the nurse and helps me into the wheelchair. The automatic doors slide open and the air outside hits me like freedom. It's bright, too bright. The sun stings my eyes. The smell of asphalt, exhaust, and distant barbecue smoke fills my chest.

Kevin opens the truck door and I climb in slow, holding my arm against me. The bandages are thick, white, and clean, but I can feel the throb deep underneath. He starts the truck, the engine rumbling low, the sound mixing with the faint ringing still buried in my ears.

As we pull out of the lot, he looks over. "You good?"

I nod, eyes on the road ahead. "Yeah. Just tired."

He laughs under his breath. "You better be. Ain't no work for you for a minute. Doc said so, right?"

I smirk. "Yeah. He said no work."

"Good," Kevin says. "Because you ain't showing up anyway. I'll see you Monday, just to make sure you're still breathing."

We drive in silence for a while. The city rolls by, lights and people moving like nothing happened. I watch everything blur past, the fast-food signs, the cracked sidewalks, the faces of strangers who don't know how close I came to disappearing. When we pull into the driveway, Kevin kills the engine and sits for a second.

"You're lucky, bro," he says. "Could've been worse. Way worse."

I nod. The words hit hard because I know he's right.

He helps me out and walks me to the door. My family's inside waiting. I can see them through the window, faces pressed to the glass, worry written all over them. Kevin claps my shoulder, then turns back toward the truck. "Call me if you need anything and hey... no fireworks."

I smile, small, tired, grateful. "Yeah. No fireworks."

He drives off and I step inside. The air in the house feels thick, full of silence and concern. My mom's eyes are red. The kids stand back, unsure, whispering. I sink onto the couch, the pain meds already dulling the edges of everything. For a long time I just sit there. Listening to the quiet. Feeling the weight of what almost was.

Alive. Hurt. But alive.

The first night back home hit hard. The quiet wasn't peaceful. It was heavy and still. My arm throbbed like something alive under the bandages, pulsing with every heartbeat. I sat on the couch with the bottle of pills the hospital sent me home with. Little white pills rattling inside like dice in a cup.

At first, I took one. Just one, like they said. The pain faded a little, but not enough. My hand was still burning, still screaming, every nerve wide awake. The next day, I took another. Then another. It was easy. Too easy. The weekend went by, and those pills slid down like candy, one after another, washing away the pain, the fear, the memory of that explosion.

Weeks would pass, and before long, I wasn't chasing pain relief anymore. I was chasing silence. Numbness. I didn't want to feel anything. The room began to soften, with sounds stretching and blurring. My thoughts slowed down, and for the first time since the fireworks, I felt like I could breathe.

I told myself it was just for recovery. Just to sleep. Just until the pain went away. But I knew what it was. I could feel it creeping back in, that same old whisper that had followed me for years. The same one that said just one more won't hurt.

I leaned back, half gone, staring at the ceiling. The kids were in the other room, cartoons humming low through the walls. I thought about everything, how close I came to losing it all, how stupid it was, how lucky I was to still be breathing. But none of that mattered at that moment. The pills had me floating somewhere between pain and peace, and I didn't care which side I landed on.

CHAPTER 39: ROCK BOTTOM BLUES

A month rolled by and the cast finally came off. The nurse unwound the wrapping slow, layer by layer, until what was left of my hand looked like something rebuilt, not reborn. Scar tissue twisted across the skin like burnt rope. I could barely move my fingers. It hurt to look at it.

Physical therapy started right after that. They gave me a stress ball, told me to squeeze it every day, told me healing takes time. But every squeeze felt like fire running up my arm. I told the pain management doctor, and he nodded like he understood. He wrote me a new script. The pills went from 5 mg to 10 mg.

A month later, I told him it still hurt, and it did. But by then, it wasn't just the pain that needed feeding. He raised me again, from 10 mg to 15 mg. The little orange bottle started showing up like clockwork. My name printed on the label made it feel legitimate, as if I was doing it right, as if this was part of the recovery process. Right?

Six months passed, and I was deep in it. They had me on 30 mg now. One hundred eighty a month. A whole army of blue soldiers waiting in the bottle. My day started and ended with them. At least ten a day, and now I was smoking them. It wasn't about healing anymore. It was about not feeling the pain.

If I missed one, I'd feel it. Cold sweats. Stomach flipping. Skin crawling. I'd get sick fast. I'd shake, get angry, desperate. It wasn't me anymore. My reflection didn't even look familiar. I was showing up to therapy high, nodding through sessions, pretending to get better while getting worse. I told myself I had it under control. I needed it for the pain. But deep down, I knew. The pills weren't helping me live. They were just helping me forget I was dying inside.

By now, word was out. People knew I had them. The pills. The good ones. The kind that hit fast and deep. The kind everybody wanted. It started small with whispers, people asking, "You still got some of them 30's?" I brushed it off at first, but in the streets, word moves faster than truth ever does. Next thing I knew, I was surrounded by familiar faces with familiar habits. People who used to just say "what's up" now hung around longer, talking softly, counting numbers in their heads. That's when I learned the game had changed. A dollar a milligram. Thirty bucks a pill. I did the math. One hundred eighty a month, half the bottle sold, that's rent, food, gas, everything paid up.

It made sense. Too much sense.

It started to feel like I'd found a loophole in life. Take half for the pain, sell the other half to pay the bills. A win-win, right? But every win came with a whisper that got louder each time, that quiet voice that said, You're not healing anymore. You're hustling. Still, when the money hit my hand, it didn't feel wrong. It felt like relief. The kind that comes wrapped in paper and pills. I'd stack the cash, tell myself it was temporary, that I'd stop once things got better. But the truth was, I was sinking slowly, smiling the whole way down.

The house was different. The kids were gone to daycare and school, and there I was, counting pills at the kitchen table, half a father, half a pharmacist. Every sound outside—every knock, every car door—made my chest tighten. I told myself it was just business, but deep down I knew it was becoming something else.

I wasn't just selling pills anymore. I was selling pieces of myself.

It had been months since the fireworks accident, months since everything changed. The pills had become part of the routine, part of me. Then came the day of Christina's release.

The sun was already dropping when we pulled up to the gates. That same desert wind that carried her away now brought her back. The yard lights buzzed over the razor wire, and when she stepped out, it felt like the world paused for a second. The same brown eyes, the same smile, but different too. Harder around the edges, something lost behind the look.

We hugged. I told her everything. About the hand. The pills. The money. I tried to make it sound like I had everything under control, but even she could see the cracks. It didn't take long before she slid right into my world. Before long, we were both chasing the same high, breathing that same empty air that never fills you.

I went back to work with Kevin. Tried to act normal. Tried to keep it together. But he saw it. He always saw it. The early mornings. The blank stares. The shakes. He pulled me aside one day, his hands still dirty from the job.

"Gabe," he said, "you're losing yourself, bro. This ain't you."

I nodded, but the words didn't hit. Not then. I thought I was fine. I had a script. I was covered. So, when the U.A.s came, they didn't say anything. I told myself I was still good. Still in control.

But deep down, I knew control was gone.

Kevin tried and I blew him off. But there's only so much you can do for someone who's already halfway gone. The day it ended, it wasn't even a fight. Just a look. He shook his head and said, "I can't do this no more."

I walked off that site, a heavy pocket and a hollow chest. Went home, and Christina was there, waiting, restless, already high.

I realized what had happened.

We weren't building anymore. We were burning slowly.

Everything started slipping again. At first, it was small, late bill payments, minor arguments, and missed work calls. Then it all just cracked open.

I had finally finished Comcor. Got my paperwork signed off. Done. Free. For the first time in years, I could breathe without somebody watching over me. My mom even said she was proud. But that kind of peace doesn't last long when the insides are still broken. She moved out not long after, saying she needed space. I told her it was fine, but deep down I knew what that really meant. She couldn't watch me fall again.

The house didn't take long to follow. Bills stacked higher than my paychecks, and the walls started feeling like a weight pressing down. One eviction notice, then another. Eventually, we lost it. Just like that. No home, no plan, just bags and boxes of what was left of our life.

We started bouncing around to cheap motels, looking for weekly rates and places that would take cash and look the other way. Rooms with cigarette burns in the blankets, stained carpets, and flickering lights that hummed louder than the silence between us. Every night was the same—the sound of people yelling down the hall, the faint smell of smoke and old grease, the kind of quiet that makes you feel like you're disappearing. Christina was restless. I could see it in her eyes. The guilt, the sickness, the hunger. She wanted to escape. We both did.

Then one night, she walked in, breathing heavy, clutching keys like she had just found salvation.

"I got us a car," she said.

I didn't ask how. I didn't want to. I just nodded. Anything that made us feel normal again, even for a night, felt worth it. But a few hours later, the lights showed up, those flashing red and blue lights that make your stomach drop. The kind of lights that never bring good news.

They had it all. The camera footage, the plates, everything that led them right to the room. We didn't even make it out the door. The cops came in loud. Knocking turned to pounding. Pounding turned to shouting. I was sleeping and woke up confused and lost. They cuffed us right there. Face pressed against the wall. The wallpaper smelled like mold and sweat. The cuffs bit into my wrists, and over the noise, the yelling, the radios, the kids crying, I could hear one of the officers saying, "They're taking the kids."

That moment broke me in two. Watching them carry my babies out of that room. Watching them disappear down that hall while I couldn't move, couldn't speak, couldn't even breathe. DHS stepped in, and they got hold of my family, and my brother took the kids. He didn't have to, but he did. I could never repay him for what he did.

And me? I just sat in county again, staring at concrete, feeling that same old burn of regret that I swore I'd never feel again. We had a bond, and we made some calls, and when we got out, nothing changed. If anything, it got darker. We went back to what we knew right away, to the only thing that made the pain fade.

At first, it was the pills again, but the pills stopped hitting. So, we chased something stronger. Fentanyl. Heroin. Meth. Whatever kept the sickness away. The world seemed to be moving in slow motion, but my heart felt like it was running out of time. Days disappeared. I'd wake up not knowing where I was, what day it was, or who I'd lied to last. Christina and I barely spoke unless it was about getting better from being dope sick. We'd sit in that smoke-filled room with foil, lighters, and broken promises scattered across the table. Sometimes we'd just stare at each other, not out of love but to have someone there.

The mirrors told the truth. Hollow eyes. Pale skin. A heartbeat that felt borrowed. I was alive, but I wasn't living. It wasn't about getting high anymore. It was about not dying from the comedown. Every sound outside made me jump, every siren, every knock, every voice.

I kept telling myself I still had control. I still had a plan. But I was lying, and I knew it.

We weren't partners anymore. We were prisoners of the same sickness. Bound together by pain, chasing a peace we'd never find at the bottom of a pipe.

The days bled into nights. I could feel that slow, steady pull toward rock bottom. Like gravity. Like fate. The world outside kept spinning, but ours had stopped. We were ghosts walking through it.

We did this song and dance for over a year, living like fugitives in our own skin. Every sunrise felt like a countdown, every night another gamble with death. I was wild and hollow, stealing anything that could be sold, traded, or smoked. Cash, cars, tools, jewelry, whatever we could grab. Kick doors, snatch and run, move fast before the sirens catch the echo.

It wasn't about the money anymore. It was about the feeling. That brief flash of power drowned the hunger clawing at our ribs.

SUSPECT was back and he didn't care who got hurt. The name wasn't just what they called me. It became a mask I wore like armor. I leaned into it. The danger. The fear. The madness. I was someone else entirely, and that made it easier not to feel.

The streets were my stage, lit by the strobe of police lights, filled with the hum of engines and the crackle of radios calling my name. The smell of burnt rubber, sweat and smoke was the only perfume I knew. Christina and I burned too hot to last. Love turned into survival, survival into silence. Eventually, she drifted one way and I another, like two sparks carried off by different winds. I didn't chase her. I didn't chase anything anymore except the next fix. My poison, my high. My mind was a haunted house I couldn't escape from. Sleep came in flashes, dreams soaked in paranoia and guilt.

Everything I'd built my kids, my home, my job, my name had turned to ash. I'd lost it all, and yet I couldn't stop. Everything I'd ever worked for fell and burned. It didn't happen all at once. It was slow, like watching yourself drown and realizing you can't swim. One mistake became two, then ten, and pretty soon the fire was everywhere. The house that once held laughter was gone, boarded up and silent. The walls were still standing, but the life inside was dead. The kids were out there somewhere, better off without me, but that truth cut deeper than any blade. Their faces haunted me every night, their tiny hands, bright eyes, memories I'd traded for a high. Every time I thought of them, my chest got tight, and the guilt crawled up my throat like smoke.

I'd sit alone in whatever broken-down spot I ended up in that night, surrounded by my wreckage, drug abuse, and cold air leaking through busted windows, and stare at the pieces of what used to be a life. I'd tell myself it wasn't my fault, but even my lies stopped believing me. The guilt hit first. Then came the shame.

Heavy. Endless. Like wearing chains that only tightened when I tried to breathe. It wasn't just that I'd lost everything. It was knowing I deserved to.

Sleep didn't come easily anymore. When it did, it brought faces I couldn't look at, voices I couldn't silence. I'd wake up shaking, sweating, sometimes screaming. I'd grab for the pipe just to make it stop, just to feel nothing but the nothing started to feel like everything. That's when I started thinking about death, not as some tragedy or fear but as a release. A way to quiet the noise. A way to stop being the monster I'd become.

I didn't cry. I didn't pray. I just accepted it.

I was chasing something that didn't exist anymore, a feeling that had died a long time ago. I'd wake up in strangers' houses, the floor littered with trash, empty baggies, the stench of sweat and regret. My heart would race, but my soul felt still. Dead still. Sometimes I'd catch my reflection in a cracked mirror, and I'd freeze. I'd stare at the man looking back, bloodshot eyes, a shadow of what used to be. I'd think, who are you? but he never answered. He just stared back, silent, broken, dangerous.

The guilt came in waves, thick, heavy, and suffocating. The faces of my kids, their voices fading like echoes in a tunnel I could never reach the end of. The shame gnawed at me. I wanted to feel something, anything but all I could feel was the emptiness where life used to live. So, I started to plan. Not for another hit. Not for another score. But for an ending. I wanted to end it all. The kind that comes when the noise finally stops. The kind that feels like freedom, even if it's the last thing you ever feel. I was so far gone that I didn't care about my life, my family, or anything. I didn't care about nothing.

I wasn't running anymore. I was just waiting for the right time to stop.

I called up two home girls, told them to come scoop me. They didn't ask why. They never did. I told them I'd get them high, and that was enough. What they didn't know was that I already had something else in mind. They pulled up in a beat-up sedan, headlights cutting through the misty night like blades. The city glowed behind us as we drove out east, the streets falling away one by one until it was just open land and black sky. The road stretched forever, empty and quiet, the hum of the tires the only sound between us.

They thought it was just another pickup, another score. They laughed, passing the pipe back and forth, smoke curling through the dim light like ghosts. I stared out the window, not saying much, watching the dark shapes of barns and fields rolling by. My chest felt tight, like something inside me was trying to crawl out. After 30-45 minutes or so, the city's lights disappeared completely. Just us and the road. The air smelled like dirt and rain. Then I saw it, an old farmhouse, leaning against the night, half swallowed by weeds and time. I pointed.

"There," I said. "That's the spot."

They looked at each other, uneasy.

"Who lives there?" one asked.

"Why out here?" the other followed, her voice small.

I told them it was fine. Nothing to worry about. My tone was calm, too calm, like I'd already left my body behind. They believed me because they wanted to. We pulled off the road, gravel crunching under the tires. The headlights hit the side of the building, revealing shattered windows and faded paint. The night swallowed the sound of the engine when it shut off, and suddenly everything felt too still.

They kept whispering, nervous, trying to piece together what we were doing. I told them again it was okay, that I just needed a minute. The lie came easily. I wasn't angry or high or scared anymore. I was empty. Earlier, I made 2 syringes full of heroin. They didn't know it yet, but they were going to give me a hot shot and leave me for dead. As I stepped out of the car, the cold air hit me like truth. The sky hung low and heavy, clouds bleeding into the darkness. The house loomed in front of me, crooked and silent, like it had been waiting for me , its roof slanted, windows black and hollow-like eyes that had seen too much. The wind rattled the loose panels, moaning through the broken wood.

I could feel their eyes on my back, their voices blending with the wind as they kept asking questions.

But I wasn't listening anymore. My mind was made up.

I turned to the girls. "Let's go inside," I said.

They froze. The laughter from earlier was gone. Their faces twisted with confusion and fear, eyes darting between me and the house.

"Why?" one whispered. "What's in there?"

"Please, let's just go back," the other said, voice trembling.

I felt something snap inside me, not rage exactly, more like pressure finally giving way. The sound of my own heartbeat filled my ears. My hands trembled, jaw tight. I'd already come too far. There was no turning back now.

"I said let's go," I barked, louder than I meant to. The words cracked through the night like thunder.

The girls flinched, tears pooling in their eyes. I could see the confusion, the betrayal; they didn't understand. Maybe I didn't either. I wasn't trying to scare them. I just needed them to move. I needed the moment to end. The gravel crunched beneath our feet as we approached the porch. Every step echoed. The boards groaned when I pushed the door open. Cold air poured out from the darkness, carrying the smell of dust and time. Inside, the house was a skeleton of a building, with empty rooms, peeling wallpaper, and faint moonlight spilling through broken windows. The silence was thick, pressing on all of us.

The girls stayed close, their breathing sharp and quick, whispering to each other as they tried to figure out what was happening. I didn't look back. My mind was already gone, drifting somewhere between guilt and determination. I told them again it was okay. That everything would be fine, but even I didn't believe it.

"Let's just… chill and get high for a minute," I said, my voice flat, hollow.

They hesitated, but they followed when I sat down. The old floor creaked under us, the sound echoing through the empty house. My hands shook as I pulled the small bag from my pocket, the one that had carried my whole world for too long. Their eyes widened. They knew what it meant. I could feel the panic start to fill the room, their breathing sharp and uneven.

"What are you doing?" one of them said, her voice cracking.

"This isn't right," the other whispered.

Tears were rolling down their faces now. Fear, confusion, pity, all of it mixing together. I told them what I wanted and explained the plan. The words came out calm, almost gentle, as if I were explaining something that had already happened. They broke. One started sobbing, shaking her head, and saying "no" over and over. The other froze, her face blank, lost somewhere between disbelief and dread.

I remember the sound of the wind outside, scraping across the windows. The weight of the night presses down. The silence between each breath. They looked at me like they really looked at me, and I saw it in their eyes...

the realization that I wasn't the same person anymore. Whatever piece of me they used to know was gone.

I sit down and they follow my lead. I take the needles out and tell them the business. They become hysterical, but they do it. Full of tears and emotion. I called them because this is how they get high. I don't shoot up. I just wanted to effect of taking too much. They tie my arm off, and they start. Try after try after try. Crying gets intense. 30 mins in and I have welts. They say. It won't go in! Try harder, I tell them. They say they are... it won't go... and they show me the needle and squeeze it. The liquid black water comes out of the top of the needle. We don't know what's wrong.

The air inside the farmhouse turned thick, almost solid. The crying, the questions, the trembling, it all pressed against my skull until I couldn't take it anymore.

"Stop!" I said, voice low but sharp. They didn't. They couldn't. Their fear filled the room like smoke, choking me, clawing at what little control I had left.

Something snapped.

I stood up fast, the old floorboards screaming under my boots. They flinched, backing away as I moved toward the door. The walls felt too close, the air too heavy, my own thoughts too loud. I couldn't breathe in there.

"Move!" I growled, pushing past them. They stumbled back, their sobs echoing through the hollow house. I didn't look at them again. Couldn't. Outside, the cold night hit me hard. The wind whipped through the dry weeds, carrying the faint smell of rain and rust. The world felt vast and empty, as if the universe had cleared a path for me and dared me to take it. The car sat there, half-lit by the moon, the engine ticking softly from the drive out. I walked straight to it, my heartbeat thundering in my ears. Every step felt heavy, as if I were marching toward something final.

I climbed in, slammed the door, and for a second just sat there, staring at the steering wheel. My reflection in the cracked rearview mirror looked like a stranger, a man hollowed out by ghosts and choices he couldn't undo. The keys were still in the ignition. I turned them, and the engine roared to life. Headlights flared against the farmhouse, washing over the girls still standing in the doorway, small, terrified silhouettes framed in white light. I didn't say a word. I just shifted into drive. Gravel spit out from under the tires as I pulled away, the beam of light cutting across the field before swallowing into darkness. In the mirror, the farmhouse grew smaller, then disappeared completely. Only the sound of the engine remained, low, steady, like a heartbeat that refused to quit.

Even as the road opened in front of me, it didn't feel like escape. It felt like punishment. Like I wasn't driving away from anything, just deeper into the wreckage I'd made of my life. The road back into town stretched like a scar through the dark. The headlights cut thin ribbons across the asphalt, bouncing off the fog that clung low to the ground. My hands gripped the wheel so tight the veins stood out in my forearms. The radio was off. The only sound was the hum of the tires and the wind knifing through a cracked window. I was running on fumes, gas, dope, life, didn't matter. The city lights were still miles away, glowing faintly on the horizon like a promise I didn't trust. My mind buzzed with static, fragments of every mistake I'd made flickering behind my eyes like old film reels.

Then it happened.

A sudden dip in the road, and it was deep, sharp, unseen until it was too late. The car slammed down hard, the impact jarring through my spine. The engine coughed once, twice, then went silent. The wheel locked, lights flickered, and everything inside me froze.

For a heartbeat, there was only silence. Then chaos.

The steering wheel jerked. Gravel sprayed. The car fishtailed, spinning out of control. The world outside blurred the sky, dirt, fence posts, and black fields, twisting into one. The headlights flashed across the inside of the windshield like lightning trapped in glass. I fought the wheel, cursing, heart slamming against my ribs. The sound of screeching tires tore through the night. Dust filled the air, swallowing the car whole. When I finally came to a stop, I sat there, gasping. My pulse was thunder. My hands were shaking, slick with sweat. For a second, I thought maybe it was over. Maybe this was the crash that finally erased me.

Then I saw the light.

Red and blue.

They bled through the dust like ghosts rising from the ground. A single spotlight cutting through the haze, landing right on me.

A cop.

Of all the roads, all the nights, all the miles I traveled and could've died on, he was right there. The siren wailed once, sharp and cold. The light filled the car, painting everything in a flickering array of colors. My breath hitched, my thoughts scattered. It wasn't just a cop... it was everything I'd been running from. Every sin, every crime, every broken promise right there in my rearview, catching up all at once.

CHAPTER 40: FORGIVEN NOT FORGOTTEN

In El Paso County, Jail once again. The patrol car slammed, and the cold El Paso County air cut through the fog of withdrawal. My skin was clammy, every nerve raw. Warrants again, same concrete kingdom, same cages, but this time I wasn't coming in angry. I wasn't trying to prove anything. I just knew I needed to be here. The booking process was a blur of fluorescent light and institutional voices. The camera flashed, my pupils swallowed the light whole. I couldn't stop sweating. The withdrawal had already started to chew its way up my spine. My body was begging for what it couldn't have.

They gave me a blanket, a wristband, and that sour jail smell, bleach, and despair. The guard led me through corridors that echoed with muffled shouts, the sound of metal slamming, and the cries of someone in a distant cell. My legs felt like jelly, my stomach twisting tighter with each step, and by the time I hit my cell, I couldn't stand straight. I crawled into the bunk, but the mattress felt like concrete wrapped in sandpaper. My skin itched like fire ants were under it. I couldn't find stillness; every position hurt. Cold sweats turned to heat waves. My bones throbbed. I threw up into the toilet next to my bed, dry heaving until there was nothing left.

The shakes came next. My legs wouldn't stop twitching. I tried to wrap myself in the blanket, but my own body betrayed me, kicking, jerking, sweating through every layer. My teeth chattered so hard I thought they'd break. My breath came in gasps, shallow, desperate. Then came the screams. Not from anyone else, from me. A sound that ripped out of my chest like an animal dying slow and loud. I punched the wall until my knuckles split. It didn't help. Nothing did. The pain inside was deeper than bone, deeper than muscle. It was in my soul. Every nerve screamed for a hit that wasn't coming.

The lights never went off. The noise never stopped. Every second stretched out, thick and heavy, like the world was punishing me in slow motion. That's what opiate withdrawal does. It takes your body hostage and drags your mind through hell. You start begging for mercy, praying to anything that might listen. At that point, I didn't care about time or pride or who was watching. I was done pretending I was strong. I just wanted out of the pain.

But there was no out, not in the fish tank. Not in that cell.

Just me, the shakes, the walls and the long road of what's ahead.

Morning came quick, but it didn't feel like morning. The lights in Warrens never went off, just that same pale hum that made you forget what time even was. I hadn't slept at all. My skin was sticky, my body shaking from the inside out. The dope sickness had me trapped, pulling me deeper into a place I didn't think I could climb out of.

I sat up on the bunk, head in my hands, sweat dripping down my face. My heart wouldn't slow down. Every nerve screamed. Every thought twisted darker. I was losing it. I wanted to end it right there. I wanted to stop breathing, stop feeling, stop existing. The pain was too real, too deep.

I stared up at the second tier. The rail looked like freedom. I thought about climbing up, leaning over, and just falling. Maybe if I landed wrong, I'd snap my neck. Maybe that would be enough. I imagined the sound, the silence after. I didn't care about anything else. Not family. Not God. Not tomorrow. Just peace. I wanted peace.

I stood up, legs weak, and walked toward the stairs. My vision was blurred from the tears and the lights. The metal rail was cold under my hands, that jail grime sticking to my palms. I could feel my heart pounding, like my chest was trying to break open. Below me was that hard concrete floor, stained and cracked from a hundred other stories like mine. I leaned forward, breathing heavy, whispering to myself that it would be quick.

Then I heard him.

"You good, bro?"

The voice cut through the noise in my head.

I turned. One of the inmates, older dude, built solid, tattoos faded like old scars. He was watching me from the table, eyes locked in. He saw it. He saw the crazy in me, the pain and the defeat. He saw the part of me that had already let go.

He stood up slow, walked closer, still calm. "You straight?" he asked again.

I shook my head. My mouth opened but the words came out broken. "I can't do this, bro. I can't handle it."

He nodded, no surprise, no judgment. Just stood there like he'd been in that same exact place before. "Yeah, I know," he said quietly. "We all been there but you ain't alone, bro. Not today." Something about how he said it hit different. It wasn't soft. It wasn't weak. It was real. Like he'd already died in here once and came back. I just stood there, shaking, staring at the floor below, trying to breathe. The urge was still there but his voice kept echoing in my head.

We sat at the steel table under that humming white light, two inmates in county jumpsuits, one shaking from withdrawal, the other steady like he'd already been through hell and made peace with it. He looked at me and said, "You want some coffee?"

I hesitated, still trying to hold myself together. "Yeah," I said quietly. My throat was dry, my hands wouldn't stop moving. He walked over, grabbed his coffee, and poured us two cups. The smell filled the pod—burnt, bitter, that cheap instant kind—but it felt warm, and that was enough. He sat down across from me and slid one cup over. Steam rose between us.

He leaned in and said, "You know, the only thing that's gonna make any of this feel better is Jesus, you know that, right?"

I looked at him and let out this half laugh, the kind that comes from disbelief and exhaustion. "Jesus?" I said. "Jesus doesn't have anything to do with this, bro."

He smiled, slow and calm. "Jesus has everything to do with this."

The way he said it wasn't like a sermon. It was like a truth he'd learned the hard way. I could see something in his eyes, a kind of peace that didn't make sense in a place like this.

We started walking circles around the pod, just talking. He asked me where I was in my faith. I told him straight, "I don't really have one. I grew up Catholic. I know about God. I know about Jesus."

He stopped, looked me dead in the eye. "Do you know Jesus?"

I frowned, confused. "It's the same thing, isn't it?"

He shook his head. "No, it's not. You said you know about Jesus. I'm asking if you actually know Him. Our Lord and Savior."

The words hung heavy between us. For a second, I didn't say anything. Then it came out sharp, almost angry. "Define Him. If there's a God, then what about the Big Bang Theory? If there's a God, and the Bible says He created man and woman and the heavens and the stars above, then where did the dinosaurs come from? If there's a God, then why would He let people like me suffer like this? Why would He let kids grow up addicted? Why would He let my life turn into this?"

My voice cracked by the end. The pod was silent, except for the distant sound of someone kicking a cell door.

He didn't interrupt. He didn't preach. He just let me pour it out—every question I had, every doubt, every bit of anger I'd buried under years of using.

Then he finally said, "You think God's scared of your questions? He made you, bro. He already knows you're broken, but He ain't done with you. You just ain't met Him yet."

Something about that hit me. Not because I believed him, not yet anyway, but because for the first time, someone in that place wasn't talking down to me. He was talking to me like I still had worth, even in jail, even sick, even lost. The coffee had gone cold, but the air between us felt alive. It was like the conversation cracked open, something in me I didn't know was still there.

We kept walking slow laps around the pod, the echo of our shoes the only sound cutting through the hum of the vents. The light above flickered, dull and tired. I could feel the sickness still in me, twisting through my gut, but something about the conversation had shifted the air.

He leaned closer, his voice lower now, like he didn't want anyone else hearing. "You ever been saved?"

I looked at him, not sure what he meant. "No," I said.

He stopped walking. We stood near the back, where the shadow from the visitation room stretched across the floor. "Then we can do it right now," he said. "We can go back there, say a prayer, give yourself to God. Repent for what you've done. Ask Jesus Christ to come into your heart."

I stared at him, my mind racing. The whole thing felt unreal. Jail clothes, cold concrete, withdrawal ripping through my body, and here this man was talking about salvation. But something inside me was listening.

He nodded toward the small visitation room, the one with the scratched glass and the heavy metal door. "Come on," he said quietly.

He took a step closer, his eyes burning with something real. "Hear me out. If I'm wrong about this, then hey, I'm wrong. But if I'm right… if I'm right, I get to go to heaven. I get to go to heaven with my Lord and Savior, Jesus Christ. Doesn't sound like a bad deal to me. Are you in?"

The room felt colder, quieter. My heart was pounding. It wasn't like a movie moment where everything clicked. It was messy, confusing. But something in his words shook me. I didn't know if I was in or not, but for the first time in a long time, I felt something other than pain. Something that almost felt like hope.

We stepped into the visitation room and the door clicked shut behind us.

The noise from the pod vanished, leaving only the hum of the light above and the sound of our breathing. The room smelled like old disinfectant and cold metal. The scratched glass windows caught the reflection of the two of us, side by side, two broken men in county jumpsuits standing in front of something unseen.

He turned toward me, eyes steady. "Give me your hands," he said.

I hesitated for a second but I did. My hands were shaking, skin clammy, knuckles still raw from the night before punching the walls. His hands were rough, scarred, and warm. He gripped tight, not soft, not gentle, but firm—like he meant to pull me out of something heavy.

"Repeat after me," he said.

We started slow. The Lord's Prayer. The words came out uneven, cracked from the dryness in my throat. Our Father who art in heaven, hallowed be thy name… My voice broke halfway through but he kept going, steady, not letting me stop. The more we spoke, the more something started to rise up in me. The weight. The guilt. The sickness. All of it started to boil over.

Then he said, "Now say this one. The Salvation Prayer."

His voice dropped, softer now. "Lord Jesus Christ, I know I'm a sinner. I know I've done wrong. I ask you to forgive me. Come into my heart. Make me new."

I repeated every word. My voice cracked. My legs shook. The room started to blur as the tears came. I couldn't stop them. They poured out of me like everything I'd buried for years was breaking loose. I was crying so hard I could barely breathe, gasping between words, choking on everything I'd never said out loud.

Then he said, "Now say this: Forgive me, Lord. I repent all my sin to you. Forgive me, Father. I am yours and yours alone."

He kept praying over me. "You are loved. You are forgiven. You are free."

I believed him, even if it was just for that moment. I could feel something—the heat, the light, maybe just hope—filling the space that had been empty for so long. When it was over, I wiped my face, embarrassed, my voice small. The tears had soaked my shirt. I couldn't even look up.

He smiled, half laughing. "Hey," he said, "you crying like a baby, bro."

I laughed too, through the tears, still shaking. "Yeah," I said, "guess I needed it."

He patted my shoulder. "Nah, you didn't need it. You were made for it."

The door opened again and the noise of the pod came back. Everything felt different. The air felt lighter. My chest felt open. For the first time in a long time, I felt alive.

The tier was quiet when I walked back to my cell. The lights buzzed overhead, that same dull hum that never stopped. My body still ached from the detox and my eyes burned from crying, but something in me felt different, softer. The guard clanked the door behind me, the lock echoing through the concrete.

I climbed onto the bunk and laid flat on my back, staring up at the ceiling, then turned my head toward the smallest window in the room. It wasn't much, just a narrow slit of glass, smudged and scratched, but through it I could see the night sky. A few stars cut through the darkness, cold and distant.

That's when it hit me again. The tears came back, slower this time. Not loud, not from pain, but from something else—something deeper. I wiped at my face but they kept falling. My chest rose and fell heavy, each breath thick with everything I'd been holding in for years.

I started talking to God. Not fancy. Not like church talk. Just me and Him.

"God," I whispered, "help me. Please help me because I can't do this on my own." My voice cracked. I pressed my hands together, gripping tight like it was the only thing keeping me alive.

"God, I want to die, Lord. Please come into my heart, Father. Please. Take this pain away. I don't know who I am anymore. Lord, help me, please. I beg you, Lord, help me. Please help me. I don't know what I'm doing. I need help."

The words spilled out of me over and over until I couldn't speak anymore. The cell was silent except for the sound of my breathing, shaky and broken. The air felt thick, heavy, like something was pressing down on the whole room.

And that's when it happened.

A sound, not loud, not outside, but inside. Clear. Calm. Close.

"Don't worry."

I froze. My body went still, every hair on my arms standing up. I looked around but there was no one there. No other voice, no movement just that whisper in my head that didn't sound like my own.

"Don't worry."

The words didn't scare me. They filled the room with warmth, like light breaking through the cracks. My body stopped shaking. My breathing slowed. The pain didn't vanish, but it didn't control me anymore. I laid there, staring at those stars, the tears still on my face, but this time they didn't burn.

For the first time in my life, in that cell, in the middle of withdrawal, locked away from the world, I felt something I hadn't felt in years.

Peace.

I ended up falling asleep. Really asleep. For two days I had been in that cell, shaking, throwing up, crying, unable to rest. But that night, after the voice, after everything, my body finally let go. I sank into the mattress like the weight of the world had slid off my back. The light above still buzzed, but it didn't bother me. My breathing slowed. My mind went quiet. For the first time in years, I didn't dream about the streets, the dope, or the chaos. Just silence.

When I opened my eyes, it was morning. The smell of instant coffee and powdered eggs drifted through the pod. The guard was yelling "Chow time," his voice bouncing off the walls. I sat up slow, confused, like waking up in another body. My head didn't hurt. My stomach wasn't turning. The ache, the sweats, the cramps... gone. I sat there for a second, waiting for the sickness to hit, but it didn't. No chills. No shakes. No pain crawling under my skin. My chest felt light, my mind clear. I pressed my hands against my face and I started laughing. Not crazy laughter, not out of shock—just disbelief.

When I tell you I had no come down from my addiction, I mean it. The feeling of the opiates was gone. The withdrawal was gone. It was like somebody reached inside and switched something off. I swung my legs off the bunk, stood up, and stretched. My body didn't feel like mine. It felt brand new. There was this calm sitting inside me, a peace I couldn't explain. It wasn't just relief, it was joy. Real joy. The kind that hums deep inside your chest and makes you want to cry all over again, but this time from gratitude.

I walked down to the dayroom, still trying to process it. The light hit different that morning. The walls didn't feel like they were closing in. The clanging and shouting didn't bother me. I was just... here. Present. Happy. Hungry.

I grabbed my tray with those runny eggs, that dry biscuit, that watery coffee, and I sat down and ate every bite. The food tasted real, like I hadn't tasted anything in years. I looked around, trying to find him—the man from the night before who prayed with me, who walked with me, who told me about Jesus.

But he wasn't there.

I checked the tables, the cells, and asked a few guys if they'd seen him. No one knew who I was talking about. They looked at me as if I were crazy.

That's when it hit me.

My chest tightened, my heart racing, but not from fear. From awe. Could this be real? Could it have been Him? Could that man have been sent for that one moment, just to reach me?

I stood there, frozen, holding my tray, as the noise of the pod faded into the background. My mind was blown. Everything I thought I knew, everything I believed about life and death, about drugs and pain, cracked wide open.

Could this really be?

Could this have been God?

Days started to move differently after that night. The sickness never came back. The dope cravings, the sweats, the pain... it was gone. I woke up each morning with something new inside me, something steady. I couldn't explain it. It wasn't like I'd earned peace; it was like it had been handed to me on a silver platter.

I started reading the Bible. At first, just a few lines here and there, trying to understand it. Then I couldn't put it down. Those thin pages turned into stories for me, and I was craving it, reading them over and over until they lived in my head.

Weeks passed. The guards started calling me for work. I signed up for the kitchen, pulling trays, stacking dishes, serving meals to the same faces that used to look just like mine, the same tired, lost, angry faces. I'd hum songs under my breath while I scrubbed pans. Something about that greasy kitchen steam and the smell of burnt toast felt holy to me. I was working again. Moving again. Alive again.

One day after lunch, I went back to my bunk to pray. I was kneeling, eyes closed, whispering the same words I'd been saying since that night. "Thank you, Lord. Thank you for saving me."

That's when I heard it again.

Not loud, not from outside. It came from deep within me.

"Write your story."

I froze. I didn't question it. I didn't second-guess it. I grabbed a stub of a pencil and asked around for paper until I had enough, and then I started writing.

I wrote about the streets. The addiction. The violence. The pain. Every word that had been rotting inside of me poured out onto that paper. I couldn't stop. My hands cramped, my eyes burned, but the Holy Spirit had me moving like I'd been waiting my whole life for that moment.

That's all I thought about. That book. My life. My story. God's story through me.

Days turned into weeks, and weeks into months. I was waiting for sentencing, but I wasn't scared anymore. Every night, I was holding Bible studies with other inmates. We'd circle around in the pod, heads bowed, voices low, and read scripture together. We would have prayer circles. Some of them came just to listen. Some cried. Some prayed. It didn't matter who they were; we were all broken, all trying to find light in a place built for darkness.

I was happy. Really happy.

Joyous in a way that didn't make sense.

I didn't want to die anymore. I wanted to live.

There were days when the sheriffs would walk by and see me smiling, wiping down tables, humming to myself. One of them stopped and asked, "What's wrong with you? Why are you so happy? You're in jail."

I looked at him and grinned. "Yeah, I'm in jail, but I'm getting my life back. I'm getting my work ethic back. I'm getting my kids back."

He just shook his head and walked off, probably thinking I'd lost my mind.

When we arrived, the guards led us through the metal detectors, the long halls, the echoing steps that made everything feel heavier. We got to the holding cell, stripped down to our jumpsuits, and we waited. Every man around me shifted, scratched, tired. Some prayed, some stared blankly at the walls, some just clenched their fists.

Then the call came. One by one, names were called. The floorboards creaked beneath our sandals as we walked to the courtroom. My knees shook with the weight of it all, but I kept my head down, hands clasped in front of me, trying to steady my breathing.

The judge's gavel hit the desk like a hammer on iron. The first man was called. He went up to the stage, face pale, shaking.

"Anything to say?" the judge asked.

"No, sir," he whispered.

"Twenty years to the Department of Corrections," the judge said.

Next. Another man. Five years. He nodded, silent.

Finally, my name: Gabriel Hinojosa vs The State of Colorado.

"Yes, sir," I said, standing. My hands were sweaty, but my heart felt steady. "I'm ready to be sentenced."

The judge looked at me, eyes sharp, pen poised over the papers. "Do you have anything to say?"

The courtroom was heavy, the air thick with tension and the scent of polished wood and fear. I stood there, hands clenched, eyes fixed on the judge, heart hammering in my chest. The weight of the past year pressed on me, every bad choice, every moment of weakness, every night lost to drugs and pain, but behind all that, something had changed. SUSPECT was dead.

"I do, Your Honor. All I want to say," I began, my voice shaking but steadying as I went on, "I take accountability for my actions. Even though my actions were drug-induced, they were still my own."

I paused, swallowing hard, feeling the lump in my throat. "Now, sitting in CJC for this last year, I feel like I've done a lot of growth. I've had a lot of realizations. Your Honor, I have written a book, and I'm still writing another book that I hope to publish. I want to help people who are like me, who were lost."

I could feel the eyes of the room on me, the silent judgments, the whispers of those waiting their turn, the pens scratching in the background. I lifted my head, looking at the judge, and I said, "See, Judge, I stand before you today. I am a completely different person. I actually found God and my faith behind the walls of CJC. I'm not the same person I was a year ago. But like I said, I take full accountability for my actions. I sincerely apologize for everything I've done, and I will accept any sentence you must impose upon me. Again, Your Honor, I just want to help people who are lost and broken, just like I was. I don't know what that looks like right now, but I know I feel it in my heart."

The judge leaned back in his chair, eyes piercing, staring straight into me. I felt like he was reading everything I had done, everything I had felt, everything I wanted to become. I could see my own reflection in his gaze, raw and exposed. I could feel my tears sliding down, warm and heavy, and I didn't hide them. I looked him in the eyes, letting him see the sincerity carved deep into my soul.

He waved his finger in my face, slow and deliberate. "Sir, I'm going to give you one chance. One chance only. You have an extensive record, but we're going to try community corrections. If you mess up one time, you're going to prison. You're going to prison."

I felt my lawyer glance at me, a quick, tense nod. My mind was spinning. I could barely process the words.

"Go ahead and take him back. Let's get him scanned. See if they'll accept him at community corrections," the judge continued.

The final words cut through the chaos of my thoughts. "Sir, I'm going to go ahead and give you six years of community corrections. Thank you, Your Honor."

My knees nearly buckled. My chest felt like it had been lifted off my back and replaced with fire. My mind was blown. Completely blown. Every prayer I had whispered in that tiny cell, every night I had cried out in pain, every step of faith, every word of my book—it all had led to this.

God showed up. God answered.

I sat back in the chair, tears streaming freely, stomach twisting, chest heaving. For the first time in my life, I could feel real grace hitting me, heavy and true. The courtroom noise faded. I wasn't thinking about the past. I wasn't fearing the future. I was alive in that exact moment, and I knew without a doubt, God had me.

The courthouse doors swung open, and the harsh light of the morning hit me like a slap. I stepped out with a handful of other guys, all dragging their chains, all moving slow and heavy with the weight of their own sentences. They started talking, voices overlapping, rough and raw.

"Bro, you got lucky."

I'd call my family on the phone and tell them, "I found Jesus. I'm writing a book. I'm going to help people."

My mom probably thought I was crazy too. Maybe I was, but I didn't care.

Because I felt it. Deep in my chest. This was just the beginning.

And I knew, without a doubt, that God was not finished with me yet.

About eleven months into my time at El Paso County Jail, my lawyer came to me in that tiny, fluorescent-lit visitation room. He sat across the table, sliding a file toward me like it carried the weight of the world, and said, "This is the best deal you're going to get with everything going on."

I already knew the numbers. I'd refused two deals before—one for fifteen to twenty, the next for twelve to fifteen—but this one was different. Everything in my life, the streets, the gangs, the drugs, all the chaos I'd survived, all the crime I'd committed, it had led to this moment.

I looked at the papers. Ten years. Ten years in the DOC.

Ten years without my kids. Ten years without my mom. Ten years.

I remember my chest tightening, my stomach dropping, my throat closing up. The world slowed down around me. Ten years. It was like someone had carved a hole in the middle of my life and I was supposed to jump into it blindfolded. I couldn't argue. I'd refused two deals already. If I didn't take this, we were going to the box. This was it.

I signed. The pen scratched against the dotted line, final and cold. It felt heavier than any weight I'd carried in jail. My hand shook. My head dropped.

I went back to my cell after the meeting. I lay on my bunk for a long time, staring at that tiny window above, the same one I'd prayed through nights before. I felt the sting of loss, the ache of separation from everyone I loved. Ten years is a long time, especially when you've already lost so much. But I prayed.

I prayed like I'd been doing all along, except now the prayer carried more weight, more depth. I gave God the years I couldn't hold, the kids I couldn't touch, the mother I couldn't hug. I gave Him the pain. I gave Him the fear. I gave Him everything I didn't know how to survive on my own.

Something shifted. Not instantly, not magically, but I felt the same peace I had found in that visitation room months ago. The joy I had discovered while reading scripture, writing my book, sharing it with the guys in the pod, it didn't leave me. The fear of ten years couldn't steal that. The heartbreak of missing birthdays, holidays, first everything with my kids couldn't touch it. Deep down, I knew God had me. I knew He wouldn't leave me alone in the darkness.

Sentencing was still two months away. Two months to sit, to wait, to reflect, to keep writing, to keep working, to keep holding on, and that's what I did. Over a year at CJC waiting to get sentenced. Each day, each hour, each moment, I held onto that truth. No matter what the world tried to take from me, no matter how much time or pain I faced, God was with me, and that was enough to keep me alive, enough to keep me whole.

The morning of sentencing came fast. My stomach churned with nerves, but beneath it all, I felt something I hadn't felt in a long time, and that was acceptance. I had made peace with what was coming. I wasn't free, not yet, but my mind was quiet. My heart was calm.

We lined up with a handful of other guys, all wearing the same county jumpsuits, all carrying the weight of their own histories. The bus ride to the courthouse was silent except for the clatter of chains and the low hum of the engine. I stared out the window, watching the world move past like I was outside it, removed. Every tree, every streetlight, every cracked sidewalk blurred together.

When we arrived, the guards led us through the metal detectors, the long halls, the echoing steps that made everything feel heavier. We got to the holding cell, stripped down to our jumpsuits, and we waited. Every man around me shifted, scratched, tired. Some prayed, some stared blankly at the walls, some just clenched their fists.

Then the call came. One by one, names were called. The floorboards creaked beneath our sandals as we walked to the courtroom. My knees shook with the weight of it all, but I kept my head down, hands clasped in front of me, trying to steady my breathing.

The judge's gavel hit the desk like a hammer on iron. The first man was called. He went up to the stage, face pale, shaking.

"Anything to say?" the judge asked.

"No, sir," he whispered.

"Twenty years to the Department of Corrections," the judge said.

Next. Another man. Five years. He nodded, silent.

Finally, my name: Gabriel Hinojosa vs The State of Colorado.

"Yes, sir," I said, standing. My hands were sweaty, but my heart felt steady. "I'm ready to be sentenced."

The judge looked at me, eyes sharp, pen poised over the papers. "Do you have anything to say?"

The courtroom was heavy, the air thick with tension and the scent of polished wood and fear. I stood there, hands clenched, eyes fixed on the judge, heart hammering in my chest. The weight of the past year pressed on me—every bad choice, every moment of weakness, every night lost to drugs and pain—but behind all that, something had changed. SUSPECT was dead.

"I do, Your Honor. All I want to say," I began, my voice shaking but steadying as I went on, "I take accountability for my actions. Even though my actions were drug-induced, they were still my own."

I paused, swallowing hard, feeling the lump in my throat. "Now, sitting in CJC for this last year, I feel like I've done a lot of growth. I've had a lot of realization. Your Honor, I wrote a book... and I'm still writing a book... that I hope to publish. I want to help people that are like me, that were lost."

I could feel the eyes of the room on me—the silent judgments, the whispers of those waiting their turn, the pens scratching in the background. I lifted my head, looking at the judge, and I said, "See, Judge, I stand before you today. I am a completely different person. I actually found God and my faith behind the walls of CJC. I'm not the same person I was a year ago. But like I said, I take full accountability for my actions. I apologize sincerely for everything I've done, and I will accept any sentence you must give me. Again, Your Honor, I just want to help people that are lost and broken, just like I was. I don't know what that looks like right now, but I know I feel it in my heart."

The judge leaned back in his chair, eyes piercing, staring straight into me. I felt like he was reading everything I had done, everything I had felt, everything I wanted to become. I could see my own reflection in his gaze, raw and exposed. I could feel my tears sliding down, warm and heavy, and I didn't hide them. I looked him in the eyes, letting him see the sincerity carved deep into my soul.

He waved his finger in my face, slow and deliberate. "Sir, I'm going to give you one chance. One chance only. You have an extensive record, but we're going to try community corrections. If you mess up one time, you're going to prison. You're going to prison."

I felt my lawyer glance at me, a quick, tense nod. My mind was spinning. I could barely process the words.

"Go ahead and take him back. Let's get him scanned. See if they'll accept him at community corrections," the judge continued.

The final words cut through the chaos of my thoughts. "Sir, I'm going to go ahead and give you six years community corrections. Thank you, Your Honor."

My knees nearly buckled. My chest felt like it had been lifted off my back and replaced with fire. My mind was blown. Completely blown. Every prayer I had whispered in that tiny cell, every night I had cried out in pain, every step of faith, every word of my book—it all had led to this.

God showed up. God answered.

I sat back in the chair, tears streaming freely, stomach twisting, chest heaving. For the first time in my life, I could feel real grace hitting me, heavy and true. The courtroom noise faded. I wasn't thinking about the past. I wasn't fearing the future. I was alive in that exact moment, and I knew without a doubt, God had me.

The courthouse doors swung open, and the harsh light of the morning hit me like a slap. I stepped out with a handful of other guys, all dragging their chains, all moving slow and heavy with the weight of their own sentences. They started talking, voices overlapping, rough and raw.

"Bro, you got lucky."

"Bro, he showed you love."

"Bro, the halfway house? That's way better than prison."

I nodded, still numb, still trying to process it. Around me, the numbers were being called, sentences handed down like cards in a deck. One got twenty, another fifteen, one got five, another ten. I couldn't help but glance at them, their faces etched with defeat, with regret, with nothing left to hold onto.

And then there was me.

I got grace. Real, unearned grace.

I could feel it hit me in waves, the relief, the disbelief, the weight lifting off my chest. I breathed it in deep, the air in my lungs burning with awe. I whispered to myself, almost in shock, "I got grace again. I got grace again." I wanted to jump for joy. The words stuck in my throat, over and over. Wow. I couldn't stop repeating it in my head. My heart was pounding. My knees felt weak. I felt like I was floating above the pavement, looking down at everything I'd been through, the streets, the drugs, the violence, the jail, the withdrawals, the fear, the pain. All of it had led to this one moment of mercy.

A couple more months back at CJC, waiting to see if they would accept me into Community Corrections, stretched long and slow. But the wait didn't shake me. I'd been broke before. I'd been lost before. But now, I was different. I had faith. I had purpose. I had a book to write.

Then the call came. They accepted me.

And I couldn't help it. I laughed out loud, tears slipping down, heart pounding with gratitude and disbelief.

Man. Can you believe it?

Can you believe it after everything I've been through?

Wow.

A couple weeks went by, slow but steady, like time was dragging its feet just to test my patience. Every day I waited, wondering if they'd call my name, if this new shot at freedom was real or just another tease. Then one morning, it happened. They told me I was getting picked up by a different community corrections center, C.A.E. I'd heard about it before. Stricter. Tighter rules. No room for games. The kind of place that either makes you or breaks you.

The van rolled up outside the county jail, a white box on wheels, the kind that doesn't look like much but means everything when your world's been four gray walls and fluorescent light. They cuffed me, loaded me up, and we drove barely a minute down Las Vegas Street. Crazy thing is, the halfway house was practically right next door to CJC. It was like God was telling me, you're close but don't forget where you came from.

We pulled up to the white building, no nonsense, surrounded by chain-link and floodlights. I stepped out, holding a plastic bag with everything I owned. My heart beat slow and heavy. New place, same rules. Same mission. Don't fall. Don't fold. Don't forget.

Intake was cold and methodical. Paperwork. Questions. Urine test. They laid it all out plain and simple:

You gotta be accountable. You can't get high. You got therapy. You got classes. You got to work and you gotta live here.

No shortcuts. No excuses.

The staff looked me over like they'd seen a thousand guys just like me come through, and most of them fail. But I wasn't trying to be like the rest.

They walked me through the large facility, which had concrete floors. Bunk beds lined against the walls. The smell of disinfectant and instant coffee mixed in the air. The rules were written big on the wall:

NO DRUGS. NO FIGHTING. NO LYING. NO EXCUSES.

I could tell right away they ran this place tighter than Comcor. Way tighter. Every move you made was logged. Every time you left, every time you came back, every word you said was clocked. Passes? You had to earn those. Level by level. No trust unless you prove yourself. And honestly, that's probably what I needed. I didn't need easy. I needed structure. I needed walls that didn't just hold me in but held me up.

The first few weeks were quiet. I worked. I prayed. I stayed out of the way. My mom and sister came to see me as often as they could. They'd pull up outside, big smiles, full of love I didn't deserve but needed more than air. They'd bring me little things, such as snacks, clothes, and a cell phone. Stuff that meant everything when you had nothing.

Every time I got a pass, I'd go to my sister's house. The smell of food cooking, the sound of laughter from my nieces and nephews, and the feeling of sitting at a real table hit deep. We'd pray before eating, and for a little while, I could breathe again. I could feel normal.

Then it was back to the grind. Classes, meetings, curfew checks, headcounts. Random searches. The same routine but with a purpose. I wasn't just surviving anymore. I was rebuilding. And every time I'd walk out the door for a pass, I'd glance down the street at CJC, the same place I'd once begged God to take my pain away, and I'd whisper to myself, look how far you've come.

To be honest, I put the book I wrote on the back burner. Not because I didn't care anymore, but because life started moving again and it was moving fast.

I was dead tired once I got off work. I worked a lot just to stay out of there. I had to get money. I had to start paying restitution, paying back what I owed not just to the courts but to life itself. To my family. To my kids. To God. The book, the dream, the fire that lit inside me at CJC, it was still there but dimmer now, like a candle flickering in a room full of wind. I wasn't getting high. I wasn't going to church either, but I knew Jesus. I knew He was inside me. I could still feel Him in quiet moments, when the noise died down, when I lay in bed staring at the ceiling after another long shift. But the intensity, that overwhelming rush of the Holy Spirit that hit me in jail, that's what had faded. What I had now was faith stripped down to its bare essentials.

C.A.E. was no place for weakness. It was rough. The walls had ears, and the people had motives. You had addicts still using, dealers still hustling, liars trying to play the system. The smell of burnt foil and cheap cologne clung to the air. Some guys were there to change, but most were just there to coast, to serve their time and slide back into the same streets that broke them. I knew if I got too close to anyone, I'd risk getting dragged right back into the chaos. So I stayed low. I kept to myself. I went to work, came back, ate my food, and stayed in my room. Headphones in, eyes down, mouth shut.

Isolation became my armor. My protection.

I didn't spend much time in the common area. Too many arguments. Too many temptations. Too many fake smiles and broken promises. I'd watch from a distance, guys sneaking around corners, passing little baggies, whispering deals, making moves like it was the same game in a different building.

And me? I wasn't playing anymore. I couldn't. I refused to lose what God gave me.

Work became my refuge. The grind was my prayer. Every shift, every hour on the clock, was another piece of my redemption. I'd wake up before dawn, lace up my boots, and go. Didn't matter what the job was—dishwasher, cook, laborer. I did it as if it were sacred because, for me, it was. At work, I didn't have to think. Didn't have to talk. Didn't have to explain myself. I just worked. Moved. Breathed. Survived and climbed the ladder. I wasn't free yet, not completely, but I was alive, and that was more than I'd been in years.

The nights were the hardest. The silence hit differently when the lights went out. I'd sit on my bunk, elbows on my knees, staring at the wall, thinking about everything, the people I hurt, the chances I wasted, the man I was trying to become. Sometimes I'd whisper a quiet prayer, not because I had to but because I needed to.

"God, just keep me here. Keep me focused. Don't let me fall."

That's when I started reaching out. One by one.

Not to get something from anyone, just to make it right.

It started with Kevin. Solid dude. Real one. He'd been there when I couldn't stand on my own two feet, when I didn't even believe I was worth saving. I called him up, and my voice cracked before I even said a word.

"Kev… I'm sorry, bro."

There was a pause on the line, just breathing. Then he said, "Thank you, I appreciate that. I love you. Just keep doing right."

I owed him everything. He helped me get to every class, every U.A., every therapy appointment. When nobody else believed in me, he pulled up early in the morning just to make sure I didn't fall off again. I told him that. He just laughed, said, "You good, bro. You're alive. That's what matters."

After Kevin, I called my brother. That one hit differently.

He picked up, quiet at first, then said, "What's up?"

I could hear kids in the background—my kids.

"Hey, bro," I said, my voice shaking, "thank you. For taking them in. For not letting them end up in the system. For being there when I wasn't."

Silence. Then he said, "They're good. They know you love 'em."

I swallowed hard. "I just want to say I'm sorry. For everything. For not being there. For all the times you had to step up when I should've."

He didn't say much after that, just, "It's alright, man. Just don't go back."

And I promised him I wouldn't.

Then came my sister, Bernadette. Always there. Always.

When everyone else got tired of my chaos, she stayed. Drove miles just to drop off food, clothes, a smile—whatever I needed.

"Bern, thank you," I told her. "You never gave up on me."

She laughed through tears, said, "You're my brother. I couldn't. I prayed for you every day when you were in the streets."

I said, "I'm sorry I always let you down."

She said, "Then stop saying sorry and just keep doing better."

That hit me deep.

Then came my mom.

I sat on my bunk, phone in hand, hands shaking. The smell of disinfectant and instant coffee in the air. The walls sweating with silence.

She answered with that soft voice that always felt like home.

"Hello?"

"Hey, Mom," I said, and before I knew it, I was crying. "I'm sorry. For everything. For all the pain. For every night you stayed up wondering if I was dead. I'm sorry for letting you down. I love you, Mom."

She started crying too. "I know, boy. I know."

And then the hardest, my daughter Nevaeh.

That one broke me.

Her voice was small, older now, wiser than it should have been.

"Hi, Dad."

Those two words hit harder than any sentence I've ever gotten.

I told her, "I'm sorry, baby. I was blind for a long time. I didn't know who I was. I didn't know how to be a father. But I'm not that man anymore. I'm trying. I promise you; I'm trying."

She didn't say much. Just whispered, "I know."

That was enough to make me drop the phone and sit there with my face in my hands.

Yeah, the outside still looked the same, tattoos crawling up my arms, scars that told stories most people couldn't stomach. But inside? My heart had changed. My spirit was new. My soul felt lighter, like I had finally laid down a lifetime's worth of weight.

And even though forgiveness wasn't guaranteed, I still reached for it. Because for the first time in a long time, I wasn't reaching for a needle, or a deal, or a lie. I was reaching for grace.

I could hear something in the background, soft cooing, the kind of sound that pulls at a man's chest.

I asked, "Who's that?"

She said, "That's Estevan, Dad."

The words stopped me cold. My baby girl had a baby. I was too caught up with drugs and running the streets to come around. I was a grandpa.

It hit me like a punch to the gut and a blessing all at once.

"Wow," I said quietly, almost to myself.

For a second, I couldn't speak. My throat burned, eyes wet. The reality sank in. I'd missed so much, and now life had kept moving without me. My daughter, grown. A mother now. Carrying the same kind of love I'd been too broken to give.

"I'm sorry, Nevaeh," I said, voice cracking. "I was blind for a long time. I didn't know who I was. I didn't know how to be a father. But I'm not that man anymore. I'm trying. I promise you, I'm trying."

She was quiet for a moment. Then she said softly, "I know, and I want you to get to know him, Dad. Estevan. He should know you."

That wrecked me. Not out of guilt but because that was grace. She was giving me another chance.

I sat there, clutching the phone, tears dripping onto the concrete floor, whispering, "Thank you, God."

Yeah, the outside still looked the same, tattoos crawling up my arms and my head, scars that told stories most people couldn't stomach. But inside? My heart had changed. My spirit was new. My soul felt lighter, like I had finally laid down a lifetime's worth of weight. And even though forgiveness wasn't guaranteed, I still reached for it. Because for the first time in a long time, I wasn't reaching for a high, or a deal, or a lie. I was reaching for grace.

That night after the call, I lay on my bunk staring at the ceiling, paint peeling, the hum of the vents echoing like a low prayer.

That thought scared me more than any sentence ever could.

What if I failed again? What if I showed up just to break another piece of all my kids' hearts? Grace is heavy. It sounds light when you say it, but when you're carrying it, when you're trying to live up to it, it weighs like iron. I felt it pressing on me now. The walls of that place felt smaller. Every noise, the keys, the footsteps, the distant yelling, reminded me how close I still was to the edge. One mistake, one bad decision, and I'd lose everything again.

But under that fear was something else. A pulse.

Out there, the streets were still waiting. The old world never forgets your name. And somewhere in that pull between grace and destruction, that's where my next chapter was forming.

I could feel it.

The real fight wasn't with addiction anymore. It was with myself. And the deeper I looked, the more I realized redemption isn't a finish line. It's a war.

And I was just getting started.

CHAPTER 41: A HEART WORTH FIGHTING FOR

One day I was heading to my sister's on a pass from the halfway house, the streets buzzing with the usual noise, tires rolling over asphalt, people shouting, lights flickering like they were alive. I pulled up at the intersection, stopped at the red, and that's when I saw her. My eyes locked from the street to hers while she was putting gas, like some kind of magnetic pull I couldn't explain. She was beautiful, but it wasn't just her face. There was something in the way she carried herself, the calm in the middle of all the chaos, like she didn't need to prove anything to anyone.

I didn't know it yet, but we were already connected, friends on social media. I didn't put two and two together until later. Small world, I guess. Time passed, and I started posting things about Jesus, about my daughter, the struggles I'd been through, the steps I was finally taking to get right. I didn't post to impress anyone. I posted to keep myself accountable, to share my journey with the world, and to remind myself that I was alive for a reason.

One day, Melissa commented. Simple words but genuine, saying something nice about what I was sharing. That one small comment lit a spark. It wasn't just a casual acknowledgment. It was recognition, understanding, maybe even respect for the grind I'd been through. That comment turned into a conversation. Just a few messages back and forth at first, testing the waters, feeling each other out. But there was something real there, like curiosity.

The conversations grew deeper, questions about each other's lives, about the paths we'd walked, the mistakes we'd made, the things that had shaped us. It wasn't shallow. There was honesty in it, something raw and unfiltered, like the city streets themselves. Before I knew it, Melissa, the woman I had just locked eyes with at a red light, was someone I wanted to know better. Not just as a connection but as a person. And for the first time in a long time, my heart felt awake again, like there was space for something new, something alive, in the middle of all the chaos that had been my life.

One day, I was at work, grinding like usual, doing landscaping, trying to keep my head down and stay in my own lane, when I got a message from Melissa. She asked if I was thirsty, said she was out and about, and wanted to bring me something to drink. I agreed, thinking it was just a little gesture, nothing more.

A little while later, I heard the pull-up of a car outside, and my chest skipped. When I saw her in person, my jaw nearly hit the floor. She was sitting in the car like she owned the sunlight, like the world paused for a second just to let me see her. My feet almost betrayed me. I might have tripped, but I kept it cool. I had to. Had to act like I wasn't about to melt right there on the asphalt.

She pulled up, I slid into the car, and I looked at her. "Thank you" barely scratched the surface. She was stunning, and I could feel the electricity between us like static buzzing through my veins. I couldn't fight it anymore. I leaned in. Bold, impulsive, maybe reckless, but I had to see if it was real. And I kissed her. Just one kiss, powerful, but it hit me like a freight train. Soul-shaking. My chest tightened. My stomach flipped. Everything I thought I knew about control, about holding back, about guarding my heart, all disappeared in that instant. I felt her, felt us, felt something I hadn't ever felt. And at that moment, I knew this wasn't just infatuation. It was something deeper, something that cut through the chaos of my past, the streets, the mistakes, the years behind bars. This kiss was raw, it was real, and it shook me down to the core.

Melissa was the kind of woman who didn't just walk into a room; she shifted the atmosphere. Standing a little over five feet, she carried herself with quiet confidence that drew eyes without ever demanding them. Her hair was long, black, and wildly curly. It fell in waves that seemed to have a life of their own, each curl catching the light like it was spun from silk. When the wind touched it, it danced, framing her face in effortless beauty.

Her eyes… her eyes. They didn't just shine, they ignited. Bright and alive, they shined with the same brilliance as the Fourth of July sky, that mix of fire and wonder that made you forget what you were about to say. You could read entire stories in her eyes, filled with mystery, strength, compassion, and just enough mischief to keep you guessing.

Melissa was the perfect painted picture. Every curve deliberates, every line a masterpiece of God's design. She moved with the kind of sophistication that couldn't be taught, part elegance, part power, part pure soul. The way she walked, the way she lifted her chin when she laughed, it wasn't just beautiful, it was breathtaking.

Her beauty went deeper than the eyes could see. Her intelligence had weight. The way she spoke, smooth, deliberate, thoughtful, you could tell she didn't waste words. She had that rare kind of mind that could disarm you with both logic and grace. Conversations with her had substance. She could talk about life, business, art, or struggle, and every word hit like poetry.

She was sophistication wrapped in fire. A woman who could sit at a dinner table with CEOs and business owners in the middle of chaos and still carry the same quiet strength. Melissa wasn't just beautiful, she had magnetic energy, the kind of woman that made you rethink the definition of the word itself. Just like that, I was drawn to her immediately.

Because beauty fades in the world, but with her... it felt eternal.

As I got to know Melissa better, I learned more about her story. She was a widow. Not a Christian or a believer by all means, but she believed in being spiritual. She carried herself with a quiet strength, a wisdom that comes from life lived fully, from love gained and loss endured. That didn't push me away. Not even close. I saw her heart. I saw her soul. It shined through every word, every smile, every gesture.

She had four kids and three grandbabies, and her family meant everything to her. That didn't intimidate me, it drew me closer. It revealed to me the depth of her love and the life she carried within her. We started going on dates, simple things at first, just enjoying each other's company, learning the rhythms of each other's lives. She asked about my past, and I told her. Everything, the streets, the mistakes, the jail, the addiction—and she listened. Really listened. No judgment, just understanding, just presence.

I soon filed for divorce from Christina. It didn't affect me. She was gone somewhere, and I let her be. That was dead years ago.

Sometimes Melissa would even drop me off at the halfway house after we hung out. Those rides were amazing and sacred to me. I felt like God placed us in each other's path, like all the chaos I'd been through had led me to her. It was as if she had fallen straight out of heaven, and God had blessed me with an angel. Everything about her felt intentional, precise, perfect. The way she laughed, the way she carried herself, the way she looked at me like I wasn't a mess, like I wasn't broken, like I was exactly where I was supposed to be.

To me, she wasn't just a woman I was dating; she was a woman I was falling in love with. She was a graceful walking in human form. She was peacefully wrapped in beauty. She was everything I didn't know I needed but had been craving all my life. Every moment with her reminded me that life could be more than survival. It could be love. It could be hope. It could be real.

A year and a half passed, and Melissa and I were living together. Every corner of the house started gaining memories of laughter, late-night talks, and moments of quiet peace I hadn't known I could feel. My kids and nephews would come over, and we would play board games and just be present in their lives.

I was still working landscaping, the cold of winter biting through my jacket as I moved mulch, trimmed hedges, and shoveled driveways, just trying to keep life steady. One night, as frost settled on the windows, Melissa brought up something that changed everything. She told me about peer coaching. Helping people. People who were struggling like I had addiction, homelessness, life lost in the streets. Showing them there was another way, a better way.

At first, I didn't know if I was ready, but her eyes told me I could do it. That she believed in me, and that was enough.

We looked into it, and I dove in headfirst. Classes, certifications, learning how to listen, how to guide, and how to show someone the door without shoving them. When I got certified, I stepped into the work headfirst. I applied to an organization doing real street-level work, and before long, I understood the rhythm of it, the ways the programs worked, the people who needed guidance, the pain, and the hope.

I rose to peer coach lead, and the work became my life. I was running groups, talking to people who were broken, beaten down by life, trying to survive. I would go to parole and explain what it was we did. Attend court with clients and represent them in court. I went out to homeless camps, places most people wouldn't drive past, and pulled people out of gutters, both literal and figurative. I sat with them, listened to them, cried with them, and challenged them. I shared my story raw and unfiltered, showing them the scars, the tattoos, the mistakes, the chains that could be broken.

Every time I saw someone step up and find a spark inside them, it hit me in the chest like a rush of electricity. This was life. This was the purpose. This was redemption in motion. I wasn't just surviving anymore. I was taking my pain, my mistakes, and my time on the streets and turning them into fuel. Fuel to lift others, to show them the door, to lead them to something better.

In the middle of all that chaos, in the brokenness of the city and the lives around me, I felt God moving through me, using me in ways I never thought possible. I felt it; this was my purpose.

Around this time, I bought a ring. Not just any ring, but something I hoped would carry the weight of everything I felt for Melissa. I knew she felt the same way. I had never felt a love like this before, not in the streets, not in chaos, not in all the mistakes and broken nights. This was different. Pure. Real.

Before I did anything, I asked her kids, asked her parents. I wanted their blessing, their permission. They all agreed. They saw what I saw: the way she talked about me, the way we fit, the way our lives were stitched together in ways that went beyond luck.

That night, I decided to do it, and we went on a simple dinner date. Nothing fancy, just food, conversation, laughter, the little sparks of connection that had carried us through months of getting to know each other. We went to a movie afterward.

I could feel my nerves bubbling under my chest, under my ribs, under my skin, but I kept it steady for her. After the movie, we walked through the park. It looked like a scene from a film, as if God Himself had set it up just for us. Stars scattered across the sky like diamonds, park lights casting a soft glow across benches and paths. The air smelled crisp, like fall hadn't quite let go, and the quiet of the night wrapped around us like a blanket.

I stopped her. My heart was pounding so loudly that I was sure she could hear it. I took a deep breath, dropped to one knee, and held out the ring. My hands were shaking, my voice barely steady as I asked her to marry me.

She looked at me, eyes wide, mouth open, excitement and love spilling out of her. Her smile lit the night, brighter than any streetlight, brighter than the stars above. She nodded and yelled, "YES!" and for a second, the world stopped. Nothing else mattered. Not the streets, not the past, not the mistakes or the pain. Just her, me, the ring, and the life we were about to step into together.

It was nerve-wracking, beautiful, and real. Every emotion hit at once: fear, joy, love, and hope. In that moment, I knew for sure that no matter what the streets threw at me, no matter what struggles came next, I had found my person, my home, my forever in Melissa.

Then, I knew we had to find a church. There was this void gnawing at me, this emptiness I couldn't ignore, no matter how much work I put in or how much time I spent trying to fix everything around me. My past had been a mess, everything falling apart like dominoes, and deep down I knew why. Jesus wasn't in our lives. We had no foundation, no anchor to hold us when the storms hit.

I wanted that for us. For me, for Melissa, for the life we were building together. But I had to be smart about it. I couldn't just drag her into something she wasn't ready for. I had to plant seeds. Slowly. Quietly. Watching Christian movies, dropping little comments about the messages, the hope, the faith in them. Subtle hints, like breadcrumbs leading somewhere bigger, somewhere sacred.

She didn't even know. At least not at first. I could see the curiosity flicker in her eyes, that spark of recognition when a line hit something deep inside her. Every moment, every conversation, every shared scene from a movie was like a gentle nudge, a small hand guiding us toward something bigger. Something real. Something eternal.

I felt the weight of it all, but also the hope. Hope that she'd see it. Hope that together, we could build something that didn't crumble, something that could hold up against the streets, the past, the mistakes, the scars. I was careful, patient, planting these seeds, trusting that one day they'd grow into faith, our faith, rooted in God, unshakable and ready to carry us through anything.

One day, my sister Bernadette called me, her voice filled with excitement. She told me she had found a new church. It was called Amazing Church Colorado, a place she thought we should check out. Bernadette had been going to church for years, faithfully, quietly, always letting her faith guide her, even when the rest of the world around us was chaos.

She described the church with a kind of fire in her voice that I hadn't heard in a long time. She said it was spirit-filled, alive, a place where you could feel God when you walked in. She wanted us to go, to see it for ourselves, to feel that presence, to let it change us the way it had changed her.

I remember standing there on the phone, the weight of my past and everything I had been through pressing down on me. Jail, addiction, broken relationships, the streets. I had come a long way, but Bernadette's tone, the way she spoke with certainty and love, cut through all of that. I could hear the hope in her words. She believed in this place. She believed in what God could do there.

Melissa was quiet when I told her about it at first, but I could see the curiosity in her.

That little spark I'd noticed before, the one I'd been planting slowly with Christian movies and quiet hints, flickered again. Maybe it was time. Maybe this was the door God had been preparing for us. So, we agreed. We decided to go, not knowing exactly what to expect, but trusting Bernadette, trusting her experience, and perhaps, just maybe, trusting that God had a plan for us, one that could finally give our lives the foundation they had been missing for so long.

When I first stepped into Amazing Church Colorado, you could feel it the moment you walked in. The Spirit was heavy in the air, thick and alive, like electricity pulsing through the room. You didn't have to understand everything to know God was there; you felt Him. The energy hit me in my chest and settled into my bones. Their teachings gave me knowledge, practical, real, and grounded in the Word. They didn't just preach, they equipped me to live, to think, to make decisions in a world that had almost destroyed me.

Every lesson, every story, every correction was a piece of armor, a tool I could use to rebuild my life. They prayed over me, called out the chains that had held me for years: addiction, fear, anger, shame. They didn't sugarcoat it. They stood firm and spoke truth, commanding the lies and spirits that tried to control me to leave and, in that moment, my spirit woke up. It hit me like lightning. Something that had been asleep suddenly came alive. Every word they spoke, every prayer they laid on me, every piece of wisdom they shared, activated my spirit. A fire, a hunger, a purpose that I didn't even know I had. I knew then that God wasn't done with me. He wasn't just saving me from the streets or from myself. He was calling me, equipping me, shaping me into someone who could walk in the life He had for me.

Those pastors weren't just guides. They were the ones who celebrated victories I thought were impossible, who prayed through nights of doubt, who believed in me when I could barely believe in myself.

Walking out of that room, my spirit felt alive, sharp, and untouchable. For the first time in a long time, everything was clear; I was ready to live, and it all started at Amazing Church Colorado, that Spirit-filled place where you could feel God in every corner, every word, every heartbeat, enveloped in the oil from the Lord our God. They move in deliverance and are part of the five-fold.

After some time and consistent attendance at Amazing Church Colorado, our relationship with Pastor Brandon and Pastor Tiffany grew deeper than I ever could have imagined. It wasn't just about Sunday services or hearing sermons anymore. It was about life, about walking alongside people who had been through the same fires I had, who understood the streets, the scars, the mistakes, and the redemption that could follow.

They started getting to know us personally. Remembering little details, asking about our days, noticing the changes, the struggles, the victories. Every interaction wasn't surface-level. My relationship with my pastors isn't just about advice or sermons. It is deeper than that. They weren't just people behind a pulpit; they were more than that. They saw through the tattoos, the scars, the street life, and into the man God was shaping inside me. Pastor Brandon Brown walked a path I knew all too well. He carried scars from drugs, trauma, and the streets, but he didn't let them define him. He used them. Every mistake, every pain, every night he thought he was lost, he turned it into strength. Into faith. Into a testimony that could reach people like me, people who had been broken, beaten and left for dead in the corners of life.

When he spoke, I heard the truth. Raw, real truth. He wasn't speaking from a pulpit; he was speaking from experience, from the fire he had walked through and survived, and he is a mighty man of God. He would sit with me after service, talk through the battles I still carried in my mind and spirit, remind me that my past didn't define my future, and guide me to use what I'd been through to help others. His words cut through the armor I'd built over the years, opening spaces I didn't even know were closed.

Pastor Tiffany Brown was equally powerful. She had a way of seeing right into your heart, reading the fear, the doubt, the hesitation beneath the surface. She spoke truth without hesitation, but in a way that made you feel loved, supported, and held accountable all at once. She challenged Melissa and me, pushing us to grow, think, act, and trust God in ways we had never done before. She was loving and gentle in a way that made you feel seen, yet fearless and strong at the same time. When it came to speaking truth, she didn't sugarcoat anything.

She didn't shy away from calling out lies, sins, or the chains that held people down. There was a fire in her eyes, a wisdom in her words, and a heart that refused to settle for anything less than real transformation.

Together, they are powerhouses. Pastor Brandon's raw strength and testimony, paired with Pastor Tiffany's love and fearless truth, it is unstoppable. The energy they carried filled the room before you even heard a word. Walking into that church, seeing them lead, praying with them, and learning from them, it isn't just inspiring, but life-changing.

They didn't just teach the Word. They activated the spirit inside you. Something that had been dormant, buried under pain, under streets, under mistakes. For me, they became more than pastors. They are mentors, guides, a mirror reflecting what is possible if you surrender fully and become obedient. If you believe fully, if you let God move in your life, miracles will happen.

They showed me a path I had thought was closed, a way to rise from the rubble of my past and step into a life I never imagined I could have. Amazing Church became my family, the place where my Father resides.

I eventually left the peer coaching organization. Our visions had drifted apart, issues around billing and direction made it clear it was time for me to step away. I still carried love and respect for the people I had worked with, but I felt a bigger call, a fire inside me that could not be ignored. At the same time, Melissa and I were diving deeper into Amazing Church Colorado. We were learning what it truly meant to live like Christ, to become disciples, to embody humility, love, and service in every part of our lives.

The day we got married, September 13, 2025, was surreal. Pastor Brandon Brown stood with us, guiding us through vows that were not just words, but promises written from our souls. Family filled every corner of the church. People had flown in from out of state. The air was thick with excitement, love, and something sacred, something bigger than both of us.

In a moment that will forever be etched in my memory, Melissa and I washed each other's feet, just like Jesus did with the disciples. It was humbling and powerful. We knelt there, side by side, no one greater than the other, letting pride fall away, showing respect and love in its purest form. Every splash of water, every touch, was a declaration that this union was not about ego, it was not about status, it was about service, devotion, and heart.

Afterward, we released doves into the sky. White wings cut through the sunlight, carrying away the past, symbolizing new life, growth, and freedom. It felt cinematic, unreal, like God had paused just for us to breathe in that moment and make the sky bright blue on a cloudy day. It was perfect.

We became Gabriel and Melissa Hinojosa. Together with all our kids, our family became one: Maleah, Mariah, Koa, Nevaeh, Makayla, Ezekiel, and Aiyannauh. Our grandbabies, Malijah, Elicia Sue, Estevan, and Rory. Every laugh, every cheer, every tear in that room felt like life itself was celebrating with us. Both of our families were there. We were no longer just two people; we were a family. Whole, broken, healed, and together.

Standing there, looking at Melissa, seeing our kids, our grandkids, and our families all around us, I felt it, the full weight of grace, the redemption that had carried me from the streets, from addiction, from jail, and brought me here. This was life rebuilt; love reclaimed a foundation solid in Christ that had never been there before. I knew, without a doubt, that no matter what storms came next, we would face them as one.

I did not know then that losing everything I had worked so hard for, being saved while sitting in a jail cell, or even writing a book I later set aside and put on the back burner, were all part of a greater plan. I did not know that meeting my wife, becoming a Christian, and helping the very people I once was like would become my true purpose, showing them there is a better way. But it did. Looking back, I can see God's hand over my life the entire time. From surviving abuse, to overdoses, to my dad taking the guns from my apartment to car accidents, to being spared from a shotgun blast to the face. Every moment of protection was Him. It was always Him, watching, guiding, and saving me every single time.

CHAPTER 42: SUCCESS IS MY DESTINY

I was a thief, a robber, a gang member, a drug dealer, a drug addict, a liar, and a manipulator. I preyed on the weak. If I wanted it, I took it. I kicked doors in for pleasure. I held temptation's hand and filled myself with lust from women. I've been shot, stabbed, blown up, and left for dead.

It makes you think... Why do you think Jesus chose wild people in the Bible? James and John were so nuts that Jesus nicknamed them the Sons of Thunder. Simon was a terrorist. Matthew was a tax collector. Jesus hand chose a group to be His disciples, full of murderers and thieves.

We ask, "What are we doing here, Jesus?" These are not the first-round draft picks. But Jesus spent all night praying for who should follow Him, and who did He choose? He chose men and women who were just wild enough to answer the call. Jesus would rather tame a mustang than inspire a mule.

The reason Jesus chooses wild-spirited people is because He knew they would go to the ends of the earth for Him, just as they did in their previous lives before meeting Him. When the Lord our God gets your heart after you have been living in sin, whatever that looks like and all of a sudden, He gets your heart and you feel His undying love, everything changes.

You feel the everlasting peace from the Lord. You will say, "I'll go wherever You tell me to go. I'll say whatever You tell me to say. I'll run headfirst into battle with no cares because I know the Lord our Savior has me." You trust Him so much. You are like Moses, getting right up to the promised land and saying, "Lord, if Your presence doesn't go with me, I don't want it."

You find that the gift is in communicating with God. He is the Master. You just follow. When you get to that place where you put it all on the altar—with all the sin, all the heavy burdens, all the stress filled with anxiety, depression, and addiction, like these men and women did, like these wild ones that Jesus chose—that's when all of a sudden He will send you on an adventure. He will say, "It's time to ride, so lace up your boots."

"I've got people for you to reach. I've got a gospel for you to preach. I've got a calling on your life, and I know I can trust you because you've lost your life."

That is the call to the Christian: to become bold with your faith and to become humble. That is why if you have a past, if you are a little wild, get ready. He chooses the wild ones above the Pharisees, above the religious people who are not truly with Him in spirit, who are not ready to sell it all and give to the poor, who are not ready to sell the field just to buy the treasure in it.

That is why God wants to call the wild ones, because He is ready. If you are ready for the change, He is ready to change you. All you have to do is listen. You cannot carry your cross and your ego at the same time. You are not called to just believe in Jesus. No. You are called to become like Jesus. The answer might not be in creating a new vision but in having a new heart.

I saw death. I looked at him right in the face many times without even knowing it.

I felt it. In those moments, it was not a thought or a story, it was real. Death and suicide. I experienced God. I experienced love. And in those moments, I knew without a doubt that Jesus is real.

Death is coming for all of us. It does not care about your hustle, your money, your fame, or your crew. It waits at the end of every street, on the corners of every block, behind every decision you try to run from. The world tells you it is the end. The grave says it is home. But I learned something that night through Jesus Christ: death is not the last word. He is.

The cross turned what was supposed to destroy me into the doorway to life. Everything I lost, every scar I carried, every night I stayed awake wondering why—He sees it all. He takes it all. He breaks the chains, and He left the tomb empty so nobody who walks with Him has to face that darkness alone. Death might take your body, but it cannot touch your soul if it belongs to Him. Those same hands that were pierced, that held the cross, reach for us now. They pull you out of the ashes of who you were and lift you into the light of who you are meant to be.

So yes, death is promised. But for those who ride with Jesus Christ, life is promised too. Real life. Eternal life. The kind that does not fade when your heartbeat stops. It is the everlasting living water, and you will never thirst again. That is the bigger promise. The one that outlives every street, every struggle, every fight you ever had. The one that says, "You are not done yet."

Jesus was not inside of me for a long time, not really. I had the head knowledge of who He was, but there was no heart change. Yes, I believed in God. I knew His name. I even talked about Him sometimes. But believing in God and knowing God are two different things. I was living lukewarm and did not even know it. One foot in, one foot out. I knew the verses. I knew how to pray when I was in trouble. But my life did not match my mouth. And God says in His Word, "If you are lukewarm, I will spit you out. Depart from me, I never knew you."

That hit me hard because I realized I was playing both sides.

I said His name a lot growing up, but nothing inside me had changed yet. I was still living the same, thinking I could hustle grace, like God didn't see what was really in my heart. Jesus said there would be people who do miracles in His name, who cast out demons, who preach the Word, and He will still say, "I never knew you." That is the kind of truth that will wake your soul up real fast.

See, I don't just want to know about God anymore, I want to know Him. Because when I leave this body, I want to make sure I have a home waiting for me. And if I had died any time before now, like I should have, multiple times with the way I was living and the choices I made, I know I would not have had a home in heaven. I would have faced real death, not just physical, but eternal separation from God.

That reality gave me a different kind of boldness. Not arrogance, but awareness. A fire to stop living for myself and start living for something that lasts. Because it is not about how long you have been in church or how many Bible verses you can quote. It is about how much of Christ has been formed inside you.

It is when your faith grows past feelings. When you stop chasing blessings and start carrying burdens for others. When obedience means more than convenience. That is when you know you are growing, when you don't just say His name, you start walking in His nature. You walk differently, you talk differently, and you leave the secular world alone. You turn away from worldly movies and music that cause disruption in your life. You won't need drugs or alcohol for personal satisfaction or even to mask feelings or emotions, because Jesus will fill you with happiness and peace. When you don't just wear a cross around your neck as jewelry, you pick it up and carry one just as Jesus did.

See, when you first come to God, it is all feelings. You get that fire, that rush, that "God's gonna bless me" mindset. But as you grow, you start to learn the blessing is not always comfort. Sometimes, it is correction. Sometimes, it is being broken so He can rebuild you right. It is when you stop saying, "God, get me out of this," and start saying, "God, teach me something in this." It is when you stop treating prayer like a wish list and start treating it like a war with a plan.

It's when you learn to love people who did you dirty, to forgive them, to walk away from drama instead of diving into it. That's real growth. When you could clap back but you let God handle it instead.

A lot of people talk about having faith, but it's when you still trust Him even when it hurts. When the bills aren't paid, when your heart is broken, when the plan falls apart, and you still say, "God, I know You got me." That's when you know you've grown. You stop chasing blessings and start being one. You stop living for attention and start living with intention. You realize it isn't about your truth; it's about His truth.

See, it doesn't mean you're perfect, it means you're consistent. It means you've been through hell and came out holy. It's when you stop asking, "What's God's plan for my life?" and start asking, "God, what's my part in Your plan?" Because the Kingdom isn't about comfort, it's about a calling.

So yes, being a Christian means you don't just believe in Jesus. You start becoming like Him.

 Even when it costs you everything. And you start... **PREVAILING TOWARDS REDEMPTION**. That's my testimony.

Today, Melissa and I run a new local nonprofit called **Prevailing Towards Redemption**, with a board of directors that includes prominent business owners and leaders from our community. What started as a calling has grown into a mission, a life dedicated to reaching the people I once was, the streets I once roamed, and the chaos I once caused.

At the heart of the organization is our peer coaching department, a place where people who have walked through addiction and the streets can connect with others who truly understand.

Our first goal is simple but life-changing: get them off the streets and sober, or work with people involved with the justice system like parole or probation. The main goal, the one that drives every step we take, is to bring them to God. We want them to find a foundation stronger than the streets, stronger than addiction, stronger than the pain and mistakes that have held them down for so long.

We show them what worked for me, how faith, accountability, and practical steps can rebuild a life from the ground up. We accept donations not for profit or recognition, but to fuel the work we do, to give hope where it feels like hope has been stripped away. Every dollar, every resource, every hand extended is a lifeline.

We help those suffering from homelessness, those lost in addiction, people stuck in cycles that feel impossible to break. We don't just talk about change, we walk with them, side by side, every step of the way.

If I could get out of that life, if I could claw my way back from the depths, I know they can too. We help them get into sober homes, connect them with jobs, teach them skills, and hold them accountable because I have been there. I have been trapped, lost, and desperate, and I know the fight it takes to rise again.

Our work is hands-on. We meet them where they are, in the streets, in the camps, in the shadows of life, and we pull them toward the light.

We are strongly partnered with **Amazing Church Colorado**. They are our covering, our protection, guiding us spiritually, supporting the mission, and giving us the foundation to do this work with integrity and power. Together, we are building a bridge from the chaos we know so well to a life of hope, faith, and purpose. This is our fight, our labor, our heart poured into the lives of others. Every time someone takes that first step toward change, every time a life turns around, every time someone finds God through the work we do, I see it, the proof that grace, persistence, and faith can rewrite the story, one soul at a time.

...I hope you enjoyed my testimony and thank you.

Thank you for taking the time to walk with me through my testimony, through the broken roads, the dark valleys, and the moments when it seemed there was no way out. These stories were the main highlights of my life, pieces of a long and painful journey. Behind them are thirty-eight years of trauma, addiction, and searching for something real. There are more stories, but those are better left unsaid. Yet even in the chaos, God was there, turning every wound into a witness and every setback into a setup for redemption.

This isn't just my story. It is proof of what God can do when you surrender. It is proof that even from the ashes, He can build something beautiful. Every scar, every failure, every tear. He used it all for His glory.

If this book reached you, it's not by accident. Maybe God is calling you, too, to rise, to heal, to forgive, to start again. Because the same grace that saved me is reaching for you right now.

My prayer is that you don't just close these pages and move on, but that you carry the message forward. That you look at the lost and broken with compassion and remember, they're not too far gone. None of us are.

— Gabriel I. Hinojosa
Prevailing Towards Redemption

Prayer for Prevailing Towards Redemption

Heavenly Father,
We come before You with hearts full of faith, seeking Your guidance and blessing over the work of Prevailing Towards Redemption. Lord, we ask that You use our hands, our hearts, and our efforts to bring hope, healing, and restoration to those who are lost, broken, and struggling.

Grant us wisdom to lead with compassion, patience to walk alongside those in need, and courage to stand firm in the face of challenges. May every action we take reflect Your love and bring people closer to You.

Lord, let the lives we touch be transformed by Your grace. Help those suffering from addiction, homelessness, and despair to find freedom, purpose, and redemption through You. Protect our team, strengthen our faith, and guide us to serve with humility, integrity, and unwavering devotion. May Your light shine through Prevailing Towards Redemption, and may our work glorify Your name, bringing healing and hope to the darkest places.

In Jesus' name, we pray. Amen.

Heavenly Father,
I lift my dad to You today. I thank You for the time we shared, for every lesson, good and hard, that shaped who I am. Even though he's gone from this earth, I know he's never far because love never dies, it just changes places.

Lord, I pray that his soul rests in Your eternal peace. Forgive him for his mistakes, just as You have forgiven me for mine. Let him feel the fullness of Your mercy and the joy that comes only from being in Your presence.

There are things I wish I could've said, hugs I wish I could've given, moments I wish I could've changed, but I trust You with all of it. You've turned my pain into purpose, and I know my dad can see now the man I'm becoming, the mission I'm living, and the redemption You've brought into my life.

Tell him I love him, Lord. Tell him I made it. Tell him his son is walking with You now and that through me, his name still carries light and meaning.

Until we meet again, keep him close to You and keep me strong to continue the work You've started in me.

In Jesus' name, Amen.

Rest in peace, David Robert Hinojosa "The Rock," my father.

July 4th, 1958 – May 18th, 2014

"Today is the first day of the rest of your life…"

Share Your Story — Join the Movement

If 'Prevailing Towards Redemption' has touched your heart or reminded you that no one is too far gone to be redeemed, we invite you to share your own story of transformation with us and be a part of this movement.

Your testimony could inspire hope in someone still battling addiction, homelessness, or brokenness. Together, we can demonstrate to the world that God's grace extends into every dark place and draws people into the light.

Stand With Us — Fuel the Mission

If something in these pages stirred your heart... if you believe, like we do, that through the pain, the mistakes, mercy can be found. This isn't just the end; it's the beginning of a new life. We invite you to join this mission.

Your support helps us reach those who are lost, broken, and battling addiction or homelessness, even a single mom struggling with 5 kids. Every donation, every prayer, and every act of kindness provides blankets, food, socks, gloves, hand warmers, toiletries, clothing, bus passes, and even emergency shelter when needed, keeping this mission alive. We are currently seeking a warming shelter on the south side of Colorado Springs. We have an issue out here, and we want to change that. You're not just giving; you're helping someone find their way back to hope, back to life, and back to God.

We can't do this alone. Together, we can bring light into dark places and continue **Prevailing Towards Redemption**.

To connect, share your story, or donate:
Email: prevailingtowardsremption@gmail.com
Facebook:
https://www.facebook.com/PrevailingTowardsRedemption

From the bottom of our hearts, thank you for believing in redemption.

www.ingramcontent.com/pod-product-compliance
Lightning Source LLC
Chambersburg PA
CBHW082247120626
46555CB00009B/2990